Cases in
Public Relations

Translating Ethics into Action

Brigitta R. Brunner
Auburn University

Corey A. Hickerson
James Madison University

New York   Oxford
OXFORD UNIVERSITY PRESS

Oxford University Press is a department of the University of Oxford.
It furthers the University's objective of excellence in research, scholarship,
and education by publishing worldwide. Oxford is a registered trade mark of
Oxford University Press in the UK and certain other countries.

Published in the United States of America by Oxford University Press
198 Madison Avenue, New York, NY 10016, United States of America.

For titles covered by Section 112 of the US Higher Education
Opportunity Act, please visit www.oup.com/us/he for the latest
information about pricing and alternate formats.

Library of Congress Cataloging-in-Publication Data

Names: Brunner, Brigitta R., 1971- editor. | Hickerson, Corey, editor.
Title: Cases in public relations : translating ethics into action / [edited by]
    Brigitta Brunner, Auburn University, Corey Hickerson, James Madison
    University.
Description: New York : Oxford University Press, [2019]
Identifiers: LCCN 2018027491 (print) | LCCN 2018029164 (ebook) |
    ISBN 9780190631734 (ebook) | ISBN 9780190631383 (pbk. text)
Subjects: LCSH: Public relations—Moral and ethical aspects—Case studies. |
    Social responsibility of business—Case studies.
Classification: LCC HD59 (ebook) | LCC HD59 .C3697 2019 (print) |
    DDC 174/.4—dc23
LC record available at https://lccn.loc.gov/2018027491

9 8 7 6 5 4 3 2 1

Printed by Sheridan Books, Inc., United States of America

TABLE OF CONTENTS

Acknowledgments   *vii*

SECTION I: *Introduction to Cases, Ethics, and Public Relations*

Chapter 1: What Is the Case Method?   3

   What Is a Case?   3
   How Is a Case Study Class Different for Students?   3
   How Do Faculty Teach via the Case Method?   6

Chapter 2: Ethical Frameworks and Professional Codes   9

   Ethics, Morals, and Laws   10
   Different Types of Ethical Frameworks   10
     Virtue   11
     Deontology   11
     Utilitarian   12
     Ethics of Care   12
   Professional Codes   13
     PRSA Code of Ethics: Preamble   14
     PRSA Member Statement of Professional Values 15
     PRSA Code Provisions of Conduct   16
     IABC Code of Ethics for Professional Communicators 16

SECTION II: *Public Relations Functions*

Chapter 3: Conflict and Crisis Management   23

   The Lands' End Content Marketing Debacle: A Cautionary
     Tale of a Retailer's Inadvertent Foray into Polarized Politics
   by Nathan Gilkerson   26

The September 11 Memorial by Hannah Karolak and Susan Mancino   35
Ethical and Effective Post-Crisis Stakeholder Relations
    by Colleen Arendt   41
"Am I Safe?": The Ethical Implications of Running and Maintaining
    a Sharing Economy Organization by Lindsey J. DiTirro, Lauren
    Berkshire Hearit, and Emilly K. Martinez   49

Chapter 4: Social Media and Technology   59

Seeing Through the Golden Arches: Transparency in the Digital
    Age by Prisca S. Ngondo and Clay Craig   63
Scrubbing and the Ethics of Digital Reputation Management
    by Alison N. Novak   71
Applebee's Social Media "Meltdown": Managing Ethics
    in an Online Brand Community by Amber L. Hutchins
    and Desirae K. Johnson   77

Chapter 5: Corporate Social Responsibility   85

All Your Clothes Are Made with Exploited Labor: Patagonia
    Takes Action to Spur Action by Jean Kelso Sandlin   88
A Tale of Two Case Studies: Comparing Coca-Cola's Divergent
    Corporate Social Responsibility Initiatives and the Resulting Ethical
    Implications by Lucinda L. Austin, MaryClaire Schulz, and
    Barbara Miller Gaither   95
Restructuring Corporate Philanthropy: Belk Strategically
    Applies Ethical Responsibility to Underpin Community
    Engagement by Alan Freitag and Jessica Martin Graham   103
Ethical Corporate Philanthropy: A Case Study on Communicating
    CSR by Heidi Hatfield Edwards   111

SECTION III: *Public Relations Contexts*

Chapter 6: Consumer Relations   119

Volkswagen the Betrayer: A Case Study of Gross Disregard for
    the Welfare of Stakeholders Worldwide by Chiara Valentini
    and Dean Kruckeberg   122
Blackfish *Backlash: SeaWorld's Attempt at Navigating a Crisis*
    Situation by Leslie Rodriguez Rasmussen and Melody Fisher   129

Food Fight: How Ethical Management Saved Market Basket
by Brenda J. Wrigley 136

Ethical Activism? Food Babe, Big Food, and the Online Pressure for Disclosure by Ashli Quesinberry Stokes 145

Chapter 7: Community Relations 154

"Do Not Use!": Ethical Implications of the 2014 Elk River Chemical Spill by Jonathan Borden and Xiaochen Angela Zhang 156

Maintaining the Public Trust: A Town Meeting About Rising Natural Gas Prices by Mary Beth Reese and Erin E. Gilles 165

Shifting Blame: Addressing the Michigan Department of Environmental Quality's Complicated Ethical Responsibility in the Flint Water Crisis by Catherine J. Bruns 171

Chapter 8: Sports Communication 179

Should the Fan Experience Impact the Game? by John Forde 181

The NFL Concussion Crisis: More Than Just a Bad Headache by Terry L. Rentner and LaMar C. Campbell 191

Paper Classes or Academic Anomalies: A Kantian Examination of UNC's Response to Its Shadow Curriculum by Christie M. Kleinmann 199

Chapter 9: Health 208

Healthcare Public Relations and Moral Obligations: Patient Safety and the Boston University Medical Center Tuberculosis Case by Heather J. Carmack and Carey M. Noland 210

Emergent Ethical Healthcare Public Relations in the Digital Age by Alisa Agozzino and Katee Fenimore 217

Healthcare Organizations and Patient Safety: Questions of Ethical Public Relations Practices by Carrie Reif-Stice, Julie A. Lasslo, and Kathryn E. Anthony 224

Chapter 10: Government Relations 232

Dealing with Subsequent Crisis Response: Timeliness and Transparency in Government Response to the New Jersey Boardwalk Fire by Mildred F. Wiggins Perreault and Anli Xiao 234

Connecting Government Relations to Ethics: Louisiana's Centralized Media Relations by Christopher J. McCollough 244

*MERS Outbreak in South Korea: A Snapshot of Government
Responses and Public Relations Considerations* by Ji Young Kim   251

Chapter 11: International   261

Skol's "Viva Redondo" ("Live Round") Crisis by Deborah de
Cillo Ottoni Teixeira and Michelle M. Maresh-Fuehrer   263

*Toshiba Accounting Scandal: Japanese National Culture,
Corporate Governance, and Public Relations Ethics* by
Koji Fuse, Jacqueline Sears, and Keyona Adaiah Butler   271

Taylor Guitars, Guardians of the Forest by Janis Teruggi
Page and William S. Page   283

Chapter 12: Nonprofit and Education   290

The Wounded Warrior Project by Pamela G. Bourland-Davis
and William Thompson   292

Why Are There So Many Crucifixes? by J. J. McIntyre and
Kristen A. McIntyre   302

*Connecting Ethics and Practice as PR Students Transition
from Learners to Educators* by Douglas J. Swanson   317

SECTION IV: *The Future of Public Relations*

Chapter 13: Trends in Public Relations, Communication, and Society
That Will Challenge Ethics   325

Taking a Swipe at Apple: The FBI v. Apple, Inc.
by Heather J. Hether   328

*Chiquita Brands, Its Illegal Payments to Paramilitary Groups
in Colombia, and the Transnational Public Relations Crisis
That Followed* by Vanessa Bravo, Juan Carlos Molleda,
Andrés Felipe Giraldo-Dávila, and Luis Horacio Botero-Montoya   343

*Making Plastic Green: Capital One's Commitment to
Sustainability* by Stephanie A. Smith   348

Index   354

ACKNOWLEDGMENTS

This book only exists because of the hard work and support of many people. Many thanks are owed to our amazing editorial team at Oxford University Press. From Paul Longo, who helped us find our wonderful and dedicated editor, to assistant editor Katlin Kocher, who guided us through the process and helped us manage our submission with expertise, to Toni Magyar, the editor who believed in us and encouraged us every step of the way, we have the greatest praise and gratitude to these people and their colleagues.

We would also like to thank the following reviewers, as well as those who have chosen to remain anonymous: Chike Anyaegbunam (University of Kentucky), Ovril (Patricia) Cambridge (Ohio University), Michelle Carpenter (Old Dominion University), Shirley Staples Carter (University of South Carolina), Katherine Cruger (Chatham University), Jennie Donohue (Marist College), Katherine R. Fleck (Ohio Northern University), Catherine Foster (Canisius College), Kirk Hazlett (APR, Fellow PRSA, Curry College), Phillip J. Hutchison (University of Kentucky), Jennifer M. Keller (Western Washington University), Marjorie Kruvand (Loyola University Chicago), Marsha Little Matthews (The University of Texas at Tyler), Deborah B. Menger (University of Texas San Antonio), Dana Alexander Nolfe (Bryant University), Hanna Park (Middle Tennessee State University), Natalie Redcross (Iona College), Burton St. John III (Old Dominion University), Robin Street (University of Mississippi), Donn J. Tilson (University of Miami), Erin Willis (University of Colorado-Boulder), and Juyan Zhang (University of Texas San Antonio). We especially want to thank John E. Forde, Amber Hutchins, Christie Kleinmann, Amber Smallwood, and Ashli Q. Stokes for their time and energy acting as our editorial board for determining the cases to include in this manuscript. We also add our sincere gratitude to our case contributors for their beautifully crafted cases and for their patience with our edits and requests.

Brigitta thanks Troy and Kai Johnson for their encouragement; she also thanks the Auburn University College of Liberal Arts and School of Communication & Journalism for the support received while conceptualizing, writing, and editing this book.

Corey thanks Laura, Lilly, and Jude for understanding the hours in front of the computer and for their constant support. He also thanks his colleagues in the School of Communication Studies at James Madison University for their backing and motivation.

INTRODUCTION TO CASES, ETHICS, AND PUBLIC RELATIONS

1 WHAT IS THE CASE METHOD?

What Is a Case?

If you think back to your childhood, some of your most vivid memories might revolve around stories. They could be nursery rhymes or tales your parents or other loved ones made up for you, but they all deal with narrative. Essentially, storytelling is at the center of case studies, too.

Storytelling is an integral part of humanity, and it becomes an educational experience with case studies (Herreid, 2005). Cases demonstrate real-life challenges faced by organizations and their leaders through stories. It is through such stories of both good and bad practice that students learn about many disciplines, including business, communication, law, public relations, and science (Herreid, 2005). Cases also give students the opportunity to learn about the consequences of organizational leaders' thoughts, actions, and lack of actions.

Typically, a case will consist of a narrative that explicates an organizational triumph or controversy such as Johnson & Johnson's Tylenol recall or the Flint water crisis. The best case studies cover topics that are relevant to students, and are likely to include dialogue and actors/characters much like a traditional story (Herreid, 2005). The dilemma or success detailed in the story will then need to be examined and analyzed through the use of students' knowledge of current events, facts, industry, ethics, theory, best practices, and critical thinking. While the case document provides information, it does not analyze the information (Foram, 2001). The analysis is left for the classroom, and it is one thing that makes case studies classes very different from lecture ones. Through discussion, students debate various approaches and perspectives to the situation, and they learn from each other.

How Is a Case Study Class Different for Students?

Many students are used to and are comfortable with a lecture-style class. If you are one of those students, you are obviously not alone. Many classes rely on lecture, which is when a faculty member speaks to students about concepts and ideas but students have little interaction with the content in the classroom. In contrast, you will find the case study classroom to be very active and engaged. A case studies class will also require you to take responsibility for your own learning.

While student–instructor interaction is still important, when case studies are used there is often more emphasis on peer-to-peer learning than the more traditional student–instructor learning of a lecture-format class (Herreid, 2005). Peer-to-peer learning means you will likely learn just as much from the other students in your class, if not more, than from your instructor. If this setup seems odd to you, that's natural. Students can be uncomfortable with learning through the case method because the structure differs from the lecture format to which they are accustomed (Herreid, 2005). In a case studies class, while your learning will be centered on learning objectives developed by your instructor, you will learn from your own knowledge and thoughts as well as through your interactions with your fellow students.

Classes using cases will be structured in a different way. For example, you will see that the class is more of a facilitated dialogue than a lecture (Foram, 2001). By this, we mean that your instructor will keep student discussion going by asking questions, summarizing, and encouraging but probably won't interject a lot of his or her thoughts into the discussion. This change is necessary so students gain confidence in their abilities to solve problems through analysis, to support their claims, and to volunteer their thoughts (Foram, 2001). I am not going to lie to you: At times the case studies classroom may push you past your comfort zone. You will be challenged to think about your own assumptions, to overcome prejudices, to test theories, and to debate solutions while developing confidence and skills.

As a student in a class using the case method, you will need to read your assigned cases carefully and think about them critically. Reading your cases on the transit system or as you wait for class to begin will not be sufficient. Before class you should think about questions, such as the following ones, to help you prepare:

What is happening?
What is the context?
When and where is the case taking place?
Who is involved?
What or who has caused the situation?
Who are the people and organizations involved?
Who is responsible for making decisions?
What is motivating the people and organizations involved?
What are their interests and goals?
What are they trying to accomplish?
What questions do they need to answer?
What problems do they need to solve?
What opportunities and constraints exist?

What might limit responses?

What should the people and organizations do or not do?

What can they do? Why?

Thinking about these questions can help you learn the facts of the situation, and will give you practice with analyzing the situation and applying your knowledge to it. By answering these types of questions you will not only have a good working knowledge of the case but will also be working on forming your own opinions about it and making arguments to support your claims (Foram 2001). You will need to apply lessons and theories you have learned in other courses to the situation. You might also analyze the situation based on experience you have had in the field, at an internship, or at a work experience. You might even need to do further research into the situation to better understand its context.

Getting the most out of a case studies class will depend on your willingness to put as much effort as you can into preparing for the discussion and for sharing your thoughts with the class. It will require you to take responsibility for your learning. When you take this step, you will see how learning expands beyond class time and the classroom as you make linkages to things you read for other classes or items you see in the news (The HBS Case Method, n.d.).

Yes, the case studies classroom might be intimidating and unfamiliar to some students, even to you. However, this experience will help you to build your critical-thinking and problem-solving skills, which are workplace skills that are highly sought after. To build these important skills, you should contribute to the discussion not only the facts of the case as needed, but also your own ideas, analysis, and personal experiences (The HBS Case Method, n.d.). To demonstrate your critical-thinking abilities, you will need to listen, and you will need to be responsible for your own learning by being prepared and ready to discuss and consider alternative plans of action. You will need to bring together material from your other classes and your own experiences. You will have to determine how your ideas fit with those of others, and vice versa. You must be willing to take risks and offer suggestions and ideas even if you are unsure about them. You should also build on your classmates' comments and not be afraid to respectfully critique and disagree with what they have said (The HBS Case Method, n.d.). Through this participation, you will not only build your critical-thinking skills but will also learn leadership skills you can bring to the workforce. Finally, as you take these steps you will find that your classroom has been transformed into a community of colleagues (Foram, 2001).

Along the way you may find that you have interpreted information in a different way than your classmates. You may miss something that others pick up upon. You may even find that others disagree with you. Due to all of this change and novelty, you may become frustrated—but don't give up. You will find that case studies replicate real-life experience. Typically, there is no one correct answer to how to handle workplace situations, good or bad. Instead you will find that "there are only choices, and the reasons behind them—some better, some worse, than others" (Foram, 2001, 4). In other words, a case methods class can be messy (Foram, 2001), and this messiness is okay because you are still learning. Since you will need to learn how to present ideas and support them in the workplace, the case studies classroom is a great place to learn these skills and to practice them. It is much better to learn these concepts in the supportive structure of a classroom, where you will have constructive feedback to help you to improve, than to learn them in the workplace, where the consequences are much steeper and support might be lacking.

How Do Faculty Teach via the Case Method?

You might be thinking to yourself, "If I am doing all this work to prepare and discuss a case, what is the instructor doing?" Well, the answer has many dimensions. Yes, instructors who teach case studies classes may not be in the typical role of pontificating their knowledge, but they are most definitely still there and involved in the learning process. They are just doing these things in a unique and, perhaps, unfamiliar way.

After instructors teach content, they can use cases to involve students in real-life situations that ask students to put themselves in the role of decision-maker. They might begin class by asking some questions about the facts of the case to make students comfortable with talking in class, but they will soon move into discussion questions that require analysis. As student discussion occurs, your instructor is listening to the conversation and guiding it.

As we have mentioned previously, listening is very important in the case studies classroom, whether it is listening to others or having others listen to your thoughts. As a student you need to be an active participant, which means you must be involved and responsible for your own learning. One way you can work toward taking this responsibility is by making a commitment to the 4 P's:

Preparation (reading and analyzing on your own)
Presence (you need to be there to discuss)
Promptness (get to class on time)
Participation (be responsible for sharing your knowledge and perspective) (Shapiro, 2014).

Taking these steps will help you to make a case studies class an integral part of your learning experience.

Typically, instructors do more listening than talking in the case studies classroom. It's not that they are lazy; rather, they have made a conscious teaching decision to encourage students to listen to one another and to demonstrate the importance of participation. The case studies classroom hinges on the involvement of and interaction among students. Class discussion has to be student-driven or else the class becomes a lecture (Shapiro, 2014).

While students are discussing, the instructor is listening and finding opportunities to guide students to greater learning and discovery. The professor might ask additional questions when something isn't clear or when he or she wants the student to provide more thought to support a claim or idea. At times the instructor may respond to some student comments and give the class some additional detail to consider. He or she might call on a student who is not already involved in the conversation to bring that student into the discussion. The instructor might follow up on the things students have said to make sure important content is covered to summarize a major point. You will see how your instructor becomes a facilitator or moderator, but at times he or she may act as a devil's advocate to encourage a different line of thinking. Faculty might even use questions to cause students to delve into conflict (Herreid, 2005). They might want opposing views to surface that are supported and reasonable so students have to consider different opinions. Sometimes there will be opportunities to foster collaboration and cooperation among the students as well as times when the instructor asks students to reflect on their thoughts and opinions.

You will find that your instructor steps to the side so students take the lead and challenge one another. The professor is not doing this due to a lack of preparation. Rather, your instructor does not provide answers, only a path to understanding and learning, because he or she does not want students to think there's only one way to look at the case situation and only one "right" solution to it (Shapiro, 2014). Instead your instructor wants you to become a class of independent thinkers.

Typically, instructors will have certain learning objectives or themes they want to cover in the class discussion, but how they arrive at these class goals may differ. At times faculty can present cases in an interrupted style, giving only part of narrative at first and then adding more information later (Herreid, 2005). This style of presenting information is meant to mimic the realities of the workplace and to help students realize that decisions often have to be made even if not all the needed information is at hand (Herreid, 2005). Faculty might also give different groups different parts of the case to analyze and then ask the whole class to come together to synthesize the ideas the smaller groups have developed. Some instructors might have students start discussions in small groups with the same questions and then bring the discussion to the larger group. Yet others might use role-playing to force students to see the case through different eyes. All of these techniques are used to help make the material "come alive" (Foram, 2001, 43).

Your instructor will wrap up the discussion of the case. After student discussion he or she might summarize the general comments made and note the students' contributions and comments so that you can use the points to help interpret a future case. Instructors typically do not share their own decision about the case because that would prevent you from analyzing the information for yourself. Instructors want you to have your own perspective and to stand by your judgments. They don't want you to learn to analyze based on what you think they expect and want to hear; that would diminish your learning experience.

In summary, the case study classroom represents a shift from the traditional instructor-centered model. It may be uncomfortable at first because you will have to take responsibility for your own learning. But by using case studies, you will more clearly see how course content directly relates to real-world contexts. You will see how many situations are not neatly defined and will come to realize that decision-makers do not always have the information they need. You will also hear many viewpoints, which can be confusing and quite different from what you're used to. You may or may not come to understand why the organizational leaders in the case studies made the choices they did. However, you will likely see how their decisions affect all publics—some negatively, others positively. You will need to consider what information is known about the situation as well as what is not. You will have to pull from and synthesize what you have learned in other classes, in previous chapters, and from your own experiences to devise solutions. You will have to take risks and participate in class discussion to share your thoughts and ideas.

The case study method will be challenging as you find your instructor using questions, debate, and dialogue to push you into an interactive experience. The case studies classroom goes beyond the transfer of knowledge to developing judgment and the ability to act despite uncertainty (Shapiro, 2014). Ideally, you should continue to learn after class as you reflect on what was discussed and think about how you can apply those insights to your professional life.

References

Foram, J. (2001, Summer). The case method and interactive classroom. *Thought & Action: The NEA Higher Education Journal, 9,* 41–50.

Herreid, C. F. (2005, May). Using case studies to teach science. Retrieved from http://www.actionbioscience.org/education/herreid.html.

Shapiro, B. P. (2014). *Hints for Case Teaching.* Cambridge, MA: Harvard Business School Publishing. Retrieved from https://cb.hbsp.harvard.edu/resources/marketing/docs/M00016_Hints_for_Case_Teaching_Brochure.pdf.

The HBS Case Method (n.d.). Retrieved from http://www.hbs.edu/mba/academic-experience/Pages/the-hbs-case-method.aspx

2   ETHICAL FRAMEWORKS
AND PROFESSIONAL CODES

By the ethical dimension . . ., we express our characters, whether or not we intend to do so.

— KENNETH BURKE *(1966, 28)*

Even without our trying, ethics reflect ourselves and the public relations profession. The decisions we make and how we decide to treat others will be viewed as our character. Our ethics reflect on our employers, clients, and profession. If you have a class project with a client, your ethics create an impression of not only the class but also the university and the public relations profession as a whole. The public relations profession has a weak reputation largely because early practitioners disregarded ethics and focused instead on persuasion (Kruckeberg & Stark, 1988; Wright, 1979). Heath (2000, 70) argued that the need to engineer consent was public relations' "ethical albatross." We in public relations cannot deny that our business is about persuasion, and this figurative albatross encumbers us and makes it imperative that we behave ethically.

Today, practitioners must address ethical concerns and not forget that part of being a professional includes serving the public (Broom, 2009, 27). Ethical issues are difficult because "practitioners are part of the public, and their growth and improvement is intertwined with the public's growth and development" (Stoker & Stoker, 2012, 42). The issues of today impact practitioners as much as everyone else. Ethics can migrate and change over time. In 1928 the "Torches of Freedom" march that encouraged women to smoke publicly was empowering and "a defiant political gesture," but today encouraging anyone to smoke has strong ethical implications (Evan, 2010, 35). This chapter explores different frameworks that can be used to interpret these complex issues and discusses how professional codes can provide guidance.

Ethics, Morals, and Laws

We often use the words *ethics, morals,* and even *laws* interchangeably (Fawkes, 2012; Grunig, 2000). While all of these words are about what is right and wrong, they can be differentiated. *Ethics* are the rules of conduct provided by an external society, group, or organization. *Morals* are personal, your individual guide to what is right and wrong. Ethics can be thought of as the customs in your group, and morals are your personal way of life. *Laws* are the formalization of ethics and morals through legislation creating either a reward or punishment.

Ethics can come from many places, such as your society, profession, or religion; these are the rules we are taught to follow because of group memberships. Ethics are not "merely what has become accepted practice within the industry," "what you can get away with," or "following the letter of the law" (Parsons, 2016, 8, 9). Ethics are broader—a system of usage that helps people decide what to do that's best not just for them, but for the larger group.

Morals are your own personal decisions about right and wrong. These can differ from your ethics. For example, you might ethically believe from your professional standards that all organizations deserve communication representation, but you might morally choose not to work for a cause with which you don't agree. For example, if you were a libertarian, you could believe that Republicans and Democrats should have public relations representation because of your professional ethics, but you might not provide those services yourself because of your morals.

Laws are different from both ethics and morals. Just because something is legal or illegal doesn't mean it is ethical to you. Instead, laws are "a basic, enforceable standard of behavior necessary in order for a community to succeed" that is enforced by a government (Ethics Center, 2016, para. 8). Laws have been influenced by a society's ethics and morals, but conflicts occur. For instance, you could say or write almost anything about a political candidate in the United States and not be subject to slander or libel laws because of the First Amendment to the Constitution's protection of free speech, and especially because of the guarantee of "free discussion of governmental affairs" (*Mills v. Alabama*, 1966, para. 3). The statements might not be prosecutable in a court, but spreading falsehoods would be ethically and morally wrong by almost any standard.

Different Types of Ethical Frameworks

Many different ways to examine ethics exist and have been debated. In examining ethics, Bowen (2016, 565) suggests that "three primary frameworks" exist: virtue, deontology, and utilitarianism. These frameworks are not presented as being in competition; all have strengths and weaknesses, and all can inform our ethical decision-making.

Virtue

Virtue is about pursuing the truth, "about right and the good, argumentation and how one should act to have a worthy life" (Bowen, 2016, 565). It asks the classic question: What makes a good person? The end result is building character and being the best version of yourself. Using this framework, people's virtues are what makes them ethical. Virtues include honesty, loyalty, justice, and courage. These are the guiding principles of your actions.

Aristotle wrote that virtue was knowing what to do at "the right times, with reference to the right objects, towards the right people, with the right motive, and in the right way" (*Nicomachean Ethics*, Book II, 6). Aristotle's "golden mean" suggests that virtues are the middle way—for example, courage is the mean of fear and confidence (*Nicomachean Ethics*, Book II, 7). At first glance, it would seem that the ethical path is always the middle, but Aristotle noted that the mean is not always in the center and sometimes you must lean to an extreme if the situation calls for it. An example could be the BBC reducing the salary of prominent male journalists to make up for past gender pay discrepancies (Freytas-Tamura, 2018). This action is not the middle way, but past actions make it necessary.

Deontology

Deontology has to do with ethical duty and is "based on obligations, principles, and rights" (Gregory & Willis, 2013, 75). It asks the question: Are there universal rules that we must follow? It examines ethics in the context that "human beings should be treated with dignity and respect because they have rights" (Gregory & Willis, 2013, 75). As all humans have rights, your individual actions should be governed only by rules that everyone can follow irrelevant of the situation. Kant called this the *categorical imperative*, meaning that all rules must be applied equally (Theaker, 2013, 103). The categorical imperative is reflected in the concept that everyone should be considered innocent until proven guilty.

Using deontology, people should act based on universal principles and should not be concerned with the consequences. But figuring out what is a universal principle is the challenge. Consider telling the truth, which seems like a good candidate for a universal principle. But say you are working for a client who has trade secrets. When a reporter asks directly about one of these secrets, you refuse to disclose the information. Did you violate your ethics? This situation seems like a violation of truth, but you also believe all organizations have the right to keep trade secrets. Is the right to keep secrets a universal principle? You understand that all organizations have the need and the right to keep some things secret, and because the principle can be applied to all, it is ethically sound.

Deontology has much in common with the idea of universal rights and John Locke's elaboration of the *social contract* (Theaker, 2013, 84–85). The social contract is an implicit agreement to cooperate for social benefits. Locke (1689/2014, 6) wrote that we all possess "life, health, liberty, or possessions," and others cannot take those away. These ideas can be found in the opening line of the preamble to the Declaration of Independence: Americans are "endowed by their Creator with certain unalienable Rights, that among these are Life, Liberty and the pursuit of Happiness."

Utilitarian

This framework bases decision-making on maximizing benefit. It asks: What must be done to provide the most benefit to the most people? John Stuart Mill and Jeremy Bentham, both English philosophers, are credited with its formulation and promotion (Theaker, 2013, 83). This framework asks you to examine the consequences of your actions. The results, not the starting principles, are what is used to judge if it is ethical. For example, you place a camera in your house to monitor the babysitter without telling her, but it helps stop a theft. Did the greater good outweigh your unacknowledged supervision?

Often utilitarianism is thought of as a brutal ethic that is only concerned about the majority, a type of "might makes right." But Elliott (2012) argues that this is a simplification, and utilitarianism is also concerned with minimizing harm. Utilitarianism is not an egoist framework where you are only out for yourself; the good to society must be considered, not just what is good for you. For example, you personally might find utility in not paying your taxes, but the government programs you benefit from are a societal benefit. Therefore, utilitarianism would say you should pay your taxes because doing so helps the greater good.

Ethics of Care

As an alternative to the frameworks of virtue, deontology, and utilitarianism, an ethics of care was introduced by Gilligan (1982). In this feminist approach, the moral question becomes how should one respond instead of simply what is just (Gilligan, 1995, 35). According to Held (2006), the core of the ethics of care is the moral requirement of "attending to and meeting the needs of the particular others for whom we take responsibility" (10). This component highlights that people are in relationships, interdependent, and not autonomous actors. Care can be defined as "everything we do to maintain, contain, and repair our 'world' so that we can live in it as well as possible. That world includes our bodies, ourselves, and our environment" (Fisher and Tronto, 1990, 40).

Additionally, emotions are valued as part of the moral process. "Sympathy, empathy, sensitivity, and responsiveness" are emotions to be "cultivated" and used in moral decision making, and even raw emotions like anger can spur moral action. (Held, 2006, 10). Tronto (1993) explains that the four elements of care are: attentiveness to needs; taking on the responsibility for care and being willing to respond; have the competence to give care; and being responsive to those receiving care and noting that they are often in vulnerable positions. This framework's concern with relationships, interdependence, and responsiveness fits well with the principles of public relations and parallels many of our professional codes (Coombs and Holladay, 2013; Fraustino and Kennedy, 2018).

Professional Codes

What is a profession? A profession is hard to define, but we all would agree careers such as law, medicine, and the ministry are professions (Brunner, 2016). Is it the high status of these jobs or the extensive training needed that makes these jobs professions? Possibly. However, consider other high-status jobs for which extensive training is needed—for instance, computer programmers, industrial designers, and boy-band members. Are those professions?

Profession can be a confusing concept, but we can set out some basic requirements. A profession "requires specialized education," "provides a unique and essential service," "emphasizes public service and social responsibility," "gives autonomy to and places responsibility on practitioners," and "enforces codes of ethics and standards of performance" (Broom, 2009, 47). The last three requirements have special import to ethics: Professionals must conduct public good, they must be responsible for their own actions, and they must follow a code of ethics.

Formulating codes of ethics defines who we are as a profession. The codes are tangible representations of what we do and how we believe practitioners should behave. They tell us who is and who isn't a member of the profession. If you violate the codes, you are not part of the profession. The codes and thus our ethics lead to public relations being a management function that "can be instrumental in fostering an organizational culture that is sensitive to ethical concerns" and "result in more responsible organizational behavior" (Bowen & Rawlins, 2013, 204). For public relations to be a legitimate profession, practitioners must define and affirm "the values by which it operates" through their actions (Heath, 2000, 69).

Ethical codes come in differing formats. Following are three of the most prominent codes followed by public relations practitioners. The Public Relations Society of America (PRSA) is the largest communication professional organization in the world, with over 30,000 members (PRSA, n.d., a, para. 1). The organization states that "ethical practice is the most important obligation of a PRSA member" (PRSA, n.d., b, para. 5). The International Association of Business Communicators (IABC) serves members in over 70 countries

(IABC, n.d., para. 1). The organization requires members to agree to its code of ethics, which is aimed at "making consistent, responsible, ethical, and legal choices" (IABC, 2014, para. 2).

The final guidelines included are the Page Principles, formulated by Arthur W. Page. He was the vice president for public relations at AT&T and the first public relations professional to become an officer and director of a major corporation (Arthur W. Page, n.d.). The Arthur W. Page Society, which is composed of senior public relations and corporate communication executives, promotes and follows these principles.

All three of codes have much in common. Each has a strong focus on being truthful and fair, improving the profession, and listening to others. The codes are not without criticism; in fact, some see them as just ideals and hypothetical concepts (Fawkes, 2012). Others criticize the focus on tactics as a list of "thou shalt nots" instead of promoting strategic ethical thinking (Kruckeberg, 2000, 38). At a practical level, little enforcement and no punishment exists for violating the codes. For example, an errant practitioner could be removed from the organization for violating the code, but that would not stop him or her from continuing to practice public relations. While these codes may not be perfect, each offers a useful perspective and guidance for being an ethical member of the public relations profession.

As you have read, there are numerous ways to understand and apply ethics. As you deliberate on the cases in this book, return to these definitions, frameworks, and codes and refresh your memory. These concepts can help guide your reflections and debates about the ethics of each situation. By applying the frameworks and codes, you will learn more about your own morals and start to develop the critical thinking necessary to be an ethical professional.

PRSA Code of Ethics: Preamble

This Code applies to PRSA members. The Code is designed to be a useful guide for PRSA members as they carry out their ethical responsibilities. This document is designed to anticipate and accommodate, by precedent, ethical challenges that may arise. The scenarios outlined in the Code provision are actual examples of misconduct. More will be added as experience with the Code occurs.

The Public Relations Society of America (PRSA) is committed to ethical practices. The level of public trust PRSA members seek, as we serve the public good, means we have taken on a special obligation to operate ethically.

The value of member reputation depends upon the ethical conduct of everyone affiliated with the Public Relations Society of America. Each of us sets an example for each other—as well as other professionals—by our pursuit of excellence with powerful standards of performance, professionalism, and ethical conduct.

Emphasis on enforcement of the Code has been eliminated. But, the PRSA Board of Directors retains the right to bar from membership or expel from the Society any individual who has been or is sanctioned by a government agency or convicted in a court of law of an action that fails to comply with the Code.

Ethical practice is the most important obligation of a PRSA member. We view the Member Code of Ethics as a model for other professions, organizations, and professionals.

PRSA Member Statement of Professional Values

This statement presents the core values of PRSA members and, more broadly, of the public relations profession. These values provide the foundation for the Member Code of Ethics and set the industry standard for the professional practice of public relations. These values are the fundamental beliefs that guide our behaviors and decision-making process. We believe our professional values are vital to the integrity of the profession as a whole.

Advocacy

We serve the public interest by acting as responsible advocates for those we represent. We provide a voice in the marketplace of ideas, facts, and viewpoints to aid informed public debate.

Honesty

We adhere to the highest standards of accuracy and truth in advancing the interests of those we represent and in communicating with the public.

Expertise

We acquire and responsibly use specialized knowledge and experience. We advance the profession through continued professional development, research, and education. We build mutual understanding, credibility, and relationships among a wide array of institutions and audiences.

Independence

We provide objective counsel to those we represent. We are accountable for our actions.

Loyalty

We are faithful to those we represent, while honoring our obligation to serve the public interest.

Fairness

We deal fairly with clients, employers, competitors, peers, vendors, the media, and the general public. We respect all opinions and support the right of free expression.

PRSA Code Provisions of Conduct

Free Flow of Information

Core Principle: Protecting and advancing the free flow of accurate and truthful information is essential to serving the public interest and contributing to informed decision making in a democratic society.

Competition

Core Principle: Promoting healthy and fair competition among professionals preserves an ethical climate while fostering a robust business environment.

Disclosure of Information

Core Principle: Open communication fosters informed decision making in a democratic society.

Safeguarding Confidences

Core Principle: Client trust requires appropriate protection of confidential and private information.

Conflicts of Interest

Core Principle: Avoiding real, potential, or perceived conflicts of interest builds the trust of clients, employers, and the publics.

Enhancing the Profession

Core Principle: Public relations professionals work constantly to strengthen the public's trust in the profession.

IABC Code of Ethics for Professional Communicators

As a professional communicator, you have the potential to influence economies and affect lives. This power carries with it significant responsibilities.

The International Association of Business Communicators requires its members to agree to the IABC Code of Ethics. This code serves as a guide to making consistent, responsible, ethical, and legal choices in all of our communications.

IABC's Code of Ethics

- I am honest—my actions bring respect for and trust in the communication profession.
- I communicate accurate information and promptly correct any errors.
- I obey laws and public policies; if I violate any law or public policy, I act promptly to correct the situation.
- I protect confidential information while acting within the law.
- I support the ideals of free speech, freedom of assembly, and access to an open marketplace of ideas.
- I am sensitive to others' cultural values and beliefs.
- I give credit to others for their work and cite my sources.
- I do not use confidential information for personal benefit.
- I do not represent conflicting or competing interests without full disclosure and the written consent of those involved.
- I do not accept undisclosed gifts or payments for professional services from anyone other than a client or employer.
- I do not guarantee results that are beyond my power to deliver.

The Page Principles

- Tell the truth.
- Let the public know what's happening with honest and good intention; provide an ethically accurate picture of the enterprise's character, values, ideals and actions.
- Prove it with action.
- Public perception of an enterprise is determined 90 percent by what it does and 10 percent by what it says.
- Listen to stakeholders.
- To serve the enterprise well, understand what the public wants and needs and advocate for engagement with all stakeholders. Keep top decision makers and other employees informed about stakeholder reaction to the enterprise's products, policies and practices. To listen effectively, engage a diverse range of stakeholders through inclusive dialogue.
- Manage for tomorrow.
- Anticipate public reaction and eliminate practices that create difficulties. Generate goodwill.
- Conduct public relations as if the whole enterprise depends on it.
- No strategy should be implemented without considering its impact on stakeholders. As a management and policymaking function, public relations should encourage the enterprise's decision making, policies and actions to

consider its stakeholders' diverse range of views, values, experience, expectations and aspirations.
- Realize an enterprise's true character is expressed by its people.
- The strongest opinions—good or bad—about an enterprise are shaped by the words and deeds of an increasingly diverse workforce. As a result, every employee—active or retired—is involved with public relations. It is the responsibility of corporate communications to advocate for respect, diversity and inclusion in the workforce and to support each employee's capability and desire to be an honest, knowledgeable ambassador to customers, friends, shareowners and public officials.
- Remain calm, patient and good-humored.
- Lay the groundwork for public relations successes with consistent and reasoned attention to information and stakeholders. When a crisis arises, remember, cool heads communicate best.

References

Aristotle. (350 BCE). *Nicomachean Ethics*. (W. D. Ross, Trans.). Retrieved February 1, 2018 from http://classics.mit.edu/Aristotle/nicomachaen.2.ii.html

Arthur W. Page. (n.d.). Retrieved February 14, 2018, from http://bellisario.psu.edu/page-center/about/arthur-w-page.

Bowen, S. A. (2016). Clarifying ethics terms in public relations from A to V, authenticity to virtue: BledCom special issue of *PR Review*, "Sleeping (with the) media: Media relations." *Public Relations Review, 42*(4), 564–572.

Bowen, S. A, & Rawlins, B. (2013). Corporate moral conscience. In Heath, R. (Ed.), *Encyclopedia of Public Relations II* (pp. 202–206). Thousand Oaks, CA: Sage.

Broom, G. M. (2009). *Cutlip and Center's Effective Public Relations*. Upper Saddle River, NJ: Prentice Hall.

Brunner, B. R. (Ed.). (2016). *The Moral Compass of Public Relations* (Vol. 8). London: Taylor & Francis.

Burke, K. (1966). *Language as Symbolic Action: Essays on Life, Literature, and Method*. Berkeley/Los Angeles/London: University of California Press.

Coombs, W. T., & Holladay, S. J. (2013). *It's Not Just PR: Public Relations in Society*. Malden, MA: Wiley-Blackwell.

Elliott, D. (2007). Getting Mill right. *Journal of Mass Media Ethics, 22*(2–3), 100–112.

Ethics Center. (2016). Ethics, morality, law: What's the difference? Retrieved February 1, 2018, from http://www.ethics.org.au/on-ethics/blog/september-2016/ethics-morality-law-whats-the-difference.

Evans, T. (2010). We are all in PR now. *British Journalism Review, 21*(2), 31–36.

Fawkes, J. (2012). Saints and sinners: Competing identities in public relations ethics. *Public Relations Review, 38*(5), 865–872.

Fisher, B., & Tronto J. (1990). "Toward a Feminist Theory of Care." In E. K. Abel & M. K. Nelson (Eds.), *Circles of Care: Work and Identity in Women's Lives* (35–62). Albany: State University of New York Press.

Fraustino, J. D., & Kennedy, A. K. Care in Crisis: An Applied Model of Care Considerations for Ethical Strategic Communication. *The Journal of Public Interest Communications, 2*(1), 18–40.

Freytas-Tamura, K. D. (2018, January 26). BBC, criticized over pay gap, cuts salaries of some male journalists. *New York Times*. Retrieved February 10, 2018, from https://www.nytimes.com/2018/01/26/business/media/bbc-pay-gap.html.

Gilligan, C. (1982). *In a different voice*. Cambridge, MA: Harvard University Press.

Gilligan, C. (1995). Moral Orientation and Moral Development. In V. Held (Ed.) *Justice and Care: Essential Reading in Feminist Ethics* (31–46). Boulder, CO: Westview Press.

Gregory, A., & Willis, P. (2013). *Strategic Public Relations Leadership*. Abingdon: Routledge.

Grunig, J. E. (2000). Collectivism, collaboration, and societal corporatism as core professional values in public relations. *Journal of Public Relations Research, 12*(1), 23–48.

Heath, R. L. (2000). A rhetorical perspective on the values of public relations: Crossroads and pathways toward concurrence. *Journal of Public Relations Research, 12,* 69–91.

Held, V. (2006). *The Ethics of Care: Personal, Political, and Global*. New York: Oxford University Press.

International Association of Business Communicators. (n.d.). About us. Retrieved February 10, 2018, from https://www.iabc.com/about-us/.

International Association of Business Communicators. (2014, July 30). Code of Ethics for Professional Communicators. Retrieved February 10, 2018, from https://www.iabc.com/about-us/governance/code-of-ethics/.

Kruckeberg, D. (2000). The public relations practitioner's role in practicing strategic ethics. *Public Relations Quarterly, 45,* 35–39.

Kruckeberg, D., & Starck, K. (1988). *Public Relations and Community: A Reconstructed Theory*. New York: Praeger.

Locke, J. (1689/2014). *Second Treatise of Government: An Essay Concerning the True Original, Extent and End of Civil Government*. Somerset, NJ: John Wiley & Sons.

Mills v. Alabama, 384 U.S. 214 (1966).

Page Principles. (n.d.). Retrieved February 10, 2018, from https://awpagesociety.com/site/the-page-principles.

Parsons, P. J. (2016). *Ethics in Public Relations: A Guide to Best Practice*. London/Philadelphia: Kogan Page Publishers.

Public Relations Society of America. (n.d., a). About PRSA. Retrieved February 10, 2018, from https://www.prsa.org/about/about-prsa/.

Public Relations Society of America. (n.d., b). Code of Ethics. Retrieved February 14, 2018, from https://www.prsa.org/ethics/code-of-ethics/.

Stoker, K., & Stoker, M. (2012). The paradox of public interest: How serving individual superior interests fulfill public relations' obligation to the public interest. *Journal of Mass Media Ethics, 27*(1), 31–45.

Tronto, J. (1993). *Moral Boundaries: A Political Argument for an Ethic of Care.* New York: Routledge.

Theaker, A. (2013). *The Public Relations Handbook.* London: Routledge.

Wright, D. K. (1979). Professionalism and social responsibility in public relations. *Public Relations Review, 5*(3), 20–33.

PUBLIC RELATIONS FUNCTIONS

3 CONFLICT AND CRISIS MANAGEMENT

Learning Outcomes

- Identify the phases in a crisis.
- Classify strategies used in crisis management.
- Understand the difference between crisis communication and risk communication.
- Apply crisis management strategies to case studies.

Definitions

Crisis: "The perception of an unpredictable event that threatens important expectancies of stakeholders and can seriously impact an organization's performance and generate negative outcomes" (Coombs, 2007, 2–3)

Crisis communication: "The collection, processing, and dissemination of information required to address a crisis situation" (Coombs, 2010, 20)

Crisis management: The plan created to deal with crisis situation

Risk communication: Communication before a crisis that aims to reduce the severity of a crisis or stop it from occurring

Most people would label the Exxon Valdez crash, Tylenol tampering, and exploding Samsung batteries as crises, but most crises that organizations face are more nuanced. If you are a communication director, one of your most important strategic decisions is whether or not what just happened is a crisis, a conflict, or just a bad incident. Furthermore, no matter the quality or type of organization, most organizations will face a crisis in the long term. Even the most prepared organizations are not immune from a crisis (Spillan, 2003).

Many definitions of crisis exist, but most have in common the attributes of involving change, producing negative or positive outcomes, and being unexpected. Coombs (2007, 2–3) provides a definition that encompasses all three. He writes a crisis is "the perception of an unpredictable event that threatens important expectancies of stakeholders and can seriously impact an organization's performance and generate negative outcomes."

Notice that it is the perception of the stakeholders that determines if it is a crisis. Understanding how the publics are viewing the event is vital. The public perception of the organization's responsibility in causing the crisis can be used to classify the type of crisis. If the organization is perceived as not being responsible for the crisis, these are *victim crises*. Items like earthquakes, workplace violence, and product tampering are examples. When the organization has a low level of responsibility, that would be an *accidental crisis*. These types of crises could include a sudden downturn in the economy, a piece of manufacturing equipment malfunctioning, or a product causing harm when used in an unforeseen way. The third type is a *preventable crisis*, which is caused by an intentional misdeed—for example, embezzlement, releasing a product that was known to be defective, and lying about earnings. Seeger (2006) used a similar set of categories: natural disasters, industrial accidents, and intentional events (234–235).

Also, crises cause serious outcomes. Crises are not normal day-to-day operations and thus require additional attention and resources. Furthermore, a crisis is not always a bad thing. Friedman (2002, 5) noted that the crisis "may be a radical change for good as well as bad." A crisis will always cause change, but the outcome can be positive or negative.

Crisis Phases

Crises can be divided into multiple cyclical parts. Wilcox (2006) suggests that crises should be thought of as having proactive, strategic, reactive, and recovery phases. The proactive phase occurs before the crisis and is characterized by issue tracking and management. In this first phase, organizations can prepare crisis plans. The strategic phase occurs next. During this time, the organization knows that a crisis is possible and engages in risk communication and conflict positioning. For example, a city official in a hurricane-prone area can provide information about preparing for a storm before the first hurricane. Risk communication is the type of communication that occurs before the crisis to prepare stakeholders and possibly prevent the crisis. Not all crises can be prevented, so preparedness is important. The better an organization is prepared, the better the response and recovery during and after a crisis (e.g., Longstaff & Yang, 2008).

The reactive phase occurs begins with the actual crisis. It aims at ameliorating the crisis event and resolving the conflict. During this stage, practitioners engage in crisis communication and crisis management. Crisis management "seeks to prevent or lessen the negative outcomes of a crisis and thereby protect the organization, stakeholders, and/or industry from damage" (Coombs, 1999, 4). Crisis communication can be defined generally as collecting, attending to, and distributing the information required to address a potential crisis.

Crisis Responses

Both Coombs (2007) and Benoit (1997) offer a typology of the crisis communication strategies that can be used during this stage. In his rhetorical studies of crisis, Benoit (1997) notes that organizations respond to crises with the strategies of denial (we didn't do it), evasion of responsibility (it wasn't our fault), reducing the offensiveness of the event (it wasn't that bad), corrective action (we fixed it), and mortification (we're sorry). Coombs (2007), in his Situational Crisis Communication Theory, posits that crises can be responded to by primary and secondary methods. Primary strategies are used to resolve the crisis and include attacking the accuser, denying the existence of the crisis, scapegoating some person or organization for the crisis, excusing organizational responsibility, justifying the perceived damage, compensating victims, and apologizing. The secondary responses are ones that bolster the organization's reputation, such as reminding the publics of past good works, ingratiating and praising stakeholders, and playing the victim of the crisis.

The final stage is the recovery phase. During this time, the organization focuses on reputation management and the future. At the end of this phase the cycle begins again with the proactive phase.

Crisis Ethics

Our discussion of crises has yet to mention ethics, but the two are intricately connected. What good is corrective action if it isn't truly corrective? What good is an apology if it is untrue? Seegar and Ulmer (2001, 375) argue that often "ethical issues are ignored during the immediacy, uncertainty, and stress of a crisis," but ethical crisis management is effective in maintaining stakeholder relationships and "rejuvenating" organizations. Transparency, two-way symmetry, and timing are three components of a test proposed by Kim (2015) to ensure ethical communication. Transparency means that an organization should communicate all the information it can about the crisis. The amount of information and the speed at which it is released can be stifled due to legal or practical needs, but organizations should strive to give out as much information as would be useful. The two-way component means that organizations should listen to the public instead of just being the mouthpiece for the organization. The practitioner should be seeking out the opinions and communications of others and taking them back to the organization. The goal is understanding and dialogue. The final test is timing: ethical crisis communication should be prompt and continue through all the crisis phases.

References

Benoit, W. L. (1997). Image repair discourse and crisis communication. *Public Relations Review, 23*(2), 177–186.

Coombs, W. T. (1999). Ongoing Crisis Communication: Planning, Managing, and Responding. Thousand Oaks, CA: Sage.

Coombs, W. T. (2007). *Ongoing Crisis Communication. Planning, Managing, and Responding* (2nd ed.). Thousand Oaks, CA: Sage.

Coombs, W. T. (2010). Parameters for crisis communication. In Coombs, W. T., & Holladay, S. J. (Eds.), *Handbook of Crisis Communication* (pp. 17–53). Malden, MA: Blackwell.

Friedman, M. (2002). *Everyday Crisis Management: How to Think Like an Emergency Physician*. Naperville, IL: First Decision Press.

Kim, Y. (2015) Toward an ethical model of effective crisis communication. *Business and Society Review, 120* (1), 57–81.

Longstaff, P. H., & Yang, S. U. (2008). Communication management and trust: Their role in building resilience to "surprises" such as natural disasters, pandemic flu, and terrorism. *Ecology and Society, 13*(1), 3.

Seeger, M. W. (2006). Best practices in crisis communication: An expert panel process. *Journal of Applied Communication Research, 34*(3), 232–244.

Seeger, M. W., & Ulmer, R. R. (2001). Virtuous responses to organizational crisis: Aaron Feuerstein and Milt Colt. *Journal of Business Ethics, 31*(4), 369–376.

Spillan, J. E. (2003). An exploratory model for evaluating crisis events and managers' concerns in non-profit organisations. *Journal of Contingencies and Crisis Management, 11*(4), 160–169.

Wilcox, D. (2006). *Public Relations: Strategies and Tactics*. Boston, MA: Pearson Education.

THE LANDS' END CONTENT MARKETING DEBACLE: A CAUTIONARY TALE OF A RETAILER'S INADVERTENT FORAY INTO POLARIZED POLITICS

Nathan Gilkerson, Ph.D., *Marquette University*

In late February of 2016, the iconic clothing retailer Lands' End found itself embroiled in a self-inflicted public relations firestorm. The company, long known for its mail-order catalogue business, customer service, and high-quality fashion basics, was facing angry calls for boycotts from customers on social media—and a wave of negative headlines from news outlets eager to report on the retailer's embarrassing marketing misstep. The backlash was in response to an interview with author and feminist activist Gloria Steinem, conducted by the company's chief executive officer Federica Marchionni, which appeared on the retailer's website and within its newly released spring fashion catalogue. Conservative customers expressed dismay that the company had featured a controversial feminist icon known for her long history of activism and support for abortion rights. In an attempt to end controversy and quickly quell consumer anger, the retailer immediately removed the Steinem content from its website and issued a carefully worded apology stressing it had not intended to cause offense. Instead of defusing the situation, however, the apology caused a new wave of customer backlash and angry posts to social media, this time from shoppers who supported Steinem and her liberal politics. The damage to the Lands' End brand was done, and instead of refreshing the classic retailer's somewhat stodgy image, it seemed the company had only succeeded in disappointing and angering a wide spectrum of its core customer base.

Background

Lands' End was founded in Chicago in 1963 as a yachting equipment supply business, with casual clothing representing just a small fraction of its products. The company was an innovator in the mail-order industry by creating catalogues with compelling visuals and detailed and appealing product descriptions, quickly shipping orders to customers, and offering shoppers a flexible and "unconditional" return policy (landsend.com, About Us, para. 5). As the company became more successful, it narrowed its product focus to clothing and luggage and, in 1978, moved its business operations to the small town of Dodgeville, Wisconsin. Becoming a publicly traded company in 1986, Lands' End expanded internationally during the 1990s and became an early adopter of internet retailing with the launch of LandsEnd.com in 1995 (landsend.com, Corporate Overview). In 2002, the company was purchased by Sears (CNN Money, 2002), a move that put Lands' End–branded clothing in hundreds of Sears retail stores across the country. In 2013, suffering profitability challenges, the Sears Holding Corporation elected to spin off Lands' End into a separate publicly traded company (Malcolm, 2013). Today the company's top three competitors are L.L. Bean, Eddie Bauer, and J.C. Penney (Hoovers.com, 2016).

Along with its website offering a variety of clothing for women, men, and kids and home furnishings, today the company generates revenue from its standalone retail Lands' End Inlet Stores located across the country, as well as its Business Outfitters workplace apparel and School Uniform websites (landsend.com, Corporate Overview). Important to this case study, the company's sales of school uniforms to private (and often religious) educational institutions represents a significant percentage of the retailer's business (Bukszpan, 2016); the company partners with thousands of private schools by offering customized websites that assist parents in shopping for school uniforms, and an incentive program that gives participating institutions a 3% cash back payment on the net sales of their school's uniforms (landsend.com, Corporate Overview).

Following separation from Sears, Lands' End has suffered declining sales and a significant reduction in its stock value (Romell, 2015c). In early 2015 the retailer hired a new Italian-born CEO, Federica Marchionni, who previously served as an executive for the Dolce & Gabbana luxury fashion house (Romell, 2015c). News articles described her plans to seek cost efficiencies in the company's operations and to reinvigorate the brand and increase its relevance with a move toward trendier, "more fashion-forward" clothes (Romell, 2015b). Shortly after Marchionni started, media reports questioned the "fit" between the high-fashion Italian executive's management style and the more traditional Midwestern brand and corporate culture of Lands' End. Articles specifically noted Marchionni's decision to maintain her primary residence in New York City, and to regularly fly back and forth between New York and Wisconsin for meetings and major corporate events, versus moving with her family to the 4,700-person town of Dodgeville, home to most of the company's employees (Kapner, 2016; Romell, 2015a).

The Situation

Sent to customers in late February, among descriptions of its latest clothes and fashionable pictures depicting well-dressed models enjoying a fancy Easter-themed picnic, the spring 2016 Lands' End catalogue featured a multi-page photo spread and interview with the headline "Gloria Steinem, The Woman Who Paved the Way." Next to a photo of a smiling Steinem wearing Lands' End clothing, the page announced: "Introducing the Legend Series, our ode to individuals who have made a difference in both their respective industries and the world at large. We honor them and thank them for paving the way for the many who follow" (Faircloth, 2016). The company's website also featured the interview and photos of Steinem, labeling the section "A Conversation with Federica Marchionni, CEO." As multiple news reports noted, the published interview, which included a photo of Marchionni and Steinem sitting and talking together, did not discuss or mention the topic of abortion but, rather, focused on challenges women encounter in the workplace (Halzack, 2016) and Steinem's longstanding support for the Equal Rights Amendment, a proposed change to the Constitution to "expressly prohibit discrimination against girls and women on the basis of sex" (ERA Coalition, n.d., para.1). The feature also advertised a promotion allowing customers to add an embroidered "ERA Coalition" logo to Lands' End products, with the company then donating proceeds to the nonprofit organization.

Outcomes

Online backlash from conservative consumers was almost immediate. Media reports described the flood of angry comments posted to the Lands' End Facebook page, with consumers expressing outrage at the company's decision to feature Steinem and calling for a boycott of the brand. Most articles included a sampling of negative social media posts. The *Washington Post*, for example, described the backlash against Lands' End as "swift and intense" and included a series of Facebook posts in its story (Bukszpan, 2016):

> "You obviously don't know who shops with you, or maybe you do and don't care," wrote one shopper on Facebook. "In the midst of the celebration of Easter (life), you interview and glorify a woman who fosters a culture of death."
>
> "Those of us who love family, love children, are completely puzzled why you would promote a very vocal pro-abortion celebrity," wrote another. "Is this who you are LandsEnd? Are you anti-child?"
>
> "How could you not understand that your family-friendly customer base does not want to see a rabidly pro-abortion woman (Steinem) honored as a hero?"

Dozens of major media outlets reported on the controversy, including the *New York Times, Washington Post, Los Angeles Times, NBC News, Forbes, Fortune*, and *The Guardian*. Most articles also included at least a portion of the formal apology statement Lands' End issued in response to the customers who had complained about the Steinem piece:

> We understand that some of our customers were offended by the inclusion of an interview in a recent catalog with Gloria Steinem on her quest for women's equality. We thought it was a good idea and we heard from our customers that, for different reasons, it wasn't. For that, we sincerely apologize. Our goal was to feature individuals with different interests and backgrounds that have made a difference for our new Legends Series, not to take any political or religious stance.

Other articles referenced a similar message, with slightly different wording (see the Appendix), which was posted on the same day to the Lands' End corporate Facebook page. The tone of the Lands' End statements reads as contrite, apologetic, and deferential. Perhaps predictably, however, many consumers who backed Steinem were quick to express their own anger at what they viewed as the cowardly decision Lands' End had made to distance itself from Steinem and her politics. Much of the media coverage included samples of social media posts from users who were irate that the company had deleted the interview from its site and apologized for its association with the feminist activist (Halzack, 2016).

> "What a terrible message to send to all the women and girls who wear your clothes," one Facebook commenter wrote. "I'm sorry you see equal rights for women as a divisive issue. I see it as a human issue."

Many articles highlighted social media posts from consumers declaring that they would never again shop at Lands' End, with declarations that they and their families would instead be taking their business to other retailers:

> "I don't intend to teach my children that anyone should do business with a company that is ashamed to even talk about feminism."
> "You see equal rights as a divisive issue? Thanks for letting me know not to give you my money."
> "Dear @LandsEnd, my kids know Gloria Steinem is a heroine, and they're also going to know why they're no longer wearing your clothes."
> "Lands' End will never get another dollar from our family. Poorly done, @LandsEnd @LandsEndPR #landsend steinem"

In deciding not to stand behind its original marketing content, although the company attempted to apologize and de-politicize its actions, analysis shows that Lands' End placed itself in a "lose–lose" public relations position. In examining this case study, it is important to explore ethical consideration along with the various factors that may have motivated these choices. How could such a well-respected company make such clumsy and seemingly ill-considered decisions?

Declining Sales, a CEO/Company Culture Clash, and the Private School Uniform Factor

Leading up to the Steinem controversy, Marchionni was quoted as citing a "challenging retail environment" and "a lack of product acceptance" as among several factors that had contributed to the company's decreased earnings and recent loss of stock value (Romell, 2015c). Reporting on the company's fourth consecutive disappointing earnings report, retail industry journalists noted that Marchionni was attempting to "tweak the brand's image" to better attract a younger and more fashion-focused clientele, while retaining the more traditional Lands' End shopper (Bhasin, 2015; Romell, 2015b). Along with trendier clothing options (Cheng, 2016), the new Legends Series of interviews with pioneering individuals was part of Marchionni's attempt to generate attention and increase the relevance of the brand.

Upon her hire as CEO, observers had noted Marchionni's background in high fashion and its stylistic contrast with the more down-to-earth Lands'

End image. However, news coverage emerging after the Steinem controversy unfolded revealed evidence of deeper tensions, including poor internal communication and a culture clash between Marchionni and some of the company's Wisconsin-based executives and employees (Romell, 2016c). One article, which relied heavily on anonymous quotes from current and former Lands' End employees, referenced Marchionni's decision to remain based in New York as contributing to colleagues' questioning of the executive's understanding of "Midwestern" culture—and depicted an atmosphere of toxic office politics, with Marchionni described derisively by one former colleague as "a princess," and her business demeanor and management style compared to the icy Meryl Streep character from the film "The Devil Wears Prada" (Romell, 2016c). Marchionni, who was described by anonymous employees as being impatient and often unwilling or uninterested in hearing dissenting ideas, is alternately quoted in the piece describing issues of stagnancy and complacency within the company (Romell, 2016c). It is perhaps an open question as to whether tensions among executives or poor communication served to hamper strategic dialogue in the development of the Legends Series initiative, and key discussions related to the decision to feature a polarizing and controversial figure like Steinem to inaugurate the series. One could also question whether a cultural disconnect—between the New York City–based CEO and the company's Midwestern employees, or between Marchionni and the more traditional (i.e., conservative) Lands' End customer base—helped to create a situation in which the benefits and risks of the Steinem interview were not fully considered.

With a professional marketing and corporate communications team on staff, it is implausible that at least some within Lands' End didn't anticipate negative feedback in the lead-up to the Steinem interview. As a public figure, Steinem has been involved in controversial politics for decades, and today's often highly charged social media environment allows anyone to easily voice an opinion. While likely expecting some resentment from a segment of customers opposed to Steinem's politics, as is evident in the company's statements the Lands' End communication team was seemingly caught off guard by both the volume of angry responses from conservative customers and the antipathy many held toward Steinem.

However, perhaps the most influential factor in the company's decision to make such a hasty public reversal and apology for its honoring of Steinem was the coordinated response and public calls for boycotts from the religious and parochial school community. In particular, many news articles covering the controversy referenced two private Christian schools in Missouri, the College of the Ozarks and Father Tolton Regional Catholic High School, which had both announced they had "ended their relationship with Lands' End" due to the Steinem interview (Berry, 2016; Schlossberg, 2016). Coverage from a Columbia, Missouri, television station reported that administrators from Tolton Catholic High School had sent a letter to parents announcing that it would no longer use Lands' End as its official uniform provider because of its alliance with Steinem, "an advocate for abortion rights" (Quick, 2016). An excerpt from the letter, which was also posted to the school's Facebook page, read: "We believe unequivocally that all life is sacred, from conception until natural death. It would be contrary to our school's very identity to support a company who celebrates the work of someone so opposed to our beliefs" (Quick, 2016). The story also quotes the regional Catholic diocese of Jefferson City (MO) as supporting the school's decision to cut ties with Lands' End, and encouraging the dozens of other elementary and high schools within its region "to be aware of the situation" when making future decisions regarding uniform company selection (Quick, 2016).

While the initial backlash Lands' End faced for the Steinem interview may have been isolated to a handful of religious schools—which were fast to publicize their discontent via social media posts and traditional media interviews—the company's quick decision to apologize and disassociate itself from Steinem was likely motivated by a larger concern that the trend of schools canceling uniform contracts might spread exponentially throughout national networks of Catholic and Christian schools. For Lands' End, the potential loss of a significant portion of its school uniform business due to offended members of the religious community likely far outweighed the reputational costs and damage to the brand image caused by backtracking on its support for Steinem. While time, and future sales, will reveal the business implications of its decision, perhaps more up for debate are the ethical considerations, for Lands' End—and other companies—striving to remain relevant and win over today's consumers, while also avoiding "any political or religious stance."

Appendix

Alternate wording of apology statement, posted to the Lands' End corporate Facebook page:

> Some customers were troubled and concerned that we featured an interview with Gloria Steinem in a recent catalog. Lands' End is committed to providing our loyal customers and their families with stylish, affordable, well-made clothing. We greatly respect and appreciate the passion people have for our brand. It was never our intention to raise a divisive political or religious issue, so when some of our customers saw the recent promotion that way, we heard them. We sincerely apologize for any offense.

References

Berry, S. (2016, February 26). Schools drop Lands' End as uniform supplier after interview with abortion activist Gloria Steinem. *Breitbart*. Retrieved from http://www.breitbart.com/big-government/2016/02/26/schools-drop-lands-end-as-uniform-supplier-after-interview-with-abortion-activist-gloria-steinem/.

Bhasin, K. (2015, August 20). Inside Lands' End's quest for a younger, cooler customer. *Bloomberg.com*. Retrieved from http://www.bloomberg.com/news/articles/2015-08-20/inside-lands-end-s-quest-for-a-younger-cooler-customer.

Bukszpan, D. (2016, February 26). How Lands' End suddenly became an abortion debate battleground. *Fortune*. Retrieved from http://fortune.com/2016/02/26/lands-end-apology-steinem/.

Cheng, A. (2016, April 16). Land' End's new designer collection: Everything you need to know about canvas by Lands' End. *InStyle*. Retrieved from http://www.instyle.com/news/canvas-by-lands-end-launch-federica-marchionni.

CNN Money. (2002, May 14). Sears buys Lands' End. *CNN Money*. Retrieved from http://money.cnn.com/2002/05/13/news/deals/sears/index.htm.

ERA Coalition (n.d.). What is the ERA? Retrieved from http://www.eracoalition.org/about.php.

Faircloth, K. (2016, February 24). Did Lands' End delete an interview with Gloria Steinem to please pro-lifers? *Jezebel.com*. Retrieved from http://jezebel.com/did-lands-end-delete-an-interview-with-gloria-steinem-t-1761106358.

Halzack, S. (2016, February 26). Lands' End put Gloria Steinem in its catalog. Then it got an earful from customers. *Washington Post*. Retrieved from https://www.washingtonpost.com/news/business/wp/2016/02/26/lands-end-put-gloria-steinem-in-its-catalog-then-it-got-an-earful-from-customers/.

Hoovers.com. (n.d.). Lands' End, Inc. company information. Retrieved from http://www.hoovers.com/company-information/cs/company-profile.lands_end_inc.de33019b0ea06bf7.html.

Kapner, S. (2016, May 6). New Lands' End CEO delivers high fashion—and a culture clash. *Wall Street Journal*. Retrieved from http://www.wsj.com/articles/new-lands-end-ceo-delivers-high-fashionand-a-culture-clash-1462547397.

Lands' End. (n.d.) About Us. Retrieved from http://www.landsend.com/aboutus/.

Lands' End. (n.d.). Corporate Overview. Retrieved from https://www.landsend.com/newsroom/corp_info/overview/.

Malcolm, H. (2013, December 6). Sears to spin off Lands' End business. *USA Today*. Retrieved from http://www.usatoday.com/story/money/business/2013/12/06/sears-to-spin-off-lands-end-business/3888811/.

Quick, J. (2016, February 24). Tolton Catholic HS to end relationship with clothing company over abortion stance. *ABC 17 News*. Retrieved from http://www.abc17news.com/news/tolton-catholic-hs-to-end-relationship-with-clothing-company-over-abortion-stance/38171048.

Romell, R. (2015a, April 25). Lands' End CEO will call New York—not Dodgeville—home. *Journal Sentinel*. Retrieved from http://www.jsonline.com/business/dont-look-too-hard-for-new-lands-end-ceo-in-dodgeville-b99486008z1-301342881.html.

Romell, R. (2015b, June 5). Changes afoot at Lands' End, new CEO Marchionni says. *Journal Sentinel*. Retrieved from http://www.jsonline.com/business/changes-afoot-at-lands-end-new-ceo-marchionni-says-b99514255z1-306333611.html.

Romell, R. (2015c, December 3). Lands' End earnings plunge again; CEO partly blames weather. *Journal Sentinel*. Retrieved from http://www.jsonline.com/business/lands-end-earnings-plunge-again-ceo-partly-blames-weather-b99 627656z1-360417891.html.

Romell, R. (2016c, April 30). One year in, CEO Marchionni shakes up tradition-minded Lands' End. *Journal Sentinel*. Retrieved from http://www.jsonline.com/business/one-year-in-ceo-marchionni-shakes-up-tradition-minded-lands-end-b99714174z1-377708931.html.

Schlossberg, M. (2016, February 25). Lands' End completely changed its marketing strategy after Catholic schools threatened to boycott the business. *Business Insider*. Retrieved from http://www.businessinsider.com/lands-end-removes-gloria-steinem-interview-2016-2.

Discussion Questions

1. Is it "ethical" for a company to become involved with controversial social and political issues, such as (support or opposition toward) abortion, LGBT rights, or gay marriage? What are some of the key factors a company should consider before wading into politics? (An alternate framing of this question: Is it ever *unethical* for a company to remain "neutral" or to refuse to take any sort of stance on a specific political or social issue?)

2. Today more and more companies and corporate CEOs are choosing to take a stand on controversial social issues, or to become involved in charged political debates. Noteworthy recent examples include Starbucks CEO Howard Schultz and the company's #RaceTogether campaign, Apple CEO Tim Cook's public support of LGBT rights, and Target Corporation's bathroom policy for transgender customers. With this trend in mind, is there ever an ethical imperative for companies (especially publicly traded, stockholder-owned firms) to *avoid* polarizing political controversies that could alienate customers and potentially harm sales and profits? Or, alternatively, should corporate executives always feel compelled to "do what's right" in offering their company's support for (or opposition to) political causes, regardless of the potential negative implications to profits and stock price and so forth?

3. Following a major public relations misstep like the Gloria Steinem controversy, how can a company such as Lands' End work to gain support and win back customers who were angered by previous marketing decisions? What unique risks and benefits might tools like social media hold in pursuing this effort?

4. Specifically related to the notion of business ethics, is there really such a thing as "corporate values"? What does it mean for a company to have strong values, and how can an organization demonstrate its values in a way that is both truly genuine and generally perceived positively and as authentic by various publics? What role should employees and consumers play in determining a company's values?

5. Following the Steinem controversy, Lands' End CEO Marchionni was quoted in an interview ("The Power of Sorry," appearing on June 27, 2016, in *Marie Claire*) saying that as part of an attempt to raise awareness, Lands' End "took a stance to support

women's equality" and that the company was surprised by the negative response from both sides of the abortion debate. Discussing the company's apology, the CEO said, "we never intended to raise that (abortion) issue." Can social and political issues be *separated* in this manner? Alternately, is there such a thing as controversy-free corporate involvement in politics? What are the key factors involved?

THE SEPTEMBER 11 MEMORIAL

Hannah Karolak, Ph.D., *UPMC Health Plan*, and
Susan Mancino, Ph.D., *Saint Mary's College*

Following the September 11, 2001 terrorist attacks, public leaders of New York City announced their commitment to rebuilding Ground Zero both to honor victims and family members of the attacks and to provide space for businesses that were housed within the towers. By 2004, development plans for Ground Zero slowed, and by 2006, construction was at a standstill. At the heart of the rebuilding effort were disagreements between the public corporation that owned the land, the Port Authority of New York and New Jersey, and the leaseholder of the land, Larry Silverstein. However, the conflict stretched far deeper, emerging from leadership changes among the "19 public agencies, two private developers, 101 different construction contractors and sub-contractors and 33 different designers, architects and consulting firms," budget constraints amid rising costs, and memorial design disagreements. Architects, members of the New York Fire Department, residents of lower Manhattan, and family members of 9/11 victims demanded voice and participation in the rebuilding effort (Ward, 2008, 5). This conflict demanded public relations professionals to be attentive to the interests and ethical commitments of each stakeholder group. This reading details how PR practitioners navigated the competing background positions that fueled the Ground Zero rebuild conflict.

Conflicts emerge as organizations and stakeholders work to protect particular goods (Arnett, Fritz, & Bell, 2009). These goods are shaped by understandings of what matters (Cooren, 2010)—what positions, rights, or interests contribute to a particular stakeholder's well-being. Often, groups disagree on what matters, and it becomes the job of PR professionals to navigate these disagreements. The mixed motives model for understanding conflicts among stakeholders, communities, and organizations describes one-way and two-way communication strategies for PR professionals handling conflict (Plowman, 2013); this model is helpful when thinking about the Ground Zero rebuild. Part 1 of this reading, "Background," contextualizes the rebuilding of Ground Zero and its relevance to public relations ethics. Part 2, "The Situation," identifies major players in the conflict and the tensions among the various stakeholders involved in the Ground Zero rebuilding efforts. Part 3 of the essay, "Outcomes and Directions," identifies the public relations outcomes of the conflict. Here, the mixed motives model of conflict resolution proves helpful for understanding the connections among public relations, communication ethics, and the conflicting interests of multiple stakeholders.

Background

The World Trade Center complex is a financial hub located in Lower Manhattan. In 1946, the World Trade Corporation, commissioned by the New York State Legislature, proposed to build this site. By 1962, the Port Authority identified the bounds of the complex as West, Church, Liberty, and Vesey Streets, which later became known as a central component of New York's Financial Center. In 1964, the design for the complex was introduced to the public. The architecture and engineering company Yamasaki designed the space. In the following years, the Port Authority of New York and New Jersey acquired the property. The construction of the Twin Towers began in August 1968 with the North Tower. The South Tower construction continued in January 1969. The "topping out" ceremonies for the construction of these sites occurred in 1970 (North Tower) and 1971 (South Tower) with the first tenants moving into the towers shortly after. In 1973, these towers were recognized as the tallest buildings in the world ("World Trade Center Timeline of History," n.d.).

The Twin Towers became symbols of commerce and American life, serving as a site for media and culture. In 1974, the famous tightrope walker Phillippe Petit crossed the towers. The observation deck in the South Tower opened in 1975 and the world-famous restaurant Windows on the World opened in the North Tower in 1976. The visibility and recognition of the Towers marked this site as a symbolic target for terrorist attacks. The first of these attacks occurred on February 26, 1993, when a van with 1,500 pounds of explosives exploded in the underground parking garage of the North Tower, and later on with the tragic attacks on September 11, 2001. Only a few months prior to the 2001 attacks, Larry Silverstein gained ownership of the "keys" of the World Trade Center. Shortly after the attacks, the Lower Manhattan Development Corporation (LMDC) was created to respond to the question: What do we build in this space? ("World Trade Center Timeline of History," n.d.).

In the months following the 9/11 attacks, three organizations emerged as primary leaders among the rebuilding efforts of Ground Zero: the LMDC, the Port Authority of New York and New Jersey, and Larry Silverstein. First, then-New York Governor George Elmer Pataki and then-NYC Mayor Rudy Giuliani formed the

LMDC, a "joint city–state agency" charged to oversee the rebuilding of Ground Zero and the coordination of a national memorial design (LMDC, n.d.). Second, the Port Authority of New York and New Jersey owned the land at Ground Zero, and finally, Larry Silverstein, a Brooklyn-born American businessman, held a 99-year lease on the land. Each stakeholder controlled particular aspects of development for the site. Constituents, victims, members, competitors, and partners of these primary organizations created a multiplicity of participants with each group devoted to their reflective goals, interests, and ethical concerns.

In 2002, the LMDC held a competition in an effort to choose a Master Planner to organize the rebuild of the 16-acre area at Ground Zero. Daniel Libeskind, a Polish-American architect, won for his submission "Memory Foundations" (Studio Libeskind, n.d.). Libeskind's plan included the construction of One World Trade Center (or Freedom Tower). Yet, Silverstein, as leaseholder, argued for his right to choose his own architect, appointing David Childs to work alongside Libeskind as Master Planner. Then, in 2003, the LMDC held an international design competition to select the National September 11th Memorial architect. The LMDC announced that designs must "inspire and engage" visitors to learn about the attacks, honor each victim without hierarchy, and work within the master plan developed by Libeskind (Wyatt, 2003, Jan. 8) The design competition and guidelines were met by public outcry. For example, the Advocates for a 9/11 Fallen Heroes Memorial, a group of firefighters who campaigned for a memorial that honored all rescue workers together, criticized the "no hierarchy" policy of the memorial contest guidelines (Wyatt, 2003, April 11). Of the 5,201 entries received from 63 nations, the 13-member board of the memorial design competition (including Maya Lin, famed architect of the Vietnam Veterans Memorial Wall, and family members of 9/11 victims) selected a junior architect, Michael Arad, and his design, entitled "Reflecting Absence." The contest resulted in the official plans for the rebuild of Ground Zero, which were released to the public in January 2003. However, following the announcement of Arad's winning design, disagreements among the primary constituents and their respective stakeholders led to a 2006 standstill in the rebuilding efforts. In the following section, we identify two major background disagreements that led to the foreground conflict among stakeholders that halted construction.

The Situation

This section tells the story of the Ground Zero rebuild as consisting of two major conflicts ultimately leading to the 2006 standstill. The background material explicated in the previous section provides insight into each of the conflicts discussed in this section. Conflicts continually evolve and escalate in various directions depending upon the background goals, interests, and ethical concerns that shape stakeholder engagement in a conflict (Arnett, Bell McManus,, & McKendree, 2014). In this case, these conflicts caused a major delay in the 9/11 commemorative efforts.

The first major conflict that resulted in the 2006 standstill took place between the Port Authority of New York and New Jersey and Larry Silverstein concerning the Freedom Tower. The conflict surrounded the Port Authority's worry that Silverstein would be unable to adequately finance the rebuilding of the site's 10 million square feet of office space and incapable of paying the annual rental payments of $110 million to the Port Authority. In 2004, the Port Authority requested that Silverstein provide a business plan detailing the rebuilding of the office space. When Silverstein submitted the proposal, the Port Authority "dismissed" the document (Neuman, 2005, para. 4). Subsequently, in 2005 security concerns caused a delay in the development of the Freedom Tower. The delay cost hundreds of millions of dollars, and the Port Authority and Silverstein argued over who would pay the construction delay fees (Neuman, 2005, para. 4). For Silverstein, delays in the project were the fault of Port Authority, who underestimated the complexities and costs of the rebuild and frequently changed their estimates (Neuman, 2005, para. 21). At the center of this dispute rested delays in insurance payouts, estimated to be over $4 billion, which both the Port Authority and Silverstein recognized as necessary to fund the rebuild of commercial space and the proposed Freedom Tower.

The second major conflict regarding the rebuild concerned the LMDC and the construction of the National September 11th Memorial and Museum. Arad's winning design for the memorial was set to occupy nearly half of the overall space of Ground Zero, invading the space dedicated to Libeskind's Freedom Tower. While Arad planned to construct ramps that would guide visitors to underground viewing areas, security concerns and budget increases resulted in arguments between and among Arad, the LMDC, and Libeskind. Due to the disagreements, in April 2004, the LMDC issued a request for proposals for an architect to assist Arad in the technical aspects of his design (Hagan, 2006). Against the wishes of Arad, the LMDC chose Davis Brody Bond. In an effort to establish further allies and support, Arad joined the Handel Architecture firm. Over the next few months, the competing firms argued over the placement of the memorial fountains and alterations of Arad's original design, which eliminated two of the proposed four pedestrian ramps to underground viewing areas. In addition to disputes concerning architecture, the rising costs of the memorial build, which came to include a $160 million Memorial Museum, angered Arad; in 2006 only $131.4 million had been fundraised while costs for the project were estimated to be over $300 million (Hagan, 2006).

In 2006, these two major background conflicts halted the rebuilding efforts at Ground Zero. These background conflicts fueled a foreground standstill, dissected within a 2008 public document released by Port Authority of New York and New Jersey. This document detailed a list of the constraints of rebuilding Ground Zero that led to the 2006 standstill and recounted the efforts of public relations professionals charged with navigating this conflict. In the document, Port Authority acknowledged 15 unresolved issues regarding the rebuild that needed to be resolved before resuming construction. Of the 15 issues, the report identified five as significant. First, the Authority recognized that the original schedules and budgets were "unrealistic" (Ward, 2008, 17). Second, the size and complexity of the planned rebuild were massive, including (in 16 acres) five major skylines, a national memorial and museum, a transportation hub serving over 150,000 persons per day, a retail venue, a performing arts center, a security hub, two new city streets, and all of the infrastructure necessary to support these projects. Third, the Authority recognized that each of these projects was being led by independent persons/organizations and that each project affected the others. Fourth, cost inflations led to significant increases in building materials. Finally, of the 15 recognized issues, the Authority recognized that within each project, conflicts existed that delayed the rebuild.

With the issues in sight, the Authority proposed three guiding principles in an effort to move forward. First, the rebuild plans needed to be certain and clear so that schedules and budgets could be made realistically. Second, the Authority urged the respective leaders of each project to put all conflicts on the table and to be honest and open about what could and could not be done. Finally, the Authority argued that "tough but practical" decisions needed to be made (Ward, 2008, 18). In moving forward from the 2006 standstill, the Authority urged continued clarity in design plans, honest and open confrontation of minor disputes, and the commitment to practical decision-making.

The controversies and difficulties that occurred in response to the Ground Zero rebuild prompted dissatisfaction and questions from constituent groups related to each group's individual wants and concerns. The events act as an exemplary case study that allows a public relations practitioner to recognize the power and import of ethical ground as a driving factor in conflict. The following section overviews the outcome of these controversies and reveals three insights relevant to public relations ethics.

Outcomes and Directions

The Ground Zero rebuild is secure but remains in progress. To date (August 2016), the National September 11th Memorial and Museum is completed and open to public visitation. The Freedom Tower is complete, with visitors granted the opportunity to visit a city overlook on the building's top floor. Despite all controversies on design, location, and purpose, the space simultaneously acts as one of commemoration, public life, and commercial business. In the midst and as the result of significant conflict, the Ground Zero rebuild efforts offers insights relevant to public relations ethics, three of which are highlighted below:

1. Public relations practitioners must recognize the inevitability of conflict as the result of differing interests, goals, and ethical positions. These interests, goals, and ethical positions represent the stakeholders' central concerns.

As PR practitioners are faced with diverse stakeholders, differing interests and conflict becomes inevitable. Conflicts are fueled by these differences, and these differences are the background to each conflict situation.

2. Public relations practitioners must attend to the background concerns that contextualize conflicts. These background concerns signal to PR professionals what matters and what is meaningful for particular groups that are directly influenced by organizational decisions. The decision-making and actions of stakeholders reflect a group's primary concerns and commitments. This recognition can inform PR professionals about sensitive and highly contested matters that fuel and escalate conflicts.

3. Public relations practitioners must understand that initial responses to stakeholder concerns shape the conflicts that occur in PR scenarios. PR professionals should reflect carefully on their responses and anticipate how those responses might prompt positive and negative feedback from stakeholder groups. Such reflection can be done by paying attention to the ways that stakeholders speak and act. Reflective responses will guide PR professionals through conflicts and help them to understand their stakeholders.

This case study of the Ground Zero rebuild conflict emphasizes that behind the 2006 construction standstill there were two primary disagreements concerning what mattered to each participating organization and its constituents. The interests, goals, and ethical concerns that emerge in the background contextualized these conflicts. This reading points to the importance of recognizing public relations, conflict, and ethical grounds as intertwined. Public relations practitioners have the task of navigating the mixed motives of these divergent and diverse stakeholder groups.

References

Arnett, R. C., Fritz, J. M. H., & Bell, L. M. (2009). *Communication Ethics Literacy: Dialogue and Difference*. Thousand Oaks, CA: Sage.

Arnett, R. C., McManus, L. B., & McKendree, A. (2014). *Conflict Between Persons: The Origins of Leadership*. Dubuque, IA: Kendall Hunt.

Cooren, François. (2010). *Action and Agency in Dialogue*. Amsterdam: John Benjamins Publishing Co.

Hagan, J. (2006). The breaking of Michael Asad. *New York Magazine*. Retrieved from http://nymag.com/arts/architecture/features/17015/.

Lower Manhattan Development Corporation. (n.d.). About us. Retrieved from http://www.renewnyc.com/overlay/AboutUs/.

Neuman, W. (2005, June 5). Getting along is a tough job at Ground Zero. *New York Times*. Retrieved from http://www.nytimes.com/2005/06/05/nyregion/getting-along-is-a-tough-job-at-ground-zero.html?_r=0.

Plowman, K. D. (2013). Conflict resolution. In Heath, R. L. (Ed.), *Encyclopedia of Public Relations* (pp. 176–180). Thousand Oaks, CA: Sage.

Studio Libeskind. (n.d.). All projects. Retrieved from http://libeskind.com/work/ground-zero-master-plan/.

Ward, C. (2008). *World Trade Center Report: A Roadmap Forward*. New York: Port Authority of New York and New Jersey. Retrieved from https://www.panynj.gov/wtcprogress/pdf/wtc_report_oct_08.pdf.

World Trade Center Timeline of History. World Trade Center. (n.d.). Retrieved from https://www.wtc.com/about/history#first-1946.

Wyatt, E. (2003, Jan. 8). Draft guidelines released for trade center memorial. *New York Times*. Retrieved from https://www.nytimes.com/2003/01/09/nyregion/draft-guidelines-released-for-trade-center-memorial.html.

Wyatt, E. (2003, April 11). Victims to be honored equally on 9/11 memorial, panel says. *New York Times*. Retrieved from https://www.nytimes.com/2003/04/11/nyregion/victims-to-be-honored-equally-on-9-11-memorial-panel-says.html.

Discussion Questions

1. Why is it important for public relations practitioners to understand the mixed motives model of conflict?
2. Why were the Port Authority's public relations efforts successful in ending the 2006 standstill?
3. Why are the background ethical commitments in conflicts not always obvious to conflict participants?
4. Who were the major parties in conflict during the 2006 standstill, and what motives were they protecting?
5. What does the case of the Ground Zero rebuild reveal about the relationship among ethics, public relations, and conflict?

ETHICAL AND EFFECTIVE POST-CRISIS STAKEHOLDER RELATIONS

Colleen Arendt, Ph.D., *Concordia University, Saint Paul*

On Wednesday, August 1, 2007, at 6:05 p.m., the I-35W Mississippi River Bridge in Minneapolis, Minnesota, collapsed during the evening rush hour, killing 13 people and injuring 145. With 140,000 cars passing over it every day, the collapse of the fifth busiest bridge in Minnesota affected more than just the victims; it severed a major artery in Minneapolis, affecting nearby businesses and the hundreds of thousands of Minnesotans who used the bridge daily until it was rebuilt and reopened 13 months later on September 18, 2008. The collapse had far-reaching and long-term impacts. It sparked a debate in the state and nation about the safety of the U.S. transportation infrastructure and how government expenditures were prioritized. The collapse affected not only the victims on the bridge but also the individuals and organizations in the area.

On a broader level, the collapse sparked concerns about the safety of other bridges both in Minnesota and across the country. On August 2, 2007, U.S. Secretary of Transportation Mary E. Peters called on states to immediately inspect their "deck-truss" bridges similar in design to the 35W bridge, and asked the Department of Transportation's Inspector General to assess the National Bridge Inspection Program (American Association of State Highway and Transportation Officials, 2008). This call to review the inspection process made sense in light of information that the bridge collapsed despite regular inspections. Speculative causes of the bridge collapse surfaced immediately, including the National Transportation Safety Board (NTSB)'s initial conclusions that the weight of construction materials on the bridge may have caused a collapse. Ultimately, the NTSB's formal investigation concluded that a design flaw in the gusset plates was a major factor in the collapse, a design flaw stemming from a simple math error made 40 years ago by designers (Diaz, 2008).

The collapse sparked intense debates over the cause of the collapse, the culpable parties, and the state and country's spending priorities. Another issue that received a lot of media attention both immediately and for months following the collapse was how to compensate victims and the families of survivors for their pain and suffering, and in 13 cases, their loss as a direct result of the collapse. This case study examines the post-crisis stakeholder relations between state officials and the victims and their families, who received settlements from the state Victim Compensation Fund (VCF).

The Situation

Compensating victims appears in both Benoit's (2015) and Coombs' (1999) typologies as one strategy for responding to a crisis. It became evident shortly after the crisis that there would be a state compensation fund for the victims. As one legislator, Senator Winkler, said, "It's only the state of Minnesota that's responsible to make sure a bridge doesn't fall down. The state needs to step up" (O'Connor, 2007, para. 15). The spokesperson for then-Governor Pawlenty released the following statement:

> At the governor's direction, our office is currently talking to legislators about addressing the needs of victims, including a possible special victims' fund, which may be appropriate in this case... We feel it's important to

have a bipartisan consensus in this regard and the governor believes the state should help survivors of the bridge collapse. (Hoppin, 2007, para. 19)

Eventually, the state legislature (consisting of a Senate and House of Representatives) approved legislation for the VCF in May 2008. Governor Pawlenty released the following statement on May 2, 2008:

I look forward to signing this legislation into law. It provides needed relief and support for victims and family members directly impacted by the I-35W bridge tragedy. I'm pleased that Senator Latz, Representative Winkler, my office and others were able to work together to craft this legislation. (Office of the Governor, 2008, para. 2)

Senator Latz, the State Senate's chief negotiator on the compensation legislation, said the following to reporters covering the bill's signing:

There is nothing we can do and nothing that we have done that can alter for them what happened on August 1, 2007. All we can do is come in after the fact and try to respond with money. It's a poor substitute, but that is what our justice system uses. (Stassen-Berger, 2008, para. 4)

Drafting and approving the legislation for a VCF took many months, in part because the legislature would not reconvene until the February following the August collapse, but also because legislators had numerous legal issues to consider. Some of the issues that arose with the idea of a compensation fund were (a) where the money would come from, (b) whether or not there would be a cap on how much monetary compensation people would receive, (c) how funds disbursements could be compared to other state incidents to make it fair for people who had been harmed in other state incidents, such as a car accident caused by a state trooper in pursuit of a criminal, and (d) who would determine the compensation.

These questions were ultimately addressed in the following ways. For the first issue, the state legislature opened a fund of $36.6 million consisting of state funds and contributions. This figure was divided into two funds:

The larger one, at $24 million, was designated to be used for pain and suffering in addition to medical and income issues. The individual cap was $400,000. The other portion, at $12.6 million, was a supplemental fund that applied only to medical bills and income loss. (O'Connor, 2009b, para. 16)

This created a "finite pie" unlike the federal September 11th Victim Compensation Fund, which had no budget cap (A job well done, 2009).

For the second issue, whether or not to place a cap on the amount per claim, the legislature decided that there would be a cap on how much victims would receive.

The cap that was in place at the time of the collapse was $300,000 per person with a $1 million limit on total damages from a single event. After the collapse, the cap moved to $400,000 and $1.2 million respectively (Foti, 2009a). Without this fund, the state's total liability would have been only $1 million, meaning the 179 claims would have been divided by $1 million, totaling only a few thousand dollars for each claim (Foti, 2009b).

Third, to make sure bridge collapse victims were not compensated exorbitantly more than victims of other state accidents, the new, higher cap applied to future incidents involving the state. For the last issue, figuring out who would decide the compensation, a special panel was created by then-Chief Justice Russell Anderson to hear victims' testimony and decide on the compensation amounts for the 179 claims. The panel consisted of three Minnesota personal injury lawyers, chairwoman Susan Holden, Steven Kirsch, and Mike Tewksbury.

Before beginning the process of deciding compensation, the panel spoke to Kenneth Feinberg, who headed the 9/11 victim's fund, and members read his book, *What is Life Worth?* (A job well done, 2009). The panel members wrestled with the question of being fair while working with a finite amount that, based on their calculations, would not be enough. According to O'Connor (2009b), after adding up how much the claims were worth and realizing that the fund did not have enough money, the panel was forced to make tough decisions about whose compensation would be reduced:

> After picking over stacks of documents and talking with victims, the panel concluded that the claims were worth nearly $100 million. Subtracting what insurance companies already had covered brought that to $46.3 million. But by law, they had $36.6 million to spend, so the panel had some hard decisions to make. "It wasn't as difficult to come up with the gross amount," Kirsch said. "What was difficult was the cutting, because they're all deserving, and we knew everybody would take significant hits." (O'Connor, 2009b, para. 9–10)

The panel not only reviewed documentation regarding lost income and medical bills, but they also listened to four months of testimony. According to O'Connor (2009b, para. 19),

> Victims could also choose whether to meet with one or all three panel members. They could request an hour or longer to explain their situations. The panel thought it was key to give people the chance to tell their stories.

Kirsch, one of the panel members, said, "The bridge case emotionally affected me. I would review a lot of these claims at night. I felt so bad for these people. I think all of us had sleeping problems" (O'Connor, 2009b, para. 3). Eventually, the panel made compensation offers to those who filed the 179 claims in February 2009 and they had until April 16, 2009, to accept or reject the offers (Nelson & Karnowski, 2009). According to the chairperson, Holden,

> Families of the deceased received the maximum $400,000 from the main fund, with most receiving varying amounts from the supplemental fund. By law, those additional amounts were based on such factors as past and future medical bills, past and future lost wages, and the number of dependents. (Foti & Lerner, 2009)

After choosing compensation amounts and making offers, as one article noted:

> Remarkably, all 179 eligible recipients accepted the compensation, with settlements ranging from $4,500 to $2.2 million, depending on the severity of individual cases. In the process, all waived the right to sue the state, although several are taking legal action against two firms that worked on the bridge. (A job well done, 2009)

The fact that all offers were accepted was not in itself remarkable because, as mentioned previously, claimants would have received less money based on the usual state liability cap. Because of the severity of the event, however, the legislature created a special fund that allowed victims to receive more than the state's usual liability cap. What was remarkable about the VCF was that the process received praise from a lot of victims.

Outcomes

Politicians and victims alike had a lot of praise for the panel and the process. Senator Ron Latz, chief architect of the fund, said, "The three panel members took their responsibilities very seriously. I think it went extraordinarily well" (A job well done, 2009). In a letter published in the letters to the editor section of the *Minneapolis Star Tribune*, Senator Latz wrote:

> This was tremendously difficult, but I feel that these three individuals did a wonderful job. They followed closely the law passed by the Legislature last year, and carefully crafted the settlements to ensure that everyone was justly compensated. (Readers Write, 2009)

During a session designed to gather feedback on how well the fund worked, Jennifer Holmes, who lost her husband, Patrick, in the collapse, said, "I thought the process went very, very well and very, very smooth," saying that the panel "did an awesome job of doing what they could to help us" (Foti, 2009b). She added: "It's not easy to talk about it. . . . They were very kind" (O'Connor, 2009b, para. 11). At one point after the collapse, friends and relatives had to help raise funds through a spaghetti fundraiser because she was unable to pay her house payment on her single salary (O'Connor, 2009a). Betsy Sathers, who lost her husband, Scott, said she would give up every dime to spend another day with her husband, to whom she had been married for just ten months before the collapse. She said of the compensation: "It gives me the opportunity to stay in our same house. I may or may not ever be a wife again, but I'm in the process of adopting a baby" (O'Connor, 2009b, para. 3).

Sandy Cermak, who along with her husband had only a few thousand dollars of out-of-pocket expenses related to their vehicle and some personal property, said: "We got very little money . . . [but] that's OK. The people who got really hurt should get the money" (Foti, 2009a). Adam Noe, who received the lowest award at just $4,500, said that he only hurt his knee and nothing was broken and therefore "more money rightly should go to Eric Paulsen, who was in the same car but was seriously injured and received $201,500" (Foti & Lerner, 2009). Alicia Harris said: "We're very grateful for the state coming up to the plate" (Foti & Lerner, 2009). While some admitted that the compensation offer was not enough to cover their expenses, they appreciated some relief. Garrett Ebling likely has years of surgeries ahead of him, with injuries including shattered face bones, a colon severed by his seat belt, two broken feet, and a broken arm. He endured an initial two-month hospital stay. He accepted his settlement, although he estimated that it was less than one-sixth of the costs he has faced or will face. Yet he said of the fund and the panel: "It was a finite pool of money, and it was what it was . . . They did a good job in allocating the funds that they had available in the fairest way that was possible" (Foti, 2009a).

The well-handled VCF, despite needing $10 million more, suggests post-crisis management can be handled ethically, transparently, and with positive outcomes. First, an organizational justice ethical lens (see Nowakowski & Conlon, 2005) examines whether people perceive fairness in terms of (a) outcomes (distributive justice), (b) procedures (procedural justice), (c) whether stakeholders felt any information provided was thorough, reasonable, truthful, candid, and timely (informational justice), and (d) whether or not they were shown sensitivity and respect from leaders (e.g., elected officials, VCF administrators) (interpersonal justice).

Although many have already filed lawsuits against the private companies working on the bridge at the time of the collapse, they received some relief from their state. Many felt as though the state listened and engaged in procedural justice by processing their claims quickly and with perceived fairness in terms of outcomes (distributive justice) and procedures (procedural justice).

Another ethical perspective critical to post-crisis stakeholder relations is an ethic of care, which calls for a responsibility to care for those in need (see Xu & Li, 2013). Creating a state fund that was roughly $10 million too small, as determined by appointed experts, does not care for those in need as real pain, death, and injury were caused by the collapse. Yet, because the four forms of organizational justice were addressed, victims and their families felt positively toward the process. This positive orientation to the fund is likely because some victims themselves were operating from an ethic of care, as they acknowledged others had greater losses and deserved more compensation.

Because the special masters' panel comprising the three personal injury lawyers was dealing with what Feinberg, the man in charge of the 9/11 compensation fund, called a "relatively modest tragedy" (Louwagie, 2007), this panel can and should serve as an example of a successful compensation effort for future disasters of similar size that require compensation from some level of government—in this case a state compensation fund.

References

A job well done on 35W bridge fund; State, survivors well-served by Legislature, legal community. (2009, April 27). *Star Tribune*, 14A.

American Association of State Highway and Transportation Officials. (2008). *Bridging the Gap: Restoring and Rebuilding the Nation's Bridges*. Retrieved from http://www.transportation1.org/BridgeReport/docs/BridgingtheGap.pdf.

Benoit, W. L. (2015). *Accounts, Excuses, and Apologies: Image repair theory and research (5th ed)*. Albany: State University of New York Press.

Coombs, W. T. (1999). *Ongoing Crisis Communication: Planning, Managing, and Responding*. Thousand Oaks, CA: Sage.

Diaz, K. (2008, November 15). Tragedy of bridge may yield new rules; Tighter oversight is urged after a federal panel found skipped calculations set the I-35W disaster in motion. *Star Tribune*, 1A.

Foti, J. (2009a, April 12). 35W panel's impossible task nears end; Bridge collapse survivors have until Thursday to accept state settlements. Almost everyone realizes the money goes only so far. *Star Tribune*, 1B.

Foti, J. (2009b, April 22). Bridge survivors testify about settlement process; Summing up the 35W panel's $36.6 million job, survivors and victim's families said it was handled well. *Star Tribune*, 2B.

Foti, J., & Lerner, M. (2009, April 19). After the Collapse; Bridge victims paid, but pain goes on; Those receiving the funds expressed gratitude, but many also said they would rather not be in the position to need help. *Star Tribune*, 1A.

Hoppin, J. (2007, October 19). For I-35W bridge collapse victims, how much compensation is enough? Retrieved from: http://www.twincities.com/2007/10/19/for-i-35w-bridge-collapse-victims-how-much-compensation-is-enough/.

Louwagie, P. (2007, November 10). After the collapse; One big question: A fund for victims?; Legislators struggled with how and whether to do something extra for victims' families and survivors of the I-35W collapse. *Star Tribune* 1B.

Nelson, T. & Karnowski, S. (2009, April 16). Individual compensation amounts of 35W settlement released. Retrieved from: https://www.mprnews.org/story/2009/04/16/state_settles_35w_bridge_collapse_victims

Nowakowski, J. M., & Conlon, D. E. (2005). Organizational justice: Looking back, looking forward. *International Journal of Conflict Management 16*(1), 4–29.

O'Connor, D. (2007, October 25). Minnesota House panel hears testimony in favor of compensation fund for victims of I-35W bridge collapse. Retrieved from http://www.twincities.com/2007/10/25/minnesota-house-panel-hears-testimony-in-favor-of-compensation-fund-for-victims-of-i-35w-bridge-collapse/.

O'Connor, D. (2009a, April 21). Two affected by the collapse say the fund's special masters were fair and kind. *St. Paul Pioneer Press.*

O'Connor, D. (2009b, April 25). Too much pain, not enough money: How three lawyers divided state funds to I-35W bridge collapse victims. *St. Paul Pioneer Press.*

Office of the Governor, Tim Pawlenty (2008). A statement from the Governor. Retrieved from https://www.leg.state.mn.us/docs/2010/other/101583/www.governor.state.mn.us/mediacenter/pressreleases/2008/PROD008863.html.

Readers Write. (2009, April 23). *Star Tribune,* 10A.

Stassen-Berger, R. E. (2008, May 8). I-35W bridge collapse victims "grateful" for compensation. Retrieved from http://www.twincities.com/2008/05/08/i-35w-bridge-collapse-i-35w-bridge-collapse-victims-grateful-for-compensation/.

Xu, K., & Li, W. (2013). An ethical stakeholder approach to crisis communication: A case study of Foxconn's 2010 employee suicide crisis. *Journal of Business Ethics, 117*, 371–386.

Discussion Questions

1. How do the VCF and victims' statements exemplify each of the four organizational justice perspectives (distributive, procedural, informational, and interpersonal)?

2. How important to the process of a VCF is the session where people provide feedback to the panel?

3. This case exemplifies what happens when, due to a crisis, citizens suddenly find themselves unable to work and pay their mortgage and mounting medical bills; sometimes a family member died. While the state legislature worked out the details on whether to raise the state cap and/or provide a special compensation fund, victims and their families were struggling. How can officials plan ahead of time to be able to provide smaller, immediate relief funds? What sort of criteria should they consider?

4. Think about how small, less visible and less powerful stakeholders can be ignored during a crisis. Think about other types of crises, such as natural disasters, terrorist attacks, mass shootings, and massive product or food recalls, and consider the various stakeholders who will be affected. What will each stakeholder group need? What would organizational justice and ethics of care look like for these stakeholders?

5. What role did the media and the transparent panel process play in shaping people's ethic of care response?

"AM I SAFE?": THE ETHICAL IMPLICATIONS OF RUNNING AND MAINTAINING A SHARING ECONOMY ORGANIZATION

Lindsey J. DiTirro, Ph.D., *University of Southern Indiana*, Lauren Berkshire Hearit, Ph.D., *Hope College*, and Emilly K. Martinez, *Purdue University*

Micaela Giles's son, Jacob Lopez, was more than 3,000 miles away, vacationing in Madrid. On July 4, 2015, she woke up to a series of horrifying texts from her son asking her for help. Jacob told her that his Airbnb host had "locked him into the fourth-floor apartment where he was supposed to be staying and removed the key" (Lieber, 2015, para. 2). He claimed his host was "rattling knives around in the kitchen drawer and pressing him to submit to a sexual act" (Lieber, 2015, para. 2). Micaela contacted Airbnb, hoping the company would help her son. According to the *New York Times*, Airbnb employees refused to give Micaela the address where Jacob was staying, nor would they contact the local Madrid police on her behalf (Lieber, 2015). They instead provided Micaela with the number for the Madrid police and withheld further assistance.

After the assault received national news attention, Airbnb fielded calls from journalists by claiming it believed the assault had already taken place and was not an ongoing crisis situation. The company tried to distance itself from the crisis, stating the attack was merely one "unique situation" on a weekend when more than 80,000 individuals had safely stayed with other Airbnb hosts (Lieber, 2015, para. 16).

A "peer-to-peer online marketplace and homestay network . . . [that enables] people to list or rent short-term lodging in residential properties," Airbnb is a twist on the traditional bed and breakfast, and a new type of organization that is part of the sharing economy (Airbnb, About us, n.d.). A sharing economy organization is a way in which individuals "collaboratively make use of under-utilized inventory via fee-based sharing" (Zervas, Proserpio, & Byers, 2016, 2). It is not yet clear what regulations should be applied to these organizations, which in addition to Airbnb include crowdfunding sites and car-hire services (The rise of the sharing economy, 2013). The question many policymakers, government officials, local cities, and customers have is: What responsibility do sharing organizations hold to their stakeholders, shareholders, communities, and customers? In traditional organizations, a basic assumption exists that the company is responsible for any crisis scenario or wrongdoing. In the new sharing economy, or in corporations that make their business a sharing economy, the lines among customer, company, and independent contractor are highly blurred. Who actually is responsible for any crisis scenario or wrongdoing in this new form of organizing? A number of ethical dilemmas emerge from sharing economy organizations, such as whether workers are considered employees (and as such should receive benefits) or contractors.

This case will examine Airbnb's response to this crisis using an ethical lens. This allows for critical inquiry as to the implications of organizations in the sharing economy using crisis response strategies such as scapegoating, denial, and excuses in emergency situations. When is it okay to use these? What is the line between needing to protect an organization's financial interests, reputation, and legitimacy and customers' well-being and concern? When should practitioners advocate less for organizational interests and instead prioritize the well-being of the consumer? Does responsibility shift in sharing economy organizations from the company to the independent contractors?

Background

Airbnb was founded in 2008 and is based in San Francisco, California. Via its website, the company works to connect "hosts" with individuals looking for a room, apartment, or house to rent for a short (or long) period of time (e.g., one night or several months). Airbnb describes itself as "a trusted community marketplace for people to list, discover, and book unique accommodations around the world" (Airbnb, About us, para. 1).

Airbnb reservations can be made in more than 34,000 cities and 191 countries (Airbnb, About us). The company allows individuals or families to rent extra space in their homes to make money. For travelers, Airbnb provides an alternative to staying in hotels or other traditional accommodations. Hosts are essentially independent contractors, working for Airbnb, but are not employees in the traditional sense (e.g., work in a physical facility, entitled to salary and benefits), as clarified by recent court rulings on sharing economy organizations (see Lien, Hsu, & Solomon, 2015 for more information).

To make this a trusted community, Airbnb takes certain precautions. Users must verify their identity by linking their Airbnb account with another website account like Facebook, providing an email address and phone number, and providing a copy of a passport or driver's license (Airbnb, Policies). Guests and hosts can review and rate each other at the end of each trip, allowing users to examine each other before booking (for the customer) or confirming (for the host) a reservation. Airbnb also provides a 24-hour support system for users.

Because Airbnb operates using private consumers and independent contractors (hosts), it is not required to follow the same laws and regulations as the hotel industry (Rocheleau, 2016). The lack of regulations for Airbnb has led the hotel industry to worry about its survival, and a report commissioned by the Hotel Association estimates that in New York City alone, Airbnb has cost hotels approximately $450 million in direct revenue each year (Mahmoud, n.d.). Additionally, neighborhood associations have gone on the record that they are concerned about strangers coming in and out of their area regularly, leading to a potential increase in crime or petty theft (Rocheleau, 2016; Walker, 2016).

In response, some cities have gone so far as to make certain types of listings illegal. In New York City, one law states that *entire* apartments cannot be rented out—an attempt to prevent the creation of illegal hotels (i.e., trying to prevent individuals from purchasing residences and renting them out in their entirety like a hotel for extra income) (Plautz, 2016). These issues have led to much political debate, and in some cities Airbnb has been outlawed, regardless of the type of listing. As a result, there has been a push to regulate Airbnb listings at the local and national levels, and to keep Airbnb true to its roots: individuals renting out space in their current residence.

Issues with safety also exist with the use of Airbnb. As there are no regulations for pre-investigation of guests and hosts before using Airbnb's services, individuals are often cautious when hosting guests and/or staying as a guest (e.g., McQuigge, 2015). There have been reports of issues between hosts and customers, like when one woman came home to her apartment that she rented out using Airbnb and found it severely damaged (e.g., Romero, 2011). In one extreme case, a group of friends found a decomposing body in the garden of their rental in Paris (Airbnb guests shocked, 2016).

In an effort to combat safety issues, Airbnb listed safety tips in its "Help Center" for both guests and hosts (Airbnb, Help Center). The suggestions focus on customers being careful, trusting their instincts, and researching the area and their host before staying at an Airbnb location. Guidelines and support hotlines alone cannot prevent all potential incidents, however, as was evidenced when Micaela's son was sexually assaulted at an Airbnb residence.

The Situation

Nineteen-year-old Jacob Lopez vacationed in Brazil in 2014 and used Airbnb for living accommodations. After an enjoyable experience, he decided to try Airbnb again when he traveled to Spain. Jacob's trip began innocuously. Upon arriving in Madrid he met his Airbnb host at the metro stop and walked with her the short distance to her apartment. When they entered the residence, however, she locked them in the apartment and tried to kiss Jacob. He ignored her advances. According to Jacob, she then ordered him to take off his pants and threatened to kick him out of the residence without his belongings if he did not do as she said. Jacob worried for his life as he feared she had a weapon, and could hear her "rattling knives" in the kitchen (Lieber, 2015, para. 2).

To get away, Jacob told his host he needed to meet up with his friends, or they would become suspicious and come looking for him (Bleier, 2015; Lieber, 2015). His Airbnb host allowed him to leave with his luggage. During this incident, Jacob texted his mother, Micaela Giles, to tell her of the horrible events and to ask her to get him help. Micaela immediately contacted Airbnb for assistance. However,

Airbnb employees would not provide the address for her son's location or call the police. They instead gave her the number for the Madrid police.

Frantically, Micaela tried calling the Madrid police, but she could only get a recording in Spanish and the call kept disconnecting (Lieber, 2015). She tried again to reach the Airbnb representative who previously helped her, but after repeated attempts she only got the individual's voice mail (Lieber, 2015).

In later interviews, Jacob claimed he was sexually assaulted by his host that evening (e.g., Bleier, 2015; Lieber, 2015). He stated he "chose not to fight his way out" and that he was "telling [him]self that [he] was going to have to kill her or she was going to kill [him]" (Bleier, 2015, para. 5–6). In an interview with the *New York Times*, an Airbnb spokesman stated,

> We realize we can learn a lot from this incident and we can do better. We are clarifying our policies so that our team will always contact law enforcement if we are made aware of an emergency situation in progress. Safety is our No. 1 priority, and we want to get our hosts and guests as much help as possible. (Lieber, 2015, para. 18)

Airbnb also issued a statement to NBC regarding the assault, stating,

> The weekend that this occurred, over 800,000 people stayed on Airbnb around the world, and 70,000 were staying on Airbnb in Spain. But even one incident is one too many, and while no industry has a 100 percent safety record, that's what we strive for. We are clarifying our policies so that our team will always contact law enforcement if we are made aware of an emergency situation. (Stump, 2015, para. 7)

With mounting criticism of its services from local governments and the hotel industry, Airbnb found itself facing another front of admonishment. This sexual assault called to the forefront what responsibilities, if any, Airbnb has to its customers, both hosts and guests. Moreover, Airbnb does not call its customers "customers" or "clients." It has rhetorically constructed customers as *users* of a service, or members of the Airbnb community. What are the implications of this? When there is an issue with an Airbnb stay, who is available to check on a guest or host? The question of responsibility comes at an especially salient time as the company was recently evaluated as one of the most successful startup businesses ever (currently, Airbnb is in talks to be valued at about $30 billion), right behind Uber (valued at $62.5 billion) (Picker & Isaac, 2016).

Following the assault in Madrid, Airbnb began using social media to post about the company, though no statements addressing the assault or any other negative issue were posted. While some posts were unlinked, like a July 15 post about how hosts decorated their apartment for a Marine's retirement (Airbnb, 2015c) and a July 13 video about a Brazilian host with the tag "This is not a hotel. It is our home, and now it is your home" (Airbnb, 2015a), others were part of a campaign. Within 10 days of the assault, Airbnb launched a #mankind campaign across its Facebook, Instagram, and Twitter platforms by creating and posting a video that asked how kind the world really is (Airbnb, 2015b). This series was designed to explore the kindness in the world and within Airbnb's community. The campaign was most prevalent on Twitter, where they used hashtags such as "humankind," "mankind," "womankind," and "transkind" to highlight acts of kindness (Airbnb, Tweets). Posts about extreme acts of kindness within the world and by their hosts and guests ran daily from July 13 to August 7 (Airbnb, 2015d). See the Appendix for some examples of these tweets.

The campaign was launched on Airbnb's Facebook page on July 14 (Airbnb, Timeline) and in addition to the video, a series of posts went up about nice things hosts had done for residents (Airbnb, Profile). A July 17 post requested stories about the best adventures guests have had with their hosts (Airbnb, 2015d). The post said,

> What is the best adventure a host shared with you? Sometimes our favorite travel stories happen when we take the unexpected detours that only a local could suggest. Thanks to her host's list of nearby gems, this guest took a plunge into the oldest marble quarry in America. #Mankind

In August, normal posting resumed; there were no posts related to safety. Instagram was comparably quiet. On July 14, posts began using the hashtag "Mankind," which also promoted Airbnb's video about kindness (Airbnb, 2015b). These posts mirrored the Facebook posts very closely. Despite Airbnb's public relations activities on social media, the company never directly addressed the assault or responded to the press attention following the attack on one of its Airbnb guests.

Outcomes

After the incident in Madrid, Airbnb received substantial coverage in the media. The *New York Times* broke the story, and it even received attention in popular press outlets like *Cosmopolitan* (Beck, 2015). Despite this attention, Airbnb has not significantly changed its policies, yet public awareness of safety concerns while using Airbnb appears to be higher, as evidenced by recent articles designed to help Airbnb users stay safe while staying with an Airbnb host. For example, *Condé Nast Traveler*, a major luxury and lifestyle travel magazine, ran an article in early 2016 entitled "Is Airbnb Safe?" designed, in part, to provide readers with safety tips (Brady, 2016).

Before and during the crisis, Airbnb did not issue any public statements, nor did it communicate on social media about the incident. Safety was not discussed in any of the company's press releases in the year leading up to this incident. After the crisis, Airbnb did issue a statement acknowledging its shortcomings (Lieber, 2015) and pledged to clarify its safety policies (Stump, 2015).

However, Airbnb did not issue a public statement about how its emergency contact policies had been clarified, nor did it take to social media to reassure stakeholders about their safety when using Airbnb. As of the time of this case's publication, Airbnb more frequently releases statements fighting regulations imposed by cities and the hotel and tourism industry (e.g., Airbnb, Airbnb news and announcements; Herrera, 2016; Kendall, 2016). The company has not developed an emergency contact protocol but recommends that guests contact local police in the event of an emergency (Airbnb, Help center).

In the year since this crisis, a lot of other websites have posted negative articles about Airbnb, identifying safety tips for those staying at an Airbnb residence. Yet the company has begun to develop new kinds of trips for its clients, and its reputation does not seem to have suffered; indeed, the company is now larger than ever (Carrol, 2016; Chafkin & Newcomer, 2016).

References

Airbnb. (n.d.). About us. Retrieved from https://www.airbnb.com/about/about-us.

Airbnb. (n.d.) Airbnb news and announcements. Retrieved from https://press.atairbnb.com.

Airbnb. (n.d.) Help center. Retrieved from https://www.airbnb.com/help.

Airbnb. (n.d.) Policies. Retrieved from https://www.airbnb.com/help/topic/250/terms---policies.

Airbnb. (n.d.). Profile [Instagram page]. Retrieved November 30, 2015, from https://www.instagram.com/airbnb/.

Airbnb. (n.d.). Timeline [Facebook page]. Retrieved November 30, 2015, from https://www.facebook.com/airbnb/.

Airbnb. (n.d.). Tweets [Twitter page]. Retrieved November 30, 2015, from https://twitter.com/airbnb?lang=eng.

Airbnb. (2015a, July 13). Meet Rio hosts Evandro and Leonardo who bring their guests into their world by welcoming them with: "This is not a hotel. It is our home, and now it is your home." [Video file]. Retrieved from https://www.facebook.com/pg/airbnb/videos

Airbnb. (2015b, July 14). We have a question: Is mankind? Our new film asks just how kind this world can be. Go and see. [Video file]. Retrieved from https://www.facebook.com/pg/airbnb/videos.

Airbnb. (2015c, July 15). What's the kindest welcome you've ever received from a host? To celebrate their guest's retirement from the Marines, these hosts surprised him with quite the welcome note. [Facebook status update]. Retrieved from https://www.facebook.com/airbnb/.

Airbnb. (2015d, July 17). What is the best adventure a host shared with you? Sometimes our favorite travel stories happen when we take the unexpected detours that only a local could suggest. Thanks to her host's list of nearby gems, this guest took a plunge into the oldest marble quarry in America. #Mankind [Facebook status update]. Retrieved from https://www.facebook.com/airbnb/.

"Airbnb guests shocked by decomposing corpse in garden." (2016, February 28). *The Guardian*. Retrieved from https://www.theguardian.com/technology/2016/feb/29/airbnb-rental-with-decomposing-corpse-in-garden-shocks-guests.

Beck, L. (2015). If you've ever stayed in an Airbnb, you have to read this horrifying tale. *Cosmopolitan*. Retrieved from http://www.cosmopolitan.com/lifestyle/news/a44908/if-youve-ever-stayed-in-an-airbnb-you-have-to-read-this/.

Bleier, E. (2015, August 15). American tourist claims he was held captive and sexually assaulted by his transsexual Airbnb host in Spain. *Daily Mail*. Retrieved from http://www.dailymail.co.uk/news/article-3199338/American-tourist-Jacob-Lopez-claims-transexual-Airbnb-host-Madrid-sexually-assaulted-him.html.

Brady, P. (2016, March 10). Is Airbnb safe? Seven tips for first-time renters. *Condé Nast Traveler*. Retrieved from http://www.cntraveler.com/stories/2014-01-14/six-tips-for-first-time-airbnb-renters.

Carrol, R. (2016, November 17). "Whole trip" service makes Airbnb bigger than ever, but many want tougher rules. *The Guardian*. Retrieved from http://www.theguardian.com/technology/2016/nov/17/airbnb-launch-new-trips-service-los-angeles-protests.

Chafkin, M., & Newcomer, E. (2016, July 11). Airbnb faces growing pains as it passes 100 million guests. *Bloomberg Businessweek*. Retrieved from https://www.bloomberg.com/news/articles/2016-07-11/airbnb-faces-growing-pains-as-it-passes-100-million-users.

Herrera, C. (2016, May 25). Airbnb and hoteliers battle over role, regulations for home-sharing in Miami. *Miami Herald*. Retrieved from https://www.miamiherald.com/news/business/tourism-cruises/article79673612.html.

Kendall, M. (2016, September 18). Airbnb fights unfriendly regulations with wave of lawsuits against San Francisco, other cities. *Mercury News*. Retrieved from https://www.mercurynews.com/2016/09/18/airbnb-fights-unfriendly-regulations-wave-lawsuits-san-francisco/.

Lieber, R. (2015, August 14). Airbnb horror story points to need for precautions. *New York Times*. Retrieved from http://www.nytimes.com/2015/08/15/your-money/airbnb-horror-story-points-to-need-for-precautions.html.

Lien, T. Hsu, T., & Solomon, D. B. (2015). Sharing economy gets a wake-up call with Uber ruling. *Los Angeles Times*. Retrieved from http://www.latimes.com/

Mahmoud, A. (n.d.). The impact of Airbnb on hotel and hospitality industry. *Hospitality Net*. Retrieved from http://www.hospitalitynet.org/news/4074708.html.

McQuigge, M. (2015, May 3). Pondering Airbnb-ing your home? Experts urge caution after Calgary ordeal. *Globe and Mail*. Retrieved from https://www.theglobeandmail.com/life/pondering-airbnb-ing-your-home-experts-urge-caution-after-calgary-ordeal/article24231984.

Picker, L., & Isaac, M. (2016, June 28). Airbnb is said to be seeking funding valuing it at $30 billion. *New York Times*. Retrieved from http://www.nytimes.com/2016/06/29/business/dealbook/airbnb-is-said-to-be-seeking-funding-valuing-it-at-30-billion.html.

Plautz, J. (2016, June 20). New York is close to making entire apartment listings illegal on Airbnb. *Travel and Leisure*. Retrieved from http://www.travelandleisure.com/hotels-resorts/vacation-rentals/new-york-airbnb-legal-challenge.

Rocheleau, M. (2016, April 04). Should Airbnb rentals be subjected to hotel taxes and regulations? *Boston Globe*. Retrieved from www.bostonglobe.com.

Romero, F. (2011, July 29). Airbnb renter wrecks woman's San Francisco home. *Time*. Retrieved from http://newsfeed.time.com/2011/07/29/airbnb-renter-wrecks-womans-san-francisco-home/.

Stump, S. (2015, August 17). Airbnb horror story reveals safety issues for lodging site. *Today*. Retrieved from http://www.today.com/money/airbnb-horror-story-reveals-safety-issues-lodging-site-t39091.

The rise of the sharing economy. (2013, March). *The Economist*. Retrieved from http://www.economist.com/news/leaders/21573104-internet-everything-hire-rise-sharing-economy.

Walker, R. (2016, March 05). Airbnb pits neighbor against neighbor in tourist-friendly New Orleans. *New York Times*. Retrieved from www.nytimes.com.

Zervas, G., Proserpio, D., & Byers, J. (2016). The rise of the sharing economy: Estimating the impact of Airbnb on the hotel industry. *Boston University School of Management Research Paper*. Retrieved from http://people.bu.edu/zg/publications/airbnb.pdf.

Appendix

PHOTO 3.1 A tweet from Airbnb on July 15, 2015, after the assault happened in Madrid.

Airbnb @Airbnb · 15 Jul 2015
A host makes the best kind of local guide. Who else has experienced the kindness of a great Airbnb host? #Mankind

spencergoldiephoto @SpencerGoldie
Airbnb has been a great experience. My host is the homie. Has showed me so much of the city already.

↩ 4   ♺ 8   ♥ 21   •••

Airbnb @Airbnb · 15 Jul 2015
On her birthday, @malala celebrates by opening a new school for Syrian refugees. abnb.co/RZmwP4 #Mankind

PHOTO 3.2 Two additional tweets from Airbnb on July 15, 2015, after the assault happened in Madrid.

Airbnb @Airbnb · 3 Aug 2015
These Airbnb hosts pay it forward by donating a portion of their profits to charity. #Mankind abnb.co/YLJPif

PHOTO 3.3 A tweet from early August, 2015, as part of Airbnb's #Mankind Twitter campaign.

Discussion Questions

1. Do you think Airbnb privileged its reputation over the future safety of its customers? If you were an Airbnb public relations practitioner assigned to answer news inquiries about this incident, what would you say differently?

2. What about the legal aspects of this case: can Airbnb ever apologize? What would you do if you were asked to scapegoat and blame a victim and a victim's family after a crisis to protect your company's reputation? Is there a situation where it is appropriate for you to advocate for the victim instead?

3. If wrongdoing happens, is it the fault of the company or the independent contractor?

4. Airbnb has safety tips listed in its "Help Center" for both guests and hosts, telling customers to be careful, to trust their instincts, and to complete research about their host/guest. Is this an effective strategy or an attempt by Airbnb to shift the locus of responsibility in advance should something go wrong? Where does Airbnb's responsibility lie, given that they facilitate relationships between homeowners and patrons but don't actually own the facility?

4

SOCIAL MEDIA AND TECHNOLOGY

Learning Outcomes

- Recognize the prominence of social media and internet communication.
- Describe the tools of social media and internet communication in the practice of public relations.
- Analyze ethical principles in relation to social media and internet communication.
- Apply ethical principles to social media case studies.

Definitions

Conflicts of interest: "Clashes between the practitioner's self-interest and a professional-interest, or their public-interest, or their client's interest" (PRSA, 2009a).

Federal Trade Commission (FTC): U.S. governmental agency that oversees consumer protection.

Ghost social media: Social media purporting to be from one author but authored by someone else.

Native content: Media placements that are styled to look like regular content but are really paid content.

Pay-for-play: The undisclosed compensation for posting content.

Social media: "Blogs, social networking sites, location-based services, microblogs, photo- and video-sharing sites, etc., in which ordinary users . . . can communicate with each other and create and share content with others online through their personal networked computers and digital mobile devices" (Bechmann & Lomborg, 2013, p. 767).

Transparency: Releasing all information that can be released "in a manner that is accurate, timely, balanced, and unequivocal" (Rawlins, 2009, p. 75).

You might call it new media, social media, digital media, or just internet communication, but regardless of the name, it has changed our society and the practice of public relations. Today the pervasiveness of these technologies is astounding, with more devices connected to the internet than there are people on the planet (Bennett, 2013, para. 1). The proliferation of internet devices is staggering, with 84% of American households owning a smartphone and a third owning three or more (Olmstead, 2017).

Defining this new type of communication can be difficult, but Bechmann and Lomborg (2013) define social media as items "such as blogs, social networking sites, location-based services, microblogs, photo- and video-sharing sites, etc., in which ordinary users (i.e., not only media professionals) can communicate with each other and create and share content with others online through their personal networked computers and digital mobile devices" (p. 767). The commanding influence of these social media services is unmissable. The Pew Research Center found that 79% of U.S. online adults use Facebook. Instagram (32%), Pinterest (31%), LinkedIn (29%), and Twitter (29%) round out the top social media services in the United States (Greenwood, Perrin, & Duggan, 2016, para. 3). And people are using these services often: 76% of Facebook users and 51% of Instagram users visit the services daily, and over half of both services' users visit more than once a day (Greenwood, Perrin, & Duggan, 2016, para. 20).

The attraction of social media to public relations practitioners is obvious. It creates a way to talk directly to a public without media gatekeepers. It also creates a method for our publics to talk back to us. The highly promoted ideas of two-way symmetrical communication and dialogue are possible using these new technologies. Internet communication has dramatically changed the speed, scope, and amount of communication that practitioners and publics can create and consume.

As with any new public relations tool, the ethical considerations need to be considered. The openness, speed, and 24/7 aspects of social media present unique ethical challenges. The Public Relations Society of America (PRSA) states that practitioners using social media should "be honest, transparent, credible and truthful, striving for meaningful social media content that fosters trusted relationships and creates value" (PRSA, 2015, 1). But what is meaningful, and how can we build trust? As a starting point, social media should be governed by honesty and fairness. Social media may seem temporary or insignificant, but a faux pas can live forever online, gain a massive audience, and ruin trust. An ethical practitioner would never use social media to mislead or alter information. Additionally, social media should be handled with fairness to your client, the publics, the media, and even competitors. The speed and ubiquity of social media can lead to quick replies that are incomplete, untrue, or unfair.

Transparency/Disclosure of Information

Two ethical guidelines that often are relevant to social media are transparency and disclosure. Practitioners need to be transparent about who is doing the communicating and what the sources of information are in their social media.

Rawlins (2009) defines transparency as "mak[ing] available all legally releasable information . . . in a manner that is accurate, timely, balanced, and unequivocal" (p. 75). This is a large commitment for organizations, especially when looking at the openness of social media. For example, the practice of ghost blogging and tweeting involves hiring someone to write content that is officially credited to another person. The information may be accurate, timely, balanced, and unequivocal— but the authorship is not true. In a study of CEO blogs, 60% of people expected that they were not actually written by CEOs, and 40% didn't think this was okay (Gallicano, Bivins, & Cho, 2014). Without transparency, positive long-term relations with a public cannot be expected.

Advertorials, native advertising, and sponsored content are other examples where practitioners must be transparent and disclose the sponsorship of the content. These are media placements that are created to look like regular or native content but are really paid content. For example, if a celebrity is compensated to promote a travel location and posts about it on Twitter, Instagram, and Facebook, should she disclose that to her fans? If her fans later find out that those posts were paid content, has this discovery damaged those relationships? The practice of paying for media mentions is called "pay-for-play," a term that comes from the era when DJs were paid to play certain songs. More specifically for public relations it means "the undisclosed compensation of reporters or media for the placements of editorial material" (PRSA, 2009b). The PRSA guidelines for social media suggest that if gifts are given to social media influencers, they should be "nominal, legal, and infrequent" (PRSA, 2015, 3). Furthermore, the Federal Trade Commission (FTC), the U.S. agency that administers consumer protection legislation, requires that people posting on the internet state anything of value given to secure that coverage (2009).

Conflicts of Interest

Conflicts of interest are closely related to disclosure. Conflicts of interest are a "clash between the practitioner's self-interest and a professional-interest, or their public-interest, or their client's interest" (PRSA, 2009a). Conflicts of interest can harm the perception of your impartiality, trustworthiness, and overall credibility. For example, if real estate agents were tweeting about property, you would expect them to reveal if they have a financial interest in those properties. Publics think the same thing about public relations practitioners. As part of our professional and personal lives, we naturally have conflicts of interests that must be disclosed to build and maintain trust. PRSA suggests disclosing **anything** that might be perceived as biasing the practitioner's judgment (PRSA, 2009a). Those could be family relationships, working for competing organizations, receiving gifts, and holding outside jobs. For example, imagine you are working for a large retailer and tweeted about the company's *great* Memorial Day sale. You may have been genuine in your praise and not doing it for a client—you just thought it was a wonderful sale—but you have opened yourself and the retailer up to criticism. Your readers may see this as dishonest and blame you and the client. If it can be perceived as a conflict of interest, address it.

References

Bechmann, A., & Lomborg, S. (2013). Mapping actor roles in social media: Different perspectives on value creation in theories of user participation. *New Media & Society, 15*(5), 765–781.

Bennett, S. (2013, Jan. 4). 100 amazing social media statistics, facts and figures [Infographic]. *Adweek*. Retrieved from www.adweek.com/socialtimes/100-social-media-stats/475180.

Gallicano, T. D., Bivins, T. H., & Cho, Y. Y. (2014). Considerations regarding ghost blogging and ghost commenting. In DiStaso, M. W., & Bortree, D. S. (Eds.), *Ethical Practice of Social Media in Public Relations*. New York, NY: Routledge.

Greenwood, S., Perrin, A., & Duggan, M. (2016). Social media update 2016. Retrieved from http://www.pewinternet.org/2016/11/11/social-media-update-2016/.

Federal Trade Commission. (2009). FTC Publishes Final Guides Governing Endorsements, Testimonials. Retrieved from https://www.ftc.gov/news-events/press-releases/2009/10/ftc-publishes-final-guides-governing-endorsements-testimonials.

Olmstead, K. (2017). A Third of Americans Live in a Household with Three or More Smartphones. Retrieved from http://www.pewresearch.org/fact-tank/2017/05/25/a-third-of-americans-live-in-a-household-with-three-or-more-smartphones/.

Public Relations Society of America. (2009a). Professional Standards Advisory PS-11: Professional Conflicts of Interest. Retrieved from http://www.prsa.org/AboutPRSA/Ethics/EthicalStandardsAdvisories/Documents/PSA-11.pdf.

Public Relations Society of America. (2009b). Professional Standards Advisory PS-10: Phantom Experience: Inflating Resumes, Credentials and Capabilities. Retrieved from http://www.prsa.org/AboutPRSA/Ethics/EthicalStandardsAdvisories/Documents/PSA-10.pdf.

Public Relations Society of America. (2015). Ethical Standards Advisory ESA-20. Retrieved from https://www.prsa.org/wp-content/uploads/2016/10/Ethics-and-Social-Media.pdf

Rawlins, B. (2009). Give the emperor a mirror: Towards developing a stakeholder measurement of organizational transparency. *Journal of Public Relations Research, 21*(1), 71–99.

SEEING THROUGH THE GOLDEN ARCHES: TRANSPARENCY IN THE DIGITAL AGE

Prisca S. Ngondo, Ph.D., *Texas State University*, and
Clay Craig, Ph.D., *Texas State University*

McDonald's expresses its ambition as being a positive force "for our customers. Our people. Our communities. Our world" (McDonald's, n.d., b). The company's emphasis on customers is displayed through the inclusion of a variety of foods from recommended food groups in their product offerings and their commitment to employees in the training and education offered, and they demonstrate their commitment to the global community through the use of sustainable practices (McDonald's, n.d., b).

While the company's goals are clear, their actions fall short. Throughout the past six decades, McDonald's has faced criticism and negative publicity. Botterill and Kline (2007) examined over 2,000 newspaper stories revealing five negative themes impacting the organization: youth as labor, community and family values, globalization and anti-Americanism, environmental issues, and fat kids and burger panic. Within each of these themes, McDonald's strategy was to defend its image through court battles, which actually harmed the brand image. A more effective strategy of transparency could have produced a more beneficial reaction from the public.

Organizational transparency has been associated with a company's ethical practices, corporate social responsibility (CSR), and trust (Rawlins, 2009). As PR practitioners start to understand the value of transparency, it is important to examine how the ever-changing digital media landscape poses some challenging ethical questions for PR professionals and opens up avenues for different viewpoints that encourage practitioners to embrace authenticity, shared interest in accuracy, and transparency. Social media allow an organization to provide transparent communication and serve as another outlet to take responsibility for its actions and efforts (DiStaso & Bortree, 2014).

In fact, 81% of PR practitioners surveyed believed social media offered organizations a low-cost way to influence organizational transparency (Wright & Hinson, 2010). Through digital media, organizations can grow and solidify their online identity via transparency (DiStaso & Bortree, 2014). Additionally, Wright and Hinson (2012) found practitioners view social media as a platform impacting corporate transparency and push for a culture that is both transparent and ethical.

McDonald's acknowledges the need to evolve their communication techniques to become more transparent. In fact, Bob Langert, McDonald's vice president of sustainability and a McDonald's Corporate Blog contributor, wrote on January 16, 2013,

> All of us need to get less uptight about the perils of opening up because the reality is that the perils are there already . . . we are no longer controlling the messaging anyway, so why pretend to do so? We are now part of a larger dialogue and need to be comfortable with discomfort. (para. 1)

Background

Ray Kroc opened the first McDonald's in 1955 in Des Plaines, Illinois, featuring the original rendition of the Golden Arches. In the 1960s, marketing efforts focused on families and promoting the child-friendly mascot Ronald McDonald. Currently, there are more than 36,525 restaurants across 118 countries serving 69 million customers daily. The expansion and profitability of McDonald's propelled the brand into the global spotlight as an exemplary capitalist enterprise, even resulting in the term "McDonaldization" (Ritzer, 2012).

McDonaldization is composed of four imperative managerial components: efficiency, calculability, predictability, and control (Ritzer, 2012). With the increase in influence and scale, McDonald's had to be mindful of the public's perception of the "soulless" modern corporation focused on only profit and growth (Botterill & Kline, 2007). Thus the primary goal was to humanize the corporate image by minimizing the social anxieties created by McDonald's exponential market domination.

Back in 2012, Morrison noted that although McDonald's was a top-6 brand and one of the largest advertisers in the U.S., it had a brand perception problem. People were not "Lovin' it" as much as McDonald's hoped. With that in mind, McDonald's started working on improving its brand image by addressing issues related to food quality, ingredient sourcing, sustainability, and working conditions (Morrison, 2012). Heather Oldani, McDonald's director-USA communications, said:

> There is an opportunity for us to answer some of the questions that customers may have, that influencers may have, about our menu, our commitments to the community and in the areas of sustainability—things that frankly we haven't been as vocal about . . . in the past . . . We're actually going out there and having a dialogue. (Morrison, 2012, para. 6–7)

With a current 3.3 million U.S. Twitter followers (McDonald's USA Twitter, 2016); nearly 68 million Facebook page "likes" (McDonald's USA Facebook,

2016); over 275,000 YouTube subscribers; and 15,348,958 total YouTube views (McDonald's USA YouTube Channel, 2016), McDonald's was and is poised to engage in a digital media transparency campaign.

The Situation

While McDonald's is attempting to be transparent and a positive force for all stakeholders, below is an example of how their best intentions failed. In 2012, McDonald's created #McDStories in the hopes of customers sharing their heart-warming interactions with the brand, but the online firestorm resulted in brand bashing through horror stories pertaining to brand experiences. Although the campaign was pulled within two hours, there was a lasting negative impact from the crowd-driven campaign (Hill, 2012). This example substantiates the fears of PR practitioners' use of social media. While the execution and intentions were clear and strategic, McDonald's had no control over how the public utilized this campaign.

In 2014 McDonald's and its PR agency Golin took a different approach and utilized digital media to enhance transparency regarding both its food and the company through the use of the "Our Food. Your Questions." originating from McDonald's 2012 Canadian campaign. The Canadian campaign received several accolades, such as *Marketing* magazine's "Marketer of the Year for 2012" award. One of the most successful videos, which had almost 8 million YouTube views by the end of 2012, showed why a restaurant-bought hamburger looks different in advertising (Laird, 2013). As of November 20, 2016, the video had over 11 million views, 30,000 likes, and 25,000 shares (McDonald's Canada YouTube Channel, 2016). According to *Marketing* magazine, through the social media campaign, McDonald's redefined transparency (Laird, 2013). While basking in the glory of the Canadian success, McDonald's turned its eyes toward the U.S. market.

On Oct. 13, 2014, the "Our Food. Your Questions." campaign was launched in the U.S. and received its own version of digital success. Through the use of websites, Twitter, Facebook, and YouTube, McDonald's answered food questions, shared multimedia content, and engaged in open conversations (Jarboe, 2015). Two notable videos featured Grant Imahara, former host of Discovery Channel's MythBusters, visiting Cargill, one of McDonald's beef suppliers in California, and the chicken nugget manufacturer Tyson plant in Tennessee. In the video, Imahara walks the viewers through the factory and exposes how the beef and chicken are inspected and processed into patties and nuggets.

The campaign represented an important step for McDonald's in its desire to be more transparent by taking the consumer behind the scenes. Although McDonald's has been providing information about its food for the past 35 years, this campaign allowed for a two-way dialogue allowing consumers to ask questions that McDonald's may not have specifically addressed before. Lainey Garcia, manager of brand reputation and PR for McDonald's USA, said McDonald's put together a team called rapid responders, who created a response inventory, handled the volume of questions, and found answers to unanticipated questions (Kane, 2015).

Birkner (2014) of *Marketing News Weekly* interviewed Julie Wenger, senior director of USA marketing at McDonald's, about the campaign's goals and objectives:

> *Birkner*: Talk about the importance of transparency, particularly in food marketing. What advice do you have for marketers who might be considering similar programs on social media?
>
> *Wenger*: It's the responsibility of any large brand to be transparent. It's really part of doing business . . . The advice I would have for other marketers is, use social media to learn about your audience and customers, and be prepared. We did a lot of work around anticipating what the questions might be, and what issues we could expect to deal with. It goes back to using social media as a tool to learn more about our customers, and to respond to their concerns. (Birkner, 2014, p. 1)

While top-level executives viewed this as a success, it is necessary to examine the digital media outcomes that followed.

Outcomes

As a result of the transparency campaign, McDonald's made some changes. In an interview with *PR Week*, Jack Russo, senior analyst at Edward Jones, noted that because of consumer cynicism McDonald's is striving to offer healthier options and continues to be transparent about its food. For example, the company plans to use antibiotic-free chicken in its restaurants by 2017 (Stein, 2015).

When asked how the campaign will be measured, Wenger said, "We'll know if it's a success in the short term based on the reaction we're seeing as we respond to customers online. Long term, we're looking to see more positive conversation around our food, in general" (Birkner, 2014, p. 1).

McDonald's and industry experts deemed the campaign a success. By March 2015, the highly visible program received 7.2 million views, 27,000 YouTube likes, 16,000 Facebook shares, and 2,937 tweets for "What are McDonald's Chicken McNuggets made of?" and "What are McDonald's USA fries made of?" had 6.2 million views, 13,000 YouTube likes, 7,130 Facebook shares, and 1,436 tweets (Jarboe, 2015, para. 12–13). Overall, the 13 videos had a total of 30.7 million views. The U.S. campaign was 1.9 times more popular than the McDonald's 2015 Super Bowl commercial and nearly 7.7 times more popular than its award-winning animated "Arch Enemies" ad (Jarboe, 2015, para. 14).

According to Garcia, one of the biggest rewards for the company was a more informed and supportive public. Based on its key performance indicators (KPI),

McDonald's saw increased traffic on its websites and social platforms and a positive attitude shift toward the brand. "It's been very successful for us . . . For the first time, we've seen customers really responding in the sense that they're *defending* us" (Kane, 2015, p. 3).

In March 2015, McDonald's USA announced new menu sourcing initiatives that include only sourcing chicken raised without antibiotics that are crucial to human medicine, and restaurants started offering low-fat white and fat-free chocolate milk from cows free of artificial growth hormones (Jarboe, 2015).

Additionally, during the campaign, customers asked about McDonald's offering an all-day breakfast menu (Kane, 2015), which came to fruition in late 2015. Garcia also noted that other customer comments were forwarded to leadership for consideration (Kane, 2015).

Overall McDonald's believes that the campaign changed how it engages with consumers across platforms by learning how to make business decisions based on actively listening to customers (Kane, 2015). Beyond changing menu items, the digital data also gave McDonald's insight on how to adjust its daily business functions from operations to sustainability (Kane, 2015).

Recently McDonald's USA hired 200 millennials to manage its digital footprint by responding to tweets and conducting digital analytics (Jargon, 2016). The millennial team is supposed to help the 61-year-old fast food chain connect with its younger consumers (Jargon, 2016).

In the spirit of its transparency campaign, in May 2016 McDonald's launched another digital campaign on Facebook and Instagram to advertise the source, quality, and taste of its juicier Quarter Pounder (Jargon, 2016). According to Jargon (2016), McDonald's USA Chief Marketing Officer Deborah Wahl realizes that millennials are harder to persuade because they are wary of anything that seems inauthentic. Reminiscent of the YouTube video used in the Canadian campaign, McDonald's recently stopped using staged food in some of its ads and instead features close-up images of burgers in their natural state as you would get it at the restaurant (Jargon, 2016).

Other Transparency Efforts

Following the "Our Food. Your Questions" campaign, McDonald's took additional steps to further its transparency efforts on social media.

McDonald's social media presence followed a similar pattern to other organizations, with Facebook and Twitter being used and updated most frequently, followed by YouTube and blogs. McDonald's attempted to harness two-way communication through consumer involvement with the most success associated with Facebook and Twitter. Consumers are more vocal on the Facebook page compared to the other social media platforms, but Twitter is updated most frequently.

Although McDonald's Twitter account allows users to retweet, favorite, and reply to tweets, the interactivity between McDonald's and its customers was not as extensive as on Facebook. McDonald's encompassed some elements of transparency; however, there is room for improvement.

Looking at the different digital platforms, although McDonald's did not initiate posting unflattering information, it did not seem to delete potentially damaging posts from consumers. By retaining the posts, McDonald's appeared to be open to criticism, exemplifying transparency. For example, comments criticizing McDonald's business practices went unanswered. On the other hand, some consumers were upset that McDonald's did not pull its support from the 2014 Winter Olympics in Sochi, Russia, despite the Russian government's anti-gay stance. Customers left numerous messages on the Facebook page and McDonald's responded with a blanket statement.

On its YouTube Channel, McDonald's has videos highlighting where its food is sourced. For example, two of the videos were on-site profiles of coffee farmers in Guatemala. Throughout the videos, McDonald's shows where, how, and who sources its coffee beans. From a transparency standpoint, the information is relevant to stakeholders interested in sustainability and ethically sourced food but fails to garner much interaction with consumers. This highlights the need for McDonald's to provide content that would offer additional dialogue between McDonald's and its publics.

Conclusion

Practitioners aiming for success must be strategic about the information they disclose on social media (DiStaso & McCorkindale, 2013). Just providing information is not transparency; the information must meet certain criteria for it to be considered transparent (Rawlins, 2009). Most importantly, the information must not only be truthful but should also increase consumers' understanding of the company's mission and business activities. Although McDonald's skeptics and critics were not convinced, some consumers appreciated McDonald's efforts and the campaign had far-reaching effects.

As Wright and Hinson (2012) found, most PR practitioners agree that digital media are changing the way companies engage with their publics and evolving how PR is practiced. Additionally, digital media are impacting corporate transparency and promoting a more ethical and transparent culture in the PR industry. McDonald's exemplifies this through its willingness to let consumers have a voice and changing its operating strategies due to consumer feedback.

Ultimately, organizations must be willing to be vulnerable by providing all pertinent and legally releasable information whether it's good, bad, or ugly. Releasing bad information might make an organization uneasy, but that can serve as motivation for the company to improve (Rawlins, 2009). As the father of modern PR, Ivy Lee, advised John D. Rockefeller Jr. in 1914, "Tell the truth, because sooner or later the public will find it out anyway. And if the public doesn't like what you are doing, change your policies and bring them into line with what the people want" (Harr & Johnson, 1998, p. 130).

It was true in 1914 and it still applies today. The people had questions about McDonald's food; it answered. The millennials demanded all-day breakfast; it obliged. Ethically sourced food and sustainability became the trend; it followed. Digital media provide a new way to interact with publics, and McDonald's is using it for transparency efforts and "We're Lovin' It."

References

Birkner, C. (2014, October 28). Transparency is the main ingredient in McDonald's social media campaign. *Marketing News Weekly*. Retrieved from https://www.ama.org/publications/eNewsletters/Marketing-News-Weekly/Pages/mcdonalds-our-food-your-questions.aspx.

Botterill, J., & Kline, S. (2007). From McLibel to McLettuce: Childhood, spin and re-branding. *Society and Business Review, 2*(1), 74–97.

DiStaso, M. W., & Bortree, D. S. (2012). Multi-method analysis of transparency in social media practices: Survey, interviews and content analysis. *Public Relations Review, 38*, 511–514.

DiStaso, M. W., & McCorkindale, T. (2013). A benchmark analysis of the strategic use of social media for fortune's most admired us companies on Facebook, Twitter and YouTube. *Public Relations Journal, 7*(1), 1–33.

McCorkindale, T., & DiStaso, M. W. (2013). *The Power of Social Media and Its Influence on Corporate Reputation*.: Blackwell Publishing Ltd.

Harr, J. E., & Johnson, P. J. (1998). *The Rockefeller Century: Three Generations of America's Greatest Family*. New York: Simon & Schuster.

Hill, K. (2012, January 24). #McDStories: When a hashtag becomes a bashtag. *Forbes*. Retrieved from http://www.forbes.com/sites/kashmirhill/2012/01/24/mcdstories-when-a-hashtag-becomes-a-bashtag/#6e21a8ac193f.

Jarboe, G. (2015, March 16). McDonald's "Our Food, Your Questions" video campaign is changing hearts, minds, and action. Retrieved from http://www.reelseo.com/mcdonalds-our-food-your-questions-video-campaign/?utm_source=reelshare&utm_medium=email&utm_campaign=email_share.

Jargon, J. (2016, October 6). McDonald's Knows It's Losing the Burger Battle—Can It Come Back? *The Wall Street Journal*.

Kane, Gerald C. (2015, November 12). How McDonald's cooked up more transparency. *MIT Sloan Management Review*. Retrieved from http://sloanreview.mit.edu/article/how-mcdonalds-cooked-up-more-transparency/.

McDonald's (n.d. a). Our Food. Your Questions. Retrieved from https://www.mcdonalds.com/us/en-us/about-our-food/our-food-your-questions.html.

McDonald's. (n.d. b). Our History. Retrieved from http://www.mcdonalds.com/us/en/our_story/our_history.html.

McDonald's Canada YouTube Channel (2016). Behind the scenes at a McDonald's photo shoot. Retrieved from https://www.youtube.com/watch?v=oSd0keSj2W8.

McDonald's Corporate Blog (n.d.). Let's talk. Retrieved from http://community.aboutmcdonalds.com/t5/tag/Food/tg-p.

McDonald's USA Facebook page (2016). Retrieved from https://www.facebook.com/McDonaldsUS/.

McDonald's USA Twitter (2016). Retrieved from https://twitter.com/McDonalds.

McDonald's USA YouTube Channel (2016). Retrieved from https://www.youtube.com/user/McDonaldsUS/about.

Morrison, M. (2012, February 20). Is McDonald's losing that lovin' feeling? *Advertising Age*. Retrieved from http://adage.com/article/news/mcdonald-s-losing-lovin-feeling/232821/.

Rawlins, B. (2009). Give the emperor a mirror: Toward developing a stakeholder measurement of organizational transparency. *Journal of Public Relations Research*, *21*(1), 71–99.

Ritzer, G. (2012). *The McDonaldization of Society: 20th Anniversary Edition* (7th ed.). Los Angeles, CA: Sage.

Stein, L. (2015, July 1). Not Lovin' It: McDonald's consumers want transparency as key ingredient. *PR Week*. Retrieved from http://www.prweek.com/article/1354282/not-lovin-it-mcdonalds-consumers-want-transparency-key-ingredient#icI29yGLz51g8RzJ.99.

Wright, D. K., & Hinson, M. D. (2012). Examining how social and emerging media have been used in public relations between 2006 and 2012: A longitudinal analysis. *Public Relations Journal, 6*(4). Retrieved from http://www.prsa.org/Intelligence/PRJournal/Documents/2012WrightHinson.pdf.

Discussion Questions

1. What factors motivated McDonald's to foster a new level of transparency?
2. Bob Langert, vice president of sustainability, wrote, "We are now part of a larger dialogue and need to be comfortable with discomfort." What did he mean by this? What type of ethical discomfort might organizations such as McDonald's face on digital media?
3. How can McDonald's and other corporations improve consumer engagement efforts on social media?
4. How was McDonald's YouTube account used after the "Our Food. Your Questions" campaign? Was it successful?
5. What were some methods used to measure the success of the "Our Food. Your Questions" campaign?

SCRUBBING AND THE ETHICS OF DIGITAL
REPUTATION MANAGEMENT

Alison N. Novak, Ph.D., *Rowan University*

Have you ever walked by a new restaurant, but wanted to read customer reviews before making a reservation? You may have gone to third-party review sites (TPRS) like Yelp, Google Reviews, or Open Table to get honest feedback and recommendations from patrons to help you decide if the restaurant is right for you. Millions of customers rely on TPRS every day to make purchase decisions. However, what if you found out that those reviews weren't entirely accurate but instead were carefully crafted and refined by companies to improve their ratings and digital reputations? Would you continue to trust online reviews? Would you be angry at the TPRS for allowing fake or revised reviews? Would you regret or rethink past purchases? This is exactly what happened to Yelp users in 2014 after they discovered TPRS were modifying prominent retailer reviews through "scrubbing." Scrubbing is a business practice where bad reviews are deleted and good reviews are promoted to artificially raise average ratings. Hundreds of users left the site and protested the unethical behavior. Yelp had no choice but to develop a popup warning that advised users when they were looking at a scrubbed profile. This case looks at the digital behavior of scrubbing and examines the ethics behind the 2014 Yelp incident to help understand digital reputation management in public relations.

Founded in 2004, Yelp was created to help users find local businesses such as mechanics, dentists, and restaurants. It boasts nearly 72 million viewers per month on its mobile application and has a total of 115 million user reviews. While controversial, Yelp claims that it exists to support the reach of small businesses who want to demonstrate services and goods in local markets. The official purpose of Yelp is "to connect people with great local businesses," demonstrating its commitment to supporting local economies and organizations.

Background

Digital sites where customers can post reviews have grown popular since 2006 as consumers look for ways to make purchase decisions based on unbiased information and examples. These TPRS allow customers to tell the story of their interaction with a company—good or bad. In many ways, TPRS take power away from advertising and public relations because of their efforts to provide a space for honest and accurate feedback that is not influenced by paid professionals. This is partially why these sites are so trusted by users. However, sites like Yelp have found a way to give public relations practitioners new control over business reviews. TPRS can ask companies to buy digital ads on the review sites in exchange for removing negative reviews and artificially raising the average rating.

This practice, where companies pay to change reviews, is called "scrubbing" because the TPRS can scrub away the negativity from a company profile. As scrubbing became more and more popular with the growth of TPRS, customers, company owners, and public relations practitioners questioned its ethics and legality. Scrubbing creates an inherently dishonest digital atmosphere where user feedback is controlled not by the user, but by corporate interests. Users have no idea which profiles are scrubbed and which ones are honest, making it difficult to trust the space and its reviews.

Scrubbing can also take place outside of the TPRS control. Companies can hire external reviewers to add fake positive reviews to profiles or fake negative reviews to those of competitors. Since 2010, anonymous online reviewers sell fake reviews for (on average) $75 a post through websites like Craigslist (Hill, 2015). These fake reviews look accurate to outside readers, making it difficult for users and the regulators of TPRS to identify and track which companies pay for reviews. Although sites like Yelp have spoken out about these paid reviews and have banned them through its "Terms and Services Agreements," it is difficult to track and prevent this type of scrubbing.

As a whole, the public is aware of the presence and potential of scrubbing and fake reviews. Novak (2016) identified ways that the public tries to overcome or outsmart these problems on TPRS, noting that most users are skeptical of the accuracy and honesty of sites like Yelp. As a result, some users leave the sites entirely, instead relying on person-to-person recommendations from friends and families. *Tech Insider* reported that many users deleted their accounts to protest what they thought were unethical practices by Yelp from 2014 to 2016 (Stenovec, 2016, para. 2).

Since 2006, Yelp has adamantly denied the presence of scrubbing on its site, despite rumors circulating for years about paid review content (Babb, 2015). However, a series of events starting in 2014 challenged Yelp's anti-scrubbing stance and required the TPRS to address user concerns and the ongoing rumors.

The Situation

In 2014, a group of small businesses in San Francisco sued Yelp for extortion over the issue of scrubbing. The small business owners claimed "Yelp's sales representatives told them their ratings would depend on their decision to buy ads" (Egelko, 2014, para. 5). The businesses claimed the act of scrubbing was detrimental to their practices because it artificially raised the ratings of competitors and created a dishonest digital atmosphere (Harris, 2014). In addition, the small business owners added that they did not have enough income to pay for digital ads, so instead relied upon TPRS for their digital reputations. Shortly after the small business owners filed the complaint, their lawsuit was denied by the San Francisco Federal Appeals Court. The justice ruled that scrubbing was a legal practice, and while it certainly did disadvantage small businesses, the TPRS was not doing anything legally wrong by demanding payments to scrub small business profiles. In the 2014 ruling, "Judge Marsha Berzon states: 'As Yelp has the right to charge for legitimate advertising services, the (alleged) threat of economic harm . . . is, at most, hard bargaining'" (Barmann, 2014, para. 3).

Yelp remained quiet during most of the court case but was quick to issue a statement on its website after the ruling in favor of its scrubbing practices. In what was called a "smug statement" the company released a blog post that read "for years, fringe commentators have accused Yelp of altering business ratings for money. Yelp has never done this and individuals making such claims are either misinformed, or more typically, have an axe to grind" (Schur, 2014, para. 1). The tone of this communication tactic seemingly had the opposite effect intended by Yelp. It enraged the small business owners further and perhaps united them against the TPRS.

Although this court case was stopped, small business owners around the country united to form Yelp-Sucks.com in early 2015, a digital protest site for customers, owners, and users to vent their frustrations over TPRS practices. The website featured testimonials about negative experiences, instructions on how to delete your business from Yelp, and online discussion boards for users to debate and discuss recent Yelp events. The online space became a place for the public to react and form collective actions against the large organization (including protests). The site also took to news media to vocalize its negative relationship with Yelp and publicize scrubbing.

Yelp continued to deny allegations of scrubbing and launched an "Advertiser FAQ" page that provided an infographic on how advertising sales work, linked to an independent academic study debunking the extortion claims, and summarized the court victory in San Francisco (Yelp, 2015). It also provided a set of instructions for how users could "prove it to yourself" by looking for negative reviews on prominent pages. This interactive FAQ page was a communication tactic intended to engage the public into the debate.

However, just months after the page's premiere, Yelp's own actions challenged this scrubbing-free FAQ page. In July 2015, Yelp removed thousands of reviews from a Minnesota dentist's office after the owner was accused and found guilty of hunting and killing a beloved lion in a protected Zimbabwe national park (Babb, 2015). Yelp defended this scrubbing by saying these posts were intended to protest the hunt, not the dentist's office. Despite Yelp's statements, the practice further identified and promoted Yelp's scrubbing abilities to the public, drawing massive criticism by users. After these three issues, it was difficult for Yelp to confidently deny scrubbing allegations anymore.

Shortly after, in a class action lawsuit, Yelp was sued by shareholders for misleading "investors into believing it was a filtering algorithm doing the behind-the-scenes work and ensuring only reliable 'first hand reviews' were featured on the site" (Phaneuf, 2014, para. 4). Even Yelp's investors no longer believed the site was scrubbing-free. The lawsuit also identified over 2,000 complaints filed with the Federal Trade Commission regarding the legality and ethics of Yelp's behavior. This caused Yelp's stock price to drop nearly 30% in just a few short months (Phaneuf, 2014, para. 8).

Despite what many see as clear evidence, Yelp never admitted to scrubbing and released few statements or official responses to allegations. Although the company lost thousands of users in protest and lost a significant amount of money from stock price drops, the company instead launched a digital initiative in June 2015 to demonstrate its commitment to being scrubbing-free.

To do this, the site launched a series of steps that would make users aware of its efforts to cut down on scrubbed profiles. The site posted popup warnings on company profiles that were accused of pursuing external fake reviews. For example, if a business attempted to hire an external reviewer for positive reviews and was caught, that profile would then permanently have a popup window that warned users not to trust the company. Yelp even provided evidence of scrubbing through screenshots of email exchanges between the company and the external reviewers (Schwartz, 2015).

The goal of this initiative was to provide evidence to users of the proactive efforts of Yelp to discredit and remove scrubbing from its site. Rather than just denying the claims like Yelp did in 2014, the TPRS now demonstrated its dedication and rejection of scrubbing. Yelp received positive reviews of this new initiative from users and bloggers who noted it was a refreshing change of tactic for the company that used to deny all claims of scrubbing (Schwartz, 2015).

Outcomes

Although Yelp never formally acknowledged scrubbing practices on its own site, the multiple lawsuits, digital protest site, and public outrage challenged the site's reputation and public trust. Today, Yelp reports that there are more users than ever on its site, and the stock price is on the rise (Wieczner, 2016). In addition, the increase in user presence in the site reflects the success of communicated messages of reliance and trust. So how did they regain public support and interest in the aftermath of an ethics crisis?

Yelp turned the scrubbing crisis into an opportunity to demonstrate a commitment to honest and accurate reviews through the popup warnings on scrubbed profiles. Whereas scrubbing violates the ethical principles of "establish responsibility" and "consistently build trust," instead, by calling out profiles with external scrubbing through popup warnings, Yelp identifies themselves as a type of protector of the public interest. The company's willingness to tell users when reviews were questionably credible was viewed as evidence that they were once again trustworthy and responsible. Although some users (like those on Yelp-Sucks.com) are still skeptical of the popup tactics, the renewed popularity of Yelp and its growing stock price suggest this tactic may be working—or, at the very least, working better than the denial tactic.

In addition, Yelp added a page to the "about us" section of the website that features a breakdown of the ad-buying process. The "Advertiser FAQ" page explains exactly what ad buying on Yelp results in (or does not result in). For example, one section of the FAQ page reads "I bought this ad on Yelp, and all I got was this ad on Yelp." This humorous quote showcased the relationship between the organization and advertisers and reminded the audience that ad sales did not result in scrubbing.

Yelp also sought to improve its relationship with digital publications who could help advocate on the organization's behalf. Yelp executives, sales personnel, and members of the technical team gave interviews to leading publications such as CNET, *LA Times*, *Wall Street Journal*, and *PC World* (Yelp, 2015). By providing interviews, giving tours of its headquarters, and giving journalists behind-the-scenes access to the website, Yelp was able to cultivate a positive relationship with the media and gain favorable reviews and news coverage.

Although it is unclear how Yelp assessed the success of popups and anti-scrubbing policies, there are multiple options for evaluation. First, to assess the success of this tactic, Yelp could look for positive and negative media coverage of scrubbing and popup warnings. This way, the organization can analyze how receptive media bloggers, journalists, and the public were to the change. Second, Yelp could engage in user research through focus groups or in-depth interviews. Yelp could talk to a sample of actual users to see how they respond to the popups and scrubbing warnings. Evaluative research could help generate information about what further steps are needed.

It is unclear if Yelp is continuing its own scrubbing practices despite the popup initiative to detect external scrubbing and fake reviews. However, scrubbing still holds ethical implications for digital reputation management. In addition to violating Bowen's (2013) principles of "clearly identify, establish responsibility, and consistently build trust," other research suggests that scrubbing may violate the utilitarian nature of online engagement. DeMers (2015) reported that 88% of the public trusts most online content because they expect other users to be honest and helpful in the online setting (para. 3). This perception of honesty and helpfulness is why the Internet is often called "utilitarian," meaning "good *for all*" (Foust, 2009, para. 18). Scrubbing violates the utilitarian principle because it deceives the user and provides reviews that are neither helpful nor honest. When scrubbing is successful at misleading the user, it is inherently unethical because it violates the utilitarian promise of the internet (Stanford University, 2015). In short, by scrubbing profiles of retailers who are willing to buy digital ads, the helpfulness and honesty of TPRS are compromised.

Although legal, scrubbing is an ethically complicated part of digital reputation management and public relations. Practitioners must make decisions to advise clients in favor or against this practice when looking to promote their brand in TPRS. Continued efforts such as Yelp's popup warnings and "Advertiser FAQ" page reinforce its commitment to identify and preventing scrubbing on its own site. The long-term implications of these tactics are still unknown, but it is likely to remain a relevant concern in public relations for the future.

References

Babb, F. (2015). Yelp is scrubbing thousands of angry comments from the page of a lion-murdering dentist. *Venturebeat*. Retrieved from http://venturebeat.com/2015/07/28/yelp-is-scrubbing-thousands-of-angry-comments-on-the-page-of-a-lion-murdering-dentist/.

Barmann, J. (2014, September 4). Yelp is allowed to manipulate rulings and remove good reviews, says court. *San Francisco-ist*. Retrieved from http://sfist.com/2014/09/04/yelp_is_allowed_to_manipulate_ratin.php.

Bowen, S. A. (2013). Using classic social media cases to distill ethical guidelines for digital engagement. *Journal of Mass Media Ethics, 28*(1), 119–133.

DeMers, J. (2015, December 28). How important are customer reviews for online marketing? *Forbes*. Retrieved from http://www.forbes.com/sites/jaysondemers/2015/12/28/how-important-are-customer-reviews-for-online-marketing/#2cfb90fa788c.

Egelko, B. (2014, September 4). Yelp can manipulate ratings, court rules. *San Francisco Gate*. Retrieved from http://www.sfgate.com/news/article/Yelp-can-give-paying-clients-better-ratings-5731200.php.

Foust, M. (2009). Scheffler's agent-centered prerogative—a viable solution to the problem of autonomy in utilitarianism. Institute for Applied and Professional Ethics at Ohio University. Retrieved July 11, 2016, from https://www.ohio.edu/ethics/tag/utilitarianism/.

Harris, S. (2014, January 17). Yelp accused of bullying businesses into paying for better reviews. *CBC-Radio Canada*. Retrieved from http://www.cbc.ca/news/business/yelp-accused-of-bullying-businesses-into-paying-for-better-reviews-1.2899308.

Hill, K. (2015, September 15). I created a fake business and bought it an amazing online reputation. *Fusion.net*. Retrieved from http://fusion.net/story/191773/i-created-a-fake-business-and-fooled-thousands-of-people-into-thinking-it-was-real/.

Novak, A. (2016). *Revenge of Cecil the Lion: Credibility in Third-Party Review Sites*. Presented at the International Communication Association Conference: Communicating with Power, Fukuoka, Japan.

Phaneuf, W. (2014, August 7). Yelp lied about allegedly shady sales tactics, new shareholder lawsuit claims. *San Francisco-ist*. Retrieved from http://sfist.com/2014/08/07/yelp_still_lying_about_shady_sales.php.

Schur, A. (2014, September 2). Ninth Circuit confirms that Yelp does not extort. *Yelp*. Retrieved from https://www.yelpblog.com/2014/09/ninth-circuit-confirms-that-yelp-does-not-extort.

Schwartz, B. (2015, June 9). Yelp starts showing evidence of review fraud. *Search Engine Land*. Retrieved from http://searchengineland.com/yelp-adds-link-to-evidence-of-review-fraud-222740.

Stanford University (2015, October 22). Consequentialism and classic utilitarianism. *Stanford Encyclopedia of Philosophy*. Retrieved from http://plato.stanford.edu/entries/consequentialism/.

Stenovec, T. (2016, March 2). People are deleting their Yelp accounts to protest the company. *Tech Insider*. Retrieved from http://www.techinsider.io/people-are-deleting-their-yelp-accounts-2016–3.

Wieczner, J. (2016, May 6). Yelp is absolutely crushing the rest of the market. *Fortune*. Retrieved from http://fortune.com/2016/05/06/yelp-stock/.

Yelp. (2015, June). "Advertiser FAQ." *Yelp*. Retrieved July 11, 2016, from http://www.yelp.com/advertiser_faq.

Discussion Questions

1. How did Yelp's communication tactics change over the course of 2012 to 2016? What elements changed and what stayed the same?

2. What would you recommend to a client who wanted to use scrubbing to remove negative reviews on TPRS? What alternative strategies might the client use?

3. If you worked for Yelp, what communication tactics would you suggest in addition to what they have already implemented?

4. Why was it important for Yelp to work with journalists? What news outlets would you recommend the organization reach out to?

5. What could Yelp do to improve relations with small business owners who feel like the TPRS creates an unethical and unfair environment by asking for advertising dollars?

APPLEBEE'S SOCIAL MEDIA "MELTDOWN": MANAGING ETHICS IN AN ONLINE BRAND COMMUNITY

Amber L. Hutchins, Ph.D., *Kennesaw State University,* and Desirae K. Johnson, *Kennesaw State University*

"I give God 10%, why do you get 18?"

Pastor Alois Bell, a customer at a St. Louis–area Applebee's restaurant, left the above note on the server's copy of the receipt. Bell was frustrated with the restaurant's policy of an automatic gratuity for large parties. An Applebee's co-worker of Chelsea Welch, the server who had served the party and received the note, posted a photo of the receipt to Reddit's atheism thread (reddit.com/r/atheism) with the caption "My mistake sir, I'm sure Jesus will pay for my rent and groceries." The post received thousands of comments, and the photo of the customer's note, which included the customer's signature, went viral on other sites beyond Reddit. When the customer, a pastor who visited the restaurant with her congregation, learned that her receipt had become public, she demanded that Applebee's fire the employee, and the company complied, citing its customer privacy policy. Reddit users and others took to Applebee's Facebook page as well as their own social media accounts to demand that the employee be rehired and to communicate their disapproval of Applebee's actions.

Communication experts, bloggers, the media, and the public at large were fascinated by what came next: As Applebee's tried to explain its company policies and communicate its position, the situation became more inflamed and, literally overnight, Applebee's Facebook page was inundated by thousands of negative comments. Commenters pointed out the company's inconsistent or unclear policies (previously, another customer's receipt with a positive note had been posted by the company but then deleted when this situation unfolded). Observers— some who chronicled the "meltdown" in real time—pointed out the numerous ways in which the company had mishandled and exacerbated the situation by censoring comments, blocking users, and responding only to selected individual posts. Many asserted that the situation would become a textbook case, serving as a cautionary tale for future public relations practitioners and online community managers.

Background

Applebee's Services Inc. is a publicly traded company that operates and franchises nearly 2,000 restaurants in the U.S. and in 15 international countries, with approximately 28,000 employees (Our History, n.d., About Us, n.d.). Applebee's is a well-established brand in social media, with more than 3.8 million Facebook likes, nearly 110,000 Twitter followers, and about 261,000 YouTube views.

Reddit is a popular online community known for its relaxed guidelines, in which members and volunteer moderators are responsible for regulating speech. The Applebee's situation is one of several high-profile instances in which the actions of members led to media coverage and controversy, including the misidentification of the suspect in the Boston Marathon Bombing (Stanglin, 2013).

Applebee's is one of a number of organizations that have experienced high-profile social media crisis situations or challenges with online community management. Because of the increased access to organizations, more and more stakeholders turn to social media sites to publicly address concerns (Coombs & Holladay, 2012).

In turn, these sites often set the stage for public relations meltdowns, making it imperative for organizations to learn how to effectively respond to key audiences in an online environment (Young & Flowers, 2012).

Public relations practitioners struggle to keep up with the accelerated pace of the 24-hour social media communication cycle (Young & Flowers 2012). In the past, professional communicators had a day (or more) to carefully craft messages to respond to public opinion, but now communication must occur within a moment's notice, especially when there is an impending crisis (Bridgeman, 2008). Not only is communication between organizations and publics happening more frequently and faster due to the internet, but social media also are empowering marginalized voices so that even average citizens on their personal computers or smart devices can influence public opinion and organizational decisions (Bridgeman, 2008; Tinker, Dumlao, & McLaughlin, 2009; Tinker, Fouse, & Currie, 2009).

Online brand communities are becoming more prevalent, and management is quickly becoming a common responsibility for public relations practitioners. While these communities can be a useful forum for creating dialogue with stakeholders and fans, they are also a venue for customers to express their dissatisfaction, and PR professionals can help brands and organizations mitigate and manage negative or harmful communication that takes place outside the brand-controlled community (Fröhlich & Schöller, 2013).

The Situation

Friends notified Bell that the photo of the receipt, including her signature, had been posted online. Bell contacted Applebee's and demanded that the server, Welch, and the restaurant manager be fired. The franchise fired Welch, stating that she had violated both the customer's privacy and company policy.

Applebee's posted a statement about the incident on the company's Facebook page on January 31, 2013, explaining the restaurant's position:

> We wish this situation hadn't happened. Our Guests' personal information—including their meal check—is private, and neither Applebee's nor its franchisees have a right to share this information publicly. We value our Guests' trust above all else. Our franchisee has apologized to the Guest and has taken disciplinary action with the Team Member for violating their Guest's right to privacy. (Applebee's, 2013a)

Soon after, the page was inundated with comments from those who opposed Applebee's actions, with many calling the company's actions "hypocritical" and pointing out that the company itself had violated its own policies in a previous situation by posting a photo of a positive customer note with the name clearly visible on their own Facebook page. In response, Applebee's removed the photo from their Facebook page, but the company did not reply to any of the negative comments from Facebook users at that time.

Applebee's posted another message on February 1, 2013, containing information from its employee handbook to further explain its position. The following excerpt from the message shows that the restaurant continued its argument that it is against company policy to publicly display guest information:

> Employees must honor the privacy rights of APPLEBEE's and its employees by seeking permission before writing about or displaying internal APPLEBEE'S happenings that might be considered to be a breach of privacy and confidentiality. This shall include, but not be limited to, posting of photographs, video, or audio of APPLEBEE'S employees or its customers, suppliers, agents or competitors, without first obtaining written approval from the Vice President of Operations.

The policy goes on to specify:

> Employees who violate this policy will be subject to disciplinary action, up to and including termination of employment. (Applebee's, 2013b)

By midnight, there were more than 17,000 negative posts on Applebee's Facebook page. At 2:53 a.m. on February 1, 2013, Applebee's began responding to negative comments on its original message rather than creating a new Facebook message, and its responses soon were buried under more negative feedback. Commenters complained that Applebee's deleted customer comments and blocked users from posting on the page, which led to more negative comments. The restaurant denied deleting comments, but commenters and bloggers shared screenshots of posts that had allegedly been deleted by Applebee's.

By 3 a.m., Applebee's response had shifted from replying to individual comments by repeatedly posting the same statement and tagging individual users in response:

> We can understand why you are upset. But the details circulating about this story do not represent all the facts. For example, the team member who posted the receipt WAS NOT the team member who waited on the group. The 18% gratuity was added to the bill. We'll be posting a statement later that explains the facts. This is an unfortunate situation but please let us assure you that Applebee's and every one of our franchisees values the hard working team members and the amazing job they do serving the guest. We appreciate your support of them too.

After a few minutes, commenters criticized the cut-and-paste response and the Applebee's representative began responding to individual posts with more personalized replies that varied in tone, from personal and emotional to comparatively formal:

"Again, a lot of the facts have been twisted."

"The disregard for an important policy left the franchisee no choice but to take the action they did."

"If you knew me or we were face to face you'd know how much I care. No one's asking me to comment at 5 a.m. in the morning. I am because I care, we care. I totally understand why you're upset and hate that I can't fix it." (Stoller, 2013)

Despite this attempt to address individual concerns, negative comments continued. Applebee's made two more status updates that reiterated their apology and included a detailed explanation of how company policies applied to the situation and led to the employee's termination. Applebee's continued to respond to Facebook comments well into the evening. Bloggers, commenters, and observers captured screenshots that became the sourse for news coverage by major news outlets including CBS and NPR, as well as trade publications and blogs such as *PR Daily* and Eater.com. International news outlets also reported the story—one headline proclaimed: "US restaurant Applebee's commits 'social media suicide'" (Porter, 2013, para. 1).

Despite Applebee's significant social media presence and reach, the company made many missteps in managing its Facebook page. While the Applebee's representative (or team) who managed the account committed significant time and effort to managing the situation, responding to numerous individual posts for many hours, the priority of timely responses resulted in efforts that suggested a lack of preparedness.

Many journalists (Payne, 2013; Porter, 2013) and critics agreed that the restaurant's crisis communication efforts on Facebook were not appropriate or effective in subduing concerns from key audience members who advocated for the fired server. In addition to the opinions of bloggers and journalists, Applebee's failed to meet many of the best practices requirements outlined by public relations scholars, who have asserted that crisis communication on social media should be a conversation, not a series of statements (Bridgeman, 2008; Veil, Buehner, & Palenchar, 2011), and that crisis communication between an organization and its publics should be a collaborative process (Tinker, Dumlao, & McLaughlin, 2009). Although Applebee's posted many responses, their communication efforts did not demonstrate a willingness to have an authentic dialogue or collaborate with its audience.

Outcomes

In the weeks after the incident, the company continued to address criticisms of the incident, mostly about the firing of Welch rather than the company's problematic communication response. CEO Mike Archer released a statement that reiterated the same key messages from the company's Facebook responses: regret that the situation had taken place, the fact that the server's firing was in accordance with the company's established policies, and understanding that the community had strong feelings about the incident. Although they did not publicly discuss any loss of income or other consequences, the company's efforts suggested that they were still working to repair their reputation.

Aside from missteps in best practices, Applebee's made several errors that raised ethical concerns, and existing ethical guidelines could have helped the organization mitigate and defuse the situation. Commenters took issue with the company's first Facebook post, which revealed that the company had violated its own policy of publicly posting customer information (when it served to benefit them), and the subsequent removal of the post when the company's error was pointed out by commenters.

Applebee's has continued to use social media and their Facebook page to communicate with customers and respond to complaints. Applebee's did not seem to suffer long-term consequences, but this situation has served as an example of the need for brands and organizations to closely monitor social media conversation and to prepare for negative responses before they happen. The situation has also raised awareness about the culture and community of Reddit (and similar discussion boards) where unmoderated conversations about brands and organizations might go unnoticed in traditional monitoring efforts.

The accelerated pace of social media communication reduces the amount of time that practitioners have to prioritize and assess communication challenges in "real time." Consideration of ethical implications can become a low (or non) priority for a practitioner trying to manage an extraordinary volume of feedback from multiple channels at once. Social media provide unprecedented access to brands and organizations, and it is the responsibility of the online community manager to facilitate open and honest communication and engage in ethical and respectful dialogue with all parties. Online community managers need to consider ethical guidelines, including the PRSA Code of Ethics (PRSA Code of Ethics, n.d.), at the beginning of social media efforts rather than waiting for an unplanned situation to occur.

References

About Us (n.d.). Retrieved from http://www.applebees.com/about-us Applebee's. (2013a, January 31). We wish this situation hadn't happened. [Facebook update]. Retrieved from https://www.facebook.com/applebees.

Applebee's. (2013b, February 1). We appreciate the chance to explain our franchisee's action in this unfortunate situation. [Facebook update]. Retrieved from https://www.facebook.com/applebee.

Bridgeman, R. (2008). Crisis communication and the net: Is it just about responding faster ... or do we need to learn a new game? In Anthonissen, P. F. (Ed.), *Crisis Communication: Practical PR Strategies for Reputation Management and Company Survival* (pp. 169–177). London: Kogan Page.

Coombs, W. T., & Holladay, J. S. (2012). The paracrisis: The challenges created by publicly managing crisis prevention. *Public Relations Review, 38*, 408–415.

Fröhlich, R., & Schöller, C. (2012). Online brand communities: New public relations challenges through social media. In Duhe, S. C. (Ed.), *New Media and Public Relations* (2nd ed., pp. 86–95). New York: Peter Lang Publishing Inc.

Our History – Applebee's. (n.d.). Retrieved 2016, from https://www.applebees.com/en/our-history

Payne, J. (2013, February 1). Applebee's taking heat on social media for firing waitress. *Yahoo! Small Business Advisor*. Retrieved from http://smallbusiness.yahoo.com/.

Porter, C. (2013, February 5). US restaurant Applebee's commits 'social media suicide.' *Herald Sun*. Retrieved from http://www.heraldsun.com.au/

PRSA Code of Ethics. (n.d.). Retrieved from https://www.prsa.org/ethics/code-of-ethics/

Stanglin, D. (2013, April 25). Student wrongly tied to Boston bombings found dead. Retrieved from http://www.usatoday.com/story/news/2013/04/25/boston-bombing-social-media-student-brown-university-reddit/2112309/.

Stollar, R. (2014, May 12). Applebee's Overnight Social Media Meltdown: A Photo Essay. Retrieved from https://rlstollar.wordpress.com/2013/02/02/applebees-overnight-social-media-meltdown-a-photo-essay/

Tinker, T. L., Dumlao, M., & McLaughlin, G. (2009). Effective social media strategies during times of crisis: Learning from the CDC, HHS, FEMA, the American Red Cross and NPR. *The Strategist, 15*, 25–39. Retrieved from http://www.oecd.org.

Tinker, T., Fouse, D. (Eds.), & Currie, D. (Writer). (2009). Expert round table on social media and risk communication during times of crisis: Strategic challenges and opportunities [Report]. Washington, DC: American Public Health Association. Retrieved February 26, 2013://www.apha.org/NR/rdonlyres/47910BED-3371-46B3-85C2-67EFB80D88F8/0/socialmedreport.pdf.

Veil, S. R., Beuhner, T., & Palenchar, M. J. (2011). A work-in-process literature review: Incorporating social media in risk and crisis communication. *Journal of Contingencies and Crisis Management, 19*, 110–122. DOI: 10.1111/j.1468-5973.2011.00639.x

Young, C. L., & Flowers, A. (2012). Fight viral with viral: A case study of Domino's Pizza's crisis communication strategies. Case Studies in Strategic Communication, 1, 93–106.

Discussion Questions

1. What could Applebee's have done differently to create a more ethical dialogue with the community?
2. How could the PRSA Code of Ethics could have provided guidance for Applebee's in this situation?
3. How could the Applebee's have been better prepared for this situation? Should they have been monitoring other communities like Reddit in order to prevent this situation?

CORPORATE SOCIAL RESPONSIBILITY

Learning Outcomes

- Recognize the consequence of corporate social responsibility (CSR).
- Describe the use of CSR in the practice of public relations.
- Analyze ethical principles in relation to CSR efforts.
- Apply ethical principles to CSR case studies.

Definitions

Corporate social responsibility: The initiatives an organization has created to assess its impact on social and societal issues and concerns such as diversity and the environment.

Social responsibility: The concept that an organization should balance its profitmaking activities with programs that benefit society.

Corporate social responsibility, CSR for short, in its simplest terms can be described as "using resources wisely and acting responsibly" (McIntire, as quoted in Jacques, 2012, 12). Often CSR is used to describe the activities corporations take on to help causes. The help could come in the form of volunteers and volunteer hours or it could be product or monetary donations. Many corporations choose to support causes with a direct link to their missions. For example, Patagonia took a stand on protecting national parks, places likely to be near and dear to its consumers. Similarly, Salt Life invests in ocean conservation efforts.

Planning CSR Activities

One suggestion for determining what social issues to address is for corporate leaders to talk with community members and listen to what they view as its greatest needs (Jacques, 2010). However, CSR efforts need to be planned; CSR cannot be a response to every request made by community members, consumers, or employees (Walton & Rawlins, 2011). Taking such an approach to CSR would not be sustainable and would therefore cause CSR efforts to fail. To be more successful, some companies have streamlined their CSR efforts so they can put their time and energy into one cause and make a greater impact (Walton & Rawlins, 2011).

Corporations play a role in society and are often known by others through their works as good citizens (Jacques, 2016). However, corporations need to do more than good or prevent harm: They need to participate in the community's development (Jacques, 2012). Texas Instruments, for example, believes the relationship between corporations and communities is reciprocal, meaning that when corporations strengthen communities, those communities then work to restrengthen those corporations (Jacques, 2012). Similarly, UPS and Coca-Cola state that organizations can only be as strong as the communities in which they operate (Jacques, 2012). Leaders at Coca-Cola add that corporations need to be a positive influence and need to make a difference in the communities in which they exist (Jacques, 2012).

While CSR can be confusing, one thing is clear. Consumers often want more than quality products and services; they want to support corporations that reflect their values when it comes to treating employees, caring for the environment, and responding to community needs (Jacques, 2010). A 2017 report conducted by Cone Communications (http://www.conecomm.com/research-blog/2017-csr-study) found that 87% of those surveyed would purchase a product because a company supported an issue the consumer found important and 76% would avoid purchasing a product or service from an organization that supported a cause or issue incongruent with their beliefs (Hessekiel, 2017).

Therefore, attention to CSR and CSR efforts done correctly can benefit a corporation in many ways. Companies with planned CSR efforts are strengthened by enhanced reputation and image, improved government relations, enhanced brand differentiation, created customer loyalty, and increased employee recruitment and retention (Walton & Rawlins, 2010). Many corporations have come to view CSR as more than just something that is nice to do to; rather, they view it as something that creates value (Walton & Rawlins, 2010). Not only do corporations need to be proactive with their CSR efforts, but they need to be reflective and think about where society is moving so that the CSR activities are part of the organization's broader strategies, objectives, and goals (Walton & Rawlins, 2010).

Not only consumers but also employees, especially younger ones, are looking for corporations with quality CSR programs. Employees want to engage in CSR activities, especially those related to causes they support (Walton & Rawlins, 2011). Employees are important to CSR activities and their success; they can be ambassadors demonstrating their commitment to causes (Walton & Rawlins, 2011). Millennial employees often want to work for companies that are working to better society (Walton & Rawlins, 2011). "Employees should be at the forefront of corporate responsibility and sustainability" (Cone as quoted in Walton & Rawlins, 2011, 16). When employees believe the companies they work for don't do enough socially, poor productivity and high turnover can result.

To sum it up, people want to buy from sustainable companies and employees want to work for corporations making a difference (3 emerging CSR trends, 2012).

CSR Cautions

Unfortunately, CSR efforts are often misunderstood. This situation makes communicating about CSR openly and effectively both important and at times tricky. Corporations need to be transparent about their CSR activities because all stakeholders deserve to know what is being done, what is working, and what is not (Walton & Rawlins, 2011). Corporate PR practitioners will find they need to have a balance when speaking about CSR activities so that they are sharing about the programs yet not raving about them (Walton, 2010). Communication about CSR activities, achievements, and failures should be steady and should incorporate more than just annual reports and CSR reports (Walton, 2010). Communicators need to ask themselves what publics are reading and watching; they also need to be where their audiences are—social media and apps (Ruggeri, 2016). In addition, CSR messages should be authentic, transparent, and supported by the corporation's actions (Jacques, 2010). Companies need to monitor social media to determine how publics are responding to and evaluating their CSR efforts (Jacques, 2012). Engage your publics in your CSR efforts and invite them to comment on and evaluate them (Sibilia, 2013). Not only does this sort of communication help to humanize the corporation, but it also strengthens the community (Jacques, 2010).

References

Hessekiel, D. (2017, December 14). Watch for these 3 corporate social impact trends in 2018. Retrieved from http://www.forbes.com/sites/davidhessekiel/2017/12/14/watch-for-these-corporate-social-impact-trends-in-2018/.

Jacques, A. (2010, July 1). Socially conscious: Companies share CSR best practices. Retrieved from http://apps.prsa.org/Intelligence/Tactics/Articles/view/8700/1017/Socially_conscious_Companies_share_CSR_best_practi#.Wmj7giOZNR0.

Jacques, A. (2012, April). At your community service: 5 companies with strong CSR initiatives. *Public Relations Tactics, 19*(4), 12–13.

Jacques, A. (2016, June 1). Soar with CSR: Take action to see coverage and reputation take flight. Retrieved from http://apps.prsa.org/intelligence/Tactics/Articles/view/11537/1127/New_Strategies_to_Get_Results_in_the_Age_of_Digita#.Wmj60SOZNR0.

Ruggeri, R. (2016, June). The future of news: Thriving in a 24/7 news cycle. *Public Relations Tactics, 23*(6), 16.

Sibilia, J. (2013 May). Be prepared: 5 CSR reporting guidelines for PR professionals. *Public Relations Tactics*, *20*(5), 15.

(2012, April). 3 emerging CSR trends. *Public Relations Tactics*, *19*(4), 11.

Walton, S. B. (2010, July). Do the right thing: Measuring the effectiveness of CSR. *Public Relations Tactics*, *17*(7), 10–11.

Walton, S. B., & Rawlins, B. (2011 September). Great expectations: Engaging employees in CSR. *Public Relations Tactics*, *18*(9), 16–17.

ALL YOUR CLOTHES ARE MADE WITH EXPLOITED LABOR: PATAGONIA TAKES ACTION TO SPUR ACTION

Jean Kelso Sandlin, Ed.D., *California Lutheran University*

How would you feel if you discovered the clothing you are wearing today was made by laborers working in slave-like conditions? In Gillian B. White's article in *The Atlantic*, "All Your Clothes Are Made with Exploited Labor" (2015), she exposed egregious human trafficking violations in the mills that produced fabric for clothing manufacturers and used the international clothing company Patagonia to illustrate her point. White wrote, "Patagonia's admission stands out in that it comes from a brand considered a leader in the movement for ethical production" (2015, para. 13).

Being linked to human rights violations in such a high-profile publication can damage a company or brand, particularly if its reputation was built on a strong record of corporate social responsibility (Servaes & Tamayo, 2013). However, Patagonia's then-director of global public relations and communications, Adam Fetcher, initiated contact with the reporter, divulged the violations the company had discovered internally, and arranged access to the company's senior leadership and suppliers. The article in *The Atlantic* was part of Patagonia's communication strategy to intentionally heighten the conversation about the use of exploited labor, frame the complex issue as an industry-wide problem, and position Patagonia as a leader in helping to solve it. In developing the public relations strategy, Fetcher said he was influenced by the history and mission of the company and its "culture of transparency" (A. Fetcher, personal communication, Feb. 5, 2016).

Social Responsibility as a Founding Value and Work in Progress

Patagonia's open culture was influenced by the company's founder. Yvon Chouinard is known today as an environmentalist and philanthropist (Archer, 2005; Casey, 2007; Welch, 2013), but back in the 1970s before he founded Patagonia, his small company manufactured rock-climbing equipment. However, the pitons (spikes hammered into rocks to help climbers get a foothold) degraded the rocks. During a climb in Yosemite National Park in California, Chouinard witnessed the degradation for himself and made the decision to phase out pitons, opting for a new approach that left the rocks "unaltered by the passing climber" (Patagonia, Beginnings and blacksmithery). Chouinard founded Patagonia in 1973 with a mission to "build the best product, cause no unnecessary harm, use business to inspire and implement solutions to the environmental crisis" (Patagonia, Mission statement, para. 1).

Since its founding, several initiatives helped boost the company's reputation as socially responsible. Patagonia was a founding member of the Fair Labor Association (n.d., para. 1), an organization "dedicated to creating lasting solutions to abusive labor practices;" 1% for the Planet (n.d.), a nonprofit organization that supports environmental causes; and the Sustainable Apparel Coalition (n.d.), an industry alliance for sustainable production based on a standardized supply chain measurement tool to understand the environmental and social and labor impacts of making and selling products and services. In 2013, the company launched the $20 Million and Change fund to help startup companies benefit the environment (Chouinard, 2013; Schwartz, 2013).

Other initiatives that earned the company recognition for being socially responsible include the Footprint Chronicles, an online resource unveiled in 2007 to offer greater transparency by detailing information about its manufacturers (Patagonia, The Footprint Chronicles), and Common Threads, an eBay partnership started in 2011 that encouraged consumer-to-consumer resale of Patagonia clothing to help reduce waste (Houpt, 2011; Kleinberg, 2014). In 2013, the company replaced Common Threads with a new initiative, Worn Wear, a program to encourage consumers to buy high-quality clothing and repair it, instead of discarding it, when it gets damaged. The program offers repair services, tutorials on garment repair, and recycling services (Beer, 2015; Cave, 2015; Patagonia, Worn Wear). The company was recognized as a Champion of Change by President Barack Obama for its generous parental leave policy and onsite childcare (White House Briefing Room, 2015). Patagonia's founder has received numerous awards and recognition for his commitment to social and environmental justice (Archer, 2005; Casey, 2007; Welch, 2013). Yet in the midst of this progress, the company discovered human trafficking violations in the mills that produced its fabrics (White, 2015).

The Issue: A New Tier of Exploited Labor

Labor issues are prevalent throughout the history of clothing manufacturing. Often referred to as "sweatshops," many clothing factories have been reported to engage in gender discrimination, underage child labor, forced overtime, safety violations, denial of sick leave, sexual harassment, physical intimidation, and other unscrupulous labor practices as documented by human rights organizations such as Clean Clothes Campaign, the Institute for Global Labour and Human Rights, Human Rights Watch, the International Labour Organization, and Worker Rights Consortium. According to Human Rights Watch, "International clothing and footwear brands have a responsibility to promote respect for workers' rights throughout their supply chains, including both direct suppliers and subcontractor factories . . . many brands have not fully lived up to these responsibilities due to poor supply chain transparency, the absence of whistleblower protections, and failure to help factories correct problems in situations where that is both possible and warranted" (Human Rights Watch, 2015, para. 8).

Starting in the mid-1990s, Patagonia hired third-party auditors to help the company monitor labor conditions at its factories. However, in 1996, it came out that Kathy Lee Gifford's line of clothing made for Walmart, which was contracted to be made by a U.S. manufacturer, was actually being made by an overseas subcontractor using child labor. This spurred more diligence within the industry and within Patagonia. Patagonia became a founding member of the Fair Labor Association. However, the company's quick growth, the ubiquity of poor labor practices in the industry, and the use of many subcontractors to meet production deadlines soon put Patagonia into a position where its clothes were being made by factories that were unknown to the company and that lacked reliable monitoring for labor violations (Patagonia, Patagonia and social responsibility). Recognizing this, Patagonia hired a manager of social responsibility and began to build a social responsibility program with a systematic approach to reduce the number of factories the company used; to monitor those factories and subcontractors; and to start an internal training program to reassert Patagonia's Workplace Code of Conduct.

As the monitoring process expanded, Patagonia began auditing the mills that supplied the raw materials, referred to as the tier 2 supply chain; few large apparel companies conducted such audits. During those audits in 2012, another layer of problems was revealed: human trafficking violations in some of the mills in Taiwan. Migrant workers from those mills often got their job through labor brokers who charged the workers exorbitant fees that could take workers up to two years to pay back. The brokers would sometimes retain the workers' passports until the fees were paid in full. Since migrant workers must renew their contracts every three years, this system, according to Patagonia's website, created "a form of indentured servitude that could also qualify, less politely, as modern-day slavery. And it's been happening in our own supply chain" (Patagonia, Protecting migrant workers, para. 2).

The Response: Taking Action to Spur Action

Patagonia did not stop using the mills that the company found to be in violation, nor did they immediately share the news with the public. According to Fetcher, "Creating a responsible supply chain is an immense challenge. It's a complex issue and so pervasive in the system that it required a holistic approach to help the workers and influence other brands to join us in our efforts" (A. Fetcher, personal communication, Feb. 5, 2016).

Patagonia's social and environmental responsibility (SER) team was the first to receive the audit results and immediately began plans for a three-phase response: research, remediation, and system-wide implementation. Fetcher followed the work of the SER team as it waded through the complex web of managers, owners, subcontractors, labor brokers, and government officials and began forming a strategic communication plan based on the company's actions. As part of its efforts to approach it as an industry-wide issue and not just a Patagonia issue, the company hosted a one-day brand forum in San Francisco in November 2013 and invited 40 brands to send representatives to address the topic of human trafficking in the supply chain. Only seven brands sent representatives; the other brands, according to Fetcher, said they were interested but not ready to tackle the complex issue.

It took 18 months of working with the nonprofit organization Verité to develop Patagonia's comprehensive migrant worker standard that covered every aspect of employment, including prehiring interactions, labor contracts, wages and fees, retention of passports, living and working conditions, grievance procedures, and repatriation. Patagonia applied this standard not only to the suppliers in Taiwan, where the problems were initially detected, but to the company's entire supply chain. In addition, the company made this standard freely available to any other brand or company that wanted to adopt it or use it as a guide to create their own standard.

During the time the standard was being developed, Patagonia hired a CSR expert to spearhead the migrant worker program in its Ventura, California, headquarters, and a CSR field manager based in Taiwan. Once the new staffing and the standard were in place, Patagonia hosted a forum for its Taiwanese suppliers to explain the new standard that, among many things, required them to stop charging fees to foreign workers hired on or after June 1, 2015, and repay currently employed workers who were hired before June 1 all fees that exceeded the legal amount. Patagonia's SER staff met with Taiwan's Ministry of Labor Workforce Development Agency and, as a result, representatives from the agency provided training to Patagonia's suppliers on the practice of direct hiring. In January 2015, Patagonia, along with Walmart, HP, and SAP Cloud, were invited to present the company's work at the White House Forum on Combating Human Trafficking in Supply Chains (Pope, 2015).

Throughout this process, Patagonia's communication strategy remained focused on the suppliers, to gain their understanding and compliance; the government entities, to gain their cooperation; and brands within the clothing industry, to gain collaboration. However, the question for the public relations and communication team was how to share the news with consumers in a way that would properly present both the complexity and the pervasiveness of the issue. How could they guard against superficial or sensationalized coverage? The foundation of the plan was to acknowledge the problem and take responsibility, demonstrate the issue's pervasiveness in the clothing industry, and communicate the actions the company was taking toward resolving the issue. To this end, they developed a detailed chronology of the company's actions and reached out to a journalist who had a reputation for treating complex issues with depth and clarity. "This was a story that required a deep look . . . due diligence, a look at the larger landscape. It could easily have been taken out of context," said Fetcher. He contacted White at *The Atlantic*, divulged the violations the company had discovered internally and the steps the company had taken to mitigate the issue, and arranged access to the company's senior leadership and unprecedented access to its suppliers. On the same day the article was published, Patagonia published the chronology and the company's explanation of the issue on its blog (Patagonia, The unacceptably high cost of labor, 2015). They also sent an email to the company's media list with a link to the blog post. "We wanted it in our own words," said Fetcher.

Reflecting on the experience, Fetcher said the willingness and support of his company to be transparent was key: "We value transparency. We can tolerate it. It's worth it for us to raise awareness," he said. Fetcher said communicators could make a difference through their work, not just by influencing their own company to be transparent but by strategically framing their own company's struggles in the context of the broader global issue in an effort to influence brands and consumers to be less tolerant of unacceptable labor practices. He admitted that labor issues still plague the clothing and fashion industry supply chains. "I would like to see the issue covered in the pages of *Vogue* and *Glamour*," Fetcher said. "It's shocking, and it might be uncomfortable to read it, but it would deepen the impact."

References

Archer, M. (2005, October 30). Founder of Patagonia became a businessman accidentally. *USA Today*. Retrieved from http://usatoday30.usatoday.com/money/books/reviews/2005-10-30-patagonia_x.htm.

Beer, J. (2015, April 1). Don't throw that jacket away—Patagonia is taking its Worn Wear program on the road. *Fast Company*. Retrieved from http://www.fastcocreate.com/3044573/dont-throw-that-jacket-away-patagonia-is-taking-its-worn-wear-program-on-the-road.

Casey, S. (2007, May 29). Patagonia: Blueprint for green business. *Fortune*. Retrieved from http://archive.fortune.com/magazines/fortune/fortune_archive/2007/04/02/8403423/index.htm.

Cave, A. (2015, May 4). We're not just about sales: Patagonia clothing is a state of mind. *Daily Telegraph*. Retrieved from LexisNexis Academic database.

Chouinard, Y. (2013, May 6). A letter from Yvon Chouinard. *Patagonia Works*. Retrieved from http://www.patagoniaworks.com/#index.

Fair Labor Association. (n.d.). About Us. Retrieved from http://www.fairlabor.org/about-us-0.

Houpt, S. (2011, September 29). Marketing with a mission. *Globe and Mail*. Retrieved from http://www.theglobeandmail.com/report-on-business/industry-news/marketing/patagonia-marketing-with-a-mission/article600919/.

Kleinberg, A. (2014, June 6). Brands from KFC to Gucci are jumping on the cause marketing bandwagon. *Advertising Age*. Retrieved from http://adage.com/article/agency-viewpoint/marketing-hot-pay-good/293537/?utm_source=daily_email&utm_medium=newsletter&utm_campaign=adage&ttl=1402617401.

1% for the Planet (n.d.). History. Retrieved from http://onepercentfortheplanet.org/about/history/

Patagonia. (n.d.) Beginnings and blacksmithery. Retrieved from http://www.patagonia.com/company-history.html.

Patagonia. (n.d.). Mission statement. Retrieved from http://www.patagonia.com/company-info.html.

Patagonia. (n.d.). Patagonia and social responsibility in the supply chain: A history. Retrieved from http://www.patagonia.com/corporate-responsibility-history.html.

Patagonia. (n.d.). Protecting migrant workers. Retrieved from http://www.patagonia.com/protecting-migrant-workers.html.

Patagonia. (n.d.). The Footprint Chronicles. Retrieved from http://www.patagonia.com/footprint.html.

Patagonia. (n.d.). Worn Wear. Retrieved from http://www.patagonia.com/worn-wear.html.

Patagonia. (2015, June 3). The unacceptably high cost of labor: How a deeper dive into our supply chain led to a new migrant worker standard [blog post]. Retrieved from http://www.patagonia.com/blog/2015/06/the-unacceptably-high-cost-of-labor-a-new-migrant-worker-standard-from-patagonia/.

Pope, A. (2015, January 29). Combating human trafficking in supply chains [blog post]. Retrieved from https://www.whitehouse.gov/blog/2015/01/29/combating-human-trafficking-supply-chains.

Schwartz, A. (2013, May 13). Patagonia launches a venture fund for environmentally responsible startups. *Fast Company*. Retrieved from http://www.fastcoexist.com/1682011/patagonia-launches-a-venture-fund-for-environmentally-responsible-startups.

Servaes, H., & Tamayo, A. (2013). The impact of corporate social responsibility on firm value: The role of customer awareness. *Management Science, 59*(5), 17. Retrieved from http://faculty.london.edu/hservaes/ms2013.pdf.

Sustainable Apparel Coalition (n.d.) The challenges facing our industry require collective action on a global scale. Retrieved from http://apparelcoalition.org/.

Welch, L. (2013, March 13). The way I work: Yvon Chouinard, Patagonia. *Inc*. Retrieved from http://www.inc.com/magazine/201303/liz-welch/the-way-i-work-yvon-chouinard-patagonia.html.

White, G. B. (2015, June 3). All your clothes are made with exploited labor. *The Atlantic*. Retrieved from http://www.theatlantic.com/business/archive/2015/06/patagonia-labor-clothing-factory-exploitation/394658/.

White House Briefing Room. (2015, April 16). The White House champions of change: Working families [video log post]. Retrieved from https://www.whitehouse.gov/photos-and-video/video/2015/04/16/white-house-champions-change-working-families.

Human Rights Watch. (2015, March 11). Work faster or get out: Labor rights abuses in Cambodia's garment industry. Retrieved from https://www.hrw.org/report/2015/03/11/work-faster-or-get-out-labor-rights-abuses-cambodias-garment-industry.

Discussion Questions

1. According to the International Association of Business Communicators (IABC) Code of Ethics for Communicators, "Professional communicators uphold the credibility and dignity of their profession by practicing honest, candid and timely communication and by fostering the free flow of essential information in accord with the public interest."
   a. Did revealing the poor conditions of the workers and having the story reported in *The Atlantic* help or hurt the reputation of Patagonia?
   b. Was it the right strategy for the company?
   c. Was it in the public interest?
   d. Was Patagonia demonstrating responsibility by inviting a specific journalist to cover the story or did that strategy conflict with the free flow of information and timeliness?

2. The IABC Code of Ethics also states, "Professional communicators are sensitive to cultural values and beliefs and engage in fair and balanced communication activities that foster and encourage mutual understanding." Patagonia made the decision not to sever ties with the mills and denounce them publicly, but to work with them to improve workers' conditions, provide training for the Taiwanese suppliers, and participate in open dialogue with migrant workers and the Taiwanese government. Should Patagonia have, instead, severed ties with the mills in an effort to punish them by cancelling the contracts and/or bringing the issue to a close more quickly?

3. The Page Principles represent high professional standards for communicators. The second Page Principle is "Prove it with action. Public perception of an enterprise is determined 90 percent by what it does and 10 percent by what it says."
   a. What are some of the actions Patagonia took in this situation?
   b. Whom did the actions benefit?
   c. Did the company's actions affect its reputation?
   d. Patagonia is a privately held company with no stockholders. Would having stockholders make a difference to how a company should respond to CSR issues?

4. A study by Servaes and Tamayo (2013) suggests that CSR activities can enhance value for firms with high public awareness, but firms with high public awareness are

also penalized more when there are CSR concerns. Do you think the CSR activities related to Patagonia's tier 2 labor issues helped or hurt the company? Explain your answer.

5. According to Human Rights Watch (2015, para. 33), "Very few international clothing brands disclose the names and locations of their production units— suppliers and subcontractors—even though disclosures can help workers and labor advocates to alert brands to labor rights violations in factories producing for them. Such disclosure is neither impossible nor prohibitively expensive and there appears to be no valid reason for brands to withhold this information."

a. Where do you buy your clothes? Do you have a favorite brand?

b. Do you know where your clothes are made? Does the company offer a way for you, as a consumer, to easily trace where your clothes are made?

c. Visit the company's website or any of the human rights websites involved with monitoring labor issues. Do they provide a way for you to check whether your clothes are being made by exploited workers?

A TALE OF TWO CASE STUDIES: COMPARING COCA-COLA'S DIVERGENT CORPORATE SOCIAL RESPONSIBILITY INITIATIVES AND THE RESULTING ETHICAL IMPLICATIONS

Lucinda L. Austin, Ph.D., *University of North Carolina at Chapel Hill*, MaryClaire Schulz, *Elon University*, and Barbara Miller Gaither, Ph.D., *Elon University*

Coca-Cola, one of the world's most renowned beverage corporations, has a diverse range of CSR initiatives to engage socially minded stakeholders. Among the most substantial of these initiatives are the company's "3Ws," a range of CSR commitments announced in 2013 devoted to societal concerns related to well-being, women, and water. In regard to well-being, Coca-Cola launched the "Coming Together" public relations campaign to fight obesity, an issue to which Coca-Cola products may directly contribute. Meanwhile, to address women's issues on a global scale, Coca-Cola established a 10-year CSR initiative that supports the empowerment of female entrepreneurs around the world to create a more stable global economy. While Coca-Cola focuses heavily on its well-being and women programs, the company has also worked to provide clean water to a number of communities through water stewardship programs.

This study explores two of these initiatives in greater depth—the well-being and women's empowerment initiatives. While Coca-Cola's well-being initiatives are high in company–issue congruence (i.e., the CSR issue connects closely to the company's products/industry) yet controversial, its women-focused initiatives are generally uncontentious but are unrelated to the company's products (Miller Gaither & Austin, 2016). This case study explores how these distinct differences have affected public attributions of motives and responses to these CSR campaigns. Additionally, examination of these initiatives sparks discussion surrounding how stakeholders perceive ethics of CSR communication and the potential for different ethical standards based on the context of CSR-focused versus advocacy-focused initiatives.

Background

As the world's leading beverage company, Coca-Cola employs a range of CSR efforts, focused on promoting sustainability across a number of "global pillars," including women and well-being (Coca-Cola Company, 2012, para. 1). According to Coca-Cola, these areas of CSR focus, which make up two of the company's "3Ws" sustainability commitments, contribute to the company's desire to sustain healthy life in global and local communities where the company conducts business. Coca-Cola explains that these efforts are not only advantageous to the communities they reach but also serve as investments in Coca-Cola's own business interests. While the well-being initiative advocates for the importance of sustaining a healthy lifestyle, the women-focused initiative promotes economic sustainability by empowering female entrepreneurs.

Although Coca-Cola promotes both its well-being and women-focused initiatives as contributions to a more sustainable world, audience responses to these two programs have been markedly different. The well-being campaign has been discussed extensively in media and criticized as "a damage control exercise, and not a meaningful contribution toward addressing obesity" (CNN, 2013, para. 15). However, the women's initiative was recognized as a Best Global Initiative for Women's Economic Empowerment at the Women in Leadership Economic Forum (Coca-Cola Company, 2014) and won a 2014 Leadership Award from the Women's Empowerment Principles group. While not as controversial, the women's initiative appears to lack a clear connection to Coca-Cola's mission and products.

This case study illustrates important distinctions between these two initiatives; while the women's empowerment initiative is reflective of traditional CSR, the well-being initiative may be more accurately described as a form of marketplace advocacy, a type of issue advocacy designed to protect or improve the market for a company's business products or services (Miller & Sinclair, 2009). In this case, Coca-Cola's well-being initiative attempts to directly address a major public concern (obesity) that pertains to the soft drink market. As Coca-Cola is a company vulnerable to recent criticism due to the perceived link between soft drink consumption and obesity, Coca-Cola provides an interesting case for investigation.

The Situation

Well-Being Initiative

In January 2013, Coca-Cola launched a global public relations and advertising campaign to fight obesity. The campaign debuted with a two-minute video on national cable news titled "Coming Together," which reminded viewers that all calories count in weight management, including those contained in Coca-Cola products. A second advertisement stated explicitly that a can of Coca-Cola has 140 calories and encouraged viewers to consider fun ways to burn calories. The company also launched a number of physical activity initiatives in local communities, such as "America Is Your Park," a call to action for Americans to go outdoors and vote for their favorite national park, and the School Fitness Centers & Governor's Physical Fitness Challenge, which dedicated $5 million to placing 100 new fitness centers in U.S. schools over the next five years. The company publicly supported Michelle Obama's "Let's Move!" initiative by placing calorie labeling on the front of many of its beverage containers and, in 2012, began working with others in the beverage industry to increase the availability of low- and no-calorie beverage options in vending machines. Coca-Cola also announced intentions to avoid advertising directed at audiences of more than 35% children under the age of 12.

With two-thirds of the American population overweight or obese, Coca-Cola called obesity "the issue of this generation" (CNN, 2013). Given the health concerns associated with sugary soft drinks, as well as increased efforts to restrict their availability in many school districts (and even in New York City by Mayor Bloomberg) (Ax, 2013), Coca-Cola's CSR campaign had the additional objective of responding to public concerns associated with the consumption of its products. The four major tenets of the campaign were (1) to offer low- or no-calorie beverages in every market, (2) to be transparent in nutritional information printed on all packaging, (3) to support physical activity programs, and (4) not to advertise to children under 12 (Harder, 2014). While this pillar of Coca-Cola's 3Ws is highlighted as part of the company's CSR commitments, given the negative implications of Coca-Cola on the social issue being addressed (i.e., obesity), this campaign may, in fact, be more reflective of marketplace advocacy. Although both CSR and marketplace advocacy are intended to portray a corporation as responsive to the needs and concerns of society, marketplace advocacy is often initiated with the additional goal of protecting the organization's position in the marketplace (Miller & Lellis, 2015). In marketplace advocacy, the focus of the good works is directly tied to the organization's own source of profit and protecting that profit in a range of ways, including deflecting criticism and avoiding public calls for potential regulation of the business or industry (Miller & Lellis, 2015; Miller & Sinclair, 2012).

Of course, the dilemma for Coca-Cola with this initiative is the contribution of the company's products to the issue of obesity. According to Harvard's School of Public Health consumption data (Department of Nutrition, 2012), men who consumed one sugary drink per day increased their risk of heart attack by 20% and children who drank one sugary drink per day increased their risk of becoming obese by 60%. While Coca-Cola's well-being initiative attempted to address growing concerns regarding obesity, the company could also been seen as trying to prevent regulation of soft drink sales and avoid public scrutiny. In regard to its "Coming Together" campaign, Coca-Cola faced the difficult challenge of being seen as a credible—and ethical—voice on the public health issue of obesity.

Women's Empowerment Initiative

Conversely, Coca-Cola's women's empowerment-focused CSR initiative, the 5by20 project, launched in 2010, focused on engaging global female stakeholders invested in becoming entrepreneurs. Recognizing women as primary buyers of Coca-Cola products and major stakeholders, Coca-Cola and the Harvard Kennedy Business School conducted research at one of the company's microdistribution centers in Africa to better understand the barriers that women entrepreneurs face (Coca-Cola Company, 2010). Based on its research, Coca-Cola launched the 5by20 project with the goal of empowering 5 million women globally by 2020 by providing business training, financial services, and mentorship opportunities to female entrepreneurs around the world (Coca-Cola Company, n.d.). Many of these programs are conducted in partnership with organizations such as UN Women, the Clinton Foundation, and local governments. As of April 2015, the initiative is active in over 40 countries, and Coca-Cola has received numerous awards for its commitment to empowering women globally.

To communicate its CSR goals and 5by20's progress, the company has used channels such as press releases, articles about new partnerships or events, and "Success Story" features and videos on female entrepreneurs aided by the program. Coca-Cola also actively shares articles and news on social media channels, including its corporate and public-facing Twitter accounts. Through these strategies and others, Coca-Cola incorporates the voices of the women in its initiative and connects them directly with other women stakeholders (McPherson, 2016). Overall, this initiative has established opportunities for dialogue between and within the company and stakeholder groups and has garnered a positive public response regarding its impact on economic structures globally.

Outcomes

Comparison of the Initiatives

Public response through social media to these initiatives has shown that the women's empowerment initiative has been received significantly more positively by stakeholders (Austin & Gaither, 2016). Ultimately, Coca-Cola's attempts at traditional CSR received a positive response from stakeholders but its attempts at marketplace advocacy faced a more negative public response. The company's initial well-being efforts were largely perceived as a "public relations ploy at damage control" rather than a genuine attempt to fight obesity (Harder, 2014, 3). The women's empowerment initiative has also been better at creating social change, as well as enhancing business profits (Coca-Cola, 2015). Coca-Cola has continued to include both well-being and women-focused initiatives in its range of CSR programs, and although some of the criticism directed at its well-being efforts has abated, the corporation is still receiving awards and praise for its female empowerment project.

Although the women's empowerment project often focuses on assisting women involved in Coca-Cola's own value chain, such as retailers who sell Coca-Cola products or artisans who use Coca-Cola packaging to create goods, the initiative has been met with little criticism from the public. Coca-Cola garnered positive attention by asking U.S. bloggers to publish posts featuring the 5by20 project on their websites to gain the attention of their followers, who responded with a multitude of comments commending the company's commitment to giving back to female entrepreneurs worldwide (Gebel & Clarke, 2015). In addition, the 5by20 project has received multiple awards for its efforts to promote female empowerment, such as a 2013 Catalyst Award for Global Women's Initiatives, an award for the Best Global Initiative for Women's Economic Empowerment, and a 2014 Leadership Award from the Women's Empowerment Principles group.

For the well-being initiative, however, health experts argued the initiative was a "desperate move" on the part of Coca-Cola to increase sales, despite calls to limit soda consumption (Ravelo, 2015). The company was accused of trying to shift the blame from its company's contribution to the obesity crisis onto consumers by encouraging them to balance their calorie consumption with exercise (O'Connor, 2015). Coca-Cola was also criticized for promoting misleading and false scientific evidence regarding wellness from scientific experts who received funding from Coca-Cola. For example, in 2012 a company executive told *USA Today* that sugary beverages have no scientific link to obesity (Horovitz, 2012). However, "media and health professionals were quick to point out that studies from the Yale Rudd Center and the American Heart Association disproved this statement" (Harder, 2014, 10; Tinker, 2013). Coca-Cola also became a target of advocacy groups. For example, to dispute some of the company's claims about "energy balance," calorie consumption, and the link with obesity, the Center for Science in the Public Interest created its own viral video "The Real Bears," which, as of 2016, had well over 2.6 million views on YouTube (Center for Science in the Public Interest, 2012).

While prevailing wisdom regarding CSR suggests that high company–cause congruence (when the cause of the CSR relates to the organization) generates more favorable public response, a content analysis of Coca-Cola's Twitter posts on its CSR initiatives revealed otherwise (Austin & Miller, 2015). In fact, tweets related to the company's initiatives for well-being and water (the third issue in the 3Ws) generated the most negative public response, perhaps due to the detrimental relationship between Coca-Cola's products and production processes and the relevant social issues. This response occurred despite the fact that posts were designed to communicate the company's efforts to address societal concerns related to the company's products, namely water scarcity/pollution and obesity.

Conversely, posts regarding the women's initiative—a cause unrelated to the company's products and services—generated significantly positive public comments. Although the initiative lacks apparent congruence with the company, it also does not appear to be in conflict with the organization's goals. Moreover, it does not appear to be a corporate response to a contentious issue or an effort to avoid regulation of the industry, as is typical of marketplace advocacy. In fact, in the case of Coca-Cola, and perhaps for other corporations whose products or production processes have some form of negative societal impact, it may very well be the lack of relevance to the company's products and services that generated a favorable outcome.

Ethical Situation and Implications

Comparing these two cases allows us to explore whether different ethical criteria should apply in different cases, as Curtin and Boynton (2001) suggest may be the case for advocacy versus CSR. Ultimately, an organization should be transparent about its motives for CSR and avoid minimizing its own responsibility and shifting blame to others, especially a company such as Coca-Cola that may already face criticism for its business practices (Austin & Gaither, 2016). When CSR messages promote individual behavior change, these messages may be viewed as shifting the blame or avoiding responsibility. Special care should therefore be taken when businesses contribute to the issue being addressed, including recognition that highly congruent CSR approaches may not be the best fit for these types of organizations.

However, if a company contributes negatively to an issue of societal concern, stakeholders may view that organization as ethically and socially bound to address that issue and work toward change. For example, public opinion reflects the idea that companies that are perceived to contribute to the issue of obesity have an obligation to help combat the problem (Darmon, Fitzpatrick, & Bronstein, 2008). Initial backlash and skepticism may diminish if the organization is seen to have a demonstrated commitment to the cause. If, on the other hand, the organization continues to contribute to the issue without effectively addressing this contribution, skepticism, increased scrutiny, and reputational and relational damage are likely to occur (Austin & Gaither, 2016). As Kim (2014) notes, backlash is increased when companies with reputational challenge declare society-serving motives without acknowledging their own self-serving motives.

These two CSR initiatives provide an interesting context for the examination of company–issue congruence in stigmatized industries and marketplace advocacy versus traditional CSR. While the 5by20 project employs a more traditional CSR approach to an uncontentious issue unrelated to Coca-Cola's own corporate goals, the obesity campaign illustrates marketplace advocacy and attempts to address a negative societal issue to which Coca-Cola products contribute. Ultimately, publics have commended the company for its involvement with the 5by20 project but criticized its attempts to speak out about obesity, an issue tied so closely with its corporate goals.

The case of Coca-Cola's diverse CSR initiatives suggests that, to foster positive perceptions of CSR initiatives among stakeholders, a corporation selling products that negatively contribute to society may engage in CSR unrelated to its marketplace or be extremely clear in communicating its intentions to offset the negative impacts of its products. Above all, corporations must consider ethics for communicating CSR goals and strategies to socially minded stakeholders who desire to see not only how companies are contributing to society but also why.

References

Austin, L., & Miller, B. M. (2015). *Campaign and Corporate Goals in Conflict: Exploring Corporate Social Initiative Types and Company–Issue Congruence*. Paper presented at the annual meeting of the Association for Education in Journalism and Mass Communication in San Francisco, CA.

Austin, L. L., & Gaither, B. M. (2016, April 6). Examining public response to corporate social initiative types: A quantitative content analysis of Coca-Cola's social media. *Social Marketing Quarterly*. Online ahead of print.

Ax, J. I. (2013, July 30). Bloomberg's ban on big sodas is unconstitutional: Appeals court. *Reuters*. Retrieved from http://www.reuters.com/article/2013/07/30/us-sodabanlawsuit-idUSBRE96T0UT20130730.

Center for Science in the Public Interest. (2012, October 12). *The Real Bears Take America*. [Press release]. Retrieved from https://www.cspinet.org/new/201210151.html.

CNN. (2013). *Coke weighs in on obesity fight*. Retrieved from http://www.cnn.com/2013/01/14/health/coke-obesity.

Coca-Cola Company. (n.d.). *5by20: What we're doing*. Retrieved from http://www.coca-colacompany.com/our-company/5by20-what-were-doing.

Coca-Cola Company. (2010). *The Coca-Cola Company pledges to empower 5 million women entrepreneurs by 2020*. [Press release]. Retrieved from http://www.coca-colacompany.com/stories/5by20-news-center/.

Coca-Cola Company. (2012, January 1). *Global pillars*. Retrieved from http://www.coca-colacompany.com/stories/global-pillars.

Coca-Cola Company. (2014, December 3). *5by20 named best global initiative for women's economic empowerment*. Retrieved from http://coca-colacompany.com/stories/5by20.

Coca-Cola Company. (2015). *2015 annual review*. Available at: http://coca-cola-ir.prod-use1.investis.com/~/media/Files/C/Coca Cola-IR/documents/ar15-final.pdf.

Curtin, P. A., & Boynton, L. A. (2001). Ethics in public relations. In Heath, R. L. (Ed.), *Handbook of Public Relations* (pp. 411–422). Thousand Oaks, CA: Sage.

Darmon, K., Fitzpatrick, K., & Bronstein, C. (2008). Krafting the obesity message: A case study in framing and issues management. *Public Relations Review, 34*, 373–379.

Department of Nutrition, Harvard School of Public Health. (2012). *Sugary Drinks and Obesity Fact Sheet*. Retrieved from http://www.hsph.harvard.edu/nutritionsource/sugary-drinks-fact-sheet.

Gaither, B. M., & Austin, L. L. (2016). Campaign and corporate goals in conflict: Exploring company-issue congruence through a content analysis of Coca-Cola's Twitter feed. *Public Relations Review, 42*, 698–709.

Gebel, J., & Clarke, E. (2015, July). Bloggers celebrate the launch of 5by20 products in stores and online. Retrieved from: http://www.coca-colacompany.com/stories/bloggers-celebrate-the-launch-of-5by20-products-in-stores-and-online.

Harder, H. (2014). Are all calories created equal? An analysis of the Coca-Cola Company's communication in the fight against obesity. *Arthur W. Page Society Case Study Competition*. Retrieved from http://www.awpagesociety.com/study_competitions/2014-case-study-competition.

Horovitz, B. (2012, June 7). Coke says obesity grew as sugary drink consumption fell. *USA Today*. Retrieved from http://usatoday30.usatoday.com/money/industries/food/story/2012-06-07/mayorbloomberg-coca-cola/55452558/1

Kim, Y. (2014). Strategic communication of corporate social responsibility (CSR): Effects of stated motives and corporate reputation on stakeholder responses. *Public Relations Review, 40,* 838–840.

McPherson, S. (2016, October 28). Lessons from Coca-Cola, Nestle, and more on investing in women workers. *Forbes*. Retrieved from http://www.forbes.com/sites/susanmcpherson/2016/10/28/how-companies-are-empowering-women-across-the-value-chain/#2480485b9881.

Miller, B. (2012). *Marketplace Advocacy Campaigns: Generating Public Support for Business and Industry*. Amherst, NY: Cambria.

Miller, B., & Lellis, J. (2015). Response to marketplace advocacy messages by sponsor and topic within the energy industry: Should corporations or industry trade groups do the talking? *Journal of Applied Communication Research, 43*(1), 66–90.

Miller, B. M., & Sinclair, J. (2009). Community stakeholder responses to advocacy advertising: Trust, accountability, and the Persuasion Knowledge Model. *Journal of Advertising, 38*(2), 37–52.

Miller, B. M., & Sinclair, J. (2012). Risk perceptions in a resource community and communication implications: Emotion, stigma, and identity. *Risk Analysis, 32*(3), 483–495.

O'Connor, A. (2015, August 9). Coca-Cola funds scientists who shift blame for obesity away from bad diets. *New York Times*. Retrieved from http://well.blogs.nytimes.com/2015/08/09/coca-cola-funds-scientists-who-shift-blame-for-obesity-away-from-bad-diets/?_r=0.

Ravelo, J. L. (2015). The 3 Ws of the Coca-Cola Foundation. *Deveeximpact*. Retrieved from https://www.devex.com/news/the-3ws-of-the-coca-cola-foundation-86792.

Tinker, B. (2013, January 16). Coca-Cola weighs in on obesity fight. *CNN*. Retrieved from http://www.cnn.com/2013/01/14/health/coke-obesity.

Discussion Questions

1. Marketplace advocacy is a form of corporate issue advocacy that is designed to improve or protect the market for a company's products or the company's position in the marketplace (Miller, 2012; Miller Gaither & Austin, 2016). How does marketplace advocacy differ from other types of corporate social responsibility? What is an example of an organization that has implemented CSR aimed at protecting its position in the marketplace (marketplace advocacy)? Was this marketplace advocacy beneficial/successful?

2. Coca-Cola was criticized in its wellness initiatives for funding its own scientists to research the problem of obesity and its connection to sugary beverages (O'Connor, 2015). Does this funding represent an ethical dilemma for Coca-Cola? If so, how could the company have handled this differently?

3. Curtin and Boynton (2001) suggest that different ethical standards may apply in different contexts, such as advocacy and CSR, although the specific context should still be taken into consideration. Do you think different ethical standards are necessary and appropriate for advocacy versus other types of CSR? If so, why? What should these ethical standards be?

4. What considerations should organizations take into account when deciding whether to address social problems to which they contribute? Although Coca-Cola received negative feedback and backlash on its wellness initiatives, would failure to do anything on the issue be unethical?

5. Following backlash from a CSR initiative gone wrong, such as the Center for Science in the Public Interest's public criticisms of Coca-Cola's wellness initiative (or the media outcry over McDonald's fitness trackers included as Happy Meal toys), how should organizations respond? What messages should organizations convey to stakeholders in situations such as these?

RESTRUCTURING CORPORATE PHILANTHROPY: BELK STRATEGICALLY APPLIES ETHICAL RESPONSIBILITY TO UNDERPIN COMMUNITY ENGAGEMENT

Alan Freitag, Ph.D., *APR, Fellow PRSA, University of North Carolina at Charlotte*,
Jessica Martin Graham, *APR, Fionix Consulting LLC*

Measuring just 22 feet by 70 feet, the "New York Racket" wasn't much of a department store, but 26-year-old William Henry Belk thought the name made the store sound bigger than it was. He was risking a lot. It was May 1888, and his $750 in savings and $500 loan (at 10% interest), combined with $3,000 worth of consignment goods, as well as his name, were on the line. When he opened the store, Mr. Belk had a vision and some innovative business ideas at a transitional period in U.S. history. This era was the Gilded Age, marked by the rapid expansion of the railroads, the opening of the Washington Monument, the first skyscrapers, and the core of the second Industrial Revolution. Mr. Belk was on retail's cutting edge, pioneering concepts such as purchasing goods in quantity for cash and selling them for cash at low markups, clearly labeling merchandise with retail prices (no haggling allowed), and allowing customers to return goods if not completely satisfied. His plucky store in Monroe, North Carolina (population about 1,800 at the time), enjoyed swift success, permitting Mr. Belk to pay off his debts and bank $3,300 profit after less than seven months.

William Henry Belk had other ideas about business, too. He believed it was important for a business to give back to the community that made success achievable for him and his company. He was also committed to valuing and respecting his employees. These were not common characteristics for business leaders in the era of the robber barons. The formula was a successful one, though, and the Belk constellation of stores quickly expanded. A second store opened in Chester, South Carolina, in 1893, followed by a third in Union, South Carolina, in 1894. The following year saw the opening of a fourth store in Charlotte, North Carolina, and store operations moved there as well. New stores and acquisitions through three generations of Belk family leadership resulted in a network of roughly 300 stores in 16 states. In 2015, Belk became a portfolio company of Sycamore Partners, a private equity firm in New York. Despite tremendous growth and changes, Belk, Inc., remains committed to its traditional principles of community involvement and volunteer time. However, as the company continues to grow, its leadership recognizes the commensurate need to align its philanthropic activities with the changing business environment.

Background

It has been more than 130 years since William Henry Belk welcomed customers to the "New York Racket" in Monroe, and the company now known as Belk, Inc., generates approximately $4 billion annually in sales and employs around 24,000 associates in the southeastern United States from Texas to Maryland and Missouri to Florida. In fiscal year 2015, Belk, Inc., distributed $6.1 million to more than 250 nonprofit organizations. Philanthropy on that scale requires a careful and strategic approach to ensure that the company's largesse aligns corporate identity with community need. Organizations, particularly corporations, have several levels of responsibilities, as described by Carroll (1991). The first layers of responsibility are *economic* (earn a profit) and *legal* (obey the law); these initial levels are required if the organization is to continue to exist. The third layer Carroll called *ethical* (do no harm), and said this obligation was expected by constituencies affected by the organization. The fourth and highest level of responsibility was discretionary (*social responsibility*, *philanthropy*), and Carroll said this was a desired responsibility. Increasingly, scholars and business thought leaders believe this highest layer, once discretionary, is increasingly expected along with ethical, responsible business behavior (Werther & Chandler 2006).

There has been an ongoing debate regarding the extent to which businesses are obligated to exercise CSR—that is, the degree to which the top layer of Carroll's pyramid is expected, desired, or even appropriate. Companies already create most of the jobs, economic prosperity, and innovation that benefit society. They carry a hefty portion of the tax burden. Isn't that enough? Nobel Prize–winning economist Milton Friedman argued forcefully against permitting CSR to distract businesses, the engines of society, from their primary economic purpose (Friedman, 1962, Chapter 7). Yet corporations and their communities are interdependently joined in complex ways that suggest the need for a deeper understanding of corporate roles and responsibilities. Heli, Li, Takeuchi, and George (2016, 534) analyzed the CSR debate, as reflected in research literature, in the decades since Friedman's declarations and describe a distinct shift, noting that "an increasing majority of corporations have proactively committed to addressing larger societal challenges." They also say the debate has evolved from simplistic questions of the appropriateness of CSR to questions of how best to make CSR an intrinsic part of corporate culture, and from questions of mere financial outcomes to questions of broader societal outcomes.

Without entering into a lengthy discussion of the nature of ethical behavior and the role of ethics in the corporate setting, it is useful to ponder the fundamental questions: What distinguishes ethical behavior? How are personal and professional ethics intertwined? Are there universally accepted ethical standards? How can an inanimate organization be held to ethical standards? How does one acquire an ethical framework? Does including a 3-credit course on ethics in an MBA program predict that its graduates will apply ethical guidelines to their decision-making in the years ahead? Of course, the public relations profession is guided by a host of standards, codes, and principles such as those of the Public Relations Society of America, the International Association of Business Communicators, the International Public Relations Association, and other groups. However, the issue of CSR takes public relations managers beyond matters of communication to considerations of corporate behavior on a grander scale.

Belk, Inc., leaders believe there is a compelling moral argument for CSR and one of its components, philanthropy. That argument centers not only on values but also on the benefits that accrue to businesses from societal contributions such as an educated workforce and a stable and secure infrastructure (Werther & Chandler, 2006, 15–17). Belk's position is supported by research demonstrating that reported CSR activities produce benefits in areas such as stock price (Jizi, Nehme, & Salama, 2016) and employee commitment (Prutina, 2016). This case explores the confluence of that moral argument with the rational and economic arguments for CSR (Werther & Chandler, 2006, 17–19).

For many years, Belk's giving was done through the Belk Foundation. As Belk, Inc., made the commitment to give a percentage of its pretax income to its local communities, the Board of Directors of the Belk Foundation adopted a new mission statement that placed a stronger focus on educational programs and initiatives. To increase the impact of its charitable investments, the Foundation today invests solely in programs that fall within their two areas of focus: K-3 achievement and excellent teachers and leaders. While the company and the foundation maintained a close working relationship for many years, their charitable efforts are now completely independent.

The Situation

The rapidly evolving retail environment compels organizations such as Belk to nimbly adjust to changing circumstances while remaining centered on the company's bedrock principles. Beginning in 2010, Belk began a careful but sweeping adjustment to emerging consumer needs and expectations. Corporate leadership saw in this process the opportunity to examine and recraft its strategic giving to better align its philanthropic efforts with its organizational identity and the community's needs.

Results of research and analysis led to a central theme: Philanthropic activities needed to be more impactful and strategic. That is, corporate giving in all forms needed to focus on tangible results that measurably and meaningfully improve conditions in key societal sectors, and those sectors needed to align logically with the Belk identity. A second result was the leadership's commitment at the time to designate 2.5% of pretax corporate income to local communities. To put this percentage commitment in context, the CECP (formerly called the Committee to Encourage Corporate Philanthropy) reports that of 271 global, multi-billion-dollar companies surveyed, the median giving level was 0.11%, and a giving level of 0.20% or more placed a company in the top quartile (CECP, 2015). Further, the report says these levels continue a multiyear trend of increasing philanthropy.

Secondary research involved a review of historical practices and data as well as an examination of efforts by other organizations and a scan of literature on strategic philanthropy. Interviews with key company leaders and community influencers along with demographic analysis provided additional background. A review of relevant media coverage also informed decisions. As a result of this assessment, Belk management elected to channel giving toward three focus areas:

- Education: Belk believed education is the cornerstone of success, and the company contributed to charities that shared this belief. The idea was that this is an investment not only in young minds, but also in the future.

- Breast cancer research and awareness: Belk leadership was inspired by the women who have helped make the company successful. Contributions supported breast cancer awareness and the quest for a cure.
- Community strengthening: Giving financially and accommodating employee volunteer time to local charities and neighborhood initiatives in the communities.

Education

An example of Belk's focus on education was its school uniform donation program. For a variety of social reasons, many public K-12 schools have instituted mandatory uniform wear for students, and proponents say results include improved academic performance, reduced violence, and so forth, though admittedly the debate is not settled (King, 1998). The program began with Belk's donation of 2,000 uniforms to Charlotte-Mecklenburg Schools. Belk partnered with the regional United Way office to coordinate the program. Success soon led to the donation of more than 7,000 uniforms to additional counties surrounding Charlotte as well as to schools in Jackson, Mississippi; Savannah, Georgia; and Dallas, Texas. In the first six years of the program, Belk donated more than $1 million in uniforms. Media outreach was an integral part of the uniform program; each donation was presented formally to the schools at a media event, and those efforts resulted in favorable coverage in those communities.

Breast Cancer Research and Awareness

The central element of Belk's efforts in breast cancer research and awareness was its Belk Mobile Mammography Center. This brand-liveried, converted recreational vehicle was launched in 2013 and traveled throughout the Belk operating area for five years. By mid-2016, the BMMC had screened more than 10,000 women (including roughly 900 Belk employees) for breast cancer and other abnormalities. The distinctly recognizable vehicle has made multiday appearances at nearly all its 300 stores. Belk's medical partner, Charlotte Radiology, handled all appointments, screening, and follow-up. Charlotte Radiology's licensed, mammography-certified female technologists performed the screening exams, and a board-certified radiologist, specialized in breast imaging, interpreted the mammograms. The confidential results were sent directly to the patient and her primary care physician. Charlotte Radiology prepared the stores for the BMMC visits by visiting them several weeks in advance, and Belk hosted monthly conference calls with host store managers to share best practices, guidelines for promoting the visits, tips for involving the stores' intimate apparel departments, and details of the upcoming visits. Belk also sent each store manager a packet of visit-related materials, including posters, appointment cards, a news release, and a visit checklist. Belk promoted BMMC visits in stores via posters and cards, in malls at kiosks and on LED signs, and via local media (television, radio, website, and social media). The screenings were open to Belk customers, associates, and members of the community. Each individual visit lasted about 30 to 45 minutes for screening, and then patients were invited to visit the store for a complimentary bra fitting. The program was promoted and managed by Belk's communications and community relations team.

Tangible results were impressive. Since the program began, more than 50 cases of cancer were diagnosed by BMMC medical staff. Roughly 14% of the visits involved women receiving their first screening, and more than a third of those who have had previous screenings had not been checked in over two years. Nearly 60% of women participating had no medical insurance.

Measurable business and relationship impact results were impressive as well. In one recent year, 5% of all media coverage of Belk involved coverage of the BMMC. There were nearly 2,000 media placements stemming from the BMMC, resulting in more than 23 million impressions and over $1.5 million in advertising equivalency value. Belk's retail marketing programs linked the BMMC with intimate apparel sales, and in FY 2015, that sector experienced a nearly 60% sales increase over the previous year.

Community Strengthening

The prominent element of this component of Belk's strategic philanthropy program was its "125 Days of Service" effort. Belk, Inc., provided $2 million to Points of Light to fund the 125 Days of Service, which provided more than 300 makeovers to Title I (low-income) schools across Belk's 16-state footprint. Projects included building bookcases, renovating playgrounds, organizing book drives, and beautifying school grounds with murals, picnic tables, and landscaping. This program delivered benefits in both community relations and internal communication. More than 10,000 Belk employees representing 100% of its stores have already participated in 300-plus projects. Those employees contributed 21,000 hours of volunteer service during the 125-day event, touching the lives of an estimated 131,000 students. Belk reached out to local media in each of the communities where it hosted these projects, and Belk's 125 Days of Service generated 432 print and broadcast stories.

One of the ways Belk communication managers gauge the value of media coverage is the extent to which that coverage conveys key message themes. The leading themes at the time of the 125 Days of Service project were that Belk is family-owned, is based in the southern United States, and is deeply involved in the communities it serves. In the months during and following this community service program, 37% of all media coverage of Belk addressed one or more of those messages, a 13-point increase over the previous year.

The success of 125 Days of Service resulted in a similar program two years later, "Angel Days." Angel Days was Belk's signature holiday campaign, held annually in

December. This campaign gave Belk customers the opportunity to purchase $5 angel pins at its stores. One hundred percent of the sales in each store went to local Title I schools. This effort raised $300,000 for local schools, and subsequent holiday sales rose 5.2%.

Outcomes

What Belk, Inc., leadership, and especially its communication managers, have learned from this multiyear process of research, analysis, planning, implementation, and assessment is that including a deliberate review and adjustment of CSR approaches in a broader business realignment will ensure that resulting CSR efforts reinforce overarching long-term business goals and vision. Communication managers, in fact, developed five fundamental guidelines they recommend organizations consider if the aim is to align philanthropic and other CSR activities with broader business functions.

First, make sure that communication managers are thoroughly familiar with overarching corporate priorities, goals, and objectives. Implied here is that communication managers should be involved in the process of developing those things, including providing advice and counsel to leaders based on ongoing constituency and issue research. Attendant is the need to develop strategic communication goals and objectives that flow logically from and support organizational goals.

Second, create unique programs that reinforce and advance organizational identity. Belk's recent reorientation of its corporate philanthropy program more sharply reflected the principles espoused by young William Henry Belk nearly 130 years ago. Further, components of the program meshed consistently with Belk's retail function, such as linking breast cancer awareness with intimate apparel, and with its traditional priorities, such as linking employee volunteerism with community engagement.

Third, be authentic. That sounds simplistic, but it's vital. It means high-minded rhetoric must be matched by commensurate behavior. Authenticity is an essential quality, but it is not easy to achieve. It is not something you have but something you are. Authenticity is immeasurably valuable, and it is painstakingly earned and easily lost. Perceptions matter to both internal and external publics, so there can be no stumbles. Lack of authenticity in the area of CSR even has a name: "greenwashing" (Laufer, 2003).

Fourth, adjust CSR programs, including philanthropy, as priorities change. This requires communication managers to actively monitor the implementation and impact of CSR programs and constantly scan the horizon for emerging and evolving issues that affect and are affected by those programs. It doesn't mean shifting focus whimsically, but it does mean being responsive to environmental dynamics.

Finally, celebrate successes. Research suggests the advantages and benefits of legitimate communication regarding organizational CSR efforts (Bachman &

Ingenhoff, 2016). Of course, it's always better when someone else tells your story, but include in CSR planning honest, transparent communication, to internal and external audiences, about your organization's activities. Wise communication managers will achieve the right balance of modest narrative, confidentiality, and principled perspectives.

Belk continues to apply these principles, and the impact to date appears positive. The retail sector is evolving rapidly as technology and lifestyle changes affect the relationship between consumer and seller. Public relations leaders need to monitor these developments and gauge how best to integrate CSR into organizational mission and vision. Public relations leaders are prepared and well positioned to advocate for strategic blending of CSR activities into business practice on both moral and economic grounds. Doing so is certainly one of our highest responsibilities.

References

Bachman, P., & Ingenhoff, D. (2016). Legitimacy through CSR disclosures? The advantage outweighs the disadvantages. *Public Relations Review*, *42*(3), 386–394.

Carroll, A. B. (1991, July/August). The pyramid of corporate social responsibility: Toward the moral management of organizational stakeholders. *Business Horizons*.

CECP. (2015). *Giving in Numbers*. Retrieved from http://cecp.co/measurement/benchmarking-reports/giving-in-numbers/2015-edition.html.

Friedman, M. (1962). *Capitalism and Freedom*. Chicago: University of Chicago Press.

Heli, W., Li, T., Takeuchi, R., & George, G. (2016). Corporate social responsibility: An overview and new research directions. *Academy of Management Journal*, *59*(2), 534–544.

Jizi, M., Nehme, R., & Salama, A. (2016). Do social responsibility disclosures show improvements on stock price? *Journal of Developing Areas*, *50*(2), 77–95.

King, K. A. (1998, January). Should school uniforms be mandated in elementary school? *Journal of School Health*, *68*(1), 32–37.

Laufer, W.S. (2003). Social accountability and corporate greenwashing. *Journal of Business Ethics*, *43*(3), 253–261.

Prutina, Ž. (2016). The effect of corporate social responsibility on organizational commitment. *Management: Journal of Contemporary Management Issues, 21*, 227–248.

Werther, W. B., Jr., & Chandler, D. (2006). *Strategic Corporate Social Responsibility: Stakeholders in a Global Environment*. Thousand Oaks, CA: Sage Publications.

Discussion Questions

1. Discuss the appropriateness of publicly owned corporations including CSR programs in their organizational priorities and goals. What are the arguments for and against this practice? Cite examples of CSR efforts that you are aware of.
2. Is it ethically appropriate for Belk to link its breast cancer awareness and research efforts with promotion of its retail intimate apparel sector?

ETHICAL CORPORATE PHILANTHROPY: A CASE STUDY
ON COMMUNICATING CSR

Heidi Hatfield Edwards, Ph.D., *Florida Institute of Technology*

W̲hat are the ethics of corporate philanthropy? The question, easily posed, is not so easily answered, as is evident in the literature on the subject. Researchers in business, economics, communication, public relations, and marketing have wrestled with the question, frequently trying to find ways to justify the practice as a component of CSR. Framed as a noble practice as long as it balances the tightrope between altruistic motives and bolstering the corporate image and bottom line, the ethical reality of corporate giving is complex. This reading explores how Harris Corporation, a multinational company, communicates its philanthropic efforts as ethical activities through the more comprehensive lens of CSR.

Background

Founded in 1895 and based in the United States, Harris Corporation is a high-tech communication company with clients in 125 countries, covering markets from defense and national intelligence to transportation, energy, utilities, public safety, and healthcare, among others (Harris Corporation, About). The company notes in an annual report that CSR has been "an integral and sustaining part of the Harris culture for more than 50 years" (Harris Corporation, Annual Report, 8). According to the Harris website, the company's mission is to "be the best-in-class global provider of mission-critical assured communications products, systems and services to both government and commercial customers, combining advanced technology and application knowledge to offer a superior value proposition" (Harris Corporation, About). The company lists its values as integrity, excellence, customers, results, innovation, and inclusion (diversity of ideas/talent).

Brothers Alfred and Charles Harris founded what would become Harris Corporation, entering the communication industry by inventing a way to automatically feed paper into printing presses, thus eliminating the need to hand-feed the machines. For decades the company grew, becoming leaders in press and typesetting innovations. As communication technology advanced, Harris shifted its business focus to electronics, acquiring and merging with companies that specialized in broadcasting and microwave communication. These acquisitions took Harris Corporation into the space age. By 1974, the company was manufacturing space and military technology, including products used in communication and weather satellites, and military missile systems (Harris Corporation, The Harris story). Currently, its four core business segments are communication systems, space and intelligence systems, electronic systems, and critical networks.

Harris's corporate headquarters are in Melbourne, Florida, with operations throughout the United States, and regional international headquarters in Europe, Central and Latin America, Asia Pacific, and the Middle East and Africa. As a global company with multinational operations, Harris has particular CSR obligations and restrictions that can impact perceptions of ethical CSR and corporate philanthropy.

The Situation

Harris has a history of corporate giving (philanthropy) as part of its CSR initiatives. The corporate story includes explanations of its philanthropic efforts, but the company is careful to communicate its range of CSR activities that go beyond philanthropy and other discretionary functions.

The primary channel Harris uses to communicate its CSR efforts is its website. Harris's webpage has multiple tabs providing information for the diverse visitors to its site. The "Company" tab includes a subsection on Corporate Responsibility with its own page and subpages, which include: Business Conduct, Community, Conflict Minerals Policy, Global Inclusion, Supplier Diversity, and Sustainability. While the Community page focuses on the company's philanthropic efforts, the other sections are important to help answer how Harris addresses ethical constraints to CSR. In addition to (and available on) the website, annual reports provide a brief overview of the company's social responsibility efforts. Occasionally, the company will also issue a press release about its CSR initiatives. However, Harris's news releases on CSR activities are infrequent, with most of them focusing on new business initiatives, contracts, awards, and technology (Harris Corporation, News).

Harris tells its story through portals on its CSR website, creating an interconnected picture of its different CSR efforts. The company shows how it is creating social, economic, and environmental value for stakeholders in several areas in which it emphasizes the corporate commitment to company stakeholders. Those stakeholders include employees, clients/customers, retirees, shareholders, and the communities in which the firm operates. The Community section on the Harris website outlines the company's primary philanthropic activities: "Our funding priorities are STEM, charitable organizations that align with our mission critical customers and some local civic, cultural and health/welfare organizations" (Harris Corporation, Community). As a high-tech organization, Harris's efforts to support education in science, technology, engineering, and math (STEM) fields help generate a qualified workforce and appreciation of its fundamental business for future clients and decision-makers. The company provides scholarships, supports student organizations, sponsors special events, backs employee volunteer outreach programs to schools, and encourages employees to serve on outside advisory boards.

Harris's primary philanthropic fundraising activity is for the United Way. The company engages employees and retirees as partners to support charitable organizations in communities in the United States. Harris matches employee giving. In 2015, the company raised $1.9 million for the United Way (Harris Corporation, Community). The website clearly communicates that the company's strategy is to engage with the communities in which it operates, creating an environment for future growth. Funding for the United Way appears to be the company's broadest reach from its fundamental business/mission statement but aligns with its commitment to improve the communities in which it operates.

Evidence suggests that Harris provides some channels for two-way communication with its stakeholders. In support of its stated value of global inclusion, the company sponsors multiple employee resource groups, including programs for women, military and veterans, different racial and ethnic groups, and graduate students, among others. In terms of philanthropic efforts, the company has a matching donation program that provides employees an opportunity to identify charitable organizations they support. An anonymous help line also allows employees and suppliers a way to ask questions about ethics and compliance.

Based on what Harris is communicating through its website and most recent annual reports, the company places economic and legal/ethical responsibilities above its discretionary activities (i.e., philanthropy). The company communicates about its philanthropic activities within the context of its other responsibilities.

Economic Responsibilities

Harris's rhetoric regarding philanthropy is careful to contextualize corporate giving as a natural outreach from the company's stated mission. Community support is to "foster an environment for future growth." The focus on support for STEM education benefits Harris directly and indirectly through a qualified employee pool and an educated public. And Harris's website clearly states that priority for charitable giving is given to those organizations that "align with our mission critical customers." Those groups include universities, science and technology programs, and veterans' and military organizations (the company has significant military and government contracts).

Legal/Ethical Responsibilities

The Corporate Responsibility section on the website includes several pages devoted to meeting legal obligations; much of this material overlaps with ethical responsibilities. For example, the company has links to detailed standards for business conduct for stakeholders, including employees, board members, non-U.S.

partners, intermediaries, and suppliers. Each group has its own document outlining expected behaviors that comply with legal and ethical standards. More specific to single issues impacting its global activities, the website has a dedicated section on complying with SEC regulations regarding "conflict minerals" (natural resources linked to funding civil wars), and to preventing human trafficking. The conflict mineral policy outlines the legal obligation Harris and its suppliers have to report sources for the minerals they procure and the ethical expectations for employees and partner organizations. The statement on human trafficking asserts the company will "neither benefit from human rights violations . . . nor remain silent when human rights violations exist" (Harris Corporation, Community).

Harris's commitment to a conflict minerals policy, preventing human rights abuses, and its employee resource groups suggests the company is engaged in minimizing the harmful effects of its operations and meeting the needs of its stakeholders. More broadly, the United Way and STEM initiatives also help satisfy stakeholder needs.

Outcomes

Harris's strategic communication about its CSR activities connects its mission to stakeholders' values and expectations. For example, the company's website and annual reports show how it carefully aligns philanthropic giving with its mission and values. Harris discusses its social responsibility initiatives as strategically designed to enhance the company's immediate and future business. With the exception of the community-based United Way funding, all other philanthropic and social responsibility efforts appear tightly controlled to match the organization's goals.

The website and annual reports provide only the company's voice; however, Harris's explanations of funding decisions indicate it is responsive to its stakeholders, both internal and external constituents. For example, the company funds military and veterans' groups, aligning with many of its employees (who are veterans) and with its customers (many of whom are military- or government-based). United Way fundraising supports a variety of charitable groups in communities in which the company operates. The company hires highly educated employees, most of whom have STEM-related degrees, which directly connects to its support of STEM education. It also provides scholarships to Harris employees' children who qualify.

By nesting communication about its philanthropic efforts within the greater CSR story, Harris provides context that both fulfills societal CSR expectations and provides counterarguments to critics concerned about the ethicality of philanthropy-related CSR. This case study indicates that Harris's communication about its CSR efforts addresses ethical constraints; however, the analysis does not necessarily support the company's ability to overcome all ethical concerns.

Harris provides a strategic and thoughtful explanation of its corporate giving decisions. The company gives money to create an environment in which the organization can thrive. A healthy, active community in which the company can grow justifies its United Way efforts. Creating a pool of educated potential employees is a strong rationale for the company's STEM education programs. In this sense, Harris is acting as what Wulfson (2001) considers a steward rather than as a philanthropic entity. A philanthropist is an individual who "believes he has a moral duty towards helping the less fortunate in society through charitable distribution of earnings . . . the steward (trustee) believes his primary mission involves an obligation to earn a profit" (Wulfson, 2001, 135). This can lead to "safe" philanthropic choices.[1]

Harris's consistent message outlines a clear strategic pattern of giving that negates the idea the company is giving to hide corporate wrongdoing or to create an illusion of social responsibility. Nevertheless, its contributions to veterans' and military groups and STEM concerns are highly calculated to reap benefits and generate goodwill among its stakeholders. Thus, the company is credible in its philanthropic efforts but does not completely eliminate concerns that its philanthropic activities are solely motivated to increase profits and cover past or future wrongdoing. Further, Harris's communication about its corporate giving initiatives does little to appease the concern that philanthropic activity is beyond the scope of corporate interests, despite Harris's clear commitment to giving purposefully to support its livelihood. The issue is much more complex when analyzed from the larger cultural context. Economic motives undermine a company's ability to truly benefit social issues.

The case study of Harris Corporation and its CSR communication illustrates how one company places its social responsibility initiatives, including philanthropy, within the larger context of the company's role as a global business. As companies increasingly engage in philanthropic activities, positioning their contributions to society as integral to their business strategy, it is critical that corporate leaders, communicators, scholars, and governmental and nongovernmental agencies—society as a whole—examine the boundaries of corporate involvement in social issues. Are corporations operating with concern for ethical constraints surrounding their actions—and if so, is it making a difference?

In Harris's case, it seems to be making a difference, at least in some CSR areas. For example, for two years in a row, its commitment to a diverse workforce has earned it recognition as one of the "Best Places to Work for LGBTQ Equality" by the Human Rights Campaign (Harris Corporation 2016). It also seems to be engendering goodwill with its compliance policies and self-reporting. Harris avoided

---

1. The "safety" factor is a concern posed by critics of corporate philanthropy. Corporations don't necessarily give to those organizations/people most in need, but to those "aligned with corporate interests" (Ohreen & Petry, 2012, 371). Social issues that are less "sellable" to companies because of fear of stakeholder backlash aren't funded, while popular, noncontroversial issues thrive (breast cancer, for example) (Lieberman, 2001). And when companies withdraw funding/support, it lends credence to the second concern that corporate giving is merely for show.

prosecution and fines after uncovering a bribery scheme by one of its subsidiaries operating in China. After an internal investigation, the company reported the violations to the SEC and U.S. Department of Justice, both of which declined to prosecute. The (former) executive involved in the bribery was fined (DiPietro, 2016).

The recognition for its CSR policies indicates that the company's communication efforts are meeting stakeholder expectations for CSR commitments while also adhering to stated corporate values. Communicating these policies and values is key to maintaining positive relationships with the global company's diverse stakeholders.

References

DiPietro, Ben (2016, September 26). The morning risk report: Harris FCPA case shows cooperation benefits. *Wall Street Journal*. Retrieved from http://blogs.wsj.com/riskandcompliance/2016/09/26/the-morning-risk-report-harris-fcpa-case-shows-cooperation-benefits/.

Harris Corporation. (n.d.). About: Our mission and values. Retrieved from https://www.harris.com/about/our-mission-and-values.

Harris Corporation. (n.d.). Community. Retrieved from https://www.harris.com/corporate-responsibility/community.

Harris Corporation. (n.d.). The Harris story. Retrieved from https://www.harris.com/about/the-harris-story.

Harris Corporation. (n.d.). News. Retrieved from https://www.harris.com/press-releases.

Harris Corporation. (2013). Annual report. Retrieved from https://www.harris.com/sites/default/files/2013-annual-report.pdf.

Harris Corporation. (2016). Harris Corporation named one of best places to work for LGBT equality [Press release]. Retrieved from https://www.harris.com/press-releases/2016/12/harris-corporation-named-one-of-best-places-to-work-for-lgbt-equality.

Lieberman, T. (2001, December 17). Companies too often look for "safe" causes: Many seek to avoid linking product sales to "scary" issues. *Los Angeles Times*, S3.

Ohreen, D., & Petry, R. (2012). Imperfect duties and corporate philanthropy. *Journal of Business Ethics, 106*(3), 367–381.

Valor, C. (2007). A global strategic plan for corporate philanthropy. *Corporate Communications: An International Journal, 12*(3), 280–297.

Wulfson, M. (2001, January). The ethics of corporate social responsibility and philanthropic ventures. *Journal of Business Ethics, 29*, 135–145.

Discussion Questions

1. What are the three main arguments against corporate philanthropy?
2. How should companies overcome ethical concerns about corporate giving (based on Valor's [2007] model)?
3. How does Harris's communication about its CSR activities adhere to ethical principles of corporate philanthropy?

PUBLIC RELATIONS CONTEXTS

6

CONSUMER RELATIONS

Learning Outcomes

- Recognize the significance of consumer relations.
- Describe the ways consumer relations is practiced in public relations.
- Analyze ethical principles in relation to consumers.
- Apply ethical principles relevant to consumer relations case studies.

Definitions

Consumer: A person who, or entity that, purchases an organization's products or services.

Consumer relations: The process of building and maintaining positive relationships with consumers. This process would include responding to consumers' needs and engaging with them to create opportunities.

While PR practitioners are often involved with consumers when a crisis such as the Tylenol scare of 1980 hits, practitioners should ideally be working with consumers to help them to discover the products and services organizations offer and to create positive experiences whenever possible (Essner, 2017). Consumer relations is what it sounds like: an organization's efforts to engage and interact with those people and publics who may purchase and use the organization's products or services. One thing consumers look for is trustworthiness (Turner, 2009). Therefore, organizations should always communicate with consumers in transparent ways. Following this advice will help your organization in both good times and bad.

Understanding the Consumer

If you turn on your TV, listen to the radio, flip through a magazine or newspaper, or even check your email or social media feeds, you will likely be greeted by ads for products and services. Consumers are overloaded with information, which makes it difficult for public relations practitioners to know what people will pay attention to and what they will tune out (Burke, 2010). When practitioners understand their publics through research and engagement, they will better know how to communicate with consumers (Jacques, 2011).

Practitioners need to grab consumers' attention and make them consider their product or service; ultimately this should result in a purchase (Rodriguez, 2016). Therefore, one challenge practitioners face is how to implement creative new approaches to providing information (Burke, 2010). This task has become more difficult because there are so many brands, products, and services from which to choose (Rodriguez, 2016). One thing practitioners can do to improve their messages and make them stand out is to listen to and interact with consumers.

Practitioners and consumers need to work together to develop product communications, because consumer messages will fail if they do not address what is important to consumers (Goldfayn, 2010). An important step many organizations fail to take is to simply ask consumers what they want (Goldfayn, 2010). Most consumers want to know about extra value, significant savings, and getting more for less (Burke, 2010). In addition, understanding what consumers want from your product, how they use your product, what features they use and why, and how they think about your product are also important to know when determining message points (Goldfayn, 2010).

Practitioners who are working to engage ethnic and multicultural consumers should be sure to be authentic and sincere to demonstrate an understanding of another culture (Rodriguez, 2016). Many ethnic and multicultural consumers not only want quality and variety in the products and services they purchase, but they also want those products and services to speak to their lifestyles and heritage (Rodriguez, 2016). Therefore, practitioners should work to develop relationships with all types of consumers. Once relationships have been formed, it is much easier for organizations to build trust and loyalty (Jacques, 2013a). Strategic organizations celebrate customers and listen to their needs (Jacques, 2013b).

Practitioners should also remember it is just as important to talk to consumers as it is to speak to employees (Jacques, 2011). Employees are likely to interact directly and more regularly with consumers than members of the PR team. How employees interact with consumers and how they speak about an organization's products and services is very important. Employees can, and should, be advocates for your brand; indeed, in many cases employees are an organization's best conduits to build loyal customers (Jacques, 2013a). If an organization's employees are not strong advocates, there is a deep and serious problem within the organization (Essner, 2017).

Engaging Consumers

When organizations engage consumers, they need to do so in an authentic way. Not only can organizations use traditional means such as broadcast and print, but they should also interact with consumers via social media. Consumers have changed the ways they receive information, and today they have control over how they consume it (Trufelman, 2005). Not only do consumers decide which media are most useful to their needs, but more and more they have become producers and publishers of their own news via blogs and social media (Trufelman, 2005). I imagine that many of you follow influencers to find out about trends and new products. With the prevalence of social media, we can see how quickly and informally consumers share information, both the good and the bad (Burke, 2010). For example, think about the fallout from the way United Airlines handled an overbooked flight and the outrage over Apple's software slowing down iPhones to conserve batteries and how these incidents were magnified via the use of social media.

One way practitioners can engage consumers is by telling stories about brands and products. People like stories. Stories are comfortable and familiar. Therefore, people are naturally drawn to them. Some consumers (e.g., Hispanic/Latino consumers) tend to desire brands that are more than just a name or product; these consumers want a family, culture, and experience, all of which can be cultivated through storytelling (Rodriguez, 2016). When practitioners are able to develop compelling brand and product stories, emotional bonds and memories can be created with consumers, which then lead to consumer loyalty (Rodriguez, 2016).

Practitioners also need to be part of the conversation to be authentic. Practitioners need to engage consumers by answering questions, providing suggestions, and sharing their organization's culture and history (Jacques, 2013a). While many conversations do take place online, practitioners should not forget that human interaction and face-to-face communication still matter (Burke, 2010).

References

Burke, C. (2010, November). Inconspicuous consumption: 5 things you need to know about reaching consumers. *Public Relations Tactics, 17*(11), 14.

Essner, D. (2017 September). 5 thoughts on brand communications from Jay Baer. *Public Relations Tactics, 24*(9), 1.

Goldfayn, A. (2010, May). Consumer reports: Communicating product messaging. *Public Relations Tactics, 17*(5), 11 and 17.

Jacques, A. (2011, December 1). Inside Belk's communications and community relations efforts. Retrieved from http://apps.prsa.org/Intelligence/Tactics/Articles/view/9497/1040/Inside_Belk_s_communications_and_community_relatio#.Wmj8zyOZNR0.

Jacques, A. (2013a, April 30). Supermarket sweep: Publix's Maria Brous on media and community relations. Retrieved from http://apps.prsa.org/intelligence/Tactics/

Articles/view/10169/1077/Supermarket_sweep_Publix_s_Maria_Brous_on_media_an#.Wmj9wiOZNR0.

Jacques, A. (2013b, Dec. 4). All-star insights: Converse's Terri Hines on global PR and communications. Retrieved from http://apps.prsa.org/Intelligence/Tactics/Articles/view/10442/1086/All_Star_Insights_Converse_s_Terri_Hines_on_Global#.Wmj9RyOZNR0.

Rodriguez, G. (2016, June). The power of communications: Once upon a time, a brand became a story. *Public Relations Tactics, 23*(6), 12.

Trufelman, L. P. (2005, May). Consumer-generated media—challenges and opportunities for public relations. *Public Relations Tactics, 12*(5), 17 and 27.

Turner, B. (2009, May). Communicating your commitment: Why public relations matters in a down economy. *Public Relations Tactics, 16*(5), 11.

VOLKSWAGEN THE BETRAYER: A CASE STUDY OF GROSS DISREGARD FOR THE WELFARE OF STAKEHOLDERS WORLDWIDE

Chiara Valentini, Ph.D., *Jyväskylä University, School of Business and Economics,* and Dean Kruckeberg, Ph.D., APR, Fellow PRSA, *University of North Carolina at Charlotte*

A lie is arguably among the most insidious of evils because it is a violation of trust, argue Tsetsura and Kruckeberg (2017). They define a lie as information that the communicator knows to be false that is presented with the intent to deceive. These authors say that lying may be among the most reprehensible of acts because the liar is attempting to mislead the individual being lied to by attempting to create, but then exploit, trust, which they define as the belief in the truth of a communicator's message. However, Valentini and Kruckeberg (2011, 99) conclude that:

> [T]rust can only exist where it is deserved, i.e., such trust cannot be betrayed. A requisite of trust is the reasonable prediction and anticipation of an action by an actor based on that actor's prior behavior and other communication.

Tsetsura and Kruckeberg (2017) ask: Whom do people trust? Their answer: those whom they perceive to be telling the truth. They emphasize that the conscious intent of the communicator to deceive is central to the definition of a lie, not just the incorrect information itself. They define truth as accurate, complete, and unbiased information that has been gathered and verified conscientiously and competently and that is presented fairly and in good faith by those who are attempting to achieve the ideal of objectivity with complete transparency in gathering, analyzing, and presenting this information.

Certainly, the concepts of a lie, trust, and truth are of critical importance in the consideration of the Volkswagen emissions scandal that began in September 2015, when the U.S. Environmental Protection Agency (EPA) issued a notice to Volkswagen of its violation of the Clean Air Act. The EPA did so after having learned that the car manufacturer had intentionally and surreptitiously prevented the accurate testing of its vehicles for emissions, resulting in false data that indicated that VW vehicles met U.S. clean air standards (Valentini, 2016). This case study examines a preventable scandal that was caused by gross malfeasance. The aftermath continues to have an immense negative impact on Volkswagen stakeholders and on VW's reputation, which perhaps has been irreparably damaged.

Background

In 2015, Forbes ranked VW as the second-largest automaker in the world (Schmitt, 2016, para. 1). This German vehicle manufacturer, established in 1946 in Wolfsburg, Lower Saxony, owns twelve brands from seven European countries (Volkswagen, 2016, para. 2). Volkswagen had enjoyed a strong reputation with high brand loyalty worldwide, and its cars had been praised for their performance and sustainable technology. In 2009, the VW Jetta TDI won the annual "Green Car of the Year" award for its "groundbreaking clean diesel" engine (Smith & Parloff, 2015, para. 1). VW also has been investing substantially in electric mobility, and the company's stated goal is to develop vehicles that offer the best possible fuel economy and resource efficiency. By the year 2018, VW is attempting to cut its specific energy and water consumption, CO_2 emissions, solvent emissions (VOC), and volume of waste per vehicle being manufactured by 25%, compared to 2010 (Volkswagen, 2014b, para. 1).

The Reputation Institute's survey on consumers' opinions from fifteen countries in 2015 found that VW was the most liked and trusted corporate brand and that the company was considered among the world's most socially responsible companies (Fombrun, 2015, para. 4). Volkswagen was known as a brand that stood for quality, honesty, and a commitment to its customers. Furthermore, the company supports worldwide corporate social responsibility (CSR) initiatives to foster social development, culture, and education and to serve the needs of regional structural development, health promotion, sports, and nature (Volkswagen, 2014a, para. 6).

Adolf Hitler had envisioned the Volkswagen automobile as a means to increase the mobility of Germans, as Henry Ford had done for Americans. Volkswagen was nationalized after World War II, and, despite its later privatization, formal and informal linkages remain to the German government, as well as to the country's politicians and labor unions. Lower Saxony owns 20% of the company's voting rights and has been granted veto power over VW's strategic decisions (Cremer, Taylor, & Prodhan, 2016). As governors of Lower Saxony, former chancellor Gerhard Schröder and Germany's current vice chancellor both had served as VW directors. By law, labor has 20 board seats. Institutional investors hold non-voting preferred shares, and the descendants of the creator of the VW Beetle own 52% of common shares (Rauwald & Kresge, 2016, para. 8, 9). Such linkages can represent immense power, and critics have argued that German regulations have been minimized because job loss can ensue in the automotive manufacturing sector—Germany's largest industry—if government legislation is viewed as unfavorable (Smith & Parloff, 2016, para. 17).

Smith and Parloff (2016, para. 1, 5) further note the company's ruthless management tradition. In earlier scandals the company had largely escaped legal consequences. In 2004 it was discovered that VW's transgressions had included providing prostitutes to high-ranking labor representatives and luxury shopping trips for these representatives' wives, among other perquisites:

> The center-left Social Democratic Party came off particularly badly in the scandal, with senior officials exposed as feasting at the trough. Peter Hartz, VW's chief of personnel and the architect of Chancellor Schröder's radical labor reforms, pleaded guilty to criminal charges. It emerged that some sitting SPD lawmakers were drawing salaries of over $5,000 a month from Volkswagen, allegedly for nothing in return. (Smith & Parloff, 2016, para. 6)

Thus, despite Volkswagen's high brand loyalty, together with its excellent reputation as a trusted brand and as a socially responsible company, the company did not have a totally clean record as a corporate citizen in September 2015, when VW had to address the emissions scandal. Nevertheless, this recent scandal is considered one of the major faux pas in this corporation's history, causing not only immense financial costs but also immeasurable reputational loss.

The Situation

Valentini (2016) identified five stakeholders in this case: investors and shareholders; the EPA; German authorities; European institutions; and customers worldwide. This case study focuses on the ethical dimension concerning Volkswagen's customers, who undoubtedly felt betrayed in their purchasing decisions (although one could argue that global society at large was the most victimized by the environmental impact of Volkswagen's malfeasance).

Shortly after the emissions violations came to public attention, VW suspended sales of cars having the company's culpable engine and recalled 8.5 million cars in Europe and 500,000 in the United States (Valentini, 2016). The company had to cover the costs of modifying these vehicles as well as expenses related to owner compensation and stockholders' earnings losses that were due to reputational damage (Hotten, 2015, para. 11, 13). Volkswagen first blamed rogue employees, although in February 2016 a memo surfaced that had referred to the emissions defeat device, together with a warning to the CEO about the impending investigation by U.S. environmental authorities (Boston, 2016a, para. 1, 2; McGee & Wright, 2016, para. 2). Of course, such deception constituted an immense ethical breach against the five stakeholder groups identified by Valentini (2016). Volkswagen continues to pay a heavy price: The company is facing regulatory and criminal investigations and in 2016 reported a 2015 net loss of $1.69 billion (the worst earnings record since the company had been established 79 years ago), because the company had to set aside $17.1 billion to cover the costs of the diesel emissions scandal (McGee & Campbell, 2016, para. 1, 2, 5). Litigation against Volkswagen continues worldwide.

After first denying and then attempting to minimize the severity of the problem, Volkswagen then acknowledged responsibility. "We've totally screwed up," said VW America boss Michael Horn (Hotten, 2015, para. 8). VW CEO Martin Winterkorn said in a statement:

> I am personally deeply sorry that we have broken the trust of our customers and the public. We will cooperate fully with the responsible agencies, with transparency and urgency, to clearly, openly and completely establish all of the facts of this case. (Volkswagen, 2015, para. 2)

Winterkorn resigned as a direct result of the scandal and was replaced by Matthias Mueller, the former boss of Porsche, whose main task is regaining the trust of customers (Hotten, 2015, para. 8).

Volkswagen launched a new advertising campaign in spring 2016 that focused on people more than on technology, and Volkswagen's brand, Audi, dropped its longtime tagline, "Truth in Engineering," in its 2016 Super Bowl commercial (Allen, 2016, para. 11). However, the rage of consumers, as reflected by massive litigation, is exemplified by this description of American consumers' anger:

> An extraordinary number of educated middle-class or affluent plaintiffs feel deliberately snookered on a subject they are passionate about. Unlike in Europe, where more than half the cars are diesels, they are rarities in the U.S.—about 0.5%—and they cost more than gasoline-powered models. Accordingly, Americans chose them specifically for a trait that turned out to be a lie. (Smith & Parloff, 2016, para. 9)

Time will tell whether VW can overcome this massive betrayal of trust, which was caused not by corporate negligence but by the intentional malfeasance of an immense lie. Will Volkswagen be able to regain its customers' trust and its reputation for quality, honesty, CSR, and sustainability? Can VW redeem its reputation, and, if so, how can public relations help? Most importantly, the ethical issues of this betrayal must be addressed and fully examined.

Outcomes

The VW scandal exemplifies unethical corporate conduct that has resulted in a damaged reputation that was caused by a gross disregard for the welfare of customers worldwide, a lie that represents a betrayal of trust. During the whole process, Volkswagen was highly unethical. First, the company denied the accusation, claiming that discrepancies on test results were mere technical glitches. When confronted with evidence, the company claimed it was an isolated, concealed action taken by few managers, but later evidence suggested that management was likely informed about the emission problem and about U.S. investigations for more than a year before the scandal erupted (McGee & Wright, 2016, para. 3).

The motives for corporate behaviors such as this suggest greed that represents selfish business self-interest. It could be argued that VW had altered the engines of several car models so that they would be allowed to enter the U.S. market to compete with domestic car brands. According to Smith and Parloff (2016, para. 17), Volkswagen "aspired to be the biggest seller of cars in the world" and "sales of U.S. diesels were crucial" to this goal. An engine that could satisfy the stringent emission regulations in the United States without sacrificing performance or fuel economy, while remaining competitive in price, was not possible without sacrificing fuel economy or drivability; thus, software alteration seemed the only means to enter the U.S. market (Smith & Parloff, 2016). Of course, concealing the impact of its cars' emissions and using software to alter test results are unethical means to achieve this goal. They caused harm to the company's stakeholders by lying and, thereby, destroying trust.

VW's ethical malfeasance has resulted in immense financial cost and obviously is a public relations crisis with long-term ramifications. The scandal has been felt around the globe, with legal cases continually appearing. In summer 2016, many governments and consumers, including those of Australia, Brazil, Canada, Germany, Ireland, Italy, the Netherlands, and Spain, began pursuing legal and regulatory demands to Volkswagen. In Europe, calls for compensation are growing, despite the fact that VW has rejected these claims. Different European consumer groups are accusing VW of not providing enough evidence and information to car owners. The European Investment Bank (EIB), which has given loans to VW for the development of low-emissions engines, stopped the loans until its own investigation into the emissions scandal is concluded (European Investment Bank puts loans to VW on hold, 2016, para. 1). In South Korea, 80 VW models were banned and 4,000 customers filed suit (Boston, 2016b, para. 7). South Korean authorities have imposed a $14.68 million fine on the company after its investigation into the emissions scandal (Saarinen, 2016).

In the United States, VW has reached a $15 billion deal with U.S. owners to buy back affected vehicles and to compensate owners (Saarinen, 2016). VW also had to handle legal prosecutions by three federal agencies, the EPA, the Federal Trade Commission, and the Department of Justice. A partial settlement was reached on June 28, 2016 (Atiyed, 2016). Almost a year after the scandal had erupted and after several denials, one of VW's engineers, James Liang, pleaded guilty in a federal court in Detroit to knowing that Volkswagen had not disclosed the "defeat devices" to regulators to help the company obtain approval to sell the cars in the United States (Viswanatha & Rogers, 2016, para. 6). Liang was the first person to be convicted in this VW scandal, but most likely will not be the last one.

By no means was VW producing and selling the incriminated cars legally, although, in many countries, car emission standards are less strict than are U.S. ones. The company arguably did not directly harm the customers, as, for example, did Toyota Motor Corporation, whose vehicles experienced unintended acceleration that caused car accidents. Yet these VW vehicles had a negative impact on air quality and, thus, people's health by causing increasing respiratory problems. More problematic is the fact that the company used devices to alter emission test screenings, and VW managers knew about the defective engines and thus deliberatively lied, exploiting people's faith in their brand while trying to limit their responsibility and the compensation claims for their customers. If we look at the consequences of such actions, the Volkswagen scandal produced more costs (reputational and financial) than benefits. VW's corporate behaviors have negatively affected its stakeholder relations, not only consumer and customer relations but also political relations, because German authorities, European institutions, and the EPA have lost trust in this car manufacturer's claims of producing sustainable and clean vehicles.

References

Allen, L. S. (2016, February 5). Volkswagen launches new ad campaign without "Das Auto" slogan. *Automotive News*. Retrieved from http://www.autonews.com/apps/pbcs.dll/article?AID=/20160205/COPY01/302059943/Volkswagen-launches-new-ad-campaign-without-das-auto-slogan.

Atiyed, C. (2016, October 7). Everything you need to know about the VW diesel-emissions scandal. *Car and Driver*. Retrieved from http://blog.caranddriver.com/everything-you-need-to-know-about-the-vw-diesel-emissions-scandal/.

Boston, W. (2016a, February 15). Volkswagen memo warned of emission issues in 2014. *Wall Street Journal*. Retrieved from http://on.wsj.com/1OcFDVy.

Boston, W. (2016b, August 23). VW facing uphill battle outside the U.S. in emissions claims. *Wall Street Journal*. Retrieved from http://on.wsj.com/2cyU5ie.

Cremer, A., Taylor, E., & Prodhan, G. (2016, June 20). Investors seeking VW reform may be disappointed at AGM. *Reuters.com*. Retrieved from http://www.reuters.com/article/us-volkswagen-shareholders-idUSKCN0Z60V6.

European Investment Bank puts loans to VW on hold. (2016, January 14). *Reuters*. Retrieved from http://reut.rs/1Q7FzfY.

Fombrun, C. (2015, October 7). About Volkswagen, reputation, and social responsibility. *Reputation Institute*. Retrieved from https://blog.reputationinstitute.com/2015/10/07/about-volkswagen-reputation-and-social-responsibility.

Hotten, R. (2015, December 10). Volkswagen: The scandal explained. *BBC News*. Retrieved from http://www.bbc.com/news/business-34324772.

McGee, P., & Campbell, P. (2016, April 22). Volkswagen falls to biggest annual loss in its history. *Financial Times*. Retrieved from https://www.ft.com/content/c8c5f6f4-08a4-11e6-b6d3-746f8e9cdd33.

McGee, P., & Wright, R. (2016, March 4). Volkswagen management back in scandal spotlight. *Financial Times*. Retrieved from http://on.ft.com/218Zv3k.

Rauwald, C., & Kresge, N. (2016, June 22). VW chairman under fire from investors for dual role in crisis. *Bloomberg*. Retrieved from http://www.bloomberg.com/news/articles/2016-06-22/volkswagen-investors-gear-up-for-showdown-over-emissions-damages.

Saarinen, M. (2016, October 13).VW emissions scandal: Latest on Dieselgate recalls, compensation and testing. *Auto Express*. Retrieved from http://www.autoexpress.co.uk/volkswagen/92893/vw-emissions-scandal-recalls-compensation-is-your-car-affected-latest-news.

Schmitt, B. (2016, January 27). Nice try VW: Toyota again world's largest automaker. *Forbes*. Retrieved from http://www.forbes.com/sites/bertelschmitt/2016/01/27/nice-try-vw-toyota-again-worlds-largest-automaker/#4880cea02b65.

Smith, G., & Parloff, R. (2016, March 7). Hoaxwagen: How the massive diesel fraud incinerated VW's reputation—and will hobble the company for years. *Fortune Magazine*. Retrieved from http://fortune.com/inside-volkswagen-emissions-scandal.

Tsetsura, K., & Kruckeberg, D. (2017). *Transparency, Public Relations and the Mass Media*. New York: Routledge.

Valentini, C. (2016). Case study—Crisis communication—Volkswagen emission scandal. In Theaker, A. (Ed.), *The Public Relations Handbook—Online Compendium*. Oxon, UK: Routledge. Retrieved from http://www.routledgetextbooks.com/textbooks/9781138890961/casestudies.php,

Valentini, C., & Kruckeberg, D. (2011). Public relations and trust in contemporary global society: A Luhmannian perspective of the role of public relations enhancing trust among social systems. *Central European Journal of Communication, 4*(1), 91–107.

Viswanatha, A., & Rogers, C. (2016, September 9).VW engineer pleads guilty in emissions-cheating scandal. *Wall Street Journal*. Retrieved from http://on.wsj.com/2cMfho2.

Volkswagen. (2014a). CSR projects. Retrieved from http://www.volkswagenag.com/content/vwcorp/content/en/sustainability_and_responsibility/CSR_worldwide.html.

Volkswagen. (2014b). Sustainability report. Retrieved from http://sustainabilityreport 2014.volkswagenag.com/environment/production.

Volkswagen. (2015, September 20). Statement of Prof. Dr. Martin Winterkorn, CEO of Volkswagen AG. Retrieved from http://www.volkswagenag.com/content/ vwcorp/info_center/en/news/2015/09/statement_ceo_of_volkswagen_ag.html.

Volkswagen. (2016, October 24). The group. Retrieved from http://www.volkswagenag .com/content/vwcorp/content/en/the_group.html.

Discussion Questions

1. Do you agree with Tsetsura and Kruckeberg (2017) that a lie is arguably among the most insidious of evils because it is a violation of trust? Provide an example of a lie that had been told to you that destroyed your trust in an organization and explain why.

2. Why do you think Volkswagen was the most liked and trusted corporate brand and was considered among the world's most socially responsible companies?

3. Do you believe that the formal and informal linkages to the German government and to the country's politicians and labor unions were necessarily unethical and contributed to Volkswagen's decision to intentionally alter testing of its vehicles to meet U.S. clean air standards?

4. After the scandal occurred, what advice would you have given Volkswagen in dealing with this crisis, in particular with consumers?

5. What recommendations would you make to Volkswagen to prevent similar issues in the future?

BLACKFISH BACKLASH: SEAWORLD'S ATTEMPT AT NAVIGATING A CRISIS SITUATION

Leslie Rodriguez Rasmussen, Ph.D., *Xavier University*, and
Melody Fisher, Ph.D., *Mississippi Sate University*

For more than 50 years, SeaWorld, a marine mammal amusement park, has been the destination for those seeking family-friendly entertainment. Adventure seekers from all corners of the world come to interact with marine animals, enjoy thrill rides, and view the famous dolphin and killer whale shows. At the height of its popularity, SeaWorld welcomed more than 11 million visitors annually and held a respectable place in the stock market. With all its successes, though, it was inevitable that issues would plague the parks: SeaWorld's work with animals has always made it a target for animal rights activists. In 2011, the People for the Ethical Treatment of Animals (PETA) filed a lawsuit on behalf of five wild-captured orcas, arguing that the parks were violating the mammals' civil rights. The case was dismissed (Zellman, 2012), but the most damaging attack came in 2013 with the release of the documentary *Blackfish*.

Blackfish focuses on Tilikum, a male orca responsible for the deaths of two trainers and a SeaWorld trespasser. Through Tilikum's tale the documentary offered audiences a persuasive view of SeaWorld's capture and mistreatment of marine animals. Interviews with former employees, video footage of animals, and commentary paint SeaWorld as cruel and inhumane. The *Blackfish* backlash occurred soon after its premiere at the 2013 Sundance festival. The documentary was selected to appear in theaters and on CNN, giving more audiences access to its claims. As a result, Willie Nelson, Trisha Yearwood, and many other entertainers cancelled shows at the SeaWorld parks, attendance declined by more than 5%, and total revenue dipped by more than $15 million by 2013 (Ahmed, 2013). The theme park suffered blow after blow and was eventually forced to hire a communications firm to help restore its image and financial standing. This case study examines SeaWorld's response to a threat capable of inflicting long-term damage.

Background

SeaWorld San Diego opened in 1964 with two aquariums and several dolphins and sea lions. The organization eventually acquired several killer whales from the defunct Seattle Marine Aquarium, including Namu, the first killer whale held in captivity. In 1989 Anheuser-Busch purchased the three SeaWorld parks and three other sister parks, but sold them to the Blackstone Group in 2009. In 1992 SeaWorld acquired four whales from Sealand of the Pacific, which shut down after orca whales were involved in a trainer's death. Tilikum, the orca believed to have drowned that trainer, was sent to SeaWorld Orlando and is now its most successful sire (Frontline n.d.). Tilikum is also the orca responsible for the 2010 death of senior trainer Dawn Brancheau at SeaWorld Orlando and is the centerpiece of the *Blackfish* documentary (CNN, 2010). With additional parks in San Antonio and Orlando, SeaWorld now owns approximately 86,000 animals, including the largest killer whale population at any zoological facility. The organization also houses several endangered species and is actively engaged in animal rehabilitation and conservation.

Over the years SeaWorld has been targeted by multiple animal rights groups, perhaps most notably PETA. The organization faced government regulation and litigation over the death of Brancheau. After Brancheau's death, the federal Occupational Safety and Health Administration (OSHA) prohibited trainers from entering tanks with orca whales. After a lengthy appeals process, the U.S. Court of Appeals maintained the ruling (Hurley, 2014). SeaWorld declined to take the case to the U.S. Supreme Court.

In the years following the *Blackfish* release, SeaWorld's public image was tarnished. Celebrities broke partnerships with the organization and spoke out against its treatment of animals. In 2013 and 2014, parade-goers at the Macy's Thanksgiving

Parade jumped a barricade to protest the SeaWorld float. A race-car driver took a *Blackfish*-themed car to the Talladega Speedway in 2014.

As mistrust mounted, financial loss soon followed. Two years after the documentary's release, *Time* Magazine reported that SeaWorld "faced an 84% drop in net second-quarter income, from $37.4 million in 2014 to $5.8 million in 2015, in the second quarter" (Rhodan, 2015, para. 2). Despite the financial crisis, SeaWorld attempted to regain consumer trust by announcing plans for the $100 million Blue World Project, a large-scale expansion of the orca habitat at the San Diego park. Plans included a $10 million commitment to orca whale research. Unfortunately, SeaWorld made this announcement before obtaining the required permits. The California Coastal Commission later granted the permits with several caveats: (1) SeaWorld could no longer transport orcas to and from California, (2) a maximum of 15 orcas could be held captive in California, and (3) SeaWorld could not breed whales. SeaWorld responded by suing the California Coastal Commission over the no-breeding condition. However, after years of public scrutiny and political pressure, SeaWorld declined to pursue the lawsuit or the Blue World Project. Instead, the organization attempted to capitalize on the imposed decision. Three years following the *Blackfish* release, to regain consumer trust, SeaWorld launched a new campaign, proclaiming that "SeaWorld has been listening and we're changing. Society is changing and we're changing with it. SeaWorld is finding new ways to continue to deliver on our purpose to inspire all our guests to take action to protect wild animals and wild places" (SeaWorld, 2016). SeaWorld stopped the fight and engaged in corrective action by shifting its focus and turning the problem into an opportunity to rebrand, reshape, and rebuild consumer relations.

Situation

On January 19, 2013, the documentary *Blackfish*, detailing the life of orca whale Tilikum, premiered at the Sundance Film Festival. The film claimed "to explore the creature's extraordinary nature, the species' cruel treatment in captivity, the lives and losses of the trainers and the pressures brought to bear by the multi-billion-dollar sea-park industry" (blackfish.com, 2016). Almost immediately, the film received national attention and was picked up by CNN and Magnolia Pictures for release on the cable channel and in theaters. After *Blackfish*'s Sundance showing, SeaWorld released a general statement refuting the film's arguments and positioning itself as a leader in animal care (Storey, 2013).

As publicity and controversy mounted, SeaWorld faced multiple challenges. Its image was undoubtedly shaken, national media attention spurred activism against the organization, and it faced litigation. The potential for financial ruin loomed. Opponents called for the release of its orca whales, and the loss of the whales would mean the end of SeaWorld's centerpiece attraction. SeaWorld eventually hired communications firm 42West to inoculate audiences before the film's theatrical opening. Vice president of communications Fred Jacobs emailed a detailed critique of the film to about 50 critics (Batt 2013). In this email, SeaWorld specifically refuted eight *Blackfish* assertions, calling them "egregious and untrue" (2013). The bulleted list primarily addressed circumstances surrounding the death of Brancheau and the treatment of Tilikum, but called the entire film "shamefully dishonest and deliberately misleading" (2013). SeaWorld also released a statement to ABC News, which was published and aired throughout networks, websites, and newspapers.

Just before the documentary aired on CNN, Jacobs cited published research on whale anatomy and conservation in a written response to the network's inquiries. Jacobs attached empirical findings from biologists, as well as bibliographies of multiple studies conducted at the park to maintain credibility. On its website, SeaWorld posted "69 reasons you shouldn't believe *Blackfish*." The document dissected the film's script and created its own shot list with rebuttals (SeaWorld, 2013).

SeaWorld consistently communicated with consumers digitally. The company took advantage of its varied presence on social media, including Facebook, Twitter, and YouTube. In addition to its usual messages of publicizing events and offering general park information, SeaWorld used social media to respond to consumer comments and questions regarding *Blackfish*. Bots were used on Facebook and Twitter to automatically answer posts that mentioned *Blackfish* and its claims. Bot responses deflected comments with material on conservation efforts. SeaWorld's Twitter campaign, #askseaworld, attempted to establish two-way symmetrical communication with consumers. The SeaWorld YouTube page showcased a series of 27 short videos with clips from *Blackfish* followed by interviews with SeaWorld experts who discredited the film.

The fallout from *Blackfish* continues to hurt SeaWorld through the present day. According to SeaWorld senior corporate affairs officer Jill Kermes, the company launched a $10 million multifaceted campaign "to start that conversation

Allie E @AllieErim · 6 Mar 2015
After watching blackfish I am severely disgusted with Sea World

♡ 2   ↻   ♡ 5   ✉

SeaWorld ✓
@SeaWorld

Follow

Replying to @AllieErim

@AllieErim Hey Allie, if you're done watching Blackfish, here are some other videos that may interest you: bit.ly/Q6IEk7

9:23 AM - 9 Mar 2015

3 Likes

♡ 1   ↻   ♡ 3   ✉

PHOTO 6.1

with consumers and give them a place to go to get the facts about SeaWorld, about our animals, about our world-class animal care, and let them make up their own minds" (Kermes, as cited in Titlow, 2015). The mixed media campaign included print advertorials, national television advertising, and a separate website devoted to promoting conservation and education efforts. Seaworldcares.com features its rescue, care, research, conservation, and education programs and testimonials. The site bolsters the park's image as being concerned for the welfare and longevity of its animals while denying any mistreatment toward animals.

The sting of *Blackfish* and protests by animal rights activists persisted and caused more damage to the SeaWorld brand. In arguably its most controversial move, Sea-World sent employees disguised as activists to join PETA to infiltrate the organization. Employee Paul McComb attended meetings and created fake social media pages under the name Thomas Jones. His Facebook account showed pictures of "Jones" attending rallies and inciting activists with action-driven posts calling for the "torching" and "draining" of SeaWorld whale tanks (theguardian.com, 2015). McComb was exposed after an address he listed was found to be that of a SeaWorld security officer. In a news release, PETA officials noted that McComb tried to "cozy up to PETA employees . . . in an attempt to incite illegal acts" (PETA, 2015). SeaWorld vice president for communications Fred Jones did not confirm or deny McCombs' involvement with PETA but evaded responsibility by saying that "PETA itself actively recruits animal rights activists to gain employment at companies like SeaWorld" (theguardian.com, 2016).

After more negative attention, SeaWorld relented to pressure and announced it would discontinue breeding orcas. In a letter published in the *New York Times*, SeaWorld CEO Joel Manby shared the plan to phase out breeding and orca entertainment shows. Manby notes that the plan was made to accommodate activists, legislators, and consumers, but takes an advocating stance with the decision not to release currently held orcas (Manby, 2016).

In this letter, Manby underscores the company's goal of being consumer-driven. He reflects on SeaWorld's early years and the positive audience responses to orca whale shows. He notes how times and activism have changed and stresses the importance of listening to the consumer when there is a shift in attitudes and behaviors. Manby illustrates the need for effective consumer relations. In essence, SeaWorld took a serious problem and transformed it into an opportunity. SeaWorld's image and financial standing suffered in the three years following *Blackfish*'s premiere (Weisberg, 2016), and its response did not please consumers or critics. The new plan may be well received as SeaWorld revisits its goal of maintaining positive relationships with consumers.

Outcomes

The post-*Blackfish* environment was multifaceted and contained multiple challenges—challenges that, if not overcome, would signal the end for SeaWorld. Initially, SeaWorld publicly and aggressively refuted *Blackfish*. The organization executed multiple tactics claiming the documentary lied about the treatment of whales and Brancheau's death. But the aggressive approach appeared to draw more attention to *Blackfish* and was polarizing; thus, SeaWorld struggled to regain credibility with consumers. A strongly advocating position can carry the potential to alarm publics.

SeaWorld attempted to regain credibility and trust by posting YouTube videos containing clips from *Blackfish* and corresponding rebuttals. Using SeaWorld experts to rebut the points made in the film, rather than an impartial source, may have left audiences in doubt of its authenticity.

Consumers voiced their disapproval of SeaWorld on a variety of social media, prompting the organization to respond using a bot. The replies directed consumers to SeaWorld's *Blackfish* response. Unfortunately, the replies did not appear organic and were nearly identified as trolling. On Twitter, SeaWorld attempted to establish two-way symmetrical communication with consumers by using the hashtag #askseaworld. The effort resulted in more negative responses than positive ones and indirectly served as a means to publicize *Blackfish*. SeaWorld invited consumers to discuss their concerns, thereby remaining transparent, but the strategy appeared to backfire. The organization struggled to regain middle ground, likely because consumers were reeling from the years-long aggressive approach.

Two years after the *Blackfish* release, SeaWorld ramped up its efforts to engage with consumers and reestablish itself as a global leader in conservation. The attempt to regain control and reframe the conversation was, by all accounts, too late: Park attendance and stock prices continued to fall (Weisberg, 2016). SeaWorld aggressively maintained a strongly advocating position during the critical time following the *Blackfish* release, rather than launching the campaign prior to or immediately following its release.

SeaWorld also attempted to discredit its most high-profile opponent, PETA, by allegedly sending in an undercover employee to incite PETA activists to perform illegal acts against SeaWorld, thus providing evidence to discredit the organization. Rather than denying the act, SeaWorld's vice president for communications, Fred Jones, claimed PETA regularly participates in similar behaviors. The vague statement is telling, leaving consumers to make their own assumptions.

Proposing the Blue World Project was a step toward image repair, though as a preemptive strike it would fail. As it stands, SeaWorld has declined to move forward with the project, opting instead to end its breeding program. Ending the breeding program was framed as SeaWorld's decision, as though SeaWorld was listening to its consumers—though it was at the mercy of the California Coastal Commission. The Coastal Commission, however, only has jurisdiction in California, not in states where other SeaWorld parks are located. SeaWorld's decision to end breeding is complex. For example, it is possible that Florida and Texas may have followed California's lead by placing restrictions on breeding, transportation, and population limitations. In the end, the decision to end breeding at all parks was the polar opposite of SeaWorld's initial response and ultimately represented a more accommodating stance. SeaWorld's effort to reposition itself as a leader in animal care and conservation will unfold in the coming years.

References

Ahmed, S. (2013, December 9). Heart cancels SeaWorld show amid "Blackfish" controversy. *CNN*. Retrieved from http://www.cnn.com/2013/12/08/showbiz/seaworld-heart-blackfish/.

Batt, E. (2013, July 13). Op-Ed: SeaWorld's strange e-mail to film antics of Blackfish. *Digital Journal*. Retrieved from http://www.digitaljournal.com/article/354375.

CNN. (2010). SeaWorld trainer killed by killer whale. Retrieved from http://www.cnn.com/2010/US/02/24/killer.whale.trainer.death/

Frontline. (n.d.). A whale of a business: The Tilikum transaction. Retrieved from http://www.pbs.org/wgbh/pages/frontline/shows/whales/seaworld/tilikum/.

Hurley, L. (2014, April 11). Court upholds ruling against SeaWorld over trainer safety. Retrieved from http://www.reuters.com/article/us-usa-courts-employment-idUSBREA3A19Q20140411.

Manby, J. (2016, March 17). Op-Ed: SeaWorld CEO: We're ending our orca breeding program. Here's why. Retrieved from http://www.latimes.com/opinion/op-ed/la-oe-0317-manby-sea-world-orca-breeding-20160317-story.html.

PETA. (2015). *SeaWorld caught spying: Employee tries to befriend activists; incite illegal acts* [Press Release]. Retrieved from http://www.peta.org/media/news-releases/seaworld-caught-spying-employee-tries-to-befriend-activists-incite-illegal-acts/.

Rhodan, M. (2015). SeaWorld's profits drop 84% after *Blackfish* documentary. *Time* Magazine. Retrieved from http://time.com/3987998/seaworlds-profits-drop-84-after-blackfish- documentary/.

SeaWorld. (2013). 69 reasons you shouldn't believe *Blackfish*. Retrieved from http://da15bdaf7154613080030c725c907c2d637068751776aeee5fbf.r7.cf1.rackcdn.com/adf36e5c35b842f5ae4e2322841e8933_4-4-14-updated-final-of-blacklist-list-of-inaccuracies-and-misleading-points.pdf.

SeaWorld. (2014, January 20). Killer whale trainer Holly Byrd discusses *Blackfish*. The truth is in our parks and people. Retrieved from https://www.youtube.com/watch?v=Oyh0PVCNFBA&index=26&list=PLPAAykANPISD6JyocYWj-cjnX0KPnzZY9.

SeaWorld. (2016, March 17). Breaking news: The last generation of orcas at SeaWorld. Retrieved from https://seaworldcares.com/2016/03/Breaking-News-The-Last-Generation-of-Orcas-at-SeaWorld/.

Storey, K. (2013, June 4). New documentary claimed to make you never want to visit SeaWorld again, coming soon to theatres and CNN. *The Daily City*. Retrieved from http://www.thedailycity.com/2013/06/new-documentary-claimed-to-make-you.html.

Theguardian.com. (2015, July 14). SeaWorld accused of sending employee to infiltrate animal rights protests. Retrieved from https://www.theguardian.com/environment/2015/jul/14/seaworld-employee-animal-rights-protests-peta.

Theguardian.com. (2016, February 15). SeaWorld CEO admits employees were asked to pose as animal rights activists. Retrieved from https://www.theguardian.com/

usnews/2016/feb/25/seaworld-ceo-admits-employees-infiltrated-peta-animal-rights-activists.

Titlow, J. P. (2015, August 4). SeaWorld is spending $10 million to make your forget about *Blackfish*. *Fastcompany.com*. Retrieved from http://www.fastcompany.com/3046342/seaworld-is-spending-10-million-to-make-you-forget-about-blackfish.

Weisberg, L. (2016, August 4). SeaWorld suffers sharp attendance drop. *San Diego Union-Tribune*. Retrieved from http://www.sandiegouniontribune.com/business/tourism/sdut-seaworld-reports-second-quarter-attendance-drop-2016aug04-story.html.

Zellman, J. (2012, February 9). PETA's SeaWorld slavery case dismissed by judge. *Huffington Post*. Retrieved from http://www.huffingtonpost.com/2012/02/09/peta-seaworld-slavery-_n_1265014.html

Discussion Questions

1. Discuss the use of bots as two-way communication. Are they effective? Why or why not?
2. Do you believe SeaWorld brought more attention to the film with its response?
3. SeaWorld did not break any laws by sending an employee to PETA to pose as an animal rights activist. If no laws were broken, was this behavior ethical?
4. What are the ethical boundaries of advocating for your organization?
5. Ending the breeding program was framed as SeaWorld's decision, as though the company was listening to its consumers. Do you believe this approach was acceptable and ethical? Why or why not?

FOOD FIGHT: HOW ETHICAL MANAGEMENT SAVED MARKET BASKET

Brenda J. Wrigley, Ph.D., APR, *Curry College*

In 2008, Arthur T. Demoulas became CEO of Market Basket Supermarkets. A successful manager who was beloved by employees, he was viewed with jealousy by his cousin, Arthur S. Demoulas. In summer 2014, Arthur S. and the board fired Arthur T. and two other key executives. The fuse was lit and the battle was on.

Background

The Market Basket Supermarkets is the trade name of Demoulas Supermarkets Inc., a private corporation owned by the Demoulas family (Hoover's, 2015). With 71 Market Basket stores in Massachusetts, New Hampshire, and Maine and more than 25,000 employees, annual revenue was estimated at $4.6 billion (Newsham & Ross, 2014).

The chain was founded in 1954 by two brothers, Mike and George Demoulas, the sons of Greek immigrants (History of Market Basket, 2012). Their father, Arthur Demoulas, started the business in 1917, and it was later purchased by his two sons (Horowitz, 2014). The brothers ran the business until George died in 1971. Mike Demoulas started to manage the business by himself following his brother's death and opened multiple stores owned wholly by himself, sidelining his brother's widow and offspring (History of Market Basket, 2012; Horowitz, 2014).

Bad blood existed for years between branches of the family, and the eventual showdown between the two cousins involved in the dispute made national headlines. But why? What made this business blowup so unusual?

The Situation

Evan Horowitz of the Boston Globe said the family feud started in 1990. The heirs of founder George Demoulas filed a series of lawsuits against their uncle, claiming he defrauded them of their share of the business because they owned a mere 8% of the chain, with the rest owned by Mike's family. In 1999, the Massachusetts Supreme Court upheld a ruling in favor of George's branch, asserting their claim to about $800 million in closely held company stock and $200 million in cash (Tosh, 1999). The court also ordered Mike Demoulas to be removed from management, and George's heirs were given 51% of the company, a controlling share (Tosh, 1999). A rivalry unfolded between two cousins: Arthur S. Demoulas, George's only remaining son at the time, and Arthur T. Demoulas, Mike's only son. Mike Demoulas died in 2003, and leadership of this family branch transferred to Arthur T. Demoulas (Ross, 2013).

The Tenure of Arthur T.

In 2008, Arthur T. Demoulas became CEO (Borchers, 2014). The *Boston Globe* noted that Arthur S. was more investment-oriented, while his cousin had more experience in retail management, having worked with his father in Demoulas Supermarkets for more than 20 years (Borchers, 2014). The person who ripped the balance in favor of Arthur T. was his sister-in-law Raphaela Evans, the widow of

George's oldest son (Bailey, 2000). Despite the 2008 financial meltdown, Arthur T. made up for the losses of $46 million in the employee profit-sharing fund (Borchers, 2014). He also opened 12 stores and renovated 11 stores in Massachusetts and New Hampshire, turning reasonable profits (Ross, 2013).

Arthur T.'s company was driven by ethics that, today, would seem old-fashioned and unsustainable: generosity toward employees in terms of pay and retirement, fairness to customers and suppliers, honesty in communicating the direction in which he hoped to take the company, and transparency in business practices that is often absent in companies of this size. These ethics were in direct conflict with other Demoulas family members, who saw the grocery chain as a means to a lucrative end rather than a public good that could be both profitable and benevolent. Arthur T.'s guiding ethical principle, "Recognize an enterprise's true character is expressed by its people," was taken right out of the Arthur Page playbook (Arthur W. Page Society, 2016).

In July 2013, the board of Demoulas Supermarkets met to consider firing Arthur T., arguing that he was spending money recklessly by being too generous with employee pensions and refusing to accept the board's authority (Ross, 2013). Arthur S.'s family had received roughly $500 million in dividends over the past decade but claimed it should have been $1.5 billion. Family board members agreed to distribute $250 million to the nine family shareholders (Market Basket's descent into greed, 2013). Arthur T. said he would be the biggest beneficiary if the company slashed its generosity to employees, but he claimed that would betray the company's values. Having one employee walk away with a $1 million pension might seem wasteful by corporate standards, but Arthur T. was proud he was able to do this for an employee (Borchers, 2014).

On June 24, 2014, the board of Demoulas Supermarkets voted to remove Arthur T. and two other executives (Ailworth, 2014). That decision would trigger one of the most epic stories of business in the United States, in which the powers of labor, consumerism, state officials, and business partners would create a perfect storm for a feud between two cousins.

The Food Hits the Fan

Arthur S. and company had been working to remove Arthur T. since early summer 2013, but employee backlash was strong. In July 2013, employees created a Facebook page named "Save Market Basket" inviting employees, customers, and contractors to stand against the move and "save this company with our united stance against a corporate raid" (We Are Market Basket, 2013, 2014). The board backed down; the Facebook page and the blog continued to operate.

The board of directors didn't try to win employees' favor. In June 2014, "Arthur T. Demoulas and two other top executives were ousted" (Ailworth, 2014). One of the ousted executives described the move as "driven by greed, pure and simple"

(Ailworth, 2014). The board did not explain the firings. Supporters were already galvanized, anticipating such a move against their boss, and prepared to fight.

On July 12, 2014, the first protest took place. Staff at the Burlington, Massachusetts, stores stuffed pamphlets in customers' grocery bags saying: "We are Market Basket and we need your help" (Fox, 2014). One employee explained, "All our jobs are in danger. We have no idea what their true goals are" (Fox, 2014). The board released a statement stating that the company's direction would not change, but many employees and customers were still suspicious. "I'm very concerned now, after following what the new regime has in mind," one customer from Belmont said, as opposed to Arthur T. and "his caring for the community and the employees" (Fox, 2014).

The first formal protest took everyone by surprise. On July 17, 2,000 employees left their posts to gather outside the Tewksbury headquarters demanding the return of Arthur T. (Ailworth & Newsham, 2014). The previous Thursday, management warned employees, "If you choose to abandon your job or refuse to perform your job requirements, you will leave us no choice but to permanently replace you." Store managers were taking a greater risk, because under the National Labor Relations Act "employees are protected but management is not" (Ailworth & Newsham, 2014). Employees said so many warehouse workers joined the protests that the supermarkets did not receive normal deliveries. At the Burlington Market Basket, shelves appeared full but inventory was beginning to dwindle; a room normally packed with seafood was down to just two crates (Ailworth & Newsham, 2014). At this stage, workers posted on *wearemarketbasket.com* an outreach letter to customers: "We firmly believe that the firing of Arthur T. Demoulas and his management team is simply the start of a process which will lead to dismantling of Market Basket as we know it . . . we cannot sit back and be silent" (Ailworth & Newsham, 2014). Blog and Facebook posts emphasized that the protest was not about Arthur T. as a person, but about what he stood for. New management couldn't convince employees that it stood for the values of Market Basket.

Market Basket management responded swiftly to the protests, firing eight employee organizers (Ailworth & Adams, 2014); on August 4, it held a job fair for new job applicants (Goodison, 2014). The firings sent a message to protesters that management wouldn't back down. But workers and consumers wouldn't back down either; a fourth rally in Tewksbury gathered around 10,000 protesters (Seelye & de la Merced, 2014). The customer boycott meant the chain was losing "millions of dollars a week in sales. The shelves are devoid of fresh produce, meat and dairy products. Supplies of nonperishables are dwindling" (Seelye & de la Merced, 2014). The board considered selling the company by late July because they were hemorrhaging money (Seelye, 2014). The "bare-shelves" strategy of workers alienated the company from customers and showed management that no store can function without employee cooperation. New management didn't change its approach to workers; it threatened again that it might replace 25,000 employees if they kept the protest going (Seelye & de la Merced, 2014). However, in the following statement, management said:

> The past month has been trying. We appreciate the strain this change of leadership has placed on our associates . . . There will be no penalty or discipline for any associate who joins in what will be a significant effort to return to the unparalleled level of performance and customer service that have been hallmarks of the Market Basket brand. (Goodison, 2014)

Protesters had one message: "Arthur T. is our boss!" Arthur T. said little. Management neither initiated outreach to workers or consumers nor attempted any crisis management. As one analyst put it, the board was playing "the waiting game" (Seelye, 2014), hoping that the protest would phase out and things would return to normal. They didn't.

Government Intervention

On August 6, 2014, co-CEO Felicia Thornton clarified management's position: "All Store Directors are to let their associates know that they are not laid off. All Store Directors as part of their normal responsibilities are able to and often do reduce hours but they need to make clear when doing so that the individuals are still employees of DSM" (McGovern, 2014). Employees complained to government officials, who responded swiftly. Massachusetts Attorney General Martha Coakley set up a hotline for Market Basket employees to "answer questions directly from workers and make sure their rights are being protected" (McGovern, 2014). The Attorney General's office received more than 100 calls from worried employees, a move supposedly initiated by the Facebook page Save Market Basket (Saffir & Reston, 2014). On August 7, 2014, New Hampshire Governor Maggie Hassan pressured management to "listen to the concerns of their employees and customers and reach a constructive resolution in order to keep these dedicated workers employed and reduce the impact on consumers." The next day, Massachusetts Governor Deval Patrick sent a letter to Market Basket's management: "By any measure, the disruption caused by your recent change in CEO has gotten out of hand, and I am writing to urge you to find a prompt resolution . . . Your failure to resolve this matter is not only hurting the company's brand and business, but also many innocent and relatively powerless workers whose livelihoods depend on you" (Ross, 2014a). There was an implicit warning he might take further action if the situation worsened.

Meanwhile, Arthur T.'s offer to buy back the company was still in play; no better bidder emerged. Hannaford offered to buy the majority of the company, but Arthur T. and his family were still holding 49.5% of the stock; any future owner had to deal with him either way (Ross, 2014b). Management's waiting game backfired.

Directors offered Arthur T. a compromise: "allow him and his entire former management team, including all individuals who resigned or were dismissed, to assist the Company's return to normal business operations and people to get back to their jobs and lives … There is no reason to not meet in the middle; Mr. Demoulas gets his management team back in place, associates can get back to doing their job, customers can get back to shopping and the company gets the breathing room needed to create an orderly and productive way forward" (Feinstein, 2014). The directors wanted Arthur T. to come back on an interim basis while they considered his bid to buy the company outright. Arthur T. rejected the offer, calling it "disingenuous" and "playing games with a serious situation," especially since he offered to rejoin the company three times before but was rejected (Feinstein, 2014). Arthur T.'s skepticism was legitimate; if they wanted him back, why didn't they reappoint him as CEO or sell him the entire business? The statement released by Arthur T. called it "an attempt to have him stabilize the company, while they consider selling it to another bidder" (Cousineau, 2014).

Four main stakeholders applied pressure: workers who made the shelves empty, consumers who stopped buying, state government worried about job and revenue losses, and contractors and bidders who might worry about the value of the brand. Sensing defeat, the majority owners decided on August 9 to sell to Arthur T., but they claimed he had insufficient financing and that his "conduct to date, including his most recent public statement, continues to undermine Market Basket and the Class B Shareholders have not indicated a willingness to engage in good faith discussions for a sale" (Caesar, 2014). Arthur T. said he hoped the matter would not be negotiated in the press. He said price was not the issue, but rather the "onerous terms" with which he had been presented "squelched a deal." He said he hoped that the next article that appeared in the press would be to announce that his bid had been accepted "and that he and his whole team are going in to stabilize the company" (DiNardo, 2014).

Arthur T. had the upper hand. Two days later Governor Patrick announced a potential deal (Vaccaro, 2014). Governor Patrick asked workers to return, a call warmly received by Market Basket's directors (Vaccaro, 2014). But active workers on the Save Market Basket Facebook page refused: "Our message remains clear: we will go back to work when Arthur T. Demoulas goes back to work with full authority or when the deal is in place to sell him the company. We will not go back to work when the Governor, the Board or any other entity tells us to."

By August 21, Arthur T. had offered $1.5 billion to purchase the majority of the company; the governors of New Hampshire and Massachusetts affirmed the deal was imminent (Ross, 2014c). The good news came on August 27: Shareholders signed the deal to sell Arthur T. the majority interest, and he would return to run the company immediately (Ross, 2014d; Vaccaro, 2014). For six weeks, the business has been decimated by employee protests, supply shortages, and customer boycotts. Protesters were successful in shutting the business down until management met their demands. It would be a challenge for Arthur T. to stabilize the business after a period of turmoil, but could he be more successful because workers supported him?

Outcome

It was a day of jubilation: on Thursday, August 28, 2014, Arthur T. returned to company headquarters in Tewksbury to greet a rally held especially for him (Semuels, 2014). Workers and customers alike gathered to welcome back "King Arthur" who would restore order to the realm (Adams, Luna, Newsham, & Holt, 2014). The workers' victory came as an anomaly considering how little bargaining power was left for labor against the employers (Sneed, 2014). This case is unique because workers actually fought to bring back their billionaire boss, not to oust him. Labor struggles aren't always about raising wages or fighting layoffs, but they can also decide who will manage the company, and how. And how would that affect the efforts of internal branding, and leadership styles in general? In the end, sound ethics and concern for employees won the day—a truly "palatable" solution.

It is interesting to note that Arthur T. used a very limited communication strategy in winning back the company. He wisely allowed the employees to communicate the values of the company, their concern about the leadership vacuum, and the need to restore the company culture and values that had made the grocery chain successful. They did this through social media and on-the-ground protests and fliers. This "less is more" communication strategy might seem weak, but it was actually a brilliant way to evoke public support and bring about the eventual return to leadership that Arthur T. sought.

References

Adams, D., Luna, T., Newsham, J., & Holt, W. (2014, August 29). For Market Basket workers, "It's time." *Boston Globe*. Retrieved from https://www.highbeam.com/doc/1P2-37121077.html.

Ailworth, E. (2014, June 24). An ouster at the top in grocery family feud. *Boston Globe*. Retrieved from http://search.proquest.com/docview/1539376143?accountid=10735.

Ailworth, E., & Adams, D. (2014, July 20). Market Basket fires 8 employees amid protests. *Boston Globe*. Retrieved from https://www.bostonglobe.com/metro/2014/07/20/market-basket-warehouse-supervisor-fired-according-protest-organizer/GP6CcpuPSvUwglQTXfw6XL/story.html.

Ailworth, E., & Newsham, J. (2014, July 18). Market Basket workers stand up for ousted CEO. *Boston Globe*. Retrieved from https://www.bostonglobe.com/business/2014/07/18/employees-gather-outside-demoulas-headquarters-tewksbury-demand-return-ousted-ceo/Ohe9yhENVFCADBTWgG5IHO/story.html.

Arthur W. Page Society. (2016, December 16). The Page Principles. Retrieved from http://www.awpagesociety.com/site/the-page-principles.

Bailey, S. (2000, May 26). Arthur S. and the widow. *Boston Globe*. Retrieved from http://search.proquest.com/docview/405340944?accountid=10735.

Borchers, C. (2014, August 22). The personal touch cuts both ways with family. *Boston Globe* Retrieved from http://search.proquest.com/docview/1555210002?accountid=10735.

Caesar, C. (2014, August 10). Market Basket majority owners: We would sell to Arthur T. *Boston.com*. Retrieved from http://www.boston.com/news/local-news/2014/08/09/market-basket-majority-owners-we-would-sell-to-arthur-t.

Cousineau, M. (2014, August 8). Arthur T. rejects board members' proposal to "move on," settle strife. *New Hampshire Union Leader*. Retrieved from http://www.unionleader.com/apps/pbcs.dll/article?template=printart&AID=%2F2 0140809%2FNEWS02%2F140809001%2F-1%2Fges%2Ful%2FTwittericon_ 75px.jpg.

DiNardo, B. (2014, August 10). Statement by Arthur T. Demoulas. *Boston Globe*. Retrieved from https://www.bostonglobe.com/business/2014/08/08/statement-from-arthur-demoulas/gJPVkbhtUIv375B47FSjqL/story.html.

Feinstein, C. (2014, August 9). Independent directors offer to bring Arthur T. Demoulas back, but not as CEO. *Lowell Sun*. Retrieved from http://www.lowellsun.com/news/ci_26306526/an-offer-take-arthur-t-back-but-not.

Fox, J. (2014, July 14). Market Basket workers seek to rally customers. *Boston Globe*. Retrieved from https://www.bostonglobe.com/metro/2014/07/13/market-basket-employees-demand-return-ousted-ceo/u1cDqVjwNg148SQcTPx2aI/story.html.

Goodison, D. (2014, Jul 26). Organizer says employees will spurn Market Basket offer. *McClatchy–Tribune Business News*. Retrieved from http://search.proquest.com/do cview/1548362644?accountid=10735 http://im.fee.uva.nl/mwiki2008/images/b/ b7/Friedman_buycott.pdf.

History of Market Basket. (2012). Retrieved from http://www.mydemoulas.net/ history/.

Hoover's. (2015). *Demoulas Super Markets Inc*. Austin: Dun and Bradstreet, Inc. Retrieved from http://www.hoovers.com/company-information/cs/companyprofile .demoulas_super_markets_inc.b1f1a730584c0f6f.html.

Horowitz, E. (2014, July 16). A Market Basket feud guide. *Boston Globe*. Retrieved from http://search.proquest.com/docview/1545135717?accountid=10735.

Market Basket's descent into greed. (2013, August 27). *Boston Globe*. Retrieved from http://search.proquest.com/docview/1427969953?accountid=10735.

McGovern, B. (2014, August 7). Market Basket cutting hours as N.H. gov says fix this mess. *Boston Herald*. Retrieved from http://www.bostonherald.com/news_ opinion/local_coverage/herald_bulldog/2014/08/market_basket_cutting_ hours_as_nh_gov_says_fix.

Newsham, J., & Ross, C. (2014, August 20). No word on Demoulas negotiations; more vendors says they cut ties to grocery. *Boston Globe*. Retrieved from https://www .highbeam.com/doc/1P2-37089353.html.

Ross, C. (2013, July 12). Family business as usual. *Boston Globe*. Retrieved from http:// search.proquest.com/docview/1399475415?accountid=10735.

Ross, C. (2014a, August 8). Patrick offers to help end Market Basket feud. *Boston Globe*. Retrieved from http://www.bostonglobe.com/business/2014/08/08/patrickletter/vfwMW8eerAEuDaPPqLQcdN/story.html?event=event12.

Ross, C. (2014b, August 19). Market Basket eyes deal this week. *Boston Globe*. Retrieved from http://search.proquest.com/docview/1554022867?accountid=10735.

Ross, C. (2014c, August 22). Arthur T. Demoulas offers $1.5 billion for Market Basket. *Boston Globe*. Retrieved from https://www.bostonglobe.com/business/2014/08/22/demoulas/MwC4vzWVVHhW73nva23dvHO/story.html.

Ross, C. (2014d, August 28). Market Basket deal reached. *Boston Globe*. Retrieved from http://search.proquest.com/docview/1539376143?accountid=10735.

Saffir, D., & Reston, L. (2014, August 7). Market Basket CEOs debunk layoff rumors. *Boston.com*. Retrieved from http://www.boston.com/news/business/2014/08/07/market-basket-ceos-debunk-layoff-rumors.

Seelye, K. Q. (2014, July 25). Grocer is open to buyers' bids amid turmoil. *New York Times*. Retrieved from http://www.nytimes.com/2014/07/26/us/ailing-grocer-open-to-bids-to-buy-chain.html?_r=0.

Seelye, K. Q., & de la Merced, M. (2014, August 5). Grocery chain reels as employees and customers rally for an ousted president. *New York Times*. Retrieved from http://www.nytimes.com/2014/08/06/us/grocery-chain-reels-as-employees-and-customers-rally-for-an-ousted-president.html.

Semuels, A. (2014, August 28). Power to the workers: How grocery chain employees saved beloved CEO. *Los Angeles Times*. Retrieved from http://www.latimes.com/nation/nationnow/la-na-nn-market-basket-ceo-arthur-t-demoulas-20140828-story.html.

Sneed, T. (2014, August 28) Power to the people: Market Basket case a rare workers' win. *USA Today*. Retrieved from http://www.usnews.com/news/articles/2014/08/28/market-basket-case-a-rare-workers-win.

Tosh, M. (1999, February). Family feud. *Progressive Grocer, 78*(2), 13. Retrieved from http://go.galegroup.com/ps/i.do?id=GALE%7CA55263283&v=2.1&u=ecl_main&it=r&p=AONE&sw=w&asid=f14a35bc116dfc986f0cab009dfbc4ba.

Vaccaro, A. (2014, August 13). Gov. Patrick calls on Market Basket workers to return. *boston.com*. Retrieved from http://www.boston.com/news/business/2014/08/13/gov-patrick-calls-on-market-basket-workers-to-return.

We Are Market Basket. (2013, 2014). Retrieved from wearemarketbasket.com

Discussion Questions

1. What makes this case unique among corporate crises, and what can we learn from this special case?

2. What role did employees and customers play in bringing about a successful reinstatement of Arthur T. as CEO?

3. What are the lessons for management in using values as the basis for management philosophy and strategy?

ETHICAL ACTIVISM? FOOD BABE, BIG FOOD, AND THE ONLINE PRESSURE FOR DISCLOSURE

Ashli Quesinberry Stokes, Ph.D., *University of North Carolina at Charlotte*

In 2011, Vani Hari began blogging about healthier eating habits from Charlotte, North Carolina. Seeking to eat more healthfully, Hari, trained as a computer scientist, set about investigating more about what she ate in a typical day, paying particular attention to processed food. By 2015, Hari and her husband quit their management consulting jobs to operate Foodbabe.com, where they offer healthy living tips and recipes and report the results of investigations into "Big Food." Today, Foodbabe.com has around four million readers a month and has been named "public enemy number one" by companies such as Kraft, McDonald's, General Mills, Subway, Starbucks, and more (Rubin, 2015). *Time* Magazine calls her one of the "30 Most Influential People on the Internet," she's one of "America's 13 most powerful women in food," and her book debuted at number four on the *New York Times* Bestseller List (Myers, 2016). Hari is known for her attention-getting tactics, like "click me headlines" ("Do you eat Beaver Butt?"), viral petitions (one against Subway garnered 50,000 signatures in less than 24 hours), and extensive use of social media through hashtag activism (#foodbabearmy), that seemingly result in rapid corporate change (Franci, 2015). Subway, for example, removed a chemical from its bread (azodicarbonamide) after Hari posted a video of herself chewing a yoga mat and claiming the sandwich maker had the same chemical in its bread (Franci, 2015). She claims that her efforts made Starbucks remove caramel color from its drinks, Chick-fil-A eliminate dyes and artificial corn syrup from its products, and Kraft replace dyes in one of its famous mac-and-cheese products in the United States. Although several of these companies argue they were already in the process of making changes, Hari claims these as victories in changing the American food landscape. Others argue that Big Food is evolving, but not because of Hari's efforts; indeed, doctors and scientists, journalists, and corporations have critiqued her methods, her lack of training and food credentials, and her reasoning.

Hari's targeted attack on Big Food might not be well known outside of the United States, but her form of viral activism deserves attention because of its implications for disclosure and transparency in contemporary public relations. This case explores how Food Babe––style viral activism pressures companies to reveal their ingredients or change their practices, calling for particular responses from targeted corporations. Despite its sometimes questionable ethics, viewing Hari's brand of viral activism as a generative source of public relations activity

(Stokes, 2013) helps corporations to better respond to these forms of pressure. This essay first gives an overview of the trend toward increasing disclosure and transparency and its relationship to viral activism. It then describes the situation for Food Babe's activism, employing Lessl (1989)'s rhetorical concepts of priestly and bardic voice to critique key strategies from 2013 to 2015. The outcomes/key factors section offers suggestions about how corporations can ethically respond to disclosure/transparency demands.

Background

Food Babe's campaigns give us the chance to explore social media in the activism context, because without today's Internet, there would be no Food Babe. Hari is savvy about social/viral media, linking her Food Babe TV website content to YouTube, collecting signatures online, tweeting her followers, and employing Facebook extensively to share her "investigations" and commentary. Butterworth (2014, para. 1) argues that Food Babe's activism in general demonstrates "the growing power of social media over corporations," but she has been roundly criticized for not including details that make the findings of her investigations far less powerful. She's frequently criticized for practicing pseudo-science and fear-mongering by academics and mainstream news outlets alike (Godoy, 2014). For example, Gorski (2014) points out that her campaign that demanded that Anheuser Busch and Miller remove isinglass (made from fish bladders) from their beer omitted important information. While headlines like "Beer Contains Fish Bladders!" garner clicks, Hari, and the journalists/followers who share her messages, do not always explain that isinglass has been used to clarify beer since the 18th century.

This type of viral "hashtag" activism presents a challenge for companies, representing one type of disclosure and transparency concerns. Though the disclosure debate in public relations sometimes involves corporate spending in political campaigns or whether or not bloggers (and others) are paid to discuss corporate products or services, this case represents a third type. Here, activists take advantage of the rapid exposure the internet offers to launch demands for companies to reveal or change their ingredients or manufacturing processes, and companies must decide how and whether to react to the "steamrolling of tweets and shares and memes and more" (Jones, 2014, para. 3). Some observers call the sharing of this often sensational information "slacktivism," where consumers just pass along corporate critiques without the attendant grassroots organizing that can follow more traditional forms of activism. This form of activism, however, carries surprising power. Ogilvy PR (2011), for example, argues that "slacktivists" are more likely to commit to meaningful social change, with surveys demonstrating them to be 50% more likely to volunteer their time and change purchasing habits to buy products from companies that support their causes.

From a traditional public relations perspective, the internet helps activists serve as mediated "viruses" to corporations, "pests" that "excel at spreading outrage" (Van Den Hurk, 2013, p. 42) and block corporations from successfully communicating with their operating environments (DiNardo, 2002; Esrock & Leichty, 2000; Karlberg, 1996). Although seeking to remain oppositional, today's activists use strategies and tactics that are not so dissimilar from other, more corporate entities (Smith, 2005). We need to better explore the activist perspective (Demetrious, 2013; Stokes, 2013), and the Food Babe case offers this opportunity, but with a twist:[1] Food Babe does not seek to shutter companies like Kraft and Chick-fil-A, but wants them to make changes in their products and offer more transparency. Her campaigns provide a look into how activists resist compromise and seek varying levels of corporate change. There are three ways in which Food Babe attacks her targets that can help us understand this type of activism. The strategies also show how the interplay between corporations and activists helps shape public discussion about Big Food.

The Situation

The key words, metaphors, themes, narratives, and images were identified in a set of Food Babe documents (available at foodbabe.com) from 2013 to 2015, suggesting that Food Babe challenges Big Food over who is the authority in determining the meaning of food in today's culture. Internet culture, along with changing ideas about authority in general (Quart, 2010), compounds the food debate by encouraging the rise of the "expert by experience" (similar to Jenny McCarthy in the anti-vaccine movement). The problem with many of these "researchers" is that they do not have the expertise to interpret data scientifically. Some widely shared statements are suspect, if not false, but gain traction through online communities that anoint their own experts and ignore conflicting voices. Journalists, too, may draw uncritically on "experts" for stories from the "cacophony" of the internet (Quart, 2010).

The debate over authority and trust can be expected in this case, as food industry scientists often speak in a "priestly voice" that renders them outside of the everyday culture experienced by nonscientists (Lessl, 1989). Priestly rhetoric is vertical, descending from above to "baptize" the people in its image; bardic communication is the voice of the people, horizontally shared "common-sense experience" (Lessl, 1989). Lessl offered these helpful metaphors when television was the primary bardic voice, sharing and creating our cultural identity; today, however, the bardic internet offers a million ways to splinter *and* unify views and people. Laypeople like Hari now claim what were formerly priestly elements of the scientific message code and mix them into the food debate.

---

1. See Stokes and Rubin (2010) for a critique of the Excellence Theory in explaining activism.

The ability of Food Babe and other viral activists to adopt the priestly, authoritative voice has some pitfalls for corporations responding to demands for disclosure. Internet culture helps anti–Big Food sentiment grow by disseminating priestly code in a bardic voice, making it more appealing and relatable to readers. Traditionally scientists' ability to speak specialized technical language elicited reverence and perpetuated their power and prestige as it was judged both by other scientists and by laypeople; in contrast, bardic communication was only reflexive, judged by its own audience. Thus, when Food Babe and others tout their own "studies" or "other data" showing that chemicals are in everything, and in often seemingly disgusting ways, scientists and food industry experts bristle. Further, because of bardic communication's tendency to "claw back" experience and information into its own reality, scientific knowledge gets filtered through a community's own perspectives and beliefs (Lessl, 1989, 187). To those committed to an anti–Big Food sentiment or those starting to lean in that direction, these voices are mutually reinforcing. The internet allows anti–Big Food activists like Hari to point out that scientific knowledge is mutable, with activists reaching out directly to like-minded publics with energizing and community-reinforcing messages.

Outcomes

Food Babe's website relies on three main strategies to deliver a seemingly scientific message in a bardic voice: Hari (1) adopts the voice of a science teacher, (2) frequently employs metonymy, and (3) employs the language of "choice." All of these not only engender viral activism but also help shape the Big Food debate.

Science (Kind of)

One of the key strategies employed on the Food Babe website is the use of scientific terminology translated into lay terms. Hari becomes a type of science teacher, using scientific terms but explaining them in easily understandable, even entertaining terms. For example, Hari points out that popular foods contain chemicals like propylene glycol, salicylic acid, and more, knowing that most readers have no clue about how these compounds work. She relies on the tendency for fear to increase among audiences in the face of uncertainty (Lessl, 1989); indeed, as Gorski (2014, p. 1) warns, "name a bunch of chemicals and count on the chemical illiteracy of your audience to result in fear at hearing their very names." One of her campaigns, for example, claimed that there was antifreeze in beer, calling for consumers to petition against a number of big American beer-makers. While it is true that American beers list propylene glycol among their ingredients, what is troubling about this claim is that Food Babe's headlines scream "Antifreeze is in beer!" without noting that the chemical that makes antifreeze is not *in* the beer, it is used in its cooling system (Butterworth, 2014). This distinction is not made clear on the Food Babe website or in headlines in the media. Hari commonly lists lots of chemicals as problematic in products, but she does not describe how they act in the body or how they are created. By employing scientific terms in ways that are not exactly representative of the actual chemical processes used in manufacturing foods, she benefits from the "mantle of science."[2] Food Babe employs the language of the priest in the trappings of the layperson, perhaps leaving consumers more fearful but ill-informed about what is truly in their food.

Metonymy

Metonymy involves substituting the name of an attribute for that of the thing meant—for example, "suit" for business executive or "the track" for horse racing (Dor, 1998). This particular rhetorical strategy is very prominent in Food Babe's messaging (Franci, 2015) and it helps cultivate consumer revulsion and anger at seemingly disgusting manufacturing practices. A famous example is the Food Babe campaign against "beaver butt," which Hari claimed was in many vanilla-flavored products. The click-bait headline "Do You Eat Beaver Butt?" made its way rapidly around the internet. What Hari was referring to, however, is not only uncommon in food products, but her strategy confuses the source and use of a compound from the chemical molecules themselves. Consumers are not in fact eating "beaver butt," but they might consume a similar synthetic compound. As Franci (2015, para. 10) complains about this strategy: "I couldn't believe there was beaver's ass in my vanilla ice cream, coal tar in my mac and cheese, yoga mat and shoe rubber in my bread"—and in reality, consumers are not eating these things, at least in those forms. While castoreum is in fact extracted from the backside of a beaver and can be used to flavor things like ice cream, the average consumer is not going to experience this stomach-turning experience because of how much it would cost to use naturally derived castoreum in the manufacturing process. Thus, when consumers are told they are eating "beaver butt" when taking a bite of vanilla ice cream or eating a yoga mat when taking a bite of their Subway sandwich, Hari is relying on metonymy to make these troubling claims. Similarly, when Hari claims that L-cysteine, an amino acid, is extracted from chicken feathers or human hair to condition bread dough, consumers have a right to horrified (Franci, 2015). What is not discussed, however, is that in this application L-cysteine is synthetically manufactured nowhere near chickens or hair. The ramifications for public discourse surrounding Big Food are troubling when the audience and opponents are not operating from representative grounds.

Consumer Choice and Transparency

With her track record of inspiring victories against corporations, the Food Babe website then calls for action. Many of Food Babe's appeals are to the power of consumer choice in forcing more corporate disclosure. From a priestly/bardic

---

2. All of the excerpts analyzed in this section are available at foodbabe.com.

perspective, this approach is noteworthy because the "choice" language appeals to common fears and rights, but uses a quasi-scientific voice to do so. Food Babe invokes freedom and human rights, speaking in the bardic voice of the people to urge changes to Big Food. By standing up for the right for better food in terms of knowing more about specific ingredients and processes, however, her #foodbabearmy becomes heroic, a minority standing up to the too powerful, willfully deceptive government and corporate systems:

> I like to call you the Food Babe Army, because that is what you are . . . an army fighting for total food awareness, holding companies and the FDA accountable and spreading the truth. Collectively, you have the power to change the world.

Through this lens Big Food and its partner Big Government become the enemy, and Food Babe calls frequently for more transparency from both. Her focus on institutional deception helps strengthen community commitment to her movement, calling out industry players like Monsanto, Dow, and DuPont for their use of chemicals and/or genetically engineered crops (GMOs). Of course, to combat Big Food, readers must respond to the danger these chemicals/toxins represent to their families and their rights with courage and conviction:

> I think it's absolutely critical for us to stick together and not be afraid to tell the truth. These bullies want to intimidate us into submission. They want us to be too scared to write, investigate and share our findings. So scared, that we quit.

These appeals draw on American belief in the individual standing up against powerful institutional forces and build on the "right to know/choose" appeals. Take together these appeals offer an example of the power of using a priestly voice in a bardic channel. Food Babe is not alone in today's food fight landscape, joined by other self-styled experts like Dr. Oz, Jamie Oliver, and Morgan Spurlock, and these activists are able to effect change from corporations. It should be clear that each rhetorical theme does not employ accommodation/compromise in the traditional sense. Hari may sit down with corporate executives, but it is often only after they have capitulated to her demands. What are the outcomes of this activist approach?

Although the topics may differ depending on the industry, the strategies that Food Babe uses, aided and delivered by "likes," shares, and viral video, present challenges in responding to disclosure and transparency pressure. They also suggest how viral campaigns change activism. The strategies analyzed here heighten consumer expectation for corporate response in ways that are difficult to address. Priestly/bardic rhetorical analysis uncovers the need for companies to better serve and respond to questions of who is an "expert" in today's world. Companies may initially scoff at needing to respond to disclosure pressure from "quasi-experts/scientists," but the trend is likely to continue (Abrams, 2015). Consumers do not know whom they can trust, with the "steady flow of misinformation" causing a "crisis of credibility" that raises the question of digital influence (Coffee, 2015, para. 5). While formally trained food experts and scientists may bristle at the type of pseudo-scientific "research" that Food Babe represents, the "authentic" appeal of relatable quasi-experts remains a force with which industries must reckon.

There are a number of ways companies can respond. One is to address consumer transparency demands more honestly and fully, while retaining the relatable quality of the bardic voice. As one industry expert suggests, "Talk to me like a real person. If you have something to say, say it, and if you don't, then find something. But say it honestly, please" (in Coffee, 2015, para. 12). Despite the science of food being unclear, the common misunderstanding of competing food terms, and the need for consumers to "look at the science behind what these 'experts' are saying" (Coffee, 2015, para. 8), this approach may temper the viral activist media buzz. Of course, standard rules of weighing the dangers of the rumor mill apply. Companies must not simply dump complex information online (Abrams, 2015); as Gorski (2014, para. 14) warns, "companies live and die by public perception" and it is important to rein in the online frenzy. It might be difficult to counter, but it is important not to conflate transparency demands with scientific illiteracy (Godoy, 2014).

Second, the rise of digital experts like Hari highlights the importance of information-age media vetting. Media outlets play a role in regulating the food industry through their decisions about which stories get printed and which experts are quoted (Coffee, 2015). One public relations adviser, for example, suggests that some networks "are really cracking down on the people they're featuring. [Guests are] not able to bring paid products on the show; it needs to be more of an organic thing that they support" (in Coffee, 2015). Other suggestions for companies facing disclosure and transparency pressure should include managerial scanning for ingredients that are trending and considering whether it may be useful, or competitively threatening, to list supplier/ingredient information (Russo, 2011).

In addition to weighing how to respond to a quasi-expert's viral campaign, like it or not, the pressure for more transparency serves a generative function (Stokes, 2013), gradually changing what we talk about when we think about food in American culture. Public relations industry observers and scientists alike decry the rise of quasi-experts like Food Babe, but their influence on public debate about food should not be discounted (Draco, Senapathy, & Alsip, 2015). One study of 30,000 people, for example, found that 88% of consumers are willing to pay more for "healthier" foods, particularly Millennials (Calahan, 2015). Activism on the part of Food Babe and others brings attention to issues about what ingredients should be in our food, how and whether employees should be exposed to chemicals in the manufacturing process, and the price of convenience, for starters. Food Babe campaigns do in fact raise the question of whether azodicarbonamide should be in commercial bread dough in the United States in any form: because it can cause respiratory issues, it is banned in the European Union (Franci, 2015). Food Babe's strategies sometimes employ questionable honesty and the misleading use of science. Her website is a business, with Hari making money through affiliate marketing. Nevertheless, she and others are changing the American food landscape, despite their lack of qualifications, which some argue may ultimately be a positive thing: "They are pushing the needle to a healthier place, and people are more interested than ever in what they're putting into their bodies" (Coffee, 2015, para. 17). The food business environment has changed from placing the emphasis on fun to focusing on ingredients, sustainability, and consumer choice (Coffee, 2015), and it is necessary in public relations to better respond to this trend despite its unseemly source.

The efforts of Food Babe and other viral activists underscore that we are in new public relations territory. Despite her aggressive strategies, the type of interplay between corporations and publics that Hari encourages creates evolutionary, not revolutionary, change. As Calahan (2015, para. 10) cautions, "Love her or hate her, one thing is clear: Hari's changing what we eat." Food Babe offers a liberal approach to change that may be comfortable for her general readership. She does not tell readers to reject the American food system wholesale; rather, she shows them a way to make different choices and interpret the avalanche of information within it. This activism actually provides Big Food with opportunities. As some of these expectations become the "new normal," smart companies will use issues management to proactively respond to them, retaining profits while also making our food better.

References

Abrams, R. (2015, October 26). Under pressure, feminine product makers disclose ingredients. *New York Times*.

Butterworth, T. (2014, June 16). Quackmail: Why you shouldn't fall for the internet's newest fool, the Food Babe. *Forbes.com*.

Calahan, S. (2015, March 29). The controversial rise of the "Food Babe." *New York Post*.

Coffee, P. (2015, April). "Food Babe" debacle underscores crisis of credibility surrounding what we eat. *Adweek*.

Demetrious, K. (2013). *Public Relations, Activism, and Social Change: Speaking Up*. London: Routledge.

DiNardo, A. M. (2002). The Internet as a crisis management tool: A critique of banking sites during Y2 K. *Public Relations Review, 28*, 367–379.

Dor, Joël. (1998). *Introduction to the Reading of Lacan: The Unconscious Structured Like a Language*. New York: Other Press.

Draco, M., Senapathy, K., & Alsip, M. (2015). *The Fear Babe: Shattering Vani Hari's Glass House*. Senapath Press.

Esrock, S., & Leichty, G. (2000). Organization of corporate Web pages: Publics and functions. *Public Relations Review, 26*, 327–341.

Franci, M. (2015, February 18). Are corporations putting feathers in your food? *Slate.com*.

Godoy, G. (2014, December 4). Is the Food Babe a fearmonger? Scientists are speaking out. *The Salt-NPR*.

Gorski, D. (2014, June 16). Vani Hari (a.k.a. The Food Babe): The Jenny McCarthy of food. *Sciencebasedmedicine.org*.

Jones, Jennifer. (2014). Hashtag activism. *Jennifer Jones* [blog].

Karlberg, M. (1996). Remembering the public in public relations research: From theoretical to operational symmetry. *Journal of Public Relations Research, 8*, 263–278.

Lessl, T. (1989). The priestly voice. *Quarterly Journal of Speech, 75*, 183–197.

Myers, D. (2016, February 19). The 13 most powerful women in food. *Thedailymeal.com*.

Ogilvy Public Relations Worldwide. (2011). Dynamics of cause engagement study. Available at http://www.csic.georgetown.edu.

Quart, A. (2010). The trouble with experts. *Columbia Journalism Review, 49*, 17–19.

Rubin, C. (2015, March 13). Taking on the food industry, one blog post at a time. *New York Times*.

Russo, M. (2011). *Companies on a Mission*. Stanford, CA: Stanford Business Books.

Smith, M. (2005). Activism. In Heath, R. L. (Ed.), *Encyclopedia of Public Relations* (pp. 5–9). Thousand Oaks, CA: Sage.

Stokes, A. Q. (2013). You are what you eat: Slow Food USA's constitutive public relations. *Journal of Public Relations Research, 25*, 68–90.

Stokes, A. Q., & Rubin, D. (2010). Activism and the limits of symmetry: The public relations battle between Colorado GASP and Philip Morris. *Journal of Public Relations Research, 22*(1), 26–48.

Van Den Hurk, A. M. (2013). *Social Media Crisis Communications*. London: Pearson Education.

Discussion Questions

1. Have you seen other examples of viral activism of questionable ethical content? What did you find to be repugnant?

2. Can viral activism succeed without resorting to inflammatory strategies and tactics like "click bait"? How?

3. How do nonprofits employ tenets of viral activism in productive ways?

4. Visit Foodbabe.com and use the three rhetorical strategies (invoking science, metonymy, and "choice" language) discussed in this chapter to analyze her most recent campaigns. What do they encourage site visitors to do? Is this an ethical use of communication campaigns?

5. The pressure for corporate disclosure and transparency is only likely to increase. How do corporations respond to this pressure while guarding proprietary information?

7 COMMUNITY RELATIONS

Learning Outcomes

- Recognize the necessity of community relations to good relationships.
- Describe the practice of community relations.
- Analyze ethical principles in relation to community.
- Apply ethical principles to community relations case studies.

Definitions

Community: The area in which an organization exists. The people who live there often share common ideas, issues, attitudes, and needs.

Community relations: An organization's interactions with the people and area in which it functions and from which it draws resources such as employees. These interactions and activities are often meant to build and maintain relationships and trust with constituents.

Much like consumer and employee relations need to be cultivated, so do community relations. Organizations need to recognize that they often need the support of the community to exist and to continue their operation (Guiniven, 2005). Community relations is about an organization's centrality to the community in which it exists, and it is becoming more important each year (Guiniven, 2005). Some people even say public relations should be renamed "community relations" due to the importance of this sector (Hallahan, 2004).

Kruckeberg and Starck (1988) and Kruckeberg (1998) state that practitioners must do eight things to practice public relations with a community orientation:

1. Make community members aware of any interests in common with organizations.
2. Become one with the community.

3. Use technology to create community.
4. Promote leisure activities.
5. Develop communication that is self-fulfilling.
6. Do charitable work.
7. Share values.
8. Develop and maintain relationships.

Ideally both the organization and members of the community recognize their commonality and work together to achieve goals.

Communities and Organizations: A Reciprocal Relationship

Communities look to organizations to provide jobs and a tax base. They also expect organizations to obey laws, protect the local environment, and be truthful about risks. Organizations expect communities to provide infrastructure for their plants and a workforce. Therefore, it is not only important for organizations to build relationships with their communities, but it is also important for communities to work with organizations. Some researchers suggest that organizations should want to become "neighbors of choice" in their respective communities (Burke, 1999). To become a neighbor of choice, an organization should build and maintain relationships with community members and community organizations; understand community issues and concerns; and develop trust by supporting programs that are important to the community (Burke, 1999). In addition, when good relationships have been built, both the organization and the community can create dialogue and times of listening. By building strategic partnerships, both can support one another and share resources in the pursuit of common goals (Guiniven, 2005).

One example of building positive organization–community relationships is the Live in the City You Protect program. The Atlanta Police Foundation works to raise funds, which are used to refurbish homes. Atlanta police officers are able to purchase these homes and live in the areas they help to protect. By living in the community, these officers have a better understanding of the issues and needs of their constituents. Engagement and communication happen in an unforced and natural way. Community members get to know the police officers; police officers get to know the people they protect. Programs such as this one help to build trust and relationships. With this increased understanding, police and community members often come together for the betterment of the local community. Not only are more cases solved because community members are more willing to work with the police, but also crime rates fall (Covington, 2015).

References

Burke, E. M. (1999). *Corporate Community Relations: The Principle of the Neighbor of Choice.* Westport, CT: Praeger.

Covington, K. (2015, September 21). 6 ways to improve police and community relations, Retrieved from https://www.azcentral.com/story/news/local/phoenix/contributed/2015/09/16/6-ways-improve-police-and-community-relations/32536565/.

Guiniven, J. (2005, November). Community relations—more than money. *Public Relations Tactics, 12*(11), 6.

Hallahan, K. (2004, January). "Community" as a foundation for public relations theory and practice. *Communication Yearbook, 28*(1), 233–279.

Kruckeberg, D. (1998, November). *Public Relations and Its Education: 21st-Century Challenges in Definition, Role and Function.* Paper presented to National Communication Association, New York.

Kruckeberg, D., & Starck, K. (1988). *Public Relations and Community: A Reconstructed Theory.* New York: Praeger.

"DO NOT USE!": ETHICAL IMPLICATIONS OF THE 2014 ELK RIVER CHEMICAL SPILL

Jonathan Borden, Ph.D., *Syracuse University*, and
Xiaochen Angela Zhang, Ph.D., *Kansas State University*

On the morning of January 9, 2014, residents of the Kanawha River Valley of West Virginia awoke to discover a thick, sweet smell of licorice in the air. Such events were not unusual in the area, which had come to be nicknamed "The Chemical Valley" for its large number of small and medium-sized chemical companies. It quickly became apparent, however, that this was no ordinary odor.

Responding to tips from concerned citizens, state investigators began to seek the source of the smell. A few miles northwest of West Virginia's capital of Charleston, the investigators discovered a storage tank owned by Freedom Industries hemorrhaging a thick liquid called 4-methylcyclohexane methanol (MCHM). According to the investigators, the chemical was leaking from the tank and "bubbling up out of the ground" (Field, Edwards, & Soichet, 2014). A cinder block and a 50-pound bag of absorbent powder (Ward, 2014) were all that was in place to keep the 35,000-gallon tank from flowing into the Elk River, the sole source of drinking water for 300,000 West Virginians.

Before the events of 2014 came to a close, nearly 600 area residents would receive treatment for acute chemical exposure from rashes and blistering, burning in the throat, severe eye irritation, nausea, and vomiting. A further 13 would require hospitalization due to extreme reactions to the chemical in the air (Manuel, 2014). Nearly a fifth of the state would be without running water for nearly two weeks.

The Freedom Industries disaster of 2014 was one of the biggest chemical accidents in U.S. history. The response of the corporation to the crisis has been described as "a case study in what not to do" (Manuel, 2014, A215). What led to the Freedom Industries disaster? How did Freedom Industries fail to meet its ethical obligations to the people of West Virginia?

Background

The Elk River spill was a significant disaster for the people of West Virginia, but it was hardly unique: It was the third chemical accident in the region within the preceding five years (Gabriel & Davenport, 2014). While startling, this statistic is not unusual when one considers West Virginia's unique relationship with the chemical industry.

West Virginia is famous for chemical manufacturing. Despite ranking 39th in overall gross domestic product (GDP) among states, West Virginia is nevertheless sixth in chemical manufacturing (U.S. Department of Commerce, 2016). The state is home to nearly 140 separate chemical companies employing more than 12,000 residents. Although West Virginia hosts many large chemical plants owned by global conglomerates such as Bayer, DuPont, and Dow, a significant portion of the West Virginia chemical industry is made up of smaller companies such as Freedom Industries (West Virginia Department of Commerce, 2016).

Founded in 1992 by Dennis Farrell and Carl L Kennedy II (Gutman, 2014), Freedom Industries was what is known as a "B2B SME." B2B ("business to business") refers to organizations that do sell products or services not directly to consumers but rather to other businesses. Because B2Bs work directly with other corporations, they seldom put much effort into reaching the general public through marketing, advertising, or public relations. Many B2Bs have few, if any, corporate communications personnel or programs.

An SME, meanwhile, is a "small and medium-sized enterprise." In the case of chemical manufacturing, SMEs are defined by employee count, and they can employ up to 1,500 workers. West Virginia's welcoming small business climate, its ready access to natural resources, and its relatively lax regulatory environment

(Davenport & Southall, 2014) have all contributed to significant growth of these SMEs, particularly in chemical manufacturing.

While SMEs contribute significantly to economic health (Coppa & Sriramesh, 2013), research also reveals that they are more than just smaller than their Fortune 500 counterparts. The differences include not only available resources, management values, and how they prioritize stakeholders, but also their ethics (Coppa & Sriramesh, 2013) and crisis response strategies (Zhang & Borden, 2015). Compared with Fortune 500 companies, SME business ethics are more easily influenced by the personal ethics and values of the owner (Quinn, 1997) and these companies are much less likely to engage in crisis response. These two factors came to the forefront during the Elk River Spill.

The Situation

At around 8:15 a.m. on January 9, 2014, the West Virginia Department of Environmental Protection (WVDEP) began to receive reports of a "strong licorice smell" (Manuel, 2014) in the Elk River area. When two WVDEP investigators first arrived at the source of the smell, a chemical tank farm owned by Freedom Industries, an employee assured them that there was no problem. When pressed further, the employee admitted that the company was dealing with a leak from tank 396. Realizing that the leak was only a few miles upstream from an inlet valve for the West Virginia American Water Company (WVAWC)'s water system (which included Charleston), the investigators insisted the employee report the leak to the WVDEP.

At the same time, the WVDEP contacted the WVAWC to warn them of the leak and order them to begin sampling their water for traces of MCHM. At around 4:30 p.m., the first traces of the chemical were discovered in treated water, according to a company spokesperson (Mistich, 2014). At 5:50 p.m., the company issued a "do not use" order on all water in the Kanawha Valley System, a call echoed by West Virginia governor Earl Ray Tomblin with the declaration of a "state of emergency" later that evening (Baxter, 2014).

The announcement spurred a run on bottled water as panicked residents sought to stock up for an indefinite ban on water use (Gabriel, 2014); it also allowed the state of West Virginia to request federal assistance. President Barack Obama declared a federal state of emergency, allowing the Centers for Disease Control and Prevention (CDC) to begin investigating the spill and the Federal Emergency Management Agency (FEMA) to begin supplying drinkable water to the citizens of West Virginia (Gabriel, 2014). Elsewhere, Governor Tomblin activated the West Virginia National Guard, allowing the army to begin supplying potable water by truck.

Yet, despite the flurry of activity elsewhere, Freedom Industries remained silent.

Concerned about the potential implications of exposure to MCHM, the frightened publics turned to government officials and first responders for answers.

They found few. Beyond the "do not use" order, local officials had little information to share with the public. Chemical safety testing is covered by the Toxic Substances Control Act of 1976 (TSCA). MCHM, however, was grandfathered into that system and therefore was never tested for its effects on the environment or human health (Kroh, 2014). CDC officials could only guess at what levels of exposure could be considered dangerous and as a result could not clearly inform the public of the risks posed by the chemical in the water and air.

As the CDC and spokespersons for the water company struggled to distribute accurate information to affected publics, Freedom Industries remained silent and retained the services of a public relations firm, Charles Ryan Associates. More than 24 hours after the initial report of the leak, Freedom Industries released a short statement at 3 p.m. and briefly met with the press on the evening of July 10. The statement summarized the situation but provided few specifics and no details about the health risks posed by MCHM (Freedom Industries, 2014). Freedom Industries president Gary Southern met with reporters outside of the corporate headquarters at around 5 p.m. that Friday night in what was to be a disastrous public relations misstep.

After more than a day with no information from the company responsible for the leak, the press and the public were desperate for answers. Southern had few to give. Even worse, the timeline of response that Southern gave did not fit with the one delivered by the WVDEP earlier in the day, generating distrust and undermining his credibility. Throughout the interview, Southern seemed distracted and distant and kept sipping from a bottle of water, seemingly rubbing in the "do not use" order. The nadir of the conference, however, came after about five minutes, when Southern attempted to leave, complaining that it had been an "extremely long day" and that he was "tired" (Freedom Industries president speaks to reporters, 2014).

The comment incited an explosion among frustrated and information-starved reporters. One headline ran, "Watch the CEO of Freedom Industries offend every West Virginian without water" (Essert, 2014). Quietly, Charles Ryan Associates dropped its newest client (PR representatives drop Freedom Industries, 2014).

Without the public relations firm pushing them to communicate to the public, Freedom Industries returned to silence. As the cleanup continued, the news media continued to unearth troubling new information about the embattled company. Several executives had served prison time or faced lawsuits for different legal violations (Gutman, 2014). The revelations of a history of ethical and legal failures by the management of Freedom Industries engendered further frustration, outrage, fear, and panic among the public.

Compounding the distrust were constant changes in the reports of the situation. The initially reported 1,500 gallons of MCHM leak was later estimated to be 7,500 gallons and then 10,000 gallons (Company increases chemical leak estimate, 2014). Given the conflicting reports between Freedom Industries and emergency officials, then conflicting reports from emergency officials themselves, West Virginians had no one to trust through the Elk River Spill.

On January 17, 2014, Freedom Industries quietly filed for bankruptcy in the midst of 30 lawsuits from local residents and businesses, putting the pending lawsuits on hold and leaving the government on the hook for the costs of the cleanup.

In October 2015, the bankruptcy of Freedom Industries was finalized. Under the settlement the company's remaining assets and insurance money would be used to pay for the cleanup, with any remaining money going to West Virginians affected by the Elk River Spill. However, the money Freedom Industries and its executives contributed represented just a fragment of the overall financial losses experienced by the community and couldn't even begin to address the physical, psychological, and emotional harm the spill had inflicted on the residents of the Kanawha Valley.

Outcomes

The declaration of bankruptcy by Freedom Industries in April 2014 insulated the company and its owners from financial liability for the spill, but it did not insulate them from legal responsibility. In December 2014, federal charges were filed against Southern and other top Freedom Industries executives for violations of the Clean Water and Refuse Acts (Department of Justice, 2016a). Four executives were indicted for their role in the chemical spill and two others were charged with the "information" violations to avoid the convocation of a grand jury (Department of Justice, 2016a).

The charges centered on four major violations:

1. Freedom Industries failed to properly maintain the containment area.
2. Freedom Industries failed to properly inspect tanks.
3. The company failed to develop and implement a spill prevention, control, and countermeasures plan.
4. The company failed to develop and implement a storm water pollution prevention plan and a groundwater protection plan, both required by federal law (Department of Justice, 2016a).

Despite the extensive charges, most Freedom Industries executives saw little to no jail time for their role in the disaster. President Gary Southern and CEO Dennis Farrell were the two exceptions, each sentenced to one month imprisonment (Aaron & Morris, 2016; Associated Press, 2016). Most Freedom Industry executives received both probation and monetary fines for their role in the disaster (Department of Justice, 2016b).

In March 2014, the MCHM containers at the Freedom Industries site were torn down as part of a West Virginia Department of Environmental Protection remediation plan to remove and decontaminate soils saturated with the MCHM (U.S. Chemical Safety and Hazard Investigation Board, 2016). In April 2014, the West Virginia government commissioned a law strengthening the regulations on aboveground storage tanks such as those at Freedom Industries' facilities on the Elk River (Howard, 2015).

However, while environmental restoration efforts have continued, little can replace West Virginian's shaken faith in the reliability of their water supply. For thousands of West Virginians still traumatized by the Elk River Spill, these improvements in industry regulation were too late to restore shattered trust. As one area resident reported more than a year after the spill, neither she nor her neighbors could yet trust the safety of the local water (Howard, 2015).

Despite changes in regulations governing chemical storage tanks, by January of the following year it had been discovered that around 1,100 storage tanks still did not meet regulatory requirements (Howard, 2015). Furthermore, research reveals that as of July 2016 MCHM was still not listed on the U.S. Environmental Protection Agency's Toxic Substances Control Act Substance Inventory (U.S. EPA, 2016), a central aspect of federal chemical regulation. MCHM's absence from the inventory was noted in the findings released by the U.S. Chemical Safety and Hazard Investigation Board (2016)'s analysis of the Elk River disaster. According to the board (2016, 99), MCHM is just one of more than 55,000 potentially hazardous chemicals absent from the inventory. Short of the adding these "grandfathered" chemicals to the inventory, there is little that regulators or the EPA can do to control the containment and usage of these chemicals. The decision to inform those at risk of exposure to these chemicals is purely at the discretion of the organizations and companies using them (U.S. Chemical Safety and Hazard Investigation Board, 2016).

Compounding the danger, few average citizens or even emergency responders have expertise in the potential health threats posed by chemical accidents. Often they may not be aware of their exposure at all, such as in Flint, Michigan. Although residents of Flint recognized the discoloration in their tap water after the city changed the source of its drinking water, few were aware that the discoloration was evidence of corrosion within the water system and the presence of highly toxic lead (Associated Press, 2015). Combined with silence or disavowals by civic leaders, few residents were aware of the serious risks present in their tap water (Lin, Rutter, & Park, 2016). This failure to respond exposed residents of Flint to highly toxic lead for years longer than was necessary or ethically acceptable.

In other cases, stakeholders may not be aware of the potential health risks of the chemical exposure. For example, it was only years after 9/11 that the health effects of the attacks came to be recognized. First responders such as firefighters, paramedics, and police officers were found to have significantly increased risks of a variety of cancers (Li et al., 2012) and impaired lung function (Grady, 2010) due to their exposure to the chemicals and toxins present in the dust released by the collapsing World Trade Center.

While the Elk River disaster is an extreme case, evidence suggests that Freedom Industries' behavior throughout the crisis recurs far too frequently within chemical crises. A lack of general expertise and a tendency of key voices to remain silent in the face of potentially hazardous chemical exposure can put stakeholders at far more risk than is necessary or ethically acceptable. Perhaps the Elk River Spill of 2014 was unavoidable; certainly, an unlikely confluence of factors and failures contributed to the disaster. However, the failure of Freedom Industries executives to meet their ethical obligations to the people of West Virginia was easily avoidable. This failure exemplified an all-too-frequent tendency for communicators in chemical crises to expose stakeholders to unnecessary risk through silence.

References

Aaron, B. & Morris, J. (2016). Ex-Freedom Industries executive Farrell receives 30 days in jail, $20,000 fine. *Wchstv.com*. Retrieved from http://wchstv.com/news/local/ex-executive-dennis-farrell-due-for-sentencing-in-wv-chemical-spill-thursday.

Associated Press. (2015). Flint city councilman: "We got bad water." *Detroit Free Press*. Retrieved from http://www.freep.com/story/news/local/michigan/2015/01/14/flint-water-resident-complaints/21743465/.

Associated Press. (2016). Former president of Freedom Industries sentenced to 1 month in prison for chemical spill. *WSAZ.com*. Retrieved from http://www.wsaz.com/content/news/Gary-Southern-to-be-sentenced-Wednesday-in-chemical-spill-case-369106801.html.

Baxter, A. (2014, January). W.Va. Gov. issues state of emergency for 9 counties, water ban for 100,000+. *WSAZ News Channel*. Retrieved from http://www.wsaz.com/news/headlines/Firefighters-Investigating-Strong-Smell-in-Kanawha-Valley--239434751.html.

Company increases chemical leak estimate. (2014, January). *Charleston Gazette*. Retrieved from http://www.wvha.org/Media/NewsScan/2014/January/1-28-Company-increases-chemical-leak-estimate.aspx.

Coppa, M., & Sriramesh, K. (2013). Corporate social responsibility among SMEs in Italy. *Public Relations Review, 39*, 30–39.

Davenport, C., & Southall, A. (2014, January). Critics say spill highlights lax West Virginia regulations. *New York Times*. Retrieved from http://www.nytimes.com/2014/01/13/us/critics-say-chemical-spill-highlights-lax-west-virginia-regulations.html.

Department of Justice. (2016a). Freedom Industries officials indicted in January chemical spill. Retrieved from https://www.justice.gov/opa/pr/freedom-industries-officials-indicted-january-chemical-spill.

Department of Justice. (2016b). Freedom Industries and former Freedom Industries plant manager sentenced for roles in chemical spill. Retrieved from https://www.justice.gov/usao-sdwv/pr/freedom-industries-and-former-freedom-industries-plant-manager-sentenced-roles-chemical.

Essert, M. (2014, January). Watch the CEO of Freedom Industries offend every West Virginian without water. *Policy Mic*. Retrieved from https://mic.com/articles/78899/watch-the-ceo-of-freedom-industries-offend-every-west-virginian-without-water#.uF8Uhw32C.

Field, A., Edwards, M., & Soichet, C. E. (2014, January 13). West Virginia chemical spill shines spotlight on loose regulation. *CNN*. Retrieved from http://www.cnn.com/2014/01/13/us/west-virigina-chemical-contamination/.

Freedom Industries. (2014). Freedom Industries issues statement on West Virginia chemical leak. *PR News Wire*. Retrieved from http://www.prnewswire.com/news-releases/freedom-industries-issues-statement-on-west-virginia-chemical-leak-239652971.html.

Freedom Industries president speaks to reporters. (2014). *WCHS & WVAH TV*. Retrieved from https://www.youtube.com/watch?v=hAGixCOj8bg.

Gabriel, T. (2014, January). Thousands without water after spill in West Virginia. *New York Times*. Retrieved from http://www.nytimes.com/2014/01/11/us/west-virginia-chemical-spill.html.

Gabriel, T., & Davenport, C. (2014, January). Calls for oversight in West Virginia went unheeded. *New York Times*. Retrieved from http://www.nytimes.com/2014/01/14/us/ban-on-tap-water-being-lifted-in-west-virginia.html?_r=0.

Grady, D. (2010, April). Lung function of 9/11 rescuers fell, study finds. *New York Times*. Retrieved from http://www.nytimes.com/2010/04/08/nyregion/08lung.html?src=m&_r=0.

Gutman, D. (2014, January). Freedom Industries execs are longtime colleagues. *Charleston Gazette-Mail*. Retrieved from http://www.sundaygazettemail.com/Ncws/201401100119?page=2&build=cache.

Howard, B. C. (2015, January). A year after West Virginia chemical spill, some signs of safer water. *National Geographic*. Retrieved from http://news.nationalgeographic.com/news/2015/01/150109-west-virginia-chemical-spill-water-quality-regulations-environment/.

Kroh, K. (2014, February). The complete guide to everything that's happened since the massive chemical spill in West Virginia. *Climate Progress*. Retrieved from http://thinkprogress.org/climate/2014/02/09/3196981/chemical-spill-timeline/.

Li, J., Cone, J., Kahn, A., Brackbill, R., Farfel, M., Greene, C., Hadler, J., Stayner, L., & Stellman, S. (2012). Association between World Trade Center exposure and excess cancer risk. *Journal of American Medical Association*, *308*(23), 2479–2488.

Lin, J. C. F., Rutter, J., & Park, H. (2016). Events that led to Flint's water crisis. *New York Times*. Retrieved from http://www.nytimes.com/interactive/2016/01/21/us/flint-lead-water-timeline.html?_r=0.

Manuel, J. (2014). Crisis and emergency risk communication: Lessons from the Elk River Spill. *Environmental Health Perspectives, 122*(8), A215–A219. Retrieved from http://ehp.niehs.nih.gov/122-a214/.

Mistich, D. (2014, July). Five things from West Virginia American Water's testimony to the PSC regarding the Elk River Spill. *West Virginia Public Broadcasting*. Retrieved from http://wvpublic.org/post/five-things-west-virginia-american-waters-testimony-psc-regarding-elk-river-spill.

PR representatives drop Freedom Industries. (2014). *WSAZ News Channel*. Retrieved from http://www.wsaz.com/home/headlines/PR-Representatives-Drop-Freedom-Industries-239821611.html.

Quinn, J. J. (1997). Personal ethics and business ethics: The ethical attitudes of owner/managers of small business. *Journal of Business Ethics*, *16*(2), 119–127.

U.S. Chemical Safety and Hazard Investigation Board. (2016). Investigation report: Chemical spill contaminates public water supply in Charleston, West Virginia. Retrieved from http://www.csb.gov/assets/1/19/Freedom_Industries_Report.pdf.

U.S. Department of Commerce. (2016). Regional economic accounts. Retrieved from http://www.bea.gov.

U.S. Environmental Protection Agency. (2016). TSCA Chemical Substance Inventory. Retrieved from https://www.epa.gov/tsca-inventory.

Ward, K. (2014). DEP inspectors describe early scene at Freedom leak site. *Charleston Gazette-Mail*. Retrieved from http://www.wvgazettemail.com/News/201401130118.

West Virginia Department of Commerce. (2016). Chemical industry sites. Retrieved from http://www.wvcommerce.org/business/topsites/colocation.aspx.

Zhang, X., & Borden, J. (2015, August). *Ethical Approaches to Crisis Communication in Chemical Crises: A Content Analysis of Media Coverage of Chemical Crises from 2010 to 2014*. Poster presented at the Annual Conference of Association for Education in Journalism and Mass Communication, San Francisco, CA.

Discussion Questions

1. Crises that threaten the public health, such as exposure to the chemical MCHM in the Elk River case, create extreme emotions. What can crisis communicators do to ensure that the risk to public health is minimized during chemical crises?

2. What are some of the emotions that people may have experienced in the Freedom Industries case?

3. Can those emotions be generalized to other crises as well? How can public relations practitioners help publics deal with these emotions?

4. If you were the owner/manager of Freedom Industries, what would you have done differently?

5. Do you feel that the public relations firm that Freedom Industries hired behaved ethically and in accordance with the principles set forth by the PRSA? If you had been the firm hired to represent Freedom Industries, would you have proceeded differently? How so?

6. Chemical crises such as the Elk River Spill can be environmental disasters and require massive, collaborative efforts to clean up. In the case of Elk River, it seemed like Freedom Industries, the CDC, and local authorities couldn't work together and didn't communicate consistent information to the public. What steps can companies and the government take to make sure they are speaking with one voice after a disaster? How could we do better in the future?

MAINTAINING THE PUBLIC TRUST: A TOWN MEETING
ABOUT RISING NATURAL GAS PRICES

Mary Beth Reese, M.B.A., *University of Southern Indiana,*
and Erin E. Gilles, Ph.D., *University of Southern Indiana*

This case study showcases the daily ethical decisions, political implications, regulatory impact, and professional decision-making involved in a routine event for a public relations practitioner working for an energy utility. Rather than responding to a major, unexpected crisis, this case study describes the process of planning and strategizing for an important, preplanned public forum. Four Midwestern utilities participated in the forum:

- **Utility A:** Investor-owned natural gas company
- **Utility B:** Municipal-owned natural gas company
- **Utility C:** Natural gas transmission company (supplier)
- **Utility D:** Municipal-owned natural gas company

The primary focus of this case study is on Utility A, a publicly traded utility providing customers with natural gas and electricity. Approximately 80% of the consumers in their service area use natural gas to heat their homes, cook their food, and heat their water. A smaller percentage of the customers heat their homes with electricity. Natural gas is a major energy source in the United States: 27.5 trillion cubic feet of natural gas was consumed in 2015 (U.S. Energy Information Administration, 2016).

Background

The events in this case study occurred when natural gas prices were escalating so significantly that the issue came to the attention of legislators, governors, regulatory agencies, and consumers. It was a national, state, regional, and local issue. Natural gas is used (1) to heat residential homes, (2) as a fuel source to generate electricity, and (3) for commercial energy, especially in the restaurant business. Increased natural gas costs meant that the prices of many consumer goods would also increase, as businesses raised their prices to offset higher production costs. The rate increases were most problematic among low-income households, forcing them to choose between paying for either utilities or housing costs and food. Monthly natural gas heating bills averaged $150 to $200 and increased by approximately $80 to $100. The governor mandated that the Utility Regulatory Commission conduct public meetings to address public concerns and share information about low-income heating programs. Three natural gas utility companies serving different regions in the area participated, along with the natural gas supplier for the three utilities.

The natural gas utilities are monopolies, so consumers cannot switch if they dislike the utility's policies, prices, or customer service. Natural gas is measured by units of 100 compressed cubic feet (ccf). The utility bill is based on the units of gas used, which are billed according to rate blocks. Rate blocks are the costs assigned to each level of usage. For instance, consumers using 300 ccf would pay a different rate per ccf than consumers using 800 ccf in a billing cycle. However, there are also extra costs, such as service fees, meter fees, and the quarterly adjustment. The utility buys the natural gas from a transmission supplier at a fluctuating market cost, which is adjusted quarterly and passed on to the consumer. Quarterly adjustments are based on last quarter's gas costs, so they do not reflect current costs. The complexity of the quarterly adjustment calculations frustrated consumers, who thought the regulatory agency was conspiring with the utilities to keep the prices high.

Utility A owns a natural gas storage facility, allowing it to buy natural gas when the cost is lower (traditionally during the non-heating season); it then uses the surplus of natural gas to reduce the cost of natural gas for the consumer during the heating months. The storage facility has limited capacity, however, so it has only a minimal role in reducing costs. Natural gas storage fields are usually formed by nature, meaning that expanding or building a new storage facility is not feasible. Utilities B, C, and D did not have storage fields to help offset the impact of price fluctuations.

Customer complaints were escalating, and the answers given by the local utility providers did not reduce consumer anger. Emotions won out over logic. Utility A tried to explain to consumers the process of setting the natural gas prices, but many complicated factors are involved. Some of these factors are the processing and labor costs for natural gas collection, utility regulations, supplier and delivery charges, natural gas storage costs, individual usage patterns, weather conditions, market pricing fluctuations, and the energy efficiency of dwellings, heating units, and appliances. Consumers had no control over the bill, aside from reducing their usage levels or adding insulation, replacing window and doors, caulking, and purchasing higher-efficiency appliances and heating/cooling units. These measures were often costly for homeowners, and renters were left at the mercy of landlords to make such changes.

One option for these households is the Low-Income Home Energy Assistance Program (LIHEAP), offered by the U.S. government. In 2014, $2.8 billion was allocated across the 50 states to help low-income residents pay their home energy bills, energy crises, weatherization, and minor home repairs. Eligibility included living in nonsubsidized housing and not receiving a utility disconnect notice (LIHEAP, 2014).

Not all eligible households participate in the low-income assistance program because individuals must apply to receive the benefits, and many elderly and low-income families did not know how and where to apply. Recipients must provide proof of income and proof of residence; in some states, a program administrator makes a home visit. There is no guarantee that applications will be approved, and disconnect/reconnect fees, which can exceed $100, are not always covered (LIHEAP, 2014).

The Situation

The public meeting included four major cities in the region, with the media invited to cover the meeting. The local public television station agreed to host the meeting and allow for call-in questions and comments. A panel was formed with the Utility Regulatory Commission, the Office of the Consumer Commission, the natural gas transmission supplier, and a representative from the governor's office. Four utilities were invited to attend the meeting and prepare to answer questions from both the panel and the public. Local government officials, the mayor, and the public attended the open forum at the television station.

After being contacted by the local public TV station and invited to speak at the public meeting, which would be televised live, PR practitioners representing Utilities A and B met and discussed individual and collective strategies for the public forum. They spoke about the issues their companies were experiencing with customers, regulatory agencies, and customer cutoff policies due to past-due bills. State regulatory agencies prevented the shutoff of services for nonpayment if the temperature was below 32 degrees Fahrenheit. This was a humanitarian measure to prevent customers from freezing during the winter. This year, winter was causing record-setting cold temperatures.

Next, PR practitioners from all four utilities met to discuss their three primary concerns about the forum. First, they agreed that the public meeting had the potential to develop into a tumultuous situation and could increase the consumer backlash they were already experiencing. The second concern was that the state and the regulatory commission, plus the Consumer Council Commission (representing the consumer), would be at the meeting taking the information back to the governor's office. The third concern was that this was a public meeting televised live with an audience of consumers and call-in questions from listeners. Upset callers could be unpredictable and difficult to handle. Each utility agreed on an open, honest approach to providing answers to the consumers while building a basis of education about the process and the rules governing how natural gas bills are determined.

Following the meeting, each public relations practitioner began preparations for the forum. Utility A's PR practitioner worked with the entire office staff to develop visual charts and graphs, Q & As, documents for reference, sample gas bills, and charts to show the cost of gas, weather trends, and usage patterns. Materials were developed to address the various publics, including the governor's office, regulatory agencies, media, consumers, legislators, employees, shareholders, and the general public. A tremendous amount of information was reviewed and compiled in an attempt to increase consumers' understanding. The more documents that could be assembled to describe the pricing patterns, the better the chance of increasing consumers' understanding.

A news conference was called by Utility A one week before the community forum due to the increase in media inquiries from the local press for individual interviews. This news conference was used to distribute a media kit that included the news release, backgrounder, FAQ, fact sheet, and charts of gas costs. In addition, a special newsletter was written to share similar information with employees. In the month preceding the forum, flyers were enclosed in utility bills to communicate the gas price increase to customers. Additional training for the customer service department was developed to reinforce and align with the public relations messages when customers called in with questions.

After a week of intense planning, it was time for the live public forum hosted by the local public TV station. Additional members of the media were also invited to cover the meeting. Media interviews focused on the regulatory representatives from the state agencies and the panel of representatives from the regional utilities. Each utility prepared and presented a 5- to 7-minute introduction of the issue. Once the utility presentations concluded, the floor was open for questions from the audience in the room and from call-ins. Needless to say, customer calls were charged with emotion and included stories of families, especially those with low or fixed incomes, making difficult choices. Many faced being shut off by the utility for nonpayment, and they would later incur reconnect fees when they paid off their overdue balance. This caused additional financial strain.

Some of the sentiments expressed by consumers during the forum revealed the amount of anger they had toward the utilities. Some thought the utilities were making excuses for the price increase. Others contended that the utilities were a big, bad business making money from the little guy. Some consumers said they felt as though the utilities could do whatever they wanted without repercussion. Despite the outcry, representatives from the utilities were able to calmly respond to each query while adhering to the PRSA Code of Ethics.

Consumer confusion increased during the forum when one of the four utilities changed its tactics, despite the preplanning by the four utilities. The PR practitioner at Utility B stated during the public forum that its gas price had slightly declined in the last three months (based on natural gas per-unit costs). He announced this at the public forum, which made his utility look good but increased pressure on the other utilities. Reporters asked why everyone else' s costs were rising if Utility B's costs declined, especially since Utilities A, C, and D presented the increase as a national trend. In actuality, Utility B's customers saw a slight decrease in their bills because Utility B had overestimated the cost of gas in the previous three months; the most recent three-month natural gas cost reflected a decrease because of the reconciliation of the cost. During the forum, Utility A's PR practitioner asked Utility B's PR practitioner whether its previous overcharge for natural gas accounted for the slight decline in gas prices. Ultimately, Utility B's representative admitted during the forum that this was the case.

Two ethical issues arose before the public forum. Utility A's vice president of communications demanded that the PR practitioner place the blame on the transmission company. The VP wanted to portray this as a fixed cost that had to be passed along to the customer. The PR practitioner disagreed with this approach, due to PRSA guidelines (PRSA, 2016). Choosing whether to blame another entity or to explain how the price increase was based on multiple, complex factors presented an ethical dilemma. Should the PR practitioner follow the mandates of management or maintain transparency? Ultimately, the PR practitioner decided not to shift the blame to the transmission company.

In another moment of conflict with management, Utility A's CEO insisted that the PR practitioner state that the increase was 40%. The PR practitioner did not agree with this strategy because it oversimplified the increase, which would vary by customer. Moreover, as it was almost spring, heating bills would soon be lower. As the PR practitioner predicted, journalists focused on that number, and many headlines declared a 40% increase. This news coverage displeased the CEO, despite the fact that he had failed to heed the advice of his PR counsel.

Outcomes

A public TV studio was the venue used for the meeting, and journalists from regional radio stations, TV stations, and newspapers attended. Newspaper headlines focused mainly on the 40% natural gas increase. While the stories were mostly accurate, there were some inaccuracies due to the confusion that even some of the journalists had with the formulas used to compute the utility bills. Interviews were scheduled with the State Utility Regulatory Commission and the Consumer Counselor's Office asking for a review of the public meeting. Individual interviews with each utility were conducted at the end of the public meeting. Overall, the message was shared with the public, even if the public did not like the message. From a political standpoint, the governor wanted the citizens of the state to see him as a caring advocate for the citizens by addressing their concerns in a public meeting. Therefore, this meeting gave a platform for the consumer's voice and forced the utilities to address the issue in a broader forum.

Media impressions, informal feedback from opinion leaders, and qualitative data were collected from consumers were analyzed after the public forum to evaluate the outcome. The media impressions were bolstered by the multiday coverage of the forum as the lead story by every news outlet in the region. Positive feedback from the governor's office, the State Utility Regulatory Commission, and the state Consumer Counselor's Office recognized the efforts of the PR staff and praised the effectiveness of the visual aids. Feedback from the customer service call department indicated that the call volume had temporarily declined, which indicated that consumers' knowledge about the natural gas rate increase had increased. Internal evaluations by the CEO and upper management were positive. In addition, utility colleagues complimented the PR department on the excellent representation of the company and the ability to deftly handle the tough questions.

References

Low-Income Home Energy Assistance Program (LIHEAP). (2014). LIHEAP 2014 initial CR release of LIHEAP block grant funds. Retrieved from http://www.acf.hhs.gov/ programs/ocs/programs/liheap.

Public Relations Society of America (PRSA). (2016). Member Code of Ethics. Retrieved from https://www.prsa.org/ aboutprsa/ethics/ codeenglish#. V46V8ZMrK3c.

U.S. Energy Information Administration. (2016, April). Independent Statistics & Analysis: Frequently Asked Questions. Retrieved from https://www.eia.gov/tools/faqs /faq.cfm?id=50&t=8.

Discussion Questions

1. If you were a PR practitioner engaged by one of the utility companies in this case study, how would you tailor your message to the audience? Who is the primary target audience? What are the demographic and geographic points to consider, as well as psychographics? How would you manage communication with the governor and the two state regulatory agencies?
2. Considering the PRSA value of transparency, how would you prepare the audience for the continued increases in the price of natural gas? Should you tell the audience that the cost of natural gas in the market is predicted to continue to increase? Would you mention the 40% increase?
3. What information needs to be shared with others in the company and which departments need to have the same information to answer consumer questions? Which players in the company will review the information for the meeting? What is the estimated preparation time needed for reviews and edits?
4. Identify and discuss at least four PRSA Codes of Professional Behavior applicable to the situation outlined in this case study.
5. In the era of digital technology, how would you engage those on social media or those who are streaming the event? What financial and human resources would be needed to use digital technology? What policies should be considered?

SHIFTING BLAME: ADDRESSING THE MICHIGAN DEPARTMENT OF ENVIRONMENTAL QUALITY'S COMPLICATED ETHICAL RESPONSIBILITY IN THE FLINT WATER CRISIS

Catherine J. Bruns, M.A., *James Madison University*

In April 2014, the town of Flint, Michigan, temporarily switched its water source to the Flint River in a last-ditch attempt to reduce city expenses (Lin, Rutter & Park, 2016). Shortly after, uneasy residents began complaining of an odd color and taste in their tap water, prompting concerns of bacterial contamination (Lin et al, 2016). Test results conducted the following year determined that the town' s corrosive pipelines were leaching contaminants, including lead, into the public water supply (Seville, Rappleye, & Connor, 2016). For months, government agencies and officials brushed off community panic over environmental and health risks, assuring residents that any potential contamination levels were still safe (Sevile, et al, 2016). However, the lies came crashing down in early 2016, when President Barack Obama declared a state of emergency in Flint and its surrounding county—a federal acknowledgement of a long-brewing catastrophe (Lin et al., 2016).

As the battle for clean water rages on, investigations into the Flint water crisis have come to question just how much local and state organizations knew about the abnormal contamination levels. One player in particular, the Michigan Department of Environmental Quality (MDEQ), has received intense criticism for failing to investigate or issue a public health warning in a timely manner, acts that could have prevented the poisoning of thousands of Michigan residents. Yet the involvement, or lack thereof, of a multitude of organizations has complicated the situation by reducing the public' s ability to discern who is to blame and lessening demand for retribution from the MDEQ specifically. As a result, a key contributor to the Flint crisis has largely succeeded in evading ethical accountability for one of the largest health and environmental disasters in U.S. history.

Background

The MDEQ evolved out of Executive Order No. 1995-18 in order to address a growing number of environmental management issues in Michigan (Department of Environmental Quality, 2018b). Most notably, the order reorganized the Michigan Department of Natural Resources (MDNR), which had previously been charged with regulation of the state's environmental programs, and shifted regulation of the state's environmental programs to the MDEQ (Department of Environmental Quality, 2018b).

In the years following the MDEQ' s establishment, the department was also charged with managing drinking water-related programs and collaborating with the newly created Water Quality Advisory Board, a long-term water quality monitoring program responsible for measuring the quality of Michigan water sources (Department of Environmental Quality, 2018b). As of 2018, the MDEQ also houses six divisions, including the Drinking Water and Municipal Assistance and the Water Resources Divisions (Michigan Department of Environmental Quality, 2018).

The MDEQ's mission promotes an organizational dedication to the "wise management of Michigan's air, land, and water resources to support a sustainable environment, healthy communities, and vibrant economy" (Department of Environmental Quality, 2018a, para. 1). To further this mission, the Department is guided by three principles: to be "leaders in environmental stewardship, partners in economic development, and providers of excellent customer service" (Department of Environmental Quality, 2018a, para. 2). In addition, the MDEQ also pursues several strategic goals that aim to counteract previous negative environmental impacts, increase conservation efforts, and improve the ecological future of the state of Michigan (Department of Environmental Quality, 2018a). Most relevant to this case study are objectives related to the protection of public health, the implementation of Michigan's Water Strategy, and the improvement of water resource quality (Department of Environmental Quality, 2018a, para. 3).

When tests of the Flint water supply were initially conducted, the MDEQ was led by Dan Wyant, who had served as director since 2011 (Eggert, 2016). Following media coverage scrutinizing the department' s mismanagement of Flint, Wyant resigned, leaving the MDEQ in the temporary leadership of MDNR Director Keith Creagh (Eggert, 2016) until Heidi Grether's appoinment by Michigan governor Rick Snyder in August 2016 (Department of Environmental Quality, 2016).

The Situation

In April 2013, Flint's new state-appointed emergency manager, Jerry Ambrose, signed an agreement to switch the town' s water supply from the Detroit Water and Sewage Department (DWSD) to the Karegnondi Water Authority (KWA) (Seville et al., 2016). The change was intended as a cost-saving measure that would enable the city to control its water prices better than it could with DWSD (Dixon, 2016). At the time, KWA was working on a new pipeline that would connect Flint and its neighboring communities to a water supply in Lake Huron (Seville et al., 2016). However, because the KWA project would not be completed for years, in April 2014 the city temporarily shifted its water supply to the Flint River (Dixon, 2016). That same month, Flint residents began complaining that the taste, color, and odor of their water was unusual, and some reported the appearance of rashes (Lin et al., 2016).

In October 2014, the MDEQ responded to Flint residents' grievances after the presence of coliform bacteria was confirmed in the city's tap water (Lin et al., 2016). Yet instead of further investigating, the MDEQ attributed the issues to a recent spell of cold weather, the general aging of pipelines, and a declining population (Lin et al., 2016). Despite continued public reports of water-related problems and an offer from DWSD to waive Flint's $4 million reconnection fee and switch the town back to its former water supply at no charge, the city continued to receive water from the Flint River (Lin et al., 2016).

After protests erupted outside Flint City Hall in January 2015, the U.S. Environmental Protection Agency (EPA) informed Michigan state officials that the toxic contaminants leaching into Flint's water system were indeed a result of the chemical makeup of the Flint River water, confirming many residents' worst fears (Seville et al., 2016). Unfortunately, per EPA water regulations, the contamination level was not yet high enough to legally require action on the part of the MDEQ, even though an EPA expert noted that testing procedures may have actually underestimated lead levels (Lin et al., 2016). Undeterred by this information, the MDEQ remained uninvolved in the quickly escalating problem (Lin et al., 2016).

As reports of high lead levels in Flint homes rose throughout the spring, the MDEQ still refused to act (Lin et al., 2016). In July 2015, Governor Snyder became entangled in the problem when his chief of staff emailed the Michigan Department of Health and Human Services (MDHHS) to express personal concern for the people of Flint (Seville et al., 2016). However, the MDHHS also did not investigate, responding instead that the rising lead levels were a "seasonal anomaly" (Seville et al., 2016, para. 18). Over the summer, the MDEQ instructed the city of Flint to "optimize corrosion control" in its pipelines, yet as late as September 2015, MDEQ and Michigan state regulators remained adamant that the water itself was still safe (Lin et al., 2016, para. 16).

In October 2015, the situation spiraled out of control when the state government's validations of lead concerns prompted city officials to urge Flint residents to stop drinking their tap water (Lin et al., 2016). The water advisory soon expanded to include cooking and bathing, and halfway through the month, the city reconnected to DWSD and ceased receiving water from the Flint River entirely (Lin et al., 2016). On October 19, 2015—after more than a year of ignoring local protests and condemnations—MDEQ Director Dan Wyant publicly acknowledged that the department had used unsuitable federal protocol for corrosion control, thus contributing to the rising lead levels (Lin et al., 2016).

National coverage of Flint skyrocketed as the media began formally labeling the issue a crisis. In December, Flint increased its corrosion controls and officially declared a citywide emergency (Seville et al., 2016). Governor Snyder rang in 2016 by declaring Flint a state of emergency (Seville et al., 2016) and President Obama soon expanded the call to Flint's surrounding county, enabling the Federal Emergency Management Agency (FEMA) to provide millions in financial assistance and send free bottled water, filters, and testing kits to the area (Lin et al., 2016). On January 20, 2016, the Michigan House of Representatives approved a request from Governor Snyder for an additional $28 million in aid (Lin et al., 2016).

Public Outrage and MDEQ Response

Public response to the crisis in Flint was vigorous and hostile. Social media networks erupted with #FlintWaterCrisis and protests began at the Michigan state capitol, where citizens demanded the resignation of Governor Snyder (Lawler, 2016). As news reports investigated how dangerous lead levels could have been denied for so long, claims of environmental racism alleged the delay was because Flint was a predominately poor, African-American town (Eligon, 2016). The crisis became further politicized by the 2016 presidential candidates, many of whom journeyed to Flint to assist with water distribution and brought attention to the disaster on the debate stage (Kutsch, Taylor, & Pizzi, 2016). However, the question of who was to blame for the tragedy in Flint remained.

One of the largest perceived culprits in the disastrous handling of the water crisis was the MDEQ. On December 29, 2015, the Flint Water Advisory Task Force, an investigatory group initiated by Governor Snyder, released a statement admonishing the MDEQ and its role in the crisis, asserting:

> We believe the primary responsibility for what happened in Flint rests with the Michigan Department of Environmental Quality (MDEQ). Although many individuals and entities at state and local levels contributed to creating and prolonging the problem, MDEQ is the government agency that has the responsibility to ensure safe drinking water in Michigan. It failed in that responsibility and must be held accountable for that failure. (Davis et al., 2015, para. 5)

Prominent community members and public figures also questioned the MDEQ's ethical practices while handling the crisis. Laura L. Sullivan, a professor at Kettering University in Flint, was quoted in *PolitiFact* as saying, "As a Flint citizen and as one of the activists who fought to raise awareness regarding water quality in Flint, I witnessed firsthand a reluctance to address citizen concerns by staff of the Michigan Department of Environmental Quality" (Jacobson, 2016, para. 22). Famous political activist Erin Brockovich (2015) posted a Michigan news article to her public Facebook page with the caption, "MDEQ, Michigan Department of Environmental Quality . . . an organization who's [sic] name bring [sic] mistrust and dishonesty. What will they do to fix it?" In his May 16 speech at Northwestern High School in Flint, President Obama remarked:

> The bad news is that this should not have happened in the first place. And even though the scope of the response looks sort of like the efforts we're used to seeing after a natural disaster, that's not what this was. This was a manmade disaster. This was avoidable. This was preventable.

The MDEQ launched into crisis mode. In an effort to appease increasingly vicious publics following the Task Force's statement in late December 2015, Director Wyant and his spokesperson, Brad Wurfel, resigned (Kennedy, 2016) and Governor Snyder appointed Keith Creagh as interim head (Egan, 2015). The MDEQ also began to revamp its website, adding sections for Flint updates and providing contact information for those directly affected. In typical crisis management and image repair protocol, the department also made efforts to cooperate with governmental investigations and demonstrate compassion for the crisis it had contributed to.

Yet less than a month after undergoing these changes, the state of Michigan, including the MDEQ, was blasted by the EPA for its "inadequate transparency and accountability with regard to provision of test results and actions taken" and its continued slow response to the Flint crisis (McCarthy, 2016, para. 3). Director Creagh (2016) responded with a scathing retort, claiming that the agency's complaints ignored ongoing crisis initiatives such as the provision of water testing kits, filters, and medical care for residents. In the emailed address, Creagh contended:

> although the Order states that the State has failed to take adequate measures or comply with the USEPA's demands, to our knowledge, the State has complied with every recent demand or request made by the USEPA . . . From a legal perspective, we also question whether the USEPA has the legal authority to order a State and its agencies to take the actions outlined in the Order. (Creagh, 2016, para. 4)

Unfortunately, some interpreted the MDEQ's response as an attempt to diminish the severity of the events in Flint, shift the blame, and reduce direct ethical responsibility. When many would have acknowledged the critical mistake through apology or brainstormed additional ways to expedite the delivery of aid to residents and communities struggling to recover, the MDEQ prioritized its own victimization and sought instead to remind the EPA that it was at least taking some action to resolve the matter. To those still without drinking water or facing serious health conditions, the lack of remorse was troubling.

In June 2016, the MDEQ released a summary of its actions since admitting to the mishandling of Flint. In addition to providing extensive financial support to the affected area, the department revised its water testing procedures to a five-prong approach involving residences, schools, blood levels, food service establishments, and sentinel sampling (Michigan Department of Environmental Quality, 2016). The report also noted increased training and monetary support, improved partnerships with organizations such as the MDHHS and the Michigan Department of Education (MDE), and extensive multilingual community outreach campaigns and events to increase awareness of lead exposure (Michigan Department of Environmental Quality, 2016). Though response efforts continue, public interest in Flint has faded away, and with it, the pressure for change within the MDEQ.

A Clearer Future?

Even now, the long-term implications of the Flint water crisis remain unclear. Though the MDEQ has taken steps to become a more transparent and responsive organization, questions remain regarding its ownership of blame and willingness to revamp internal ethical practices.

One such example is the MDEQ's appointment of new leadership, which was a vital opportunity to appease public opinion and speak to the oranization's more ethical future. Unfortunately, the transition from Creagh to current director Grether was anything but smooth, and Grether's long-held previous position at BP has prompted significant controversy due to her association with a separate environmental disaster: the 2010 Deepwater Horizon oil spill (Eggert, 2016). Rather than use the transition to reemphasize MDEQ's key principles of environmental stewardship, economic initiatives, and customer service, Grether's appointment caused another public relations nightmare—an additional crisis that the MDEQ cannot afford.

MDEQ's dedication to public engagement in environmental decision making processes has also been questioned: In January 2017, the EPA accused the department of failing to address and encourage minority participation in public dialogues related to the placement of a chemical plant (Warikoo, 2017b). In a 35-page letter, the EPA asserted that the MDEQ discriminated against Flint's African-American communities nearly 24 years ago when it constructed the Genesee Power Station, a wood-fired plant in Flint that spewed lead and other pollutants into the air (Warikoo, 2017a). Although the EPA did not call for the still-burning plant be shut down, the allegation contributes to ongoing claims that MDEQ's commitment to human and environmental rights stops short of including the voices of the underprivileged (Warikoo, 2017a).

Much action has taken place since Flint residents' first complaints in 2014. Two lawsuits have been filed against companies involved in the crisis and nine city and state officials now face criminal charges (Kennedy, 2016). Yet the complicated issue of blame remains: "This was a failure of government at all levels," stated Governor Snyder in testimony before the House Committee on Oversight and Government Reform, continuing, "Local, state and federal officials – we all failed the families of Flint" (Kennedy, 2016, para. 50). As long as Flint's narrative includes confusion over the many entities responsible for the crisis, the MDEQ's ability to evade ethical accountability in future environmental injustices remains all but sealed.

References

Brockovich, E. (2015, December 20). MDEQ Flint involvement. [Facebook post]. Retrieved from https://www.facebook.com/ErinBrockovichOfficial/posts/1015 6322049535494.

Creagh, K. (2016, January 22). Emergency administrative order, Michigan Department of Environmental Quality. Retrieved from https://www.epa.gov/sites/production/files/2016-01/documents/mdeq-response_0.pdf.

Davis, M., Kolb, C., Reynolds, L., Rothstein, E., & Sikkema, K. (2015, December 29). Flint Water Advisory Task Force Snyder letter. Retrieved from http://flintwaterstudy.org/wp-content/uploads/2015/12/FWATF-Snyder-Letter-12-29-15.pdf.

Department of Environmental Quality. (2016, August). Meet the Director. Retrieved from http://www.michigan.gov/deq/0,4561,7-135-3306_70582-391508-00.html.

Department of Environmental Quality. (2018a). DEQ mission. Retrieved from http://www.michigan.gov/deq/0,4561,7-135-3306_70582-276848-00.html.

Department of Environmental Quality. (2018b). History of DEQ. Retrieved from http://www.michigan.gov/deq/0,4561,7-135-3306_70582-13142-00.html.

Dixon, J. (2016, February 28). Q&A: How things went wrong in Flint water crisis. *Detroit Free Press*. Retrieved from http://www.freep.com/story/news/local/michigan/flint-watercrisis/2016/02/28/flint-water-crisis-began/81010314/.

Egan, P. (2015, December 30). Snyder names DNR chief Keith Creagh to head DEQ. *Detroit Free Press*. Retrieved from http://www.freep.com/story/news/local/michigan/2015/12/30/snyder-names-keith-creagh-head-deq/78068188/.

Eggert, D. (2016, August 10). DEQ head says lobbying past doesn't define her. *The Detroit News*. Retrieved from http://www.detroitnews.com/story/news/local/michigan/2016/08/10/heidi-grether-deqcriticism/88545998/.

Eligon, J. (2016, January 21). A question of environmental racism in Flint. *New York Times*. Retrieved from https://www.nytimes.com/2016/01/22/us/a-question-of-environmental-racism-in-flint.html.

Jacobson, L. (2016, February 15). Who's to blame for the Flint water crisis? *PolitiFact*. Retrieved from http://www.politifact.com/truth-o-meter/article/2016/feb/15/whos-blame-flint-water-crisis/.

Kennedy, M. (2016, April 20). Lead-laced water in Flint: A step-by-step look at the makings of a crisis. *NPR*. Retrieved from http://www.npr.org/sections/thetwoway/2016/04/20/465545378/lead-laced-water-in-flint-a-step-by-step-look-at-the-makings-of-a-crisis.

Kutsch, T., Taylor, M., & Pizzi, M. (2016, February 10). Flint water crisis makes its way into 2016 presidential campaign. *Aljazeera America*. Retrieved from http://america.aljazeera.com/articles/2016/2/10/presidential-candidates-on-flint-water-crisis.html.

Lawler, E. (2016, January 15). 150 crowd Michigan capitol in protest over Flint water crisis. *MLive*. Retrieved from http://www.mlive.com/news/index.ssf/2016/01/150_crowd_michigan_capitol_in.html.

Lin, J. C. F., Rutter, J., & Park, H. (2016, January 21). Events that led to Flint's water crisis. *New York Times*. Retrieved from https://www.nytimes.com/interactive/2016/01/21/us/flint-lead-water-timeline.html.

McCarthy, G. (2016, January 21). Letter to Governor Snyder from U.S. Environmental Protection Agency. Retrieved from https://www.epa.gov/sites/production/files/2016-01/documents/letter_to_governor_snyder_1-21-16.pdf.

Michigan Department of Environmental Quality. (2016, June 23). Summary of Flint response activities. Retrieved from https://www.michigan.gov/documents/flintwater/DEQ_and_Partner_Response_to_Flint_Water_Crisis_062316_527365_7.pdf.

Michigan Department of Environmental Quality. (2018, February). DEQ guide. Retrieved from http://www.michigan.gov/documents/deq/deq-guide-divisions-offices_376636_7.pdf.

Obama, B. (2016, May 4). Water crisis speech. Lecture presented at Northwestern High School, Flint, MI.

Seville, L. R., Rappleye, H., & Connor, T. (2016, January 19). Bad decisions, broken promises: A timeline of the Flint water crisis. *NBC News*. Retrieved from http://www.nbcnews.com/storyline/flint-water-crisis/bad-decisions-broken-promises-timeline-flint-water-crisis-n499641.

Warikoo, N. (2017a, January 20). EPA backs Flint residents' 24-year bias fight over dirt-spewing plant. *Detroit Free Press*. Retrieved from http://www.freep.com/story/news/local/michigan/2017/01/20/epa-backs-flint-residents-waging-bias-fight-over-dirt-spewing-plant/96854762/.

Warikoo, N. (2017b, January 23). MDEQ denies EPA claim that it discriminates against minorities. *Detroit Free Press*. Retrieved from http://www.freep.com/story/news/local/michigan/2017/01/23/mdeq-denies-epa-claim-discriminates-againstminorities/96966066/.

Discussion Questions

1. Consider the timeline in which the situation in Flint shifted from a local issue to a national crisis. What made this issue become a national one?
2. Why did it take so long for someone to address the issue?
3. How did media coverage of the events in Flint contribute to this change in framing?
4. What role does the media play in shaping public perceptions of organizational ethics?

8 SPORTS COMMUNICATION

Learning Outcomes

- To distinguish sports communication from other public relations practices.
- To understand the complicated number of organizations necessary in sports communication.
- To apply ethics principles to sports communication cases.

Definition

Sports communication: Public relations practice that connects various publics and audiences related to sports activities.

The North American sports industry's worth is projected to be $75 billion by 2020, with $21.2 billion in media broadcast rights alone (Jones, 2016, 1). The classic sports of baseball, football, and basketball may dominate, but newer areas are emerging like the e-sports market, which is estimated to be $1.9 billion in 2018 (Gaudiosi, 2015, para. 2). Sports, regardless of form, is big business—and so is the communication around it.

Sports communication serves "as a positive communication link with a variety of the institution's publics, including the staff, media, fans, community members, alumni, student-athletes, parents and prospective students" (College Sports Information Directors of America, 1993, in Moore, 2012, 1). People in sports communication include "public relations specialists, event managers, media liaisons, publications and Web professionals, and administrators" (Moore, 2012, 47). Some have argued that sports are necessarily connected to communication, because it is only through communication that sports are produced, reproduced, consumed, and organized (Kassing et al., 2004, 358).

Lumping together all the communication around sports treats it as one unified item, but in reality there are numerous types of sports communication. There are numerous jobs in sports communication, from athletic director to content creator to agent. These practitioners all interact with different aspects of the industry. As with the rest of public relations, ethics are part of the daily considerations. The cases that follow examine fan and organizational relations.

Fan Relations

Sports fans are a special type of public. They are dedicated to their teams, but expect, or at least want, to be on the winning side. Effective public relations with fans is similar to any active public (Grunig & Hunt, 1984). These active fans are highly informed about the team and expect a high level of communication. They are seeking out information about their teams. Practitioners must actively communicate with this public and maintain high visibility. While these fans are the team's biggest supporters, their high expectations can create communication problems that have ethical considerations. Morgan (2010, 1579) argues that market pressures and fans' large appetite for sports leads to unethical and untrue communication that can be "immediately and effortlessly digested rather than critically dissected, pondered, and understood." In other words, one might say anything to make and keep fans happy.

Organizational Relations

Sport is also full of powerful interconnected organizations. If we take collegiate lacrosse as an example, practitioners need to communicate not only with the athletes, alumni, fans, and staff but also with numerous organizations like the National Collegiate Athletic Association, the athletic conference, the Association for Intercollegiate Athletics for Women, the Association for Intercollegiate Athletics for Women, and the Women's Collegiate Lacrosse Associates. Some of these organizations are regulatory, and some support aspects of the sport, but all are important stakeholders and often have differing goals that lead to ethical problems.

The complicated organizational relations is obvious in the recent court case against Larry Nassar, the former doctor for the U.S. gymnastics team, who is charged with abusing 140 women and girls (Garcia-Navarro, 2018, para. 1). Questions are being asked about when and what Michigan State University, the U.S. gymnastics governing body, the Great Lakes Gymnastics Club, medical organizations, and even the International Olympic Committee knew and why this wasn't communicated for over 20 years (Barr & Murphy, 2018).

References

Barr, J., & Murphy, D. (2018, February 5). The enablers of Larry Nassar. *ESPN Magazine*, *21*(1), 40–48.

College Sports Information Directors of America. (1993). Sports information and your institution. Quoted in Moore, J. (2012). Strategic influence in college sports public relations. *CoSIDA E-Digest*, 47–54.

Garcia-Navarro, L. (2018, January 21), Nassar testimony brings one sexual abuse survivor sadness—and then some relief. *National Public Radio*.

Gaudiosi, J. (2015, October 28). Global e-sports revenues to surpass $1.9 billion by 2018. *Fortune*. Retrieved January 7, 2018, from http://fortune.com/2015/10/28/global-esports-revenues-nearing-2-billion/.

Grunig, J. E., & Hunt, T. (1984). *Managing Public Relations*. San Diego: Harcourt Brace Jovanovich College Publishers.

Jones, A. W. (Ed.). (2016). *At the Gate and Beyond: Outlook for the Sports Market in North America Through 2020*. PWC.

Kassing, J. W., Billings, A. C., Brown, R. S., Halone, K. K., Harrison, K., Krizek, B., . . . Turman, D. (2004). Communication in the community of sport: The process of enacting, (re)producing, consuming, and organizing sport. *Annals of the International Communication Association, 28*(1), 373–409.

Moore, J. (2012). Strategic influence in college sports public relations. *CoSIDA E-Digest*, 47–54.

Morgan, W. J. (2010). Bullshitters, markets, and the privatization of public discourse about sports. *American Behavioral Scientist, 53*(11), 1574–1589.

SHOULD THE FAN EXPERIENCE IMPACT THE GAME?

John Forde, Ph.D., *APR, Fellow PRSA, Mississippi State University*

Mississippi State University (MSU) is one of the 14 schools that make up the Southeastern Conference (SEC), one of the most powerful college sports leagues in the country. Founded in 1933, SEC schools now compete in 21 sports (12 for women and 9 for men). The league has led the country in average football attendance for 17 straight seasons, and football stadiums are typically filled to near capacity (over 99% on average) for each season (Southeastern Conference, 2016).

Like most colleges, MSU has traditions. The cowbell has become known widely as a university symbol, originating sometime in the late 1930s or early 1940s. Although stories vary, the most enduring legend is that a cow wandered onto the football field during an MSU game with archrival Ole Miss that MSU won handily. Students started bringing a cow to games for good luck, and eventually the practice was streamlined to bringing just a cowbell. During the 1950s and 1960s the cowbell became a popular symbol of the university, and during the 1960s two professors welded handles onto bells to make them easier to ring. The SEC enacted a rule in 1974 banning artificial noisemakers during football and basketball games, but in 2010 the league legalized the use of cowbells during certain times of games for a one-year probationary period. This permission to ring the beloved cowbells led to new slogans promoted by the university asking fans to "respect the bell" and "ring responsibly," which have continued (Mississippi State University Alumni Association, 2016). Fans, players, and coaches (including many opponents) have felt that the cowbells provide the Bulldogs with a distinctive home field advantage.

Background

Fans typically will follow winning teams much more than losing teams, so it makes sense for colleges to strive to win as much as possible, as long as they follow the rules. Universities spend fortunes on athletic programs to attract future athletes, potential students in general, fans for games, and donors. Winning is often a key attraction, but in some cases spectators will return to the stadium if teams provide a unique experience even if they don't dominate on the field or court. The Chicago Cubs organization (until the 2016 World Series Championship year) has been a prime example of loyal fans who continue to support their team, often despite the team's winning percentage. In addition, fans frequently want to feel that they are part of the action and have an impact on their team's performance.

Much has been written about the home advantage in sports. A great deal of research has found that crowds at sporting events may affect the performance of players, and home advantage is often considered a factor in game results. One study of the Auburn University/University of Alabama football rivalry found that a major priority for athletic teams desiring to enhance their winning percentages should be to increase the proportion of home fans through various means. If sellout crowds are not typical, giving away tickets to home fans to increase attendance can make a positive impact on the home team's performance. In addition, since the SEC allots the same number of visitor tickets per game, teams with larger stadiums inherently should have a greater home field advantage (Caudill & Mixon, 2007). This research could provide evidence for teams who want to expand their stadiums to increase the number of home fans. MSU has one of the smallest football stadiums in the SEC.

In a recent analysis of the four major sports leagues (Major League Baseball, National Basketball Association, National Football League, and National Hockey League), several factors were identified that could affect the outcomes of games. Sometimes referees or umpires may be influenced by a home crowd so that they are inclined to make calls that benefit that team. Especially in football, loud home crowds may affect the ability of visiting teams to communicate. Arenas alone typically do not have an impact on outcomes for basketball, football, or hockey since most of them are very similar. However, baseball stadiums are unique to each team and may help the home team because of familiarity. The analysis found that home field advantage varies greatly depending on the team. Some teams in the study won every home game during certain seasons but were just average on the road. Other teams actually won a higher percentage of away games than home games during certain seasons (Which team, 2015).

Often the positive effect of a home crowd in football is called the "twelfth man" (the equivalent of having an extra player). One psychologist believes athletes gain a testosterone boost playing at home because of animal instincts related to territoriality and defending their home turf. Another possibility is that the visiting team could be unfamiliar with the field or court. Still others believe that the home crowd has more of an effect on game officials, which could lead to a home field advantage (BBC News, 2008).

Having larger supporting crowds at games has long been viewed as increasing the home field advantage. Smith and Groetzinger (2010, 19) concluded that "fans do matter and can increase baseball players' ability to perform." However, they also found that "good teams attract more fans, which in turn further increase that team's chances for winning" (2010, 19). The amount of fan noise at three Penn State football games was measured and compared based on whether the home or visiting team had the ball. Due to the increased noise targeted toward the visiting team, they found a "distinct, measurable home field advantage" (Barnard, Porter, Bostron, terMuelen, & Hambric, 2011, 667).

College football continues to be big business, with athletic expenditures at the "Power Five" conference schools ranging from $40.3 million (at Rutgers) to $193.9 million (at the University of Oregon). In the SEC specifically (in 2014), Alabama had the highest expenditure for athletics ($147.2 million) and MSU had the lowest ($59.6 million). Both of these schools showed a profit for the year, and MSU's expenditures increased from $28.2 million in 2004. For 2014, MSU earned a $5.2 million profit in athletics (Hobson & Rich, 2015).

The Situation

MSU experienced a challenge during the 2013 football season when fans complained about the major increase in the number of commercials shown on the video scoreboard during games. These larger-than-life ads seemed to reduce the crowd's involvement in the game, which some thought may have stalled the home team's momentum. One specific ad that irritated fans was a Mercedes-Benz commercial that used a Janis Joplin song ("Oh Lord, Won't You Buy Me a Mercedes-Benz"); sometimes it was played just as timeouts started and the crowd was loudly cheering for the Bulldogs. Many of the complaints were expressed via Twitter, apparently while fans were attending the game. In addition, some of the tweets were replies to inquiries from the athletic department about fans' game experiences.

In early September 2013, Andy Atkinson tweeted that fans should not direct any hate toward the opposing team's band, but they should focus on disliking the Mercedes-Benz commercial (Atkinson, 2013a). He followed up that he was starting a fundraising campaign to keep the commercial off the video scoreboard (Atkinson, 2013b).

In late September, another fan tweeted that he thought there were too many commercials being played, but he seemed to plan forgiveness if the team kept winning (Nanney, 2013). On an October game day, a student stated that the Mercedes commercial was very motivational, but in this short phrase there is no indication of whether it was meant as sarcasm (Gerhart, 2013). On that same game day another fan tweeted that the game experience was great, but he still hated the Janis Joplin Mercedes commercial (Ueltschey, 2013).

In response to complaints that there were too many commercials during critical game times, Scott Stricklin (2013), then the athletic director, tweeted that they were open to ideas and were trying hard but also had contractual obligations concerning the commercials. Therefore, MSU athletics faced an ethical dilemma: To whom was the university most accountable—the fans, expecting a certain type of experience; the football team, wanting to make the most of fan support and home advantage; or the paying corporate sponsor?

Another tweet appeared a few days later on a game day saying that the Mercedes commercial was the worst thing he had ever seen; he begged for them to stop playing it (Burns, 2013). On the same day another fan wrote that he was excited to watch the commercials on the Godzillatron that day, and then questioned hypothetically if there would also be a game (Patterson, 2013). Still another stated on the same day that he would not be returning to a game unless the Mercedes commercial were played, again with no indication of whether he was being sarcastic (Williamson, 2013).

Outcomes

As the 2013 football season concluded, some changes were implemented concerning commercials on the video scoreboard, often in direct response to fan tweets. Many fans may not realize that commercials are typically scheduled well in advance, when the flow of the game cannot be anticipated. However, the athletic department can have some input into when commercials are played.

During the annual Egg Bowl, the concluding regular season game with archrival Ole Miss, some changes were appreciated by fans. One tweeted prior to the game that he was excited not to have Janis Joplin during the Egg Bowl (Chandler, 2013). Another added a humorous photo of the opposing team's coach "watching" the Mercedes commercial (Nations, 2013). Still another reminisced about the great atmosphere at a long-ago game where there were no stadium commercials, and he provided a YouTube game link (Adams, 2013). One fan was complimentary of Mercedes-Benz for not having a true commercial during the Egg Bowl (Nix, 2013);

they simply showed a Mercedes logo with words and no music in some instances toward the end of this season. Some fans loudly cheered this silent offering.

The day after the Egg Bowl, more compliments were tweeted toward the athletic department and Scott Stricklin specifically. One fan thanked him for eliminating some of the commercials and said it made the experience much more enjoyable (Gable, 2013). The Bulldogs finished the season with a 7–6 record, including a Liberty Bowl win over Rice University (FBSchedules.com, 2013). After the 2013 season concluded, the athletic department staffers implemented major plans with ethics in mind. For example, they decided to listen to fans' concerns and reduce the number of commercials played in upcoming seasons in order to provide the best fan experience possible.

According to Stricklin, in 2008 the first big video scoreboard was built in the south end zone. At first, fans seemed to like the commercials being played because in earlier seasons that was just dead time and fans were often unsure what to do. Many of the early spots were MSU-oriented and tailored directly to that audience. From 2011 to 2013, however, he said they went overboard on commercials that intruded on the positive game-day atmosphere that had been created, thereby diminishing the fan experience. Adjustments to the ads played during the games had to be considered. Everyone involved also had to understand that the scoreboard ads generated a great deal of revenue, helping to make the athletic department self-sufficient. The athletic department also supports academic units on campus with its excess funds (personal communication, S. Stricklin, July 20, 2016), thereby making ethical choices about accountability even more difficult.

Much of this proactive listening and planning process had been implemented years before. Stricklin's philosophy is that they could not guarantee wins in the competitive SEC, but they could do everything possible to give fans a positive experience so they will want to return (personal communication, S. Stricklin, July 20, 2016), demonstrating a commitment to fans.

Stricklin also believes that this positive game-day experience goes beyond the stadium to include tailgating. The Junction (just outside the football stadium) has become a mainstay of fans who arrive hours before games to celebrate with family and friends (personal communication, S. Stricklin, July 20, 2016).

The full game-day experience also potentially affects fundraising. "We can't sell the outcome of the game, but we can sell an experience," said Ali Reardon, coordinator of the Bulldog Club, the fundraising unit of the athletic department. The campus experience includes the game atmosphere, events for kids, tailgating, and the video scoreboard. Several targeted programs and areas have been enhanced in recent years and are very successful, including Bully's Kids Club, the Fan Zone, the Gridiron Member Zone, the Junction, and expanded concessions. The main focus in the Bulldog Club is to listen to donors and fans and make as many people happy as possible. Reardon also believes that having Journey's "Don't Stop Believin'" as a motivational anthem near the beginning of the fourth quarter has become a great tradition. The content displayed to fans is very important, along with the timing during the game (personal communication, A. Reardon, July 20, 2016).

According to the owner of a local video production company, moves were made in recent years to add more 15-second spots and reduce the number of 30-second ads in the stadium. Another factor helping the athletic department in its comprehensive effort to enhance video production and related entertainment during games is employing dedicated broadcast personnel. "Game day is now an experience and not just about the score" (personal communication, R. Coblentz, July 20, 2016).

These proactive responses by the athletic department also occurred prior to a 2014 stadium expansion and renovation that would provide even more in-game amenities for fans. In the next two seasons the Bulldogs enjoyed excellent season records of 10–3 and 9–4, even reaching a number-one ranking in the country in 2014 (FBSchedules.com, 2014, 2015).

Just prior to the 2014 season, Stricklin tweeted that he could confirm that Janis Joplin would not be heard that year (Stricklin, 2014). One fan said his favorite part of the opening 2014 season game was that there was no Mercedes commercial on the video scoreboard (Crace, 2014).

Later in that season, some fans expressed appreciation that the athletics department had listened to their concerns and reduced the number of commercials (Harrington, 2014). Another thanked the athletic director directly for not playing commercials during a "momentum" time and for playing "Don't Stop Believin" instead (Petro, 2014). Even with the reduction of commercials during prime game time, though, not everyone was happy. One apparent musician (based on her Twitter photo) said she would prefer to have more band at halftime and fewer commercials (Banks, 2014). One fan said he actually missed the Mercedes commercial and the song (Bailius, 2014).

Detailed planning and coordination go into every game. According to Leah Beasley, assistant athletic director for marketing, members of the athletic department encourage feedback; listen to fans, donors, and sponsors; and want to provide the best experience for everyone. They make changes based on this input. She stated that this attitude starts from the top with the athletic director and continues on down (personal communication, L. Beasley, July 20, 2016).

Beasley added that they learned a great deal from the 2013 season and made modifications the following year that fans recognized. The university now does not play commercials during critical times in football games, and the focus is on playing ads during quarter breaks, pregame, and halftime. Athletic department leaders also have focused on including more sponsored elements in the game that are not commercials, such as the honorary captains program. Fans seem to enjoy these sponsored activities that focus on relationships more than just traditional advertising (personal communication, L. Beasley, July 20, 2016).

Therefore, it seems that MSU took the ethical concerns of all parties seriously as it attempted to find solutions that were fair to all—fans, players, and sponsors.

The game-day experience does not just fall on the marketing professionals. According to Beasley, the athletic department staffers have to create "something that you won't see from your couch." The marketing team (dispersed throughout the stadium) works with the band, cheerleaders, deejays and sound technicians in the audio booth, and video board crews. They all communicate simultaneously to enhance the game-day experience and attempt to make the behind-the-scenes work seamless and unnoticeable to those enjoying the game. This coordination includes run-throughs by the staff several days before each game. "I hope the fan experience affects the game positively or my department is out of business," Beasley concluded. Stricklin currently chairs the SEC Fan Experience Committee and serves specifically in the football area (personal communication, L. Beasley, July 20, 2016).

Overall, Stricklin believes the athletic department works well as a unit to build positive relationships with all constituencies. Some teams, especially women's squads, go into the stands and visit with fans after games. The athletic staff reviews Twitter feeds on the Sunday after football games to look for positive and negative comments and respond accordingly: "If we win and the atmosphere is a dud, then we failed." His focus is on developing such a positive atmosphere that fans can't wait to return for the next game (personal communication, S. Stricklin, July 20, 2016).[1]

Athletic directors and media relations professionals must constantly monitor fans' perceptions of game experiences to entice them to return, purchase season tickets and merchandise, and otherwise support teams and schools. However, to be ethical, they also must consider providing a positive atmosphere for their players and a fair venue for opposing teams.

Successful athletic directors and other administrators have realized that the philosophy of "if you build it they will come" only works fully in the movies. Effective public relations strategies must be constantly implemented, including fan input, traditional media involvement, social media engagement, positive player interactions with fans and others, and immersive research. Those outside the athletic department and university must feel a connection with teams to build the best fan base and therefore be fully successful.

In addition to establishing winning programs that engage fans through effective public relations and being attentive to the ethics of those efforts, colleges also have to be concerned with the continuing broader ethical issues of scholarship

1. In the fall of 2016, Stricklin became athletic director at the University of Florida, leaving his alma mater at MSU for one of the largest athletic programs in the country. He brought almost 25 years of experience in the SEC to the position and replaced Jeremy Foley, who had been Florida athletic director for 25 years (Parler, 2016).

athletes—for example, athletes who are paid or provided with additional support; "one-and-done" basketball players who plan to attend college for only one year before "graduating" to the NBA; relationships of college officials with professional league representatives; drug and alcohol use by athletes and others connected to programs; and overall questions of whether student-athletes are students first or just attending school to play sports. All of these issues need to be addressed. To further muddy the ethical waters, when public universities struggle with funding issues for academic programs, how should athletics fit into the full picture? Would college supporters protest if a prominent professor left because he or she were underpaid or otherwise insufficiently supported? (How would this differ from a winning football coach who receives multiple raises and contract extensions, even in lean state budget years?) Ethical public relations professionals are needed to help navigate these and other complex issues and determine how to develop relationships that provide long-term benefits to the internal and external publics of the college while still maintaining a competitive edge for athletic programs.

References

Adams, H. [MSUBoneYard]. (2013, November 28). This was a gameday atmosphere #hailstate http://www.youtube.com/watch?v=JI79AzdmBGE&feature=share . . . No commercials [Tweet]. Retrieved from https://twitter.com/MSUBoneYard/status/405980981863002113.

Atkinson, A. [n8chaboy508]. (2013a, September 7). #HailState fans, don't direct any hate toward Alcorn's band playing during the game. Focus your hate on the Mercedes Benz commercial. [Tweet]. Retrieved from https://twitter.com/n8chaboy508/status/376461196540805120.

Atkinson, A. [n8chaboy508]. (2013b, September 7). I'm starting a fund raiser to get that Mercedes Benz commercial off of the video board for good. #HailState [Tweet]. Retrieved from https://twitter.com/n8chaboy508/status/376422177631117312.

Bailius, M. [MikeBalius]. (2014, October 11). Ok . . . hate me if you will, but I miss hearing "Oh lord, won't you buy me a Mercedes Benz." @stricklinMSU #HailState [Tweet]. Retrieved from https://twitter.com/MikeBalius/status/521055508854493184.

Banks, J. [bachnbaseball]. (2014, October 4). Booooo commercials!!!! I want more @maroonband!!!!! #HailState #FMB [Tweet]. Retrieved from https://twitter.com/bachnbaseball/status/518458829324173312.

Barnard, A., Porter, S., Bostron, J., terMuelen, R., & Hambric, S. (2011). Evaluation of crowd noise levels during college football games. *Noise Control Engineering Journal*, 59(6), 667–680.

BBC News. (2008, July 1). Does the crowd affect the result? Retrieved from http://news.bbc.co.uk/2/hi/uk_news/magazine/7482972.stm.

Burns, A. [maburns635]. (2013, October 24). The Mercedes-Benz commercial is the worst thing I've ever heard. STAHP PLAYING IT! #DWS #HailState [Tweet]. Retrieved from https://twitter.com/maburns635/status/393513125334380545.

Caudill, S. B., & Mixon, F. G. (2007). Stadium size, ticket allotments and home field advantage in college football. *Social Science Journal, 44*(4), 751–759.

Chandler, W. [willchandler2]. (2013, November 25). A Janis Joplin free Egg Bowl? "@HailStateFB: Exciting news. Look for a tweet at 10 a.m. #HailState" [Tweet]. Retrieved from https://twitter.com/willchandler2/status/405001968466153472.

Crace, N. [lipouts]. (2014, August 30). Best part of the first half of the #hailstate vs USM game? No more Janis Joplin/Mercedes Benz commercial on the jumbo tron. [Tweet]. Retrieved from https://twitter.com/lipouts/status/505882762923245568.

FBSchedules.com. (2013). Retrieved from http://www.fbschedules.com/ncaa-13/sec/2013-mississippi-state-bulldogs-football-schedule.php.

FBSchedules.com. (2014). Retrieved from http://www.fbschedules.com/ncaa-14/sec/2014-mississippi-state-bulldogs-football-schedule.php.

FBSchedules.com. (2015). Retrieved from http://www.fbschedules.com/ncaa-15/sec/2015-mississippi-state-bulldogs-football-schedule.php.

Gable, D. [dwgfans]. (2013, November 29). @stricklinMSU thank you for eliminating some of the commercials on the dawgzilla tron. Much more enjoyable game experience. #HAILSTATE [Tweet]. Retrieved from https://twitter.com/dwgfans/status/406311284461035520/

Gerhart, J. R. [jr_gerhart]. (2013, October 5). Nothing pumps me up more than the Mercedes Benz commercial #HailState [Tweet]. Retrieved from https://twitter.com/jr_gerhart/status/386621641637126144.

Harrington, E. [E_J_Harrington] (2014, October 4). I gave MSU a lot of grief for commercials etc last year. Only fair that I say they have NAILED it today. Amazing! @HailStateFB #HailState [Tweet]. Retrieved from https://twitter.com/E_J_Harrington/status/518459738666061824.

Hobson, W., & Rich, S. (2015, November 23). Playing in the red. *Washington Post*. Retrieved from http://www.washingtonpost.com/sf/sports/wp/2015/11/23/running-up-the-bills/.

Mississippi State University Alumni Association. (2016). Retrieved from http://www.alumni.msstate.edu/s/811/index.aspx?sid=811&gid=1&pgid=761.

Nanney, B. [GTHOM1084]. (2013, September 22). @HailState @HailStateFB regressed to too many commercials on the jumbotron. Hard to complain when the team plays so well #hailstate [Tweet]. Retrieved from https://twitter.com/GTHOM1084/status/381657155201662976.

Nations, W. [Will_B_Nations]. (2013, November 25). Hugh Freeze watching the Mercedes-Benz commercial on the jumbotron at State. #GTHOM #HailState [Tweet]. Retrieved from https://twitter.com/Will_B_Nations/status/405008766955180032.

Nix, H. [HaydenNix]. (2013, November 28). A commercial free jumbotron brought to you by Mercedes Benz of Jackson . . . thank you. #Hailstate [Tweet]. Retrieved from https://twitter.com/HaydenNix/status/406227724462600194.

Parler, D. (2016, September 27). Florida hires Scott Stricklin as athletic director. Retrieved from http://floridagators.com/news/2016/9/27/florida-hires-scott-stricklin-as-athletic-director.aspx.

Patterson, G. [GrantP22]. (2013, October 24). Ready to be in Starkville & #DWS to watch all those commercials on #Godzillatron tonight! #HailState! Oh wait, there's a game? @stricklinMSU [Tweet]. Retrieved from https://twitter.com/GrantP22/status/393439708916613120.

Petro, L. P. [CowbellTales4]. (2014, October 4). Yes! Journey!! Thank you @stricklinMSU for NO COMMERCIALS DURING THIS MOMENTUM!!! #HailState [Tweet]. Retrieved from https://twitter.com/CowbellTales/status/518475217950507008.

Southeastern Conference. (2016). About the Southeastern Conference. Retrieved from http://www.secsports.com/article/11067695/about-the-sec-conference.

Smith, E. E., & Groetzinger, J. D. (2010). Do fans matter? The effect of attendance on the outcomes of Major League Baseball games. *Journal of Quantitative Analysis in Sports, 6*(1), 1–21.

Stricklin, S. [stricklinMSU]. (2013, October 21). @M_W_Pittman We're trying hard, Mark. There are contractual obligations involving commercials, but we are open to any ideas. #HailState [Tweet]. Retrieved from https://twitter.com/stricklinMSU/status/392396596928737280.

Stricklin, S. [stricklinMSU]. (2014, August 28). BREAKING: I can confirm that Janis Joplin will not be heard at Davis Wade Stadium this season. #HailState [Tweet]. Retrieved from https://twitter.com/stricklinMSU/status/505008069555007488.

Ueltschey, A. [Andrewulchy]. (2013, October 5). @KyleNiblett @HailStateFB Great Experience. Still hate Janis Joplin Mercedes commercial. Overall, very well done. #hailstate [Tweet]. Retrieved from https://twitter.com/Andrewulchy/status/386704790354657280.

Which team has the best home-field advantage? (2015, July 6–13). *Time.* Retrieved from http://eds.b.ebscohost.com/eds/pdfviewer/pdfviewer?sid=4760801e-77d4-4de3-879e-425d97135fc6%40sessionmgr104&vid=7&hid=103.

Williamson, B. [BWilliamson11]. (2013, October 24). I'm not coming to another game if the Mercedes commercial is not played on that big screen. @stricklinMSU #hailstate [Tweet]. Retrieved from https://twitter.com/BWilliamson11/status/393547689419239424.

Discussion Questions

1. How can colleges conduct research on what fans want or need at games?
2. Should the "fan game experience" actually affect the play on the field?
3. Does home field advantage really exist?
4. Do fans expect too much from their attendance at sporting events?
5. Can university athletic departments develop a positive atmosphere though effective public relations and also win games at an acceptable level?

THE NFL CONCUSSION CRISIS: MORE THAN
JUST A BAD HEADACHE

Terry L. Rentner, Ph.D., *Bowling Green State University,*
and LaMar C. Campbell, *Chicago Bears*

Upon my death, my brain will be donated to science to further the study of chronic traumatic encephalopathy (CTE). As co-author of this chapter and a former NFL player for five seasons with the Detroit Lions, I know and have worked with players who died from brain injury–related problems, some of whom committed suicide. I played football at the University of Wisconsin–Madison, where the legendary Mike Webster played, one of only three Badgers to be inducted into the Pro Football Hall of Fame. Sadly, his greatest impact on the game of football would come after his passing in 2002. Webster died of a heart attack at 50. Neuropathologist Dr. Bennet Omalu performed his autopsy and was quoted in a Frontline article stating, "I saw changes that shouldn't be in a 50-year-old man's brains and also changes that shouldn't be in a brain that looked normal" (Kirk, Gilmore, & Wiser, 2013).

I met Andre Waters, my idol, at our Lions training camp in 2005. We became friends and I told him that I modeled my game after him. He said, "Yeah, how do you feel?" That response would later haunt me. Waters committed suicide in 2006, and Dr. Omalu, who examined his brain, concluded that Waters' brain tissue was damaged by numerous concussions, which led to his depression and suicide.

Dave Duerson, a safety for the 1986 Super Bowl Champion Chicago Bears, mentored me when I started my post-football radio career on Voice America Sports in 2011. Shortly after, Dave would be found in his Florida home dead of a self-inflicted gunshot wound to the chest. A letter he wrote to his family requested that his brain be studied, and results showed Duerson suffered from CTE.

—LaMar C. Campbell

Introduction

For years the NFL has been defiant in denying that it was aware of any links between football and brain injuries, but reached a surprise settlement in 2013 with more than 4,500 former players who sued the NFL over concussion-related issues for $765 million (Belson, 2013). The core of the concussion lawsuit contended that the NFL "was aware of the evidence and risks associated with traumatic brain injuries for many decades, but deliberately ignored and actively concealed the information from players" (Rubin, n.d., 1). One of the documents submitted stated that the NFL expects one-third of all retired players to develop some form of a long-term cognitive problem (Breslow, 2014), yet the settlement included no admission of liability (*Turner and Wooden v. National Football League and NFL Properties, LLC*, 2014) for CTE.

Attempting to rebuild its reputation and meet the expectations of government, stakeholders, and fans, the NFL initially committed $10 million from the class-action settlement for concussion research and later pledged another $100 million for the study of head injuries and safety in football (Chappell, 2016). This amount is about 1% of the approximately $10 billion in annual income that the league and teams make (Chappell, 2016).

In this chapter, a health communication campaigns scholar and a former NFL player who has testified before Congress on CTE take a critical look at the ethical issues surrounding the NFL's knowledge of brain injuries and the safety of the sport. Specifically, if the NFL has long known about brain-related injuries, it could have shared valuable research and made efforts in prevention and treatment that could have allowed football players to make better-informed health decisions. Suicides by former players, declines in the number of children participating in sports like football that place them at risk for concussions, high media attention, and portrayals of the problem in documentaries and films generate public relations challenges for the sport, making CTE a public health issue and creating more than just a bad headache for the NFL.

Background

In 1994, the NFL convened the Mild Traumatic Brain Injury (MTBI) committee headed by rheumatologist and New York Jets team doctor Elliott Pellman. Based on scientific reports produced by this committee, the NFL held firm that there was no link between football and traumatic brain injuries from repeat concussions (Breslow, 2015). Pointing to contradictory scientific evidence from the MTBI committee, the American Academy of Neurology established guidelines in 1997 for athletes to return to play after a concussion, but in 2000 the NFL rejected these (Coates, 2013). In 2002, Dr. Bennet Omalu, a forensic pathologist, discovered a relationship between mental problems and brain diseases in football players (Omalu et al., 2005). Facing mounds of scientific evidence, the MTBI committee started pushing back in 2003 with a 13-part study published in the medical journal *Neurosurgery* over a three-year period (Ezell, 2013). The MTBI committee's findings were clear and consistent: "No NFL player had ever suffered chronic brain damage as a result of repeat concussions" (Breslow, 2015, para. 15). The committee further claimed that on-field evaluation by team physicians is effective for identifying cognitive and memory problems (Pellman, Viano, Casson, Arfken, & Feuer, 2005). These publications provided the NFL with an opportunity to refer to the problem as "mild traumatic brain injury," downplaying the seriousness. Omalu's findings, first published in 2005, sparked harsher criticisms by the MTBI committee, who accused Omalu of using "fallacious reasoning" and called for a retraction of his publication (Ezell, 2013, para. 51). By 2007, the NFL disbanded the MTBI committee and distanced itself from Pellman and his colleagues, claiming issues with the methodology and a conflict of interest (Coates, 2013). At the same time, a concussion summit was convened in June 2007 that included NFL doctors and outside researchers. Outcomes included new concussion guidelines on return-to-play standards and an NFL-sponsored pamphlet stressing that research results on the long-term impacts of concussions are inconclusive. The pamphlet was later withdrawn on the advice of the NFL legal team. The summit also helped to shape NFL Commissioner Roger Goodell's key messages for the next few years—the NFL is studying the problem and much of the current research is flawed. In particular, an NFL spokesperson denounced a 2009 study that found retired players were 19 times more likely to have dementia than the average population (Ezell, 2013), but acknowledged to the *New York Times* that concussions can lead to long-term problems (Wilner, 2016).

During the same year, scientists from the Center for the Study of Traumatic Encephalopathy announced several new cases of CTE just as members of the media were gathering for the Super Bowl in Tampa (Ezell, 2013). The head of the research team, Dr. Ann McKee, presented her findings to the MTBI committee five months later and said the panel was dismissive of her team's research (Ezell, 2013). McKee then spoke at a congressional hearing in which she linked the way the NFL is addressing the concussion issue to how the tobacco industry denied the link of smoking to health problems (Ezell, 2013). Commissioner Goodell responded by saying the NFL is continuing to research the problem and improve safety standards, but one month later the MTBI members resigned and Goodell replaced them with what he referred to as "independent sources of expertise and experience in the field of head injuries" (Ezell, 2013, para. 1).

In 2010 the NFL gave $30 million to the National Institutes of Health (NIH) to study brain injuries and $1 million to McKee's Center for the Study of Traumatic Encephalopathy, and launched a poster campaign in players' locker rooms warning of possible dangers from concussions (Ezell, 2013; Petchesky, 2013). This would be seen as "too little, too late" by the more than 4,500 former players who originally filed the class-action lawsuit in 2011 claiming the NFL did not properly warn players of the dangers of concussions, despite research that showed otherwise (Farrar, 2013).

In 2012, 34 of 35 brains donated to the Boston University Center for the Study of Traumatic Encephalopathy were found to have CTE (Petchesky, 2013). This was the same year that former San Diego Chargers linebacker Junior Seau shot himself in the chest and was found to have CTE and when the NFL funded a new program, *Heads Up Football*, to address safety in youth football (Wilner, 2016).

More recently, *Frontline*'s Concussion Watch reported that over two seasons, 306 players suffered a combined 323 concussions (Breslow, 2014). Researchers with the Department of Veterans Affairs and Boston University found that 96% of the NFL players they examined have this degenerative disease (Breslow, 2015). Even more alarming is the high number of CTE cases discovered in the brains of 131 of 165 players who, before they died, played football at some level, ranging from high school to professional (Breslow, 2015).

The movie *Concussion* was released in 2015, the same year 49ers linebacker Chris Borland abruptly retired from football, becoming the first player to walk away in his prime out of fear of long-term brain damage (Wilner, 2016).

The Situation

The link between CTE and concussions has produced research ranging from denials to direct links. Omalu was among the first to discover and later name the CTE disease when he examined the brain of former NFL star Mike Webster. The league refuted his findings, instead conducting its own research and concluding there was no increased risk of concussions in football players (Greenhow & East, 2015). This led to accusations that the NFL had started a campaign to minimize the issue, discredit the independent research, and ignore safety recommendations that came after the NFL Concussion Summit (Heiner, 2008). For two more years the league denied a relationship while scientific evidence continued to mount in what became known in a PBS *Frontline* documentary as the "concussion crisis" (Kirk, Gilmore, & Wiser, 2013).

In an attempt to be transparent, the NFL pledged $30 million to the NIH Health to produce impartial research, but this backfired when congressional investigators accused the NFL of attempting to influence the NIH's selection of a researcher to study CTE in numerous living patients (Fainaru & Fainaru-Wada, 2016). The NIH awarded $16 million of the funding to Dr. Robert Stern at Boston University to study how CTE can be diagnosed in living persons (now it can only be diagnosed after death). The NFL backed out of funding Stern, whom they viewed as a potential critic. A congressional report reprimanded the NFL's health and safety officials; U.S. Representative Frank Pallone (D-NJ) criticized the NFL for "meddling with scientific research into the link between football and brain disease" (Vrentas, 2016, para. 2).

While much of the blame for "who knew what when" rests on the NFL itself, it is the team doctor who decides when a player is fit to play and is often the person who is between the proverbial rock and hard place. Greenhow and East (2015, 68) explain that while team doctors are the ultimate decision-makers, they operate within "a tripartite relationship involving contractual obligations owed to the team, yet ethical obligations owed to the player." Partridge (2014) further describes the dilemmas physicians face when making medical decisions that could affect the success of the team, the same team that is paying the doctor's salary. Medicine's ethical principle of "do no harm" means that team physicians are ethically and morally accountable if, due to pressure from coaches, owners, and other stakeholders, they clear a player who should not medically return to the field.

Of great concern to coaches and owners is the backlash they would face if fans knew that players were unknowingly risking their mental health each time they played (Gove, 2012). This could result in loss of revenue for the most successful professional sport in the nation. Therefore, coaches and owners may be reluctant to change the rules, preferring to rely on the skewed MTBI committee's findings.

The NFL first acknowledged a link between concussions and what they described in general terms as "long-term health effects" in 2009 (Schwarz, 2009, para. 1). It would be another seven years, in March 2016, before Jeff Miller, the NFL's executive vice president of player health and safety, would tell the House of Representatives' Committee on Energy and Commerce in a carefully crafted statement that there is a link between football and degenerative brain diseases such as CTE, although "there are also a number of questions that come with that," and he pointed to a lack of research on the prevalence of CTE (Dale, 2016, para. 5).

Outcomes

The NFL clearly missed opportunities to be transparent in its communications with various publics, resulting in unethical behavior so egregious that players are suffering from long-term health issues or have died because the NFL withheld information. This has also created confusion and mistrust among the parents of youth players: although 87% of parents cannot define concussions, 32% fear their children will get them and 25% will not let their children play contact sports because of these fears (University of Pittsburgh Medical Center, 2015). This has translated into a 25% drop in youth participation over the last six years, despite a modest 1.9% increase in 2015 (Moore, 2016).

Recent public relations efforts by the NFL are attempting to shift the conversation from what the NFL knew about traumatic brain injuries and when to what they are going to do about it. To start, the NFL has implemented changes over the past five years in an effort to improve safety on the field. These include changes in league rules (most notably changes in kick-off rules), mandated certified athletic trainers and independent neurologists at every game, and harsher fines and suspensions for players who violate these rules (Thomas, 2013). *Frontline* reported that despite these rule changes, the 2012 season saw a 14% increase in concussions over the 2011 season. The changes did seem to contribute to a decline in reported cases for the next three years, but the 2015 season saw an alarming 58.3% rise during regular-season games (Shpigel, 2016).

The fourth annual NFL Health and Safety Report is a proactive effort to engage key publics in what Commissioner Goodell described in the 2015 report as "the opportunity to share the important work the NFL is leading to advance safety, from the science lab to the playing field, for current, former and future players, and for athletes in all sports" (NFL, 2015, 4).

Facing a decline in participation numbers, the NFL also has developed educational and safety programs to build relationships with current and future players and their parents. The NFL launched the *Heads Up* football safety and concussion awareness campaign in youth football. Initiatives include the *Heads Up Football Camp* run by coaches who have been trained in head injury prevention and Moms Clinics, free programs to help mothers understand what their children experience during practice and games. Both are examples of strategic moves to restore credibility and trust among key publics and at the same time increase participation numbers.

However, some are still in denial. For example, following the hearing on the lawsuit by the retired players, an NFL spokesperson denied that the league withheld any information or misled players (Ezell, 2013). Some team owners disagree with Miller's public statement to the House of Representatives linking football and degenerative brain disorders. Indianapolis Colts owner Jim Irsay compared the risks of football to the risks of taking an aspirin (Thomas, 2016), and Dallas Cowboys owner Jerry Jones said, "We don't know or have any idea that there is a consequence as to any type of head injury in the future" (Gardner, 2016, para. 44). As McKee pointed out earlier, these denials are reminiscent of the tobacco industry's denial that smoking causes cancer until litigation forced the industry to admit the link.

Football always has been and will continue to be a violent sport, and while the relationship between football and CTE is relevant and can no longer be denied, it is important to remain vigilant about the gatekeepers of the game. The NFL has a responsibility to protect the well-being of its employees—past, present, and future.

In an interview with CNN in 2011, I shared some staggering statistics. Among those are that 65% of players leave the game with permanent injuries and 20% are clinically depressed. Considering the NFL average career is only 3.5 seasons and the average age of retirement is age 28, this is quite disturbing. Most startling, however, is that the average life expectancy for retired NFL players is 53–59 years. When you look at these statistics, coupled with CTE symptoms from repeated concussions, I wonder if "NFL" stands for "Not For Long."

—LaMar C. Campbell

References

Belson, K. (2013, August 29). N.F.L. agrees to settle concussion suit for $765. *New York Times.* Retrieved from http://www.nytimes.com/2013/08/30/sports/football/judge-announces-settlement-in-nfl-concussion-suit.html.

Breslow, J. (2014, September 19). The NFL's concussion problem still has not gone away. *Frontline.* Retrieved from http://www.pbs.org/wgbh/frontline/article/the-nfls-concussion-problem-still-has-not-gone-away/.

Breslow, J. (2015, September 15). New: 87 deceased NFL players test positive for brain Disease. *Frontline.* Retrieved from http://www.pbs.org/wgbh/frontline/article/new-87-deceased-nfl-players-test-positive-for-brain-disease/.

Chappell, B. (2016, September 14). NFL pledges another $100 million for study of head injuries, safety in football. *NPR*. Retrieved from http://www.npr.org/sections/thetwo-way/2016/09/14/493971205/nfl-pledges-another-100-million-for-study-of-head-injuries-safety-in-football.

Coates, T. (2013, January 25). The NFL's response to brain trauma: A brief history. *The Atlantic*. Retrieved from http://www.theatlantic.com/entertainment/archive/2013/01/the-nfls-response-to-brain-trauma-a-brief-history/272520/.

Dale, M. (2016, March 15). NFL stands behind top executive's acknowledgement that brain disease CTE can be linked to football. Retrieved from http://www.usnews.com/news/sports/articles/2016-03-15/nfl-official-links-football-cte-could-it-affect-1b-deal.

Ezell, L. (2013, October 8). Timeline: The NFL's concussion crisis. *Frontline*. Retrieved from http://www.pbs.org/wgbh/pages/frontline/sports/league-of-denial/timeline-the-nfls-concussion-crisis/.

Fainaru, S., & Fainaru-Wada, M. (2016, May 24). Congressional report says NFL waged improper campaign to influence government study. *ESPN*. Retrieved from http://www.espn.com/espn/otl/story/_/id/15667689/congressional-report-finds-nfl-improperly-intervened-brain-research-cost-taxpayers-16-million.

Farrar, D. (2013, August 29). NFL, retired players reach $765 million settlement in concussion lawsuits. *Sports Illustrated*. Retrieved from http:www.si.com/nfl/audibles/2013/08/29/nfl-concussion-lawsuit-settlement.

Gardner, S. (2016, March 29). What NFL owners have said about CTE. *Fox Sports*. Retrieved from http://www.foxsports.com/nfl/story/cte-nfl-owners-comments-jim-irsay-jerry-jones-robert-kraft-john-mara-dan-rooney-032916.

Gove, J. P. (2012). Three and out: The NFL's concussion liability and how players can tackle the problem. *Vanderbilt Journal of Entertainment & Technology Law, 14*(3), 649–691.

Greenhow, A., & East, J. (2015). Custodians of the Game: Ethical Considerations for Football Governing Bodies in Regulating Concussion Management. *Neuroethics, 8*(1), 65–82. doi:10.1007/S12152-014-9216-1

Heiner, J. A. (2008). Concussions in the National Football League: Jani v. Bert Bell/Pete Rozelle NFL player ret. plan and a legal analysis of the NFL's 2007 concussion management guidelines. *Journal of Sports and Entertainment Law, 18*(1), 255–371.

Kirk, M., Gilmore, J., & Wiser, M. (2013, October 8). League of denial: The NFL's concussion crisis. *Frontline*. Retrieved from http://www.pbs.org/wgbh/frontline/film/league-of-denial/.

Moore, J. (2016, March 16). Youth football is plummeting. *Vocativ*. Retrieved from http://www.vocativ.com/298019/youth-football-participation-is-plummeting/.

National Football League. (2015, August). *2015 NFL Health and Safety Report*. Retrieved from http://static.nfl.com/static/content/public/photo/2015/08/05/0ap3000000506671.pdf.

Omalu, B. I., DeKosky, S. T., Minster, R. I., Kamboh, M. I., Hamilton, R. I., & Wecht, C. H. (2005). Chronic traumatic encephalopathy in a National Football League player. *Neurosurgery, 57*(1), 128.

Partridge, B. (2014). Dazed and confused: Sports medicine, conflicts of interest, and concussion management. *Bioethical Inquiry, 11*(1), 65–74.

Pellman, E. J., Viano, D. C., Casson, I. R., Arfken, C., & Feuer, H. (2005). Concussion in professional football: Players returning to the same game—part 7. *Neurosurgery, 56*(1), 79.

Petchesky, B. (2013, August 30). A timeline of concussion science and NFL denial. *Deadspin*. Retrieved from http://deadspin.com/a-timeline-of-concussion-science-and-nfl-denial-1222395754.

Rubin, M. (n.d.) NFL players' concussion litigation master complaint. *Washington Post*. Retrieved from http://www.washingtonpost.com/wp-srv/sports/NFL-master-complaint.html.

Schwarz, A. (2009, December 20). N.F.L. acknowledges long-term concussion effects. *New York Times*. Retrieved from http://www.nytimes.com/2009/12/12/sports/football/ http://www.nytimes.com/2009/12/21/sports/football/21concussions.html?pagewanted=all&_r=0.

Shpigel, Ben. (2016, January 29). Diagnoses of concussions increase by nearly a third over last season. *New York Times*. Retrieved from http://www.nytimes.com/2016/01/20/sports/ football/diagnoses-of-concussions-increase-by-nearly-a-third-over-last-season.html.

Thomas, D. (2013, December 13). Helmet-to-helmet contact: Avoiding a lifetime penalty by creating a duty to scan active NFL players for chronic traumatic encephalopathy. *Journal of Legal Medicine, 34*(4), 425–452.

Thomas, J. (2016, March 28). Colts owner Jim Irsay compares the risks of football to the risks of taking an aspirin. *SB Nation*. Retrieved from http://www.sbnation.com/nfl/2016/3/28/_____11320054/nfl-owners-cte-jim-irsay-aspirin-daughter-colts.

Turner and Wooden v. National Football League and NFL Properties, LLC (2014).

University of Pittsburgh Medical Center. (2015, October 1). Concussions misunderstood and feared by most Americans, according to Harris Study. [Press release]. Pittsburgh: UPMC/University of Pittsburgh Schools of the Health Science.

Vrentas, J. (2016, May 24). The NFL, the grant money, and the business of concussion research *Muscle and Medicine*. Retrieved from http://mmqb.si.com/mmqb/2016/05/24/nfl-concussion-research-espn-otl.

Wilner, J. (2016, January 30). The NFL's concussion crisis: A timeline. *Mercury News*. Retrieved from http://www.mercurynews.com/2016/01/30/the-nfls-concussion-crisis-a-timeline/.

Discussion Questions

1. Do you think the NFL's reputation will suffer long-term damage as a result of the concussion crisis? Why or why not?
2. Can you think of another organization beside the NFL and the tobacco industry that withheld or denied information that could potentially harm individuals? Describe what happened and discuss the ethical implications.

3. If you were in public relations for the NFL 10 years ago when Dr. Omalu released his findings, would you have recommended the league handle things differently? If so, what would you have recommended? If not, explain how you think the league's reactions were appropriate.
4. What role should public relations and ethics play in possible future liability claims?

PAPER CLASSES OR ACADEMIC ANOMALIES: A KANTIAN EXAMINATION OF UNC'S RESPONSE TO ITS SHADOW CURRICULUM

Christie M. Kleinmann, Ph.D., *APR, Belmont University*

University of North Carolina (UNC) defensive tackle Marvin Austin tweeted many things in 2010, but only one was "heard 'round the college football world" (Kennedy, 2010). On May 29, Austin tweeted a line from Rick Ross, leading to a NCAA investigation on improper benefits from agents (Barbour, 2015). In the ensuing media coverage, one Associated Press article (2010) included a seemingly innocuous aside reporting that the NCAA investigation revealed possible academic violations. At the time, this comment received little attention—but that changed a year later.

In July 2011, the NCAA brought allegations against UNC football player Michael McAdoo for receiving improper tutor assistance for a class in the African and Afro-American Studies (AFAM) department. McAdoo was released from the team and the academic tutor was dismissed (Former UNC football player, 2011). A few months later *Raleigh News & Observer* investigative reporter Dan Kane (2011) reported that Austin had taken a 400-level course in AFAM *before* the fall of his freshman year. Subsequent media reports revealed that football players had enrolled in AFAM classes that rarely if ever met and only required a paper at the end of the term. These "paper classes" resulted in "artificially high grades" for athletes, allowing them to maintain athletic eligibility (Judge dismisses, 2011). In response, UNC launched its first internal investigation and concluded that the "class irregularities" were confined to the AFAM department (Kane, 2012a, 2013a). The AFAM department chair resigned, and UNC concluded that the crisis was an academic, not an athletic, problem (UNC professor resigns, 2011; Kane & Carter, 2012). The NCAA agreed, announcing in August 2012 that UNC had not committed any athletic violations (Barbour, 2012b).

However, news reports soon implicated men's basketball in the unfolding academic scandal. An online UNC "test transcript," identified as former football and basketball player Julius Peppers, noted that Peppers earned a B-minus, B, and B-plus in suspected AFAM paper classes dating back to 1998, helping him maintain athletic eligibility (Kane, 2012b). UNC never confirmed the authenticity of the transcript, but Peppers did, although he denied any presence of academic fraud (Julius Peppers, 2012). More importantly, Peppers' transcript planted a seed of suspicion surrounding UNC's assertion that the crisis was an academic one. The crisis now encompassed two revenue-generating sports and three men's basketball national championship teams.

Frustrated with UNC's denial of an athletic scandal, UNC athletic learning specialist Mary Willingham revealed that athletic counselors steered athletes into AFAM classes that never met. Willingham described a fraudulent system where athletic counselors worked with AFAM department assistant Deborah Crowder to create easy classes for athletes to maintain their eligibility (Kane, 2012c). Paper classes were either lecture-style or independent studies that typically did not meet and required only a paper in return for a high grade. Tutors often wrote the paper, and some courses were offered without a professor assigned to the class (Ganim, 2014a, 2014b; Norlander, 2012).

UNC admitted to the irregular classes but again maintained that the issue was confined to the AFAM department. The unfolding crisis prompted UNC's chancellor to request former governor Jim Martin to conduct an external investigation. The resulting Martin Report found 216 anomaly AFAM course sections dating back to 1997 and 454 suspected unauthorized grade changes, later reported as 560, often with forged faculty signatures. The report did not find irregularities beyond the AFAM department (Barbour, 2012c; George, 2012; Kane, 2012d; Martin, 2012). While athletic counselors were aware of the "paper courses," there was no evidence of steering athletes into these classes. The Martin Report endorsed UNC's rhetoric that the crisis was academic (although three years later Martin would rescind this statement). Martin affirmed UNC's message that the immediate problems were a result of academic, not athletic, wrongdoing (Martin, 2012).

The new year brought national media attention to the crisis. A front-page *New York Times* article reported that 18 of the 19 students enrolled in AFAM's "Blacks in North Carolina" course were football players; the sole non-athlete was a former member of the football team (Lyall, 2013). Steered there by academic advisors, this course never met, and students received grades for papers they supposedly submitted. A follow-up *New York Times* editorial described the fiasco as "another shameful lesson in the multibillion-dollar entertainment industry euphemistically referred to as collegiate sports" (Acting the course, 2014). The editorial also criticized UNC's handling of the crisis: "Chapel Hill officials have clung to the fiction that the dummy courses were not designed to protect athletes' eligibility. The university says the fact that non-athletes also had access to the courses shows that the scheme was not designed to protect athletes. But the *News & Observer* found that counselors were steering athletes to the no-show classes, and that athletes accounted for nearly two-thirds of those in many of the phantom classes" (Acting the course, 2014).

Rashad McCants, the second-leading scorer on UNC's 2005 championship basketball team, confirmed these assertions. In an interview with *ESPN*, revealed that he was steered to bogus AFAM classes designed to keep athletes academically eligible. He said the paper classes did not require students to go to class, but they had to submit a term paper written by tutors. McCants made the dean's list in 2005 for receiving straight A's (Ganim & Sayers, 2014). In a follow-up *ESPN* interview, UNC head basketball coach Roy Williams said he was "shocked and in disbelief" over McCants' statements and denied knowledge of the "paper class" system (Delsohn, 2014). A few days later the *News & Observer* would question these denials in a report showing that five members of the 2005 basketball championship team, including at least four key players, accounted for 39 enrollments in "no show" classes and 13 independent studies (Bilas, 2014; Carter, 2014a; McCants, 2014; Kane, 2014). Amid the escalating evidence, the NCAA announced that it would reopen its investigation (Adelson, 2014; Carter, 2014b).

Throughout 2014, UNC was criticized for its response of "killing the messenger," "bashing the media," and engaging in "public records battles" (O'Neill, 2015; Smith & Willingham, 2015). Yet UNC did many things to foster greater transparency. The university launched the Carolina Commitment website, dedicated to disseminating information regarding the scandal. A one-way dissemination tool, the website exemplified the university's commitment to review and respond, as well as take action and move forward (Carolina Commitment, n.d.). The UNC chancellor hired prominent prosecutor Kenneth Wainstein to conduct the third UNC investigation in three years (UNC Campus Updates, 2014a, 2014b).

The resulting Wainstein report contradicted UNC's earlier rhetoric, revealing a "shadow curriculum" that helped athletes stay eligible. The 131-page report asserted that the scheme remained in place for nearly two decades and encompassed 3,100 students in over 188 lecture-style classes and independent studies that required little more than a term paper for a high grade. Nearly half of those students were athletes (Smith & Willingham, 2015; Wainstein, 2014). The report established the athletic nature of the crisis, finding clear evidence that academic counselors from the football, men's basketball, and women's basketball teams asked for players to be enrolled in bogus classes in order to maintain their athletic eligibility (Saacks, 2014).

As a result, the Southern Association of College and Schools Commission placed UNC on a one-year probation, the harshest penalty short of losing its academic accreditation. The Commission believed UNC had not addressed the scandal and noted seven separate findings, including a lack of institutional integrity and a loss of control over college sports (Dodd, 2016). In a letter to the UNC chancellor, the Commission expressed concern over the institution's integrity in its attempt to "narrow the scandal to the unethical actions of two people" (Folt, 2014). The NCAA used similar language in its renewed allegations against UNC, noting that the university showed "a lack of institutional control" (NCAA notice, 2015).

One week before its response to the NCAA's concerns was due, UNC announced that it had found additional instances of wrongdoing, implicating two minor sports in the scandal (UNC News, 2015). The announcement drew fire from sports fans, including comments from the Facebook group *UNC Cheats*, a group dedicated to documenting "the stories and investigations into further impropriety of the University of North Carolina" (UNC Cheats, n.d.). One fan termed the move a shady public relations tactic. Another mockingly applauded UNC's "transparency" to implicate non–revenue-generating sports. "Personally, I think it was great politics on UNC's part to self-report some minor violations in minor sports. They can now claim, 'Hey, we are coming clean, we're honest (wink, wink)' ... it's like turning yourself in for being double parked or expired plates yet the car is stolen and there is a dead body in the trunk" (Carter, 2015).

The unfolding drama caught UNC in a series of contradictions. Throughout the crisis, UNC had maintained that a 12-hour limit was placed on independent studies in 2006. The 2006 year was crucial as it exonerated the 2005 men's national championship basketball team from the scandal; however, the *News & Observer* established that the limit on independent studies began in 2003 (Kane, 2016; UNC academic scandal, 2014). Another key point was whether the academic irregularity was an isolated case; amid mounting evidence, the chancellor admitted that there had been academic oversight for years (Ganim, 2014c).

Many contend that UNC mishandled the crisis, "issuing statements" and trying to "ride out the problems" (UNC academic scandal, 2014). Others contend that the university's rhetoric focused on scapegoating (Wrenn, 2015). Throughout the crisis, the university blamed 10 different individuals: an academic tutor, the football coach, the athletic director, the chancellor, the faculty president, a department chair, a department assistant, an athlete, a learning specialist, and a news reporter. As the crisis continued, many grew tired of the blame rhetoric: "Watching the university do everything possible to minimize, delay, and otherwise squirm out of this disaster has been infuriating" (King, 2016). The call for transparent leadership and institutional reform had sounded.

The university's response to the Wainstein Report addressed this growing sentiment and ushered in a new level of institutional transparency. The chancellor acknowledged that the scandal was both an academic and athletics problem. "It is just very clear that it was an academic issue with the way the courses were administered, and it is clearly an athletics issue" (Saacks, 2014). The chancellor made the report "absolutely and completely public" through the Carolina Commitment website and included 900 pages of supporting documents of emails and course assignments. In a news release, the chancellor apologized to students and the UNC community: "I apologize first to the students who entrusted us with their education and took these courses; you deserved so much better from your University, and we will do everything we can to make it right. I also want to apologize to the Carolina community—you have been hurt both directly and indirectly by this wrongdoing, even though you had no knowledge or responsibility for it" (UNC Campus Updates, 2014a). The university also announced sweeping reforms in seven key areas: admissions and preparedness, academic excellence and accountability, course integrity, athletics integrity, athletics excellence and accountability, advising and support, and institutional leadership (Carolina Commitment, n.d.).

Due to these reforms, the Southern Association of College and Schools Commission lifted UNC's accreditation probation (Barbour, 2016; Stancill, 2016). The chancellor released the news to UNC alumni, faculty, and staff in a video message: "Where we are today has taken deep introspection. It's taken admission that we needed to focus more in certain key areas. We've been working closely with our accreditation board to address the academic irregularities that ended in 2011" (UNC response, 2016). The university's response received acclaim from public relations professionals, who noted that the transparency embodied in the Carolina Commitment website "should be commended" (Pace, 2015).

Outcomes

Ethical philosopher Immanuel Kant (1785/1993) believed ethics are based on duty, dignity/respect, and good intention. Duty requires an individual/organization to do the right thing and show dignity/respect through honest communication to help publics make rational decisions. These ideas are reflected in the PRSA Code of Ethics' commitment to honesty and the disclosure and free flow of information (Public Relations Society of America, n.d.). UNC's reactive stance early in the crisis created ethical uncertainty concerning its ability to foster a genuine search for truth. Incomplete information crumbled beneath the scrutiny of external investigations, causing UNC to contradict itself early in the crisis.

An important shift occurred with the Wainstein Report and the Carolina Commitment website, which offered a sense of transparency that had previously been absent. The website provided stakeholders complete access to investigative reports, university updates, and explanations of university reforms. Through such endeavors, UNC illustrated a commitment to honesty/transparency and the disclosure and free flow of information that had not been evidenced in the university's earlier responses.

The website also offered a platform for the university to illustrate what Kant called ethical duty. The university outlined more than 70 reforms and a comprehensive plan to ensure that widespread "academic irregularities" did not recur (Carolina Commitment, n.d.). However, ethical duty could have been strengthened if UNC had offered opportunities for two-way communication. Much of the university's response was one-directional, through the Carolina Commitment website, news releases, open letters to stakeholders, and video messages, with news conferences offering limited two-way communication to some stakeholders. Even institutional social media sites did not facilitate stakeholder engagement. Such a one-dimensional approach contrasted sharply with the news media and rival forums that hosted robust discussion about the crisis. As a result, UNC missed important opportunities to enhance its ethical stance of duty and dignity/respect through managed stakeholder engagement.

In addition to duty and dignity/respect, Kant (1785/1993) valued goodwill or good intention as the strongest ethical goal. He argued that the organization that bases its actions on goodwill, rather than self-interest, would be ethical. The PRSA Code of Ethics provides a similar assertion, admonishing professionals to be loyal to the client while also honoring their obligation to society (Public Relations Society of America, n.d.). The public interest obligates professionals "to look beyond the organization's own selfish interest and to the public's well-being" (Martin & Wright, 2016, 120) Public relations practitioner Richard Edelman suggested that an organization could simultaneously promote its self-interest and meet public interest if it provided a forum for "rigorous debate" (Edelman, 1992, 32). The Carolina Commitment website fell short of the "rigorous debate" that would foster greater public interest.

Beyond the website, UNC's response floundered in illustrating the priority of public interest. In three separate instances, UNC displayed an institutional priority in its ethical response. When it received the NCAA's initial notice of allegations, the university said it was committed "to continue pursuing a fair and just outcome *for Carolina*" (UNC News, 2015). When UNC identified new information for NCAA's investigation, the university noted its desire to be completely transparent and to gain "a fair and just outcome *for Carolina*," and when it received NCAA's amended allegations, the university stated it was "working tirelessly to secure a fair outcome *for Carolina*" (Carolina Commitment, n.d.). Such statements underscored the prominence of organizational interest in the university's response and gave little attention to the greater public interest Kant deemed most ethical.

References

Acting the course at Chapel Hill. (2014, January 5). *New York Times*.

Adelson, A. (2014, June 30). NCAA again investigating UNC. *ESPN*.

Barbour, B. (2012b, August 31). NCAA knows everything about AFAM and has not found a violation (for now). *Tar Heel Blog*.

Barbour, B. (2012c, December 20). Martin report released. *Tar Heel Blog*.

Barbour, B. (2015, May 29). Marvin Austin's "Club Liv" tweet was five years ago today. *Tar Heel Blog*.

Barbour, B. (2016, June 16). UNC off SACS probation. *Tar Heel Blog*.

Bilas, J. (2014, June 8). Williams: McCants doesn't ring true. *ESPN*.

Carter, A. (2014a, June 11). Back on ESPN McCants responds to Williams, UNC players. *News & Observer*.

Carter, A. (2014, June 30b). NCAA reopens investigation of academic misconduct at UNC. *News & Observer*.

Carter, A. (2015, October 28). UNC coach Roy Williams fighting perception problem. *News & Observer*.

Delsohn, S. (2014, June 5). UNC's McCants: "Just show up, play." *ESPN*.

Dodd, D. (2016, May 1). UNC scandal leaves university in peril beyond athletics. *CBS Sports*.

Edelman, D. (1992, November). Ethical behavior is key to field's future. *Public Relations Journal, 48*(11), 32.

Folt, C. (2014, November 13). *SACS letter to UNC*. Retrieved from http://carolinacommitment.unc.edu.

Former UNC football player sues NCAA after being suspended for accepting improper tutoring benefits. (2011, July 7). *Business Insider*.

Ganim, S. (2014a, January 8). CNN analysis: Some college athletes play like adults, read like 5th graders. *CNN*.

Ganim, S. (2014b, January 16). UNC will investigate claims over athletes' reading ability. *CNN*.

Ganim, S. (2014c, January 29). UNC: We failed students "for years." *CNN*.

Ganim, S., & Sayers, D. (2014, October 23). UNC report finds 18 years of academic fraud to keep athletes playing. *CNN*.

George, R. (2012, December 20). Highlights of the Martin Report on UNC academics. *USA Today*.

Judge dismisses Michael McAdoo suit. (2011, November 14). *Associated Press*. Retrieved from http://www.espn.com/.

Julius Peppers: Transcript mine. (2012, August 18). *Associated Press*. Retrieved from http://espn.go.com/

Kane, D. (2011, August 21). Austin's UNC transcript raises questions. *News & Observer*.

Kane, D. (2012a, May 4). Report finds academic fraud evidence in UNC department. *News & Observer*.

Kane, D. (2012b, August 13). Pepper's transcript might point to broader academic issues at UNC. *News & Observer*.

Kane, D. (2012c, November 17). UNC tolerated cheating, says insider Mary Willingham. *News & Observer*.

Kane, D. (2012d, December 21). Martin Report: Suspect UNC classes stretched back to 1997. *News & Observer*.

Kane, D. (2013a, June 8). Former UNC African studies chairman had close ties with athletic counselors. *News & Observer*.

Kane, D. (2014, June 6). 2005 UNC champs relied on suspect classes, records show. *News & Observer*.

Kane, D. (2016, March 31). Long-ago UNC report contradicts university's latest stance on independent studies. *News & Observer*.

Kane, D., & Carter, A. (2012, June 8). UNC football players flocked to suspect class. *News & Observer.*

Kant, I. (1785/1993). Metaphysical foundations of morals. In Friedrich, C. J. (Ed.), *The Philosophy of Kant: Immanuel Kant's Moral and Political Writings* (pp. 154–229). New York: Modern Library.

Kennedy, Doc. (2010, July 26). Austin's Twitter feed casts doubt on Club Liv tweet [blog post]. Retrieved from http://www.tarheelblog.com/2010/07/austins-twitter-feed-casts-doubt-on-club-liv-tweet.

King, J. D. (2016, April 28). More perspective on the UNC scandal: Jay Bilas and Dave Gleen. *Duke Basketball Report.* Retrieved July 2018 from http://www.dukebasketballreport.com.

Lyall, S. (2013, December 31). A's for athletes, but charges of fraud at North Carolina. *New York Times.*

Martin, J. (2012, December). *Governor Martin's academic review report of findings: The Martin Report.* Retrieved from http://carolinacommitment.unc.edu/reports-resources/governor-martins-academic-anomalies-review-report-of-findings-updated-with-addendum-the-martin-report/.

Martin, D., & Wright, D. K. (2016). *Public Relations Ethics: How to Practice PR Without Losing Your Soul.* New York: Business Expert Press.

McCants: "All I know is the truth." (2014, June 11). *ESPN.*

NCAA notice of allegations report. (2015, May 20). Retrieved from http://carolinacommitment.unc.edu/files/2015/06/NCAA-NOA.pdf.

Norlander, M. (2012, November 18). UNC whistleblower goes public, claims school tolerated academic cheating. *CBS Sports.*

O'Neill, (2015, June 1). What UNC needs to do: Fire Williams, remove banners, forfeit wins. *News & Observer.*

Pace, R. D. (2015, October 27). University of North Carolina-Chapel Hill spends $10MM on law and crisis PR. *Everything PR: Public Relations News.* Retrieved from http://everything-pr.com/edelman-paid-millions-university-crisis-pr/72237/.

Public Relations Society of America (n.d.). *PRSA Code of Ethics.* Retrieved from https://www.prsa.org/aboutprsa/ethics/codeenglish#.V6feWI7SEuw.

Saacks, B. (2014, October 22). Wainstein report reveals extent of academic scandal at UNC. *The Daily Tar Heel.*

Smith, J., & Willingham, M. (2015). *Cheated: The UNC Scandal, the Education of Athletes, and the Future of Big-Time College Sports* [digital edition]. Washington DC: Potomac Books.

Stancill, J. (2016, June 16). UNC removed from probation by accrediting agency. *News & Observer.*

UNC academic scandal more than just a public relations problem.. (2014, June 6). *Winston-Salem Journal.* Retrieved from http://www.journalnow.com/opinion/editorials/.

UNC Campus Updates. (2014a, January 16). *Chancellor Folt sends message to campus* [Press release]. Retrieved from https://www.unc.edu.

UNC Campus Updates. (2014b, October 22). *Wainstein's report into irregular classes released* [Press release]. Retrieved from http://www.unc.edu/spotlight/wainsteins-report-into-irregular-classes-released/.

UNC Cheats (n.d.) UNC Cheats [Facebook page]. Retrieved July 2016 from https://www.facebook.com/UNCCheats/.

UNC News. (2015, August 14). *UNC-Chapel Hill reports new information to NCAA* [Press release]. Retrieved from http://uncnews.unc.edu/2015/08/14/unc-chapel-hill-reports-new-information-to-ncaa/.

UNC professor resigns amid football investigation. (2011, August 31). *ABC 11*.

UNC response to NCAA amended notice of allegations. (2016, August 1). Retrieved from http://carolinacommitment.unc.edu/unc-chapel-hill-posts-response-to-ncaas-amended-notice-of-allegations/.

Wainstein, K. L. (2014, October 16). *Investigation of irregular classes in the Department of African and Afro-American Studies at the University of North Carolina at Chapel Hill*. Retrieved from http://carolinacommitment.unc.edu/reports_resources/investigation-of-irregular-classes-in-the-department-of-african-and-afro-american-studies-at-the-university-of-north-carolina-at-chapel-hill-2/.

Wrenn, C. (2015, July 7). The jewel in the crown. *NC Spin*. Retrieved from http://www.ncspin.com/the-jewel-in-the-crown/.

Discussion Questions

1. How might UNC have facilitated two-way communication that engaged its stakeholders throughout the crisis?
2. How did UNC's shifting rhetoric impact the ethical stance of the university?
3. In your opinion, how could UNC have strengthened its ethical response to the crisis?
4. What guidance does the PRSA Code of Ethics offer to UNC's response to the crisis?
5. What is the role of public relations in UNC's ethical response?

HEALTH

Learning Outcomes

- Discuss the complicated ethical issues of health-related public relations.
- Demonstrate understanding of the Health Insurance Portability and Accountability Act.
- Analyze the connections between health-related public relations and patient safety.
- Evaluate communication acts using ethical concern for patients.

Definitions

Food and Drug Administration: The U.S. federal agency that oversees the medical drug-approval process as well as other public health programs (e.g., food safety, vaccines, veterinary products).

Health advocacy organization: An organization that communicates to publics for a health-related cause.

Health communication: "The study and use of communication strategies to inform and influence individual and community decisions that enhance health" (Centers for Disease Control and Prevention, 2011, para. 15).

Health Insurance Portability and Accountability Act of 1996: U.S. law regulating what and how information can be shared by health-care professionals and organizations.

Health promotion: A strategic communication plan to improve the health of one or more publics.

When communicating about a person's health, the ultimate ethical concern should be a person's well-being, but health-related public relations is complicated by complex health conditions, various publics, privacy issues, and a large health infrastructure. Health communication is defined by the Centers for Disease Control and Prevention

(2011, para. 15) as "the study and use of communication strategies to inform and influence individual and community decisions that enhance health." Public relations intersects with health communication to help health organizations "earn the respect, understanding, and good will of their publics or of society in general" (Ristino, 2007, 56). The connection between healthcare and public relations has been a longstanding one. "Public relations has always been a key part of any hospital's strategy in getting out its message and increasing its visibility" (Berkowitz, 2008, 118). The health industry and health advocacy groups use public relations to reach consumers, raise funds, and work toward changing health behaviors.

When looking at public relations in a healthcare context, a smart place to start is with patients. Hospitals can't exist without consumers who want, or at least need, their services. While hospitals can be organized as for-profit or not-for-profit businesses, the need for strong consumer relations will always be a focus for public relations practitioners. And health consumers have special legal rights, among them privacy. Privacy is always an ethical consideration, but the privacy of a patient's healthcare information is guaranteed and regulated by the Health Insurance Portability and Accountability Act of 1996 (HIPAA). We see HIPAA in action when we visit a new physician or a hospital and have to sign paperwork acknowledging our legal right to privacy.

PR practitioners need to learn about privacy rights so they know what kind of information can be shared. For example, if you were a PR person working for a hospital, could you legally tell a reporter when and where someone was treated and released by your organization? HIPAA allows for a statement to the media "that someone has been 'treated and released,' but including where and when would require patient approval" (Guide to HIPAA Compliance in News Media Relations, 2015, 7). Privacy can be a complicated issue, and you must become aware of the laws, rely on strong legal counsel, and use "your own good judgment and understanding of circumstances" (Guide to HIPAA Compliance in News Media Relations, 2015, 2).

Another area where public relations interacts with health organizations is communicating about healthful living. Sometimes this involves assisting a health advocacy organization, like the American Heart Association or the Michael J. Fox Foundation, to create a campaign aimed at health behavior change and/or to raise money for research and support. Health promotion sounds like an area that would have few ethical considerations, but the process can become complicated. For example, consider the ethical implications of a health advocacy group that endorses a popular weight-loss plan for which there is no scientific evidence. The group would gain more media attention and increase its fundraising, but is that really promoting health?

Another area is the promotion of new drugs before, during, and after Food and Drug Administration approval. Promoting new drugs is a large undertaking: in 2017 43 new drugs were approved by the FDA, a 21-year high (Hirschler, 2018). Health communicators have a legal and ethical responsibility to make sure the product is promoted in a manner that puts patient safety first and abides by the law. Ristino (2007, 56) summarizes the interaction between health and public relations as relationship building between organization and publics: "for health care organizations to earn the respect, understanding, and good will of their publics or of society in general, they must have respect for the public's needs and opinions."

References

Berkowitz, E. N. (2008). The evolution of public relations and the use of the internet: The implications for health care organizations. *Health Marketing Quarterly, 24*(3–4), 117–130.

Centers for Disease Control and Prevention. (2011). Gateway to health communication & social marketing practice. Retrieved from https://www.cdc.gov/healthcommunication/healthbasics/WhatIsHC.html.

Guide to HIPAA Compliance in News Media Relations. (2015). Lincoln, NE: Nebraska Hospital Association.

Hirschler, B. (2018, January 2). New drug approvals hit 21-year high in 2017. Retrieved February 8, 2018, from https://www.reuters.com/article/us-pharmaceuticals-approvals/new-drug-approvals-hit-21-year-high-in-2017-idUSKBN1ER0P7.

Ristino, R. J. (2007). Communicating with external publics: Managing public opinion and behavior. *Health Marketing Quarterly, 24*(3/4), 55–80.

HEALTHCARE PUBLIC RELATIONS AND MORAL OBLIGATIONS: PATIENT SAFETY AND THE BOSTON UNIVERSITY MEDICAL CENTER TUBERCULOSIS CASE

Heather J. Carmack, Ph.D., *University of Alabama* and
Carey M. Noland, Ph.D., *Northeastern University*

In the summer of 2005, residents of the Boston area were shocked to learn that their health might have been at risk from the very people who were there to heal them. Local news outlets reported that a surgical resident exposed up to 5,600 patients and healthcare workers to tuberculosis (TB), a bacterial infection of the lungs that causes weakness, extreme coughing, chest pain, and weight loss (Doctor worked, 2005). TB is passed through the air through coughing, sneezing, or even singing (CDC, 2016). TB can be treated if it is caught early, and many individuals who contract TB show no signs of illness (known as latent TB; CDC, 2016).

The surgical resident had rotations at five area hospitals—Boston University Medical Center (BMC), the Veterans Administration Medical Center (VAMC) in West Roxbury, Brockton Hospital, Cape Cod Hospital, and the VAMC in Jamaica Plain (Smith & Allen, 2005)—although BMC was her primary residency hospital and was responsible for completing all health and safety testing for new trainee physicians beginning their residencies.

Exposed patients and healthcare workers were tested, and four patients and 13 healthcare workers tested positive for TB. According to Dr. Anita Barry, chief disease tracker at the Boston Public Health Commission, these individuals were "probably exposed" to TB by the surgical resident (Doctor worked, 2005, para. 6).

Background

BMC is located in the South End in Boston and is the primary teaching affiliate hospital of the Boston University Medical School. BMC's mission is to provide care to disadvantaged, underserved, and indigent populations in the metropolitan Boston and surrounding areas (Boston University Medical Campus, para. 1). Patient demographics show that approximately 34.4% of patients are white, 31.5% are black or African American, and 17.6% are Hispanic/Latino. Fewer than 30% of the patients have private health insurance (Boston University Medical Campus, Tables 2 and 3).

One of the biggest questions raised by this crisis was how a physician could continue to work after learning she was positive for a highly contagious and possibly deadly infectious disease. This crisis began in June 2004, when the surgical resident was beginning her residency at BMC. As part of the onboarding process, all incoming health providers must be tested for a number of communicable illnesses, including TB. The resident's TB skin test tested positive, meaning an induration (skin bump) appeared at the injection site, indicating that she might have TB. A follow-up chest X-ray was scheduled for July 2004 to confirm TB, but the resident never showed up for her X-ray and began treating patients (TB testing, 2005). An investigation by the U.S. Occupational Safety and Health Administration (OSHA) revealed that the resident contracted TB between June 2003 and June 2004. She began showing symptoms in January 2004 but was misdiagnosed and treated for pneumonia (TB testing, 2005). Her doctors estimated that she became infectious sometime between December 2004 and June 2005 (Smith & Allen, 2005). In May 2005, she developed a phlegm- and blood-laced cough, which promoted a chest X-ray. A June 2005 chest X-ray confirmed that she had TB (TB testing, 2005).

The Situation

BMC and additional health organizations engaged in a number of communication tactics to address the crisis. First, the hospitals mailed letters or sent emails to patients who might have come into contact with the resident, encouraging them to come in for testing. The letters did not specifically state if or where the patients might have been exposed to TB. As Dr. Michael Charness, chief of staff of the VA Boston Healthcare System, stated, "We don't want the public to panic, but we also don't want to belittle the importance of this . . . The important perspective is that people exposed don't automatically become infected" (Abel, 2005, para. 4).

Second, the BMC, in conjunction with the Boston Public Health Commission (BPHC), held a press conference to address the issue. They identified the hospitals where the resident worked, the timeframes of potential infection, and the free screenings the facilities were offering to patients and family members. They also encouraged patients to either call a toll-free number or to schedule an appointment immediately to get screened (Kunzelman, 2005).

Finally, an OSHA team was deployed to work with BPHC to investigate the crisis and identify recommendations (Doctor worked, 2005).

There were many organizational and communication failures in how the case was handled. An OSHA investigation found both the surgical resident and BMC to be at fault for the way they handled or failed to handle the case (Doctor worked, 2005). The resident was obviously found to be negligent for failing to follow up on a positive TB skin test and not reporting that she had symptoms. BMC, as the primary hospital responsible for the resident, failed at the beginning by not following up on her positive TB skin test result. The hospital did not have a flagging system in place for employee health records, which would have notified medical chiefs that a resident had tested positive and had not shown up for the follow-up chest X-ray. The other hospitals, especially the VAMCs, were also faulted for not having mechanisms in place for gathering and sharing health information about rotating residents (Doctor worked, 2005).

Communication about the case was also poorly handled. The press and general public became aware of the case only because the resident had rotations at VAMC facilities (Smith & Allen, 2005). The VA has a national database that requires all adverse events to be reported to a National Veterans Affairs Congressional committee. These federal memos are available to the public. BMC cited federal privacy laws as the primary driver for its silence about the resident and the outbreak. Her name was never released to the general public (this is the case with most outbreaks). The hospital was also slow to reach out to patients, mailing letters about the potential threat only in mid-June 2005, despite requests from community activists to reach out to patients via telephone or in person (Smith & Allen, 2005). The issue of the resident's privacy stands in sharp contrast to the safety and well-being of the community and calls into question how public relations practitioners working in healthcare organizations should balance the conflicting values that govern the practice of healthcare.

Deontology is a common ethical approach used in the practice of healthcare (Mandal, Ponnambath, & Parija, 2016; Panditrao, 2011). Recall that the deontological ethical approach is governed by the *categorical imperative*—an individual has a moral duty to uphold absolute, universal principles and apply them equally, fairly, and consistently to all people and situations (Bowen, 2005a, 2005b). For example, a common value in healthcare is an ethic of practice, which asks providers to acknowledge the art and science of medicine and be mindful of the patient during healthcare encounters (Carmack, 2010). From this value rule, providers should try to do this for all patients. For providers, who are primarily taught values from a deontological approach, this means focusing on the long-term therapeutic relationship with patients (Garbutt & Davies, 2011; Mandal et al., 2016). This can occasionally be problematic, however, because providers (using deontology) work in healthcare organizations with managers, educators, and public relations specialists who are traditionally trained to use a utilitarian approach (Bowen, 2005b; Mandal et al., 2016).

Outcomes

Healthcare practice is guided by a number of values, including beneficence, non-maleficence (the traditional "do no harm" motto), dignity, justice, honesty, medical privacy, and confidentiality (Panditrao, 2011). Although these values should work in concert with each other, having multiple moral rules connected to multiple values can make it difficult for an individual to determine how to act in an ethical manner (Parsons, 2008). This is especially a concern when these moral rules conflict with each other. Parsons (2008, 37) provided an apt example of these types of conflict:

> For example, if there is one rule to avoid telling lies and another to avoid harming people, what do you do in a situation where to tell the complete truth to the media about what's going on with your client would harm one or more people? You have rules to follow, but you still have a dilemma.

For providers and public relations practitioners working in healthcare organizations, this is a recurring conflict, especially when they communicate with publics about issues such as medical errors, maleficence, and outbreaks. It can be a challenge to explain to these publics how providers made decisions about care and communication. At the center of this case are the two primary competing governing values in healthcare: non-maleficence and privacy. A deontological ethics lens shows how BMC used both these values as frames for its communication with the Boston area public.

Frame 1: Non-maleficence

One of the consistent justifications made by the BMC (and the other hospitals by extension) was their moral obligation to "do no harm" to their patients and the general Boston-area public. Non-maleficence is the guiding value ensuring patient safety while in the care of providers (Panditrao, 2011). The BMC system serves many vulnerable Boston populations, including low-income and immigrant communities. These communities are typically distrustful of medical providers (Spector, 2013), so publicizing an outbreak resulting from a healthcare provider's ignoring medical requirements and the hospital's failure to have in place appropriate safeguards may not be in the best interest of patients.

> "If somebody who is a healthcare professional is made aware there is a potential that he or she has tuberculosis, there is a duty to protect patients that would require vigilance on their part," said Nancy Achin Audesse, executive director of the Board of Registration in Medicine . . . But Achin said regulators' focus is now on making sure that potentially exposed people are tested and treated, if necessary. "Then, we can all look together at what happened and look at what role various agencies might play in the future to make sure it doesn't happen again." (Smith & Allen, 2005, para. 4–5)

The hospitals and other medical governing boards emphasized that communication about the outbreak was specifically chosen to protect their patients, emphasizing that maintaining public trust was paramount.

Patient safety was also emphasized by the constant communication about how the facilities were addressing the problem and finding ways to prevent a similar outbreak for occurring again. Medical directors at several hospitals, including the VA facilities, stated that increased surveillance and tracking were top priorities to prevent potential outbreaks.

> Dr. Michael Charness, chief of staff at the VA Boston Health Care System, said the health care facilities are reviewing their procedures to ensure this doesn't happen again. "As this is analyzed by each institution, we recognize that there are aspects to our surveillance and tracking that could be improved," he said. "We will tighten up our systems." (TB testing, 2005, para. 4–5)

The statement from the VA Boston system underscores the moral obligation of non-maleficence and patient safety. Increasing security, tracking, and ensuring the health of providers communicates the facilities' commitment to "do no harm" to the patients in their care.

Frame 2: Privacy

The primary conflicting value of non-maleficence is privacy. A number of privacy concerns dictated communication about the TB outbreak to patients and the general Boston public. Perhaps the most important conflict with privacy is the need to balance the privacy of the provider and the privacy of potentially infected patients and healthcare workers. No information about the provider was ever publicly released, with the BMC citing federal patient privacy laws (Doctor working, 2005). In fact, the only reason the general public learned about the outbreak was because of the federal memo to the VA committee; the hospital released the information immediately before the memo was released. However, this privacy protection conflicts with non-maleficence because the hospital did not disclose if the provider, once treated, returned to the hospital to see patients.

The need to protect the provider's privacy (and thus the privacy of the outbreak) also conflicts with patients' safety. Widespread publicity about the outbreak would help those potentially exposed to TB to seek diagnosis and treatment, decreasing the chances that TB would spread. However, to maintain privacy, the information that is communicated to patients is often limited. Legally, hospitals are not required to inform patients if they have been exposed to a particular event, disease, or substance; they are only obligated to invite patients to come in and get tested. This lack of information as to why they need to be tested explains why the number of patients seeking testing was so high; some hospitals contacted all patients to come in for testing, whether they interacted with the provider or not.

The private way (letters in the mail) by which information was communicated to patients was problematic. Mail is perhaps the most private way to communicate information to patients who do not want family member to know about their health issues. However, it is not an effective or timely way to communicate with publics, especially because many low-income patients move frequently and may fail to update their addresses. After criticism of this method, John Rich, BPHC medical director, stated they would use additional methods, including emailing and calling patients (About 1600 patients, 2005).

Frame 3: Public Health Beneficence

One of the dangers of communicating about infectious disease outbreaks is the risk of moral panic. Widespread publicity about the error and a potential outbreak could have created widespread panic within the populace if people thought they had been exposed to TB. The BMC in particular relied on beneficence, or engaging in actions that benefit patients, as a value to guide its communication about the situation by downplaying the threat of the error and assuring patients that BMC had not violated any federal laws (stating only that BMC was not as vigilant as it could be).

To reassure patients and the general public, the facilities downplayed the seriousness of the situation to prevent moral panic. This strategy was established at the first BMC press conference: "'From a physician's standpoint, the statement I would like to make at the beginning is that TB is a very treatable disease and a relatively small percentage of people exposed to the bacterium will actually contract the disease,' said Dr. Keith Lewis, of Boston Medical Center" (About 1600 patients, 2005). BMC brought in several other health organizations to help with this communication strategy, including the BPHC and OSHA. John Rich, medical director at BPHC, reinforced this, stating "patients have a lower risk of becoming infected than the woman's co-workers because employees spent more time with her. There is no risk to members of the public who did not have direct contact with the woman" (Kunzelman, 2005, para. 4). BMC spokesperson Kristin O'Connor also downplayed the threat, stating that the 1,600 possible exposures was "a very liberal number" (Kunzelman, 2005, para. 5). Minimizing the seriousness of this situation was tricky, however, because TB is highly contagious and can spread easily if not treated. However, because many facilities do not have the capacity to test for and treat TB, the hospital did not want to create panic and a rush of patients, which would overwhelm facilities across the city.

Healthcare organizations must address conflicting values when communicating about serious health issues to the general public. As this case underscores, it can be difficult to provide the general public with all the information they feel they need while maintaining patient safety and privacy. Outbreaks also pose a unique moral challenge to facilities because of the opportunity to create panic among their publics. PR practitioners need to find ways to successfully communicate the healthcare values that guide how facilities disseminate information while maintaining the trust of those they diagnose, treat, and heal.

References

Abel, D. (2005, June 16). 4 hospital cite possible TB exposure: Officials alert hundreds of patients, staff. *Boston Globe*. Retrieved from http://archive.boston.com/yourlife/health/diseases/articles/2005/06/16/4_hospitals_cite_possible_tb_exposure/.

About 1600 patients, health care workers exposed to TB. (2005, June 16). *Boston Channel*. Retrieved from http://www.thebostonchannel.com/news/4617168/detail.html.

Boston University Medical Campus. (2012, July, 15). Retrieved from http://www.bumc.bu.edu/.

Bowen, S. A. (2005a). A practical model for ethical decision making in issues management and public relations. *Journal of Public Relations Research, 17*(3), 191–216.

Bowen, S. A. (2005b). Ethics in public relations. In Heath, R. L. (Ed.), *Encyclopedia of Public Relations* (pp. 295–297). Thousand Oaks, CA: Sage.

Carmack, H. J. (2010). Bearing witness to the ethics of practice: Storying physicians' medical mistake narratives. *Health Communication, 25*(5), 449–458.

Centers for Disease Control and Prevention. (2016, March 20). Basic TB facts. Division of Tuberculosis Elimination. Retrieved from https://www.cdc.gov/tb/topic/basics/default.htm.

Doctor worked six months infected with TB, OSHA finds. (2005, November 11). *ISHN Magazine*. Retrieved from http://www.ishn.com/articles/84258-doctor-worked-six-months-infected-with-tb-osha-finds.

Garbutt, G., & Davies, P. (2011). Should the practice of medicine be a deontological or utilitarian enterprise? *Journal of Medical Ethics, 37*, 267–270.

Kunzelman, M. (2005, June 17). Hospital worker might have exposed more than 2,000 to TB. *South Coast Today*. Retrieved from http://www.southcoasttoday.com/article/20050617/news/306179975.

Mandal, J., Ponnambath, D. K., & Parija, S. C. (2016). Utilitarian and deontological ethics in medicine. *Tropical Parasitology, 6*(1), 5–7.

Panditrao, M. M. (2011). Medical deontology: The fading science and need of the hour. *Indian Journal of Pain, 25*(1), 6–8.

Parsons, P. J. (2008). *Ethics in Public Relations: A Guide to Best Practice* (2nd ed.). London: Kogan Page.

Smith, S., & Allen, S. (2005, June 18). Organizers assail care for doctor in TB case: Lynch is seeking better patient alert. *Boston Globe*. Retrieved from http://archive.boston.com/yourlife/health/diseases/articles/2005/06/18/organizers_assail_care_for_doctor_in_tb_case/?page=full.

Spector, R. E. (2013). *Cultural Diversity in Health and Illness* (8th ed.). Boston: Pearson. TB testing at Massachusetts hospitals begins [Press release]. (2005, June 18). *WNBC*. Retrieved from http://www.freerepublic.com/focus/f-news/1425817/posts.

Discussion Questions

1. Why do the values of "do no harm" and privacy conflict with each other in this case?
2. Do you agree with how the BMC PR team handled the TB case? Why? If not, what should they have done?
3. If another illness outbreak were to occur, what could the PR team do to more effectively communicate with the community?
4. According to the deontological approach, what was the morally correct thing to do in this case? Do you agree with this? Why or why not?
5. This case study mentioned three ethical issues related to an illness outbreak. What are other potential ethical issues that could arise from illness/disease outbreaks?

EMERGENT ETHICAL HEALTHCARE PUBLIC RELATIONS IN THE DIGITAL AGE

Alisa Agozzino, Ph.D., APR, *Ohio Northern University*, and
Katee Fenimore, *St. Rita's Medical Center*

Social media platforms continue to evolve and grow. Capitalizing on the next big social media platform seems to be the dangling carrot for strategists who are looking for a better way to connect, engage, and collaborate with stakeholders. The healthcare industry, like other highly regulated industries, tends to lag behind in adopting these ever-changing platforms out of an abundance of caution. But by sticking with well-known one-way communication strategies such as billboards, fliers, and brochures, patients, who are accustomed to two-way communication in their daily interactions, are left wanting more. Public relations and communication professionals are challenged to find a social media strategy that is both engaging and effective as well as compliant with the myriad of rules and regulations governing the U.S. healthcare industry.

This reading examines how PR practitioners in healthcare organizations can share important information with patients, families, and other key stakeholders in the digital arena. Social media is all about two-way, real-time communication, allowing organizations to connect with stakeholders in new ways. One key issue that communicators must address is how an organization should respond to patients who use social media to complain about their care. Should they ignore or block negative comments to protect the organization's reputation? Or should they respond and risk breaching a patient's privacy or exposing proprietary information? This case study will review the social media approach used by one hospital in West Central Ohio and will highlight best practices for ethical social media engagement. With proper research, collaboration between departments, and a solid social media policy, social media can add value to contemporary healthcare organizations by strengthening patient relationships.

Background

The use of online doctor reviews, social media interactions, do-it-yourself health apps, and medical tourism has quickly moved the healthcare industry into a highly competitive retail environment. Added pressures from increased regulations, patient care costs, and hospital revenue fluctuations have forced the largest industry in the United States to undergo change like never before. While some healthcare providers have been waiting to shift their public relations strategy, others are only taking baby steps in the direction of change.

Part of this reticence can be attributed to the learning curve in healthcare public relations. Not everyone working in healthcare communications comes from a clinical background. Thus PR practitioners must spend hours, sometimes weeks, learning the content so they can explain it simply, yet engagingly, to the public. Proper training on the use of social media can be key to working within the social space in the healthcare arena (Horowitz, 2014). When social media platforms are used effectively, they have the potential to promote individual and public health. However, when used carelessly, platforms can be intimidating and frightening (Panahi, Watson, & Partridge, 2014, Ventola, 2014).

Advantages of Using Social Media

Looking to how social media may add value to contemporary health care is important (George, 2012). The advantages of using social media platforms in the healthcare industry are similar to those in other industries. Social platforms allow the organization to build relationships with key stakeholders—a primary foundational tool in the public relations toolbox. Healthcare professionals can use social channels—specifically Facebook in the current case study—to build communities and relationships with key publics while sharing their messages. Facebook allows the user to share information with "friends" and vice versa. To build a relationship, communicators must make an effort to fully engage these "friends" in meaningful two-way communication. Facebook holds promise for improving patient engagement and empowerment and community building (Househ, Borycki, & Kushniruk, 2014).

Because Facebook can include photos and video as well as text, it is an excellent way to share information quickly to those engaged on the platform. As part of a solid strategy for building the relationship, PR practitioners can use visuals to connect with consumers in a way that is memorable and engaging. As part of that social media strategy, monitoring what target publics think of the Facebook content (both text and visuals) can help organizations determine what is important to target publics (Agozzino, 2014). By using a planned social strategy, the organization can benefit by providing posts that are engaging and informative to patients who want to connect with and support the organization.

Disadvantages of Using Social Media

While social media platforms offer the potential to connect and promote organizations, when used carelessly the results can be frightening. Two examples of the inappropriate use of social media in the healthcare industry are included here. These examples include breaches of patient privacy and damage to the organization's professional image.

A major concern regarding the use of social media in the healthcare field is the risk of an accidental breach of patient confidentiality. HIPAA sets guidelines for the use and disclosure of protected health information, and unauthorized disclosure of this information can lead to a breach of HIPAA. HIPAA violations regarding patient privacy breaches on social media continue to increase (Bouldrick, 2015), and even unintentional violations are still punishable by law.

Another major concern includes the damage that can be done to the professional image of an organization and its employees. An organization is at "reputational risk if its processes and procedures for handling social media conversations and managing expectations are not well planned or their engagement with wider communities is not strategized" (Kaul et al., 2015, 459). Public relations professionals handling social media inquiries must understand that their responses will affect what the public thinks of the entire organization.

The Situation

St. Rita's Medical Center has provided healthcare to the people of West Central Ohio since 1918 (Virtual Tour, n.d.). It is a part of Mercy Health (formerly Catholic Health Partners), the largest health system in Ohio. The services that St. Rita's provides include cardiovascular care, trauma and emergency, cancer treatment, women's health, pediatrics, orthopedics, sports medicine and rehabilitation, behavioral services, and more. St. Rita's provides millions of dollars annually in community benefit for poor, underserved, and uninsured community members.

St. Rita's uses its various social media channels to connect with a variety of publics, especially patients. Rather than using social media as a platform to offer medical advice that is specific to each patient, St. Rita's shares general medical information such as wellness tips and pointers for healthy lifestyles. Their posts encourage patients and the general public to proactively take control of their health and to be active participants in their own wellness.

However, when choosing to engage on social media, an organization opens the door for two-way discussion, and sometimes patients will share their personal healthcare information and/or ask for medical advice on social platforms. When patients share this personal information, a number of ethical considerations can arise. In one case, St. Rita's posted a video clip on Facebook featuring a new physician and the pain management services he offers patients. More than 1,000 people viewed the video, more than 20 followers "liked" the video, and it was shared more than 15 times. Although the feedback seemed generally positive, one unhappy patient commented: "This doctor sent my test results to a lab not in my network, so I was charged $2,500!"

St. Rita's PR team replied to the comment and thanked the follower for connecting with them on social media. They explained that "We are unable to discuss patient-related matters via social media, but we recommend you reaching out to our Patient Relations Department. We want to help get your concerns addressed." A direct link to contact Patient Relations was provided with the comment.

St. Rita's encountered a number of opportunities and challenges with this single comment. First, the comment was posted publicly and contained an unhappy sentiment, which had the potential to harm St. Rita's brand and reputation. Second, because the comment referenced a patient's health information, St. Rita's faced the risk of breaching privacy and violating HIPAA regulations by even engaging in the conversation.

The PR professionals at St. Rita's wanted to respond to this patient, restore a positive relationship, and rectify the situation. They could have chosen to ignore the comment and avoid the risk of crossing HIPAA boundaries, but responding to the negative feedback gave St. Rita's the opportunity to show followers that they take customer service seriously and they care about patients and their concerns.

St. Rita's PR professionals developed a social media plan to respond to similar comments appropriately and ethically. Regular meetings between public relations, health information management, and patient relations professionals helped to establish a logical communication flow when these issues arose on social media. With a plan in place, social media managers were able to respond to this particular comment quickly, confidently, and in a timely fashion, and direct the patient to the appropriate department. The appropriate response from St. Rita's in this example was effective and beneficial for public relations (the organization's image was maintained), health information management (there was no breach of patient privacy), and patient relations (the patient was encouraged to contact St. Rita's so the situation could be rectified and the relationship could be restored).

Outcomes

Results of Opportunity

Social media never sleeps. One of St. Rita's social media strategies is to ensure that its patients are taken care of around the clock on all channels, just like in a hospital setting. The goal is to attempt to respond to comments/private messages as soon as possible. This requires vigilant monitoring of all channels and prompt action when needed. St. Rita's has built groups of words and phrases into the social listening tools in order so they can monitor the effectiveness of their social media activity. The PR team needs to analyze each post so they can understand the context in which the comment was made. Since others are watching, in addition to the original commenter, St. Rita makes a conscious effort to stay positive and pleasant no matter what type of comment is made.

On St. Rita's Facebook page, this patient in the case study (and countless others since) was asked to reach out to the Patient Relations Department. In an attempt to present the organization as welcoming and appreciative, the PR person always thanks the follower for connecting with them. To remain in compliance with ethical guidelines, St. Rita's explained in the response why it was unable to answer the question directly on the platform. By following through with these instructions, the follower had the ability, with permission, to have her medical record reviewed. If there is an issue, the follower is directed to the proper person who can handle the issue. If there is not an issue, which is fortunately the case most of the time, the follower is still thankful for the follow-through for investigation and the willingness of others to lend an ear.

As previously mentioned, one of the disadvantages of using social media is the potential for breaches of patient privacy and damage to professional image, which is demonstrated in this case study. According to the director of marketing and communications at St. Rita's Health Partners, when the organization is presented with situations like this on social media, the strategy is to take the conversation offline with the commenter via private message, email, or phone call, and to offer additional support to resolve their concerns. By acknowledging the commenter, showing appreciation, and then transferring the conversation to a different format, St. Rita's can maintain a professional image without discussing patient information in a public forum.

St. Rita's Health Partners uses social media not as a forum to discuss medical advice or patient records with followers, but instead as a channel to share the organization's story, promote its mission, and introduce its staff and services. For example, St. Rita's has posted a series of doctor videos that allow followers to get to know a little more about their physician, what they do, and why they chose to work at St. Rita's. These videos not only introduce St. Rita's staff to new patients, but current patients often comment about their connection with the doctor. Second, St. Rita's has implemented regular "Throwback Thursday" posts, which highlight the organization's history and mission. Third, St. Rita's shares a weekly blog post from a sports medicine physician, who writes about timely topics and offers tips for an active and healthy lifestyle.

These posts are just a few examples of St. Rita's content strategy. So that posts are made on a consistent and strategic basis, a content calendar was created to align with business objectives and keep things in order. The content calendar benefits the organization if it is running a campaign for the month and helps the team choose the best times to make specific posts. When building the content calendar out for the month, St. Rita's constructs organic content that is shareable. By using the art of storytelling, the organization lets its followers promote these types of posts. As a nonprofit with a tight budget, St. Rita's rarely is offered the opportunity to pay for content to be boosted. When it does boost content, every effort is made to find an area where there is a business need.

Even though the organization is careful not to post health information that could breach HIPAA policy, social media opens the door to two-way communication. When followers and patients post information that could jeopardize the organization's professional image and disclose patient information, as demonstrated in this case study, St. Rita's public relations professionals have a plan in place to ensure ethical communication. With a timely response to acknowledge the commenter's concern, and thanks to a close working relationship between hospital departments (including Marketing, Patient Relations, and Health Information Management), public relations professionals are able to quickly direct their followers to the appropriate contact, ensuring that the patient's concern is addressed and that the relationship is maintained without breaching confidentiality.

Also worth noting is the public social media policy that is visible on the organization's Facebook page. This policy allows St. Rita's to protect its social community by allowing the organization to hide or possibly delete any inappropriate engagement shared to its page. If someone is not following the social media policy, the social media specialist can give the user a warning and direct that user back to the policy. This policy can help mitigate risks while creating effective and consistent social communication between the organization and the public.

Ethical Implications

The Public Relations Society of America (PRSA) has outlined a code of ethics for all of its members practicing public relations within any field. It is important to review these foundational guidelines in an effort to practice ethical public relations. These guidelines provide professionals with a useful guide in upholding ethical responsibilities. Some ethical issues are not as clear as we would like, but these guidelines do provide insight regarding best practices when faced with ethical dilemmas.

When examining this situation, the first ethical concern that arises is patient privacy and potential HIPAA violations. Your first instinct might be to investigate the matter and send a private message to the commenter to build a positive relationship with the patient, but this would involve accessing patient records without obtaining proper identification of who is sending the correspondence. Those in charge with responding to the Facebook post understood that making any comment regarding the situation was a violation of patient privacy. By redirecting the Facebook user to the Patient Relations Department, St. Rita's public relations professionals helped the Facebook user obtain answers while still protecting patient privacy in a public arena.

Another major concern is the damage that could be done to the professional image of an organization and its employees. In this particular case study, damage was avoided to the company brand by responding to the negative posts. Some communication professionals tasked with handling social media responses want to delete or debate negative posts, but this is actually frowned upon (Rim & Song, 2016). Best practices for communications professionals involve responding in the social space appreciatively, quickly, and completely. St. Rita's thanked the follower for posting and redirected her to the Patient Relations Department to help resolve the problem. This action displayed to other followers that St. Rita's responded to the matter in a timely and polite manner.

References

Agozzino, A. (2014). Building and maintaining relationships through social media. In Bauer, J., & Stevenson, C. (Eds.), *Building Online Communities in Higher Institutions* (pp. 69–90). Hershey, PA: IGI Global.

Bouldrick, D. (2015). HIPAA violations on social media: think before you post! *AMT Events, 1*, 24.

George, D. R. (2012). Making "social" safer: Are Facebook and other online networks becoming less hazardous for health professionals? *Journal of Clinical Ethics*, *23*(4), 348–352.

Horowitz, A. C. (2014). Social media challenges for healthcare employers, employees. *Long-Term Living for the Continuing Care Professional*, *63*(8), 13–15.

Househ, M., Borycki, E., & Kushniruk, A. (2014). Empowering patients through social media: The benefits and challenges. *Health Informatics Journal*, *20*(1), 50–58.

Kaul, A., Chaudhri, V., Cherian, D., Freberg, K., Mishra, S., Kumar, R., & Carroll, C. E. (2015). Social media: The new mantra for managing reputation. *Vikalpa: The Journal for Decision Makers, 40*(4), 455–491.

Panahi, S., Watson, J., & Partridge, H. (2014). Social media and physicians: Exploring the benefits and challenges. *Health Informatics Journal, 22*(2), 99–112.

Public Relations Society of America (n.d.). PRSA Member Code of Ethics. Retrieved July 28, 2016, from https://www.prsa.org/AboutPRSA/Ethics/CodeEnglish/index.html?seMobiPref=true.

Rim, H., & Song, D. (2016). "How negative becomes less negative": Understanding the effects of comment valence and response sidedness in social media. *Journal of Communication, 66*(3), 475–495.

Ventola, C. L. (2014). Social media and health care professionals: Benefits, risks, and best practices. *Pharmacy and Therapeutics, 39*(7), 491–520.

Virtual Tour. (n.d.). Retrieved July 28, 2016, from http://www.ehealthconnection.com/regions/mercy_st_ritas/overview_virtual_tour.aspx.

Discussion Questions

1. Pertaining to its replies to all Facebook posts, how could St. Rita's Medical Center employ an evaluation method to assess what is working?
2. The PRSA Code of Provisions of Conduct includes six core principles. What two provisions do you find most prevalent in this case study?
3. In the healthcare industry, why is it important to have a social media plan that has been reviewed and approved by several departments (e.g., health information management/medical records, compliance and risk, and patient relations)?
4. What are the pros and cons of allowing social media users to comment publicly on a healthcare organization's Facebook page?
5. Where is the St. Rita's social media policy found?

HEALTHCARE ORGANIZATIONS AND PATIENT SAFETY: QUESTIONS OF ETHICAL PUBLIC RELATIONS PRACTICES

Carrie Reif-Stice, M.A., *Columbus State University* Julie A. Lasslo, *Eastern Kentucky University* M.A., and Kathryn E. Anthony, Ph.D., *University of Southern Mississippi*

According to the CDC (2016), there were approximately 35.1 million hospital stays in the United States in 2015, representing a hospitalization rate of 1,139.6 stays per 10,000 people. When patients are admitted to the hospital, they enter a complex organization; healthcare organizations must manage the competing goals of providing excellent patient care while remaining profitable, financially stable entities. Hospitals must provide quality care while achieving a high degree of patient satisfaction.

The Patient Protection and Affordable Care Act (ACA), signed into law in March 2010, is the most significant reform of the healthcare system since the institution of Medicare and Medicaid, and it directly affects the ways in which healthcare organizations balance patient and financial responsibilities (U.S. Department of Health & Human Services [HHS], 2015). The overarching goal of the ACA is to improve the accessibility, affordability, and quality of medical care (HHS, 2015). To achieve this goal, the ACA specifically includes the hospital version of the Consumer Assessment of Healthcare Providers & Systems survey (HCAHPS, 2013) as a way to calculate value-based incentive payments to hospitals (HHS, 2015). The HCAHPS survey, originally developed in 2005, is the first nationally standardized survey for collecting and publicly reporting patients' perceptions and experience with hospital care (Centers for Medicare & Medicaid Services, 2015). The inclusion of the HCAHPS aims to enhance transparency through public reporting of survey results, allows for hospital comparisons, and creates incentives for hospitals to improve patient care (HCAHPS Fact Sheet, 2013).

While prioritizing patient health is a cornerstone of good medical practice, it often brings with it increased operating costs and the potential for additional financial constraints for hospitals (Everhart, Neff, Al-Amin, Nogle, & Weech-Maldonado, 2013). Because of this, most hospitals continually seek ways to reduce expenditures and increase profitability. However, providing responsible patient-centered care is inextricably tied to ethical behavior (Opel et al., 2009). Thus, healthcare organizations should never sacrifice quality care for financial performance. Healthcare organizations that favor financial gain over patient-centered care run the risk of damaging their organizational reputation and legitimacy (Anthony & Sellnow, 2011; Veil, Wickline, & Sellnow, 2013). In this case study, we will consider how one hospital managed a potential ethical dilemma between patient care and financial gain.

The Situation

St. Joseph's Hospital in Syracuse, New York, is a not-for-profit hospital offering primary, specialized, and urgent care services in central New York and northern Pennsylvania (St. Joseph's Health, 2016). St. Joseph's has been listed by *U.S. News & World Report* (2016) as a Best Regional Hospital, with high rankings in heart bypass surgery and hip and knee replacements.

St. Joseph's came under scrutiny for the way it handled staff members' claims that Dr. Michael Clarke, an orthopedic surgeon who specializes in hip replacement and resurfacing, was physically and verbally assaulting anesthetized patients. Specifically, 11 hospital employees claimed that he slapped patients and eight claimed that he made sexual comments about patients (Huff, 2014). A federal investigation revealed that Dr. Clarke inappropriately touched unconscious patients and called them derogatory names. According to the report by the Center for Medicare & Medicaid Services, staff members witnessed the surgeon "wind up" to deliver forceful slaps, which often left a handprint on the buttocks or hips, while calling patients names like "fat ___ " (Lerner, 2014, 1). Dr. Clarke was also accused of making sexually charged jokes and directing explicit language at staff members during surgery.

Dr. Clarke denied any wrongdoing and claimed the complaints were from operating room staff who were "intent on revenge" and ruining his reputation (Mulder, 2015c, 1). He insisted the inappropriate language in the operating room was "back and forth banter" and "light-hearted exchanges" between co-workers (Mulder, 2015c, 1). He also denied referring to patients by offensive names. However, he admitted to performing a single slap over the incision site to ensure patients were adequately sedated. Staff members told investigators that slapping patients is an uncommon surgical practice (Mulder, 2014a).

Rather than taking these complaints seriously, the hospital ignored them. One staff member told federal investigators that operating room officials knew about Dr. Clarke's behavior in early 2013, but hospital administrators failed to take disciplinary action at that time. Staff members also refused to confront him for fear of jeopardizing their jobs (Mulder, 2014a). Even after a formal complaint was filed in December 2013, hospital officials continued to allow Dr. Clarke to operate. The hospital all but turned a blind eye to his behavior. However, in February 2014, a federal investigation into Dr. Clarke's conduct began. Subsequently, St. Joseph's placed him on administrative leave (Mulder, 2014a). Following his departure, the hospital issued a press release insisting that it had followed proper protocol and taken prompt action to address these issues (Lerner, 2014).

After Dr. Clarke's dismissal from the hospital, the Onondaga County District Attorney's Office investigated him for criminal misconduct. While evidence of inappropriate behavior was found, the office could not charge Dr. Clarke because there were problems identifying the victimized patients and there was no proof of sexual motivation (Kenyon, 2014). The State Board of Professional Medical Conduct also launched a separate medical misconduct investigation. Dr. Clarke was found to have practiced with negligence on more than one occasion (Mulder, 2015b); he was fined $10,000 and ordered to complete anger-management therapy. His medical license was also put on probation for three years, with strict monitoring regulations on his surgical practice (Mulder, 2015b).

St. Joseph's faced potential consequences for failing to protect patients from abuse. The Center for Medicare & Medicaid Services threatened to terminate the facility from participating in Medicare and Medicaid programs. The hospital kept its status only after firing two nursing supervisors, revising patient abuse policies, and retraining employees on patient safety (Mulder, 2014b).

Despite the misconduct of the surgeon while operating, St. Joseph's placed profit over ethical behavior and patient-centered care by ultimately inviting the surgeon to return. Dr. Clarke, the third-highest-volume orthopedic surgeon, was a top money-maker for the facility, with 480 surgeries per year. Following his departure, the hospital reported decreased inpatient volume and posted a $4.1 million operating loss during the first six months of 2014 (Mulder, 2014c). In fact, the hospital administrators fully believed that the operating loss was a direct outcome of releasing Dr. Clarke.

After a seven-month suspension, the St. Joseph's Board of Trustees reinstated his hospital privileges in October 2014. According to a staff memo, Dr. Clarke could resume practicing if he pledged to adhere to the hospital's Code of Conduct. The hospital claimed it was not money that was the major factor in its decision to reinstate him (Kenyon, 2014; Mulder, 2014d). The memo stated that the actions taken to reinstate the surgeon "were each taken with the strongest consideration of St. Joseph's mission, vision, and values. The Board of Trustees believes that the hospital has acted appropriately in upholding those values throughout this process. The decision to reinstate Dr. Clarke's privileges was made with that same thoughtful deliberation" (Deptula, Ruscitto & Waldman, 2014). Further, the memo claimed that "Based upon Dr. Clarke's completion of actions we considered to be conditions for his return, as well as his professional conduct as a surgeon over the last 8 months, the St. Joseph's medical executive committee recommended to the Board of Trustees that Dr. Clarke have his privileges restored, subject to his agreement to adhere to our code of conduct" (para. 3).

The board was vague in the ways it discussed the conditions of Dr. Clarke's return. The language employed in the memo was strategically ambiguous concerning the ways in which the board was upholding the values of the hospital by reinstating the physician (Ulmer & Sellnow, 1997). According to Eisenberg (1984, 236), strategic ambiguity is an essential organizational response during a crisis situation because it "allows the source to both reveal and conceal, to express and protect, should it become necessary to save face." Strategic ambiguity encourages organizations to communicate with stakeholders using concise messages containing vague language. Although this open but brief communication can produce positive outcomes (save face), it potentially allows organizations to engage in unethical behavior by manipulating the public's perception with incomplete or inaccurate information (Sellnow, 1993; Ulmer & Sellnow, 1997). While organizations may favor strategic ambiguity when they do not want to be forthcoming, they should never use it to intentionally hinder stakeholders' sense-making abilities (Ulmer & Sellnow, 1997).

In terms of its public relations presence, the hospital released only a couple of communications concerning the rehiring, neither of which was very public. The internal staff memo reinstating the surgeon served as one communication; CEO Kathy Ruscitto's hospital blog was the other. The CEO appeared to deny accusations that the decision to reinstate the physician had to do with financial incentives. She stated, "Sometimes people agree with the results of a decision; sometimes they don't. Moreover, it's during the times of disagreement that I may hear 'it's about the money'" (Mulder, 2014d, para. 3). She later stated, "Money is not among those first criteria. In fact, in issues of ethics or conduct, it's nowhere even on the list. Ever" (Mulder, 2014d, para. 6). However, in her post, she spent far more time articulating that the decision was not about financial incentives rather than discussing the importance of patient safety. In terms of the hospital's response in the internal memo and the blog post, both seemed to have been written in a vague manner. Neither document was specific concerning the conditions surrounding the reinstatement of the surgeon, and neither document was specific concerning the missions and the values of the hospital. The organization was strategically ambiguous in its communication surrounding the physician's reinstatement.

Additionally, the CEO's blog post appeared to be the only statement made available to the public following the scandal. In other words, it seems as though the hospital was relatively silent from a public relations perspective, particularly concerning Dr. Clarke's reinstatement.

The Outcome

The physician's inappropriate actions garnered both local and national media attention and cast the hospital in a negative light. Rather than prioritizing patient protection, the hospital appeared to prioritize its bottom line, and this choice did not go unnoticed by the community. Susan Peck, a Syracuse resident who said she had once been a patient of Dr. Clarke's, wrote in a letter to the editor of Syracuse. com, "In response to Dr. Michael T. Clarke's reinstatement to the surgical staff of St. Joseph's Hospital, it's disheartening to learn that once again money trumps ethics" (2014, para. 1). She continued, "as a woman I distrust with healthy skepticism his colleagues and hospital administrators who circled the wagons in support of his return" (para. 2). She was not alone: The online comments below her letter revealed the frustrations of other Syracuse residents who believed that the hospital had acted less than responsibly when faced with the choice between patient safety and monetary gain.

Although reinstated, Dr. Clarke did not return to St. Joseph's but resumed practice at the competing Crouse Hospital. Following the scandal, St. Joseph's continued to suffer financial repercussions. Initially, the hospital had projected a net gain of $5.9 million for 2014. While the hospital earned $641.7 million in revenue in 2014, officials reported a significant loss of $21.6 million in operating costs (Mulder, 2015a). St. Joseph's attributed $19 million of the loss to updating its electronic medical system; however, the hospital also saw a slight decline in the number of inpatients, from 27,956 in 2013 to 27,635, in 2014 (Mulder, 2015a).

The hospital's bleak financial outlook strained its ability to provide adequate healthcare and stay afloat. To remain financially stable and meet patients' needs, Trinity Health, a large nonprofit health system, acquired St. Joseph's in April 2015. A statement released by president and CEO Kathryn Ruscitto emphasized that the merger offered "St. Joseph's purchasing power and expertise in clinical and administrative practices that are needed to survive the changing health care world" (Moriarity, 2015). St. Joseph's was able to stay operational but lost its 150-year-old status as an independent not-for-profit Catholic hospital. St. Joseph's poor handling of the Clarke situation not only caused inadequate patient care but also contributed to poor financial performance and ultimately the merger with Trinity Health.

While many public relations practitioners urge organizations to use core values to guide their decision-making processes, St. Joseph's demonstrated irresponsibility and negligence by compromising patients' safety. Prioritizing profits over patient care violates ethical public relations practices (Anthony & Sellnow, 2011) and any healthcare organization's core values. Because of St. Joseph's actions, patients were not given the highest standard of care and were potentially subjected to harm. Greater than the loss to its reputation, the hospital likely damaged its organizational legitimacy (Boyd, 2000).

In conclusion, rather than being concerned for the safety and well-being of patients, it appears that St. Joseph's was more concerned with its financial bottom line. Hospital administrators consistently ignored the complaints of staff members about the doctor's misbehavior. Even after suspending him, the hospital welcomed him back once it became clear that a federal investigation would yield no concrete charges. Finally, they claimed that reinstating the physician had nothing to do with financial gains despite the monetary losses sustained in his absence. St. Joseph failed not only its patients but also its stakeholders by remaining virtually silent, except for an internal memo and a blog entry from the CEO. The hospital did not issue formal statements or press releases.

Public relations practitioners should consistently strive to position their stakeholders' safety and needs above profit or fear of damage to the organization's reputation. Ultimately, all will be lost if lesser goals are pursued first. The importance of ethical public relations cannot be understated for the longevity of an organization.

References

Anthony, K. E., & Sellnow, T. L. (2011). Beyond Narnia: The necessity of CS Lewis' first and second things in applied communication research. *Journal of Applied Communication Research*, 39(4), 441–443.

Boyd, J. (2000). Actional legitimation: No crisis necessary. *Journal of Public Relations Research*, 12(4), 341–353.

Centers for Disease Control and Prevention. (2016). Hospital utilization (in non-federal short-stay hospitals). Retrieved from http://www.cdc.gov/nchs/fastats/hospital.htm.

Centers for Medicare & Medicaid Services (2015). Hospital CAHPS. Retrieved from https://www.cms.gov/Research-Statistics-Data-and-Systems/Research/CAHPS/hcahps1.html.

Deptula, G., Ruscitto, K., & Waldman, R. (2014). Letter to St. Joseph's employees and volunteers [Memorandum]. Retrieved from media.syracuse.com/news/other/2014/10/06/stjosephs-letter.pdf.

Eisenberg, E. M. (1984). Ambiguity as strategy in organizational communication. *Communication Monographs, 51,* 227–242.

Everhart, D., Neff, D., Al-Amin, M., Nogle, J., & Weech-Maldonado, R. (2013). The effects of nurse staffing on hospital financial performance: Competitive versus less competitive markets. *Health Care Management Review, 38*(2), 146–155.

HCAHPS Fact Sheet. (2013, August). Centers for Medicare & Medicaid Services (CMS). Retrieved from http://www.hcahpsonline.org.

Huff, E. A. (2014, April 26). Surgeon routinely slaps patients on buttocks before surgery. Retrieved from http://www.naturalnews.com/044878_surgeon_sexual_harassment_assault.html.

Kenyon, J. (2014, October 6). Butt-slapping surgeon reinstated at St. Joseph's Hospital. Retrieved from http://cnycentral.com/news/local/butt-slapping-surgeon-reinstated-at-st-josephs-hospital.

Lerner, W. (2014, April 7). Surgeon accused of slapping sedated patients' behinds. Retrieved from http://news.yahoo.com/blogs/oddnews/surgeon-accused-of-slapping-sedated-patients%E2%80%99-behinds-181952054.html.

Moriarity, R. (2015). St. Joseph's Hospital joins one of the nation's largest Catholic health care systems. Retrieved from https://www.syracuse.com/business-news/index.ssf/2015/07/st_josephs_hospital_joins_trinity_health.html.

Mulder, J. T. (2014a, April 6). Syracuse surgeon slapped sedated patients, called them insulting names, feds say. Retrieved from https://www.scribd.com/embeds/216383339/content?start_page=1&view_mode=scroll&show_recommendations=true.

Mulder, J. T. (2014b, June 16). Syracuse hospital passes follow-up inspection in wake of patient butt-slapping complaint. Retrieved from https://www.scribd.com/embeds/229947982/content?start_page=1&view_mode=scroll&show_recommendations=true.

Mulder, J. T. (2014c, August 31). Ouster of doc accused of slapping patients' butts hurts Syracuse hospital's bottom line. Retrieved from http://www.syracuse.com/news/index.ssf/2014/08/post_1116.html.

Mulder, J. T. (2014d, October 14). Syracuse hospital says mission, not money, guides its decisions after reinstating controversial doc. Retrived from https://www.syracuse.com/news/index.ssf/2014/10/st_joes_says_mission_not_money_guides_its_decisions_after_reinstating_controvers.html

Mulder, J. T. (2015a, Feb. 18). Syracuse hospital loses $21.6 million, wants to join big health system. Retrieved from https://www.syracuse.com/health/index.ssf/2015/st_joes_which_lost_216_million_last_year_looking_to_join_big_health_system.html.

Mulder, J. T. (2015b, May 20). Syracuse doc accused of slapping patients fined $10,000, ordered to get therapy. Retrieved from http://www.syracuse.com/health/index .ssf/2015/05/syracuse_doc_accused_of_slapping_patients_fined_10000_ ordered_to_get_therapy.html.

Mulder, J. T. (2015c, May 20). Syracuse doctor says he never slapped anesthetized patients' butts. Retrieved from http://www.syracuse.com/health/index .ssf/2015/05/post_8.html.

Opel, D. J., Wlfond, B. S., Brownstein, D., Diekma, D. S., & Pearlman, R. A. (2009). Characterization of organizational issues in pediatric clinical ethics consultation: A qualitative story. *Journal of Medical Ethics, 35*(8), 477–482.

Peck, S. M. (2014, October 8). Reinstatement of butt-slapping doctor proves that money trumps ethics. Retrieved from http://www.syracuse.com/opinion/index .ssf/2014/10/reinstatement_of_buttslapping_doctor_proves_that_money_trumps_ ethics_your_lette.html.

Sellnow, T. L. (1993). Scientific argument in organizational crisis communication: The case of Exxon. *Argumentation and Advocacy, 30*, 28–42.

St. Joseph's Health. (2016). Who We Are. Retrieved June 28, 2016, from https://www .sjhsyr.org/who-we-are.

Ulmer, R. R., & Sellnow, T. L. (1997). Strategic ambiguity and the ethic of significant choice in the tobacco industry's crisis communication. *Communication Studies, 48*(3), 215–233.

U.S. Department of Health & Human Services. (2015). Read the law. Retrieved from http://www.hhs.gov/healthcare/about-the-law/read-the-law/.

Veil, S. R., Sellnow, T. L., & Wickline, M. C. (2013). British Petroleum: An egregious violation of the ethic of first and second things. *Business and Society Review, 118*(3), 361–381.

Discussion Questions

1. Were St. Joseph's public relations practices adequate? Why or why not?
2. What public relations responses should St. Joseph's have implemented to resolve this issue?
3. What is the danger of organizations prioritizing financial gain over stakeholders?

10 GOVERNMENT RELATIONS

Learning Outcomes

- Recognize the scope of government relations.
- Critique the practices of government relations.
- Analyze the influence of public relations on government relations.
- Choose appropriate ethical communication tactics for government relations.

Definitions

Astroturfing: Creating fake grassroots communication that "makes each message appear authentic and original" (Berkman, 2008, 7).

Lobbying: Directly or indirectly trying to influence legislation.

Public affairs: The branch of public relations "that deals with the political environment" (Lattimore, Baskin, Heiman, Toth, & Van Leuven, 2004, 302). Also known as government affairs.

Communication, politics, and government have been connected throughout history. In the United States, documents like *The Federalist Papers, Common Sense*, and the Bill of Rights can be viewed as strong "examples of the power of public relations" and set up the foundation of the government (McKinnon, Tedesco, & Lauder, 2001, 557). Today, government relations is a broad field encompassing public affairs, elections, and lobbying.

Public affairs, also called government affairs, is a commonly used term for the branch of public relations "that deals with the political environment" (Lattimore et al., 2004, 302). You can find public affairs officers in all branches of government. These practitioners have multiple functions that can be viewed as attempting to meet seven goals:

- Informing constituents
- Ensuring cooperation in government programs
- Fostering citizen support
- Advocating to government administrators

- Managing internal information
- Facilitating media relations
- Building community and nation (Broom, 2009, 406–407).

As these goals show, public affairs practitioners are just like any other public relations practitioners, but in the context of government. The standard ethical considerations of public relations must be used here, but the added aspect of working for the government muddies ethical practices.

For example, in selling a consumer product, practitioners need to abide by ethical guidelines, but what changes when the product you are promoting is a governmental program supported by only one political party? Informing constituents appears ethically neutral—just give out the information—but what if the elected officials control what can be said? For example, the *Washington Post* reported in 2017 that the Centers for Disease Control and Prevention was "forbidden" from using the words "vulnerable, entitlement, diversity, transgender, fetus, evidence-based and science-based" (Sun & Eilperin, 2017, para. 2). Having to avoid prohibited words complicates the ethical and practical tasks of informing constituents.

Another area of government relations involves working on elections. Here the practitioner might serve as a candidate's media spokesperson but is probably also a "trusted adviser who helps formulate campaign strategy and position on issues" (Lattimore et al., 2004, 317). Modern elections are built around fundraising, media coverage, and volunteer engagement, and all three of these activities have extensive communication elements. When practitioners were asked about the difference between informing voters and "selling" a candidate, the overwhelming opinion was that "the line is drawn between truth and lies"—but others suggested that the line has moved recently. In fact, one respondent argued that practitioners have no ethical responsibility "to inform unless that helps sell the candidate" (McKinnon, Tedesco, & Lauder, 2001, 561). As a practitioner in the political realm you will have to decide about your line and how much you can ethically do to help your candidate or policy to win.

Lobbying is also a substantial activity in government relations. Hendrix (2004, 183) states that the "core" activity of public affairs is direct and indirect lobbying. Direct lobbying involves contacting legislators and providing information about legislative changes your organization would like to see implemented. Indirect lobbying involves communicating with supporters of a legislative action and having them contact legislators. For example, meeting with a member of Congress to give information about a proposed gas pipeline is direct lobbying; organizing a rally of supporters in the home district where the proposed pipeline would be built is indirect lobbying.

One problematic type of indirect lobbying is astroturfing, which involves creating fake grassroots communication that "makes each message appear authentic and original" (Berkman, 2008, 7). Astroturfing is "usually sponsored by large corporations to support any arguments or claims in their favor, or to challenge and deny those against them" (Cho, Martens, Kim, & Rodrique, 2011, 572). Creating a rally of pipeline supporters who truly support the pipeline would not be astroturfing, but requiring the employees of the sponsoring energy company to attend that rally would be ethically questionable. Public relations and politics have been together throughout history—and so have the ethical considerations.

References

Berkman, R. I. (2008). *The Art of Strategic Listening: Finding Market Intelligence Through Blogs and Other Social Media*. Ithaca, NY: Paramount Market Publishing.

Boom, G. M. (2009). *Cutlip and Center's Effective Public Relations*. Upper Saddle River, NJ: Prentice Hall.

Cho, C. H., Martens, M. L., Kim, H., & Rodrigue, M. (2011). Astroturfing global warming: It isn't always greener on the other side of the fence. *Journal of Business Ethics*, *104*(4), 571–587.

Hendrix, J. A. (2004). *Public Relations Cases*. Belmont, CA: Wadsworth Publishing Company.

Lattimore, D., Baskin, O., Heiman, S. T., Toth, E. L., & Van Leuven, J. K. (2004). *Public Relations: The Profession and the Practice*. New York: McGraw-Hill.

McKinnon, L. M., Tedesco, J. C., & Lauder, T. (2001). Political power through public relations. In R. L. Heath & G. M. Vasquez (Eds.), *Handbook of Public Relations* (pp. 557–563). Boston: Sage.

Sun, L. H., & Eilperin, J. (2017, December 15). CDC gets list of forbidden words: Fetus, transgender, diversity. Retrieved February 9, 2018, from https://www .washingtonpost.com/national/health-science/cdc-gets-list-of-forbidden-words-fetus-transgender-diversity/2017/12/15/f503837a-e1cf-11e7-89e8-edec16379010_story.html?utm_term=.c968fb9f8758.

DEALING WITH SUBSEQUENT CRISIS RESPONSE: TIMELINESS AND TRANSPARENCY IN GOVERNMENT RESPONSE TO THE NEW JERSEY BOARDWALK FIRE

Mildred F. Wiggins Perreault, Ph.D., *Appalachian State University*, and Anli Xiao, Ph.D., *Texas A&M University - Corpus Christi*

A year after Hurricane Sandy destroyed the New Jersey beachside boroughs of Seaside Park and Seaside Heights, they experienced another crisis: A fire destroyed a large portion of the recently rebuilt boardwalk. Later, authorities determined that faulty wiring left unattended after Hurricane Sandy had caused the fire.

The state of New Jersey and governments in the two boroughs released formal messages less than three hours after the fire on social media and state and community websites. This chapter examines the messages that were shared formally about the crisis, which overall resulted in a positive crisis recovery narrative in the news media. Transparency is vital in crisis and disaster response and can create a positive narrative and understanding of the situation and the responsibilities of the different publics involved. In this case those groups were the citizens of the two towns, and the state and local governments. Transparency provides a platform for honesty, credibility, and trust during disaster recovery (Balkin, 1999; Rawlins, 2009).

Background

Hurricane Sandy was a tropical storm that became a hurricane on October 24, 2012. The storm's sustained winds reached 74 mph when it first made landfall at Jamaica on October 24. In the United States, Sandy was responsible for the deaths of at least 74 people in the Northeastern United States (48 in New York, 12 in New Jersey, 5 in Connecticut, 2 in Pennsylvania, and 5 in other states and 75 outside of the U.S. (CNN, 2016). New Jersey's governor, Chris Christie, estimated that as of November 28, 2012, the costs accrued from Sandy-related storms were about $36.8 billion: $29.4 billion in repair and restoration and $7.4 billion in supplemental mitigation protection and prevention coverage (CNN, 2016). Moreover, Hurricane Sandy created problems with funding and insurance payouts for businesses. In an effort to build back before the following summer, businesses were reopening, resources were stretched, and inspections were delayed for new construction and renovations.

A little less than a year later, in September 2013, the Seaside Heights boardwalk was devastated by a fire that destroyed 68 buildings and as well as the Funtown Pier attraction. Funtown Pier included amusement park attractions like go-karts, a Ferris wheel, and carnival games (Funtown Pier Amusements, 2017). The New Jersey shoreline is dotted with towns with attractions such as small amusement parks, casinos, souvenir shops, restaurants, hotels, and aquariums.

Hurricane Sandy destroyed more than half of Funtown Pier's rides in 2012 and the fire destroyed the remainder (Funderburk, 2014). With the subsequent crisis of the boardwalk fire, borough officials were expected to stretch their resources yet again.

The political situation in New Jersey was difficult in the period following Hurricane Sandy. Christie was running for reelection, but the state government was being criticized for the delay in providing funding to the communities affected by Hurricane Sandy. Christie's governing practices were being called into question, including some negative interactions he had with locals during a speech in Seaside Heights shortly after the hurricane. The economic situation in these communities was difficult due to the decrease in tourism income and a lack of emergency funding from the state. After the fire, Christie appeared in Seaside Heights and made several public statements that were released in the media. However, in this case, officials established solid lines of communication both online and offline with public and media sources.

Despite mixed feelings on the part of local residents and local officials about Christie's support of the communities of Seaside Park and Seaside Heights, the state funds were needed to get them back on their feet. The communities are small and have few full-time employees. The town managers in both communities are full-time and serve as spokespeople for their communities as well as key political figures. The governor's office does not have an office near the towns, but state officials had been in and out of the communities throughout the 2012–13 year.

Town websites and state government media blasts used phrasing that expressed the issues facing the boardwalk communities, such as the need for economic stability, the importance to continue to rebuild after the hurricane, and a desire to rebuild quickly but in compliance with town and state building codes. However, while transparency strategies may lack long-term scope, they reveal strategic crisis recovery and response.

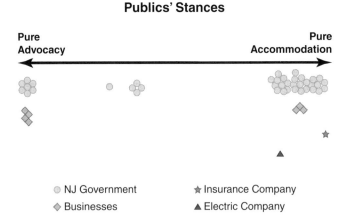

FIGURE 10.1 A plot graph of the stances conveyed in the local news coverage and press releases.

This graph was informed by Cancel, Mitrook, & Cameron, 1999; Coombs, 2007; and Coombs & Holladay, 2001.

The Situation

To communicate concern around the boardwalk fire, local officials and business owners spoke about their desire to discover its cause as soon as possible. Many locals were quick to assume the fire was a result of arson. The local fire chief and mayor made statements to the press within eight hours of the fire. Press releases were distributed and placed on the website within 24 hours. Officials emphasized the desire to share all the information they had about the cause of the fire to help the local community to move on. These statements were made in public appearances and written communications.

Analyzing the responses of the governor's office and the towns provides context for the conversation around community crisis narratives as well as an ethical perspective on that response. In a statement directly following the boardwalk fire, Christie stated, "I feel like I want to throw up and that's me." Christie emphasized his own identity as a New Jersey resident and the value of resilience and solidarity in the local community and created a shared zone of meaning with the community. He also provided immediate help to businesses damaged by the fire by extending the deadline for paying taxes or filing tax returns: "This will help them get back on their feet and back in operation as quickly as possible," he said. Press releases from local governments that were published online and news coverage also echoed Christie's statements, and dialogues were created between the local business owners, citizens, and government officials. Information was shared by state and local governments, such as the cause of the fire, who would pay to fix the problem, and whether the Federal Emergency Management Agency (FEMA) would cover the damages as part of the federal government's allotted Hurricane Sandy funds. Different departments, such as state and local government, the insurance companies, and businesses, also cooperated. This cooperative network helped to shoulder the burden of the fire's financial costs and enhanced the community's ability to cope and recover. Consistent messaging on the part of all those involved helped to create a positive overarching crisis narrative.

As the information becomes richer, more transparency occurs (Rawlins, 2009). Early on, Christie issued a number of press releases containing new information and made public appearances, but these tapered off after about a week. Most of the statements made by the governor were made in the first five days following the fires:

- "My Heart Goes Out to the People of Seaside" (September 12): In his statement directly following the boardwalk fire, Christie stated, "I feel like I want to throw up and that's me." By using informal language (conversational voice), he identifies with the residents affected by the disaster, even though he doesn't live there—he comments that he is a New

Jerseyan and therefore the boardwalk is part of his identity. He also made several statements about the shared value of resilience in the community following Hurricane Sandy, and expressed solidarity with those who survived the first disaster in 2012. An accommodative "stance is operationalized as the position an organization takes in the decision making, which is supposed to determine which strategy or tactic to employ" (Cameron, Pang, & Jin, 2007, 147). An accommodative stance is seen in the way Christie created a "zone of meaning" with the community (Heath, 1997). In his first statement on the boardwalk Christie stated, "We are providing immediate help to businesses in the fire-damaged area by giving them extra time before they have to make scheduled tax payments or file returns."

- "Christie Administration Announces Debris Removal Assistance for Seaside Park and Seaside Heights in the Aftermath of Boardwalk Fire" (September 16): Dialogue is also important when bringing attention to crisis response. The news coverage echoed the sentiments expressed in formal statements and press releases as well on local government websites. The governor held a "Mobile Cabinet Forum" on September 16 to address issues at a local level. He also released information when it became available and provided the press with information via press conferences and news releases. Community business owners, officials, and others were involved in these events and were quoted in the news media.

- "Christie Administration Announces Tax Relief for Businesses Impacted by Seaside Boardwalk Fire" (September 17): Again, Christie focused on helping the community however he can. He said he could not provide more monetary compensation because New Jersey was already dealing with expenses from Hurricane Sandy, but he could extend the deadline for local taxes. He stated, "This will help them get back on their feet and back in operation as quickly as possible." Offering compensation showed that the governor was sympathetic to the residents' plight (according to Situational Crisis Communication Theory). Two forms of compensation were being offered here: (1) $15 million in recovery funds and (2) an extension of the tax deadline. In this speech Christie outlined how money would be provided through tax relief, mostly because of the lack of funding available to help with the second round of destruction. This lack of resources was emphasized in news coverage, although Christie was still criticized for not doing more.

Businesses involved in the response to the fire, such as the local electric company and local insurance agencies, were also included in news coverage. Seaside Heights posted on its website information to help businesses connect with resources, using the same tactics they had used to address Hurricane Sandy recovery.

Timeliness is vital in crisis communications. Christie responded to the fire within five hours, and the cause was announced within a week. By providing information quickly Christie acknowledged the severity of the crisis and gained control over the crisis narrative. The narratives of the local governments and the state government worked in tandem to provide a positive recovery narrative: Seaside Park and Seaside Heights are strong and will not let the fire set them back. The community will unify to continue with its rebuilding efforts.

As noted earlier, transparency allows the spokesperson to relate to the audience and adopt an accommodative stance. Christie used this connection to the people to establish his concern and credibility. When interviewed by the media, community members spoke about various rumors that were circulating (e.g., the fire was deliberately set), and local officials and the governor addressed these in their press conferences. Many of these statements were made before it was clear what the cause of the fire was or how much it would cost to fix what had been damaged. The rumor period lasted less than a week, and rumors were dispelled quickly with public statements. As soon as information was available it was shared with the public. Rather than ignoring the rumors, statements addressed them head on and thus eliminated them from the community conversation. For example, one of the rumors was that the fire was started by a gang. Public officials denied this and asked for the community's assistance in finding the true source of the fire. Ethical public relations strategies encourage the spokesperson not to cast blame or make a scapegoat of a particular group without having evidence. After a thorough investigation officials discovered that the fire was due to the faulty wiring in Kohr's Frozen Custard shop.

The response to the fire involved many different departments. Based on the messages released, state and local governments appeared to be coordinating their

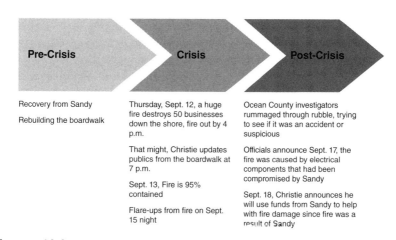

FIGURE 10.2

actions, and insurance companies and businesses appeared to be cooperating with the governments. While the amount of cooperation that appeared in these messages might not in reality have been the complete truth, the information being released created a consistent, positive narrative.

Outcomes

The transparent communication strategies fully informed the publics, especially the local residents and businesses. Local residents were able to discuss their concerns in person at town meetings and virtually by contacting local officials through the town website and via Facebook groups (Seaside Heights Boardwalk, n.d.; Seaside Park, NJ, n.d.). Aside from providing rich information and clarification, the government provided emotional support by sympathizing with the publics, making sure they felt understood. For example, Christie stated that "after all the effort and time and resources that we've put in to help the folks of Seaside Heights and Seaside Park rebuild . . . to see this going on it's just unthinkable." And when expressing his safety concerns, Christie said, "My advice to you, in fact my admonition to you, is—do not come here . . . Do not travel. Stay away." One of the Facebook pages provided links back to the town website.

The dialogic strategy allowed the publics' thoughts and concerns to be heard. These communication strategies, together with temporarily postponing tax deadlines, provided the publics with not only enough information to cope with the physical damage and emotional distress, but also a safe space to deal with the financial loss.

Media Coverage

At the end of the response, the national media ceased to cover the event. Local media outlets took Christie's word that the issues had been resolved, and their formal news coverage was also reduced. It appeared that the fire has been wrapped up into the Sandy recovery narrative.

Although local news stories included the accounts of local residents and business owners for the most part, these stories were dominated by the language from the formal statements made by Christie and the local governments. The local newspapers were not critical of these statements, and most media questioning and speculation was followed by an official response.

The local media moved very quickly from issue to resolution, perhaps missing an opportunity to examine the issues more deeply. However, the news media have revisited the boardwalk and written follow-up stories since the disaster. But perhaps the fire and Christie's empathy were overshadowed by another crisis, "Bridgegate," which involved the closure of the George Washington Bridge from Ft. Lee, New Jersey, to Manhattan during the morning rush hour on September 9, 2013 (Kaufman, Levenson, & Jorgensen, 2017). Staff members of Christie's reduced the number of lanes open from three to two and closed several entrances. The local and national media were far more critical of Christie over Bridgegate. He was accused of holding back information and scapegoating his staff. His actions were almost the opposite of those after the boardwalk fire.

With respect to the boardwalk fire, crisis communication was straightforward. The releases stated the facts that were known and expressed a desire to find out additional facts. When those facts were discovered, they were shared openly with the media and public. Even a year later, administrators for the two boroughs were concerned that rebuilding the 500-square-foot portion of the boardwalk could cost more than $2 million; in spring 2016 plans to rebuild Funtown were still just beginning to take shape (Mikie, 2016).

While it is clear that planning went into the social media and press conference responses, there was little follow-through for these commitments. What appeared to be transparency in 2013 seemed to be a lackluster and hollow response in 2016. In line with the above observations, in 2013 the news media continued to focus on recovery for the New Jersey seaside region. Perhaps this focus on recovery might be because Hurricane Sandy was still fresh in the minds of residents, as many of them had not returned to their homes—or had just recently done so. As of fall 2013, "more than 30,000 residents of New York and New Jersey . . . remain displaced by the storm, mired in a bureaucratic and financial limbo" (McHeehan & Palmer, 2013). Many people were still waiting for funding from FEMA or other insurance programs. The fire was an opportunity to bring many of these issues up again. But the fire was controlled and became a "rallying point" for the community rather than an opportunity to bring attention to unresolved issues about the hurricane recovery.

In this case study, the publics involved wrapped the response to the fire into the ongoing recovery from Hurricane Sandy. Local institutions bear the majority of the burden in a crisis, and communication, the influence of the news media, and the support the community can provide for itself all play into the recovery efforts. A buildup of social capital is often considered to result from the adverse conditions of a crisis and can serve as a resource for a community when dealing with subsequent crises (Wicke & Silver, 2009). The messages conveyed by local news outlets vary due to many factors; for instance, limited resources could mean that journalists will do less investigative work and focus more on what will make their readers happy or even contribute to a more resilient narrative.

The desire to resume a recovery narrative may explain why the boardwalk fire lost intensity in the news media within two months of the fire. It also helps to explain why the government response appeared to be transparent. In addition, government communication and action can shape news coverage and in turn contribute to the public crisis recovery narrative.

A collaborative narrative of "recovery" became the dominant platform for the crisis response. The government's strategies appeared to be transparent but primarily reactive, based on Rawlins' (2009) criteria, and represented an accommodative stance to the crisis. This case study shows how the fire was quickly couched within the Hurricane Sandy recovery narrative. The actions of public officials and the information they provided in formal messages conveyed this narrative through the recommended framework and hid other narratives that might distract the community from moving on after the crisis. The disaster also provided a chance for the community to once again rally together to address the disaster and once again focus on what was needed to recover.

Ethical Challenges

This case provides a practical example for how crisis communicators might approach subsequent crises in the wake of a devastating crisis. It also helps to contextualize how formal messages are used in mainstream news media. The crisis communication response aligns with the concept of transparency in government communication. By examining the narratives at play in the six crisis strategies, the government crisis response provides a practical evaluation of government response to natural disasters as well as a perspective concerning the messages produced by the government and the news media during a crisis. While both government structures have separate roles, their responses work in tandem to create one community crisis narrative. This produces a much more cohesive response and a more consistent message to the affected publics.

There are ethical implications for taking a certain stance in a crisis if it might result in the neglect of long-term issues. For instance, even three years later in 2016 the Funtown Pier has not been entirely reconstructed. Governor Christie has moved on and there is little accountability for his commitment to help Seaside Park and Seaside Heights in the long term. Public relations practitioners need to think about the long-term implications for their initial crisis response and what that means for the publics involved.

References

Balkin, J. M. (1999). How mass media simulate political transparency. *Cultural Values, 3*, 393–413.

Cameron, G. T., Pang, A., & Jin, Y. (2007). Contingency theory: Strategic management of conflict in public relations. *Public Relations: From Theory to Practice* (pp. 134–157). Boston: Pearson Allyn & Bacon.

Cancel, A. M., Mitrook, M. A., & Cameron, G. T. (1999). Testing the contingency theory of accommodation in public relations. *Public Relations Review, 25*(2), 171–197.

CNN. (2016 November 2). Hurricane Sandy Fast Facts. Retrieved from http://www.cnn.com/2013/07/13/world/americas/hurricane-sandy-fast-facts/.

Coombs, W. T. (2007). *Ongoing Crisis Communication: Planning, Managing, and Responding.* Thousand Oaks, CA: Sage.

Coombs, W. T., & Holladay, S. J. (2001). An extended examination of the crisis situations: A fusion of the relational management and symbolic approaches. *Journal of Public Relations Research, 13*, 3112–3340.

Funderburk, K. (2014, March 3). Seaside Heights, Park closer to connecting boardwalks again. *Asbury Park Press*. Available at http://www.app.com/story/news/2014/02/28/seaside-heights-park-closer-to-connecting-boardwalks-again/5908073/.

Funtown Pier Amusements. (2017, April 7). Retrieved from https://www.facebook.com/pages/Funtown-Pier-Amusements/115665318463291.

Heath, R. L. (1997). Issues communication: Argument structures and zones of meaning. In *Strategic Issues Management: Organization and Public Policy Challenges* (pp. 80–118). Thousand Oaks, CA: Sage.

Kaufman, E., Levenson, E., & Jorgensen, S. (2017, March 19). Bridgegate scandal: Ex-Christie allies sentenced to prison time. *CNN*. Available at http://www.cnn.com/2017/03/29/us/bridgegate-sentencing/.

McHeehan, P., & Palmer, G. (2013, December 6). Displaced by Hurricane Sandy, and living in limbo. *New York Times*. Available at http://www.nytimes.com/2013/12/07/nyregion/displaced-by-hurricane-sandy-and-living-in-limbo-instead-of-at-home.html?_r=0.

Mikie, J. (2016, February 27). Seaside's missing boardwalk could be rebuilt. *Asbury Park Press*. Available at http://www.app.com/story/news/local/redevelopment/2016/02/26/seasides-missing-boardwalk-could-rebuilt/80944214/.

Rawlins, B. (2009). Give the emperor a mirror: Toward developing a stakeholder measurement of organizational transparency. *Journal of Public Relations Research, 21*(1), 71–99.

Seaside Heights Boardwalk (n.d.). Facebook. Retrieved from https://www.facebook.com/groups/44664699737/.

Seaside Park, NJ (n.d.). Facebook. Retrieved from https://www.facebook.com/njseasidepark/?hc_ref=PAGES_TIMELINE&fref=nf.

Wicke, T., & Silver, R. C. (2009). A community responds to collective trauma: An ecological analysis of the James Byrd murder in Jasper, Texas. *American Journal of Community Psychology*, 44(3–4), 233–248.

Discussion Questions

1. What makes a subsequent crisis more challenging for public officials and communicators?
2. Are there ethical implications for sharing information upfront and early?
3. What are the challenges of having both a local and state-level spokesperson?
4. How might social media messages be different than the official releases from the state and local governments?
5. Is a more accommodative stance always the best stance to take when dealing with subsequent crises? Why or why not?

CONNECTING GOVERNMENT RELATIONS TO ETHICS:
LOUISIANA'S CENTRALIZED MEDIA RELATIONS

Christopher J. McCollough, Ph.D., *Columbus State University*

Each state government in the United States has three branches, just like the federal government—legislative, executive, and judicial branches. Governors preside over the execution of state law through executive order and through the appointment of their state agency directors, who hire or maintain staffs that serve the state (often maintaining employment independent of the political forces in play in the state government). The focus of this case falls on the executive branch of the state of Louisiana, specifically the media relations strategies in place among the governor's press secretary and the public information officers (PIOs) who conduct media relations and public communication on behalf of each of the governor's state agencies.

PIOs are the communications coordinators or spokespersons for certain governmental organizations. Much like practitioners in private organizations, PIOs can perform media relations, plan and implement communication campaigns, manage internal communications for their government agency, and coordinate and conduct public events. Workforce and department funding typically explain the focus of the PIO's work (Garnett, 1992; Graber, 1992). The duties of PIOs differ from public relations departments of private organizations in that marketing plays a more limited role (Garnett, 1992; Graber, 1992). The reason behind this limited marketing role is grounded in the Gillette Amendment of 1913, which limited the budgeting and application of funding for lobbying as part of the traditional public relations functions of a PIO (Turney, 2009).

The primary responsibility of a PIO is to provide open information to the media and public as required by law and according to the standards of the profession. PIOs do so through media relations, direct communication with the public, and responding to citizen queries for information legally mandated by the Freedom of Information Act (Garnett, 1992; Graber, 1992). Many PIOs are former journalists, bringing unique and relevant experience in reporting to the position. Government relations are instrumental in shaping public opinion, which can strengthen or weaken the position of those who govern. Two key functions in this process are media relations and public communication practices.

Governor Bobby Jindal held office in Louisiana from 2008 to 2016. Louisiana is a state historically known for governmental corruption. It was his stated goal to clean up corruption in Louisiana and his personal goal to elevate his reputation on the national stage in pursuit of national office. To seek higher office, he chose to centralize all communication strategy and messaging through his press office, severely limiting the strategic autonomy of practitioners in each of Louisiana's 36 state agencies. The goal was to control the narrative about Jindal's administration by maintaining tight control over all communication from the state government. In doing so, however, the administration created a prevalent negative perception among reporters that the civil servants in the state government were serving a single individual's political ambitions rather than the needs of the state's citizens. This ethically questionable strategy ultimately proved to damage media relations and public approval of Jindal while having minimal impact in damaging the reputation of state PIOs. The case further outlines these aspects and considers how the Jindal administration violated key elements of the Public Relations Society of America's (PRSA) Code of Ethics.

Background

The state government of Louisiana has one of the most colorful reputations in the United States for the manner in which its governor's office and state agencies execute state law. Since the days of former governor Huey P. Long, the state has been associated strongly with political corruption and has a reputation for questionable practices. In the wake of Hurricane Katrina in 2005, then-governor Kathleen Blanco and the agencies under her received heavy criticism for ineffective conduct during the storm and in the recovery process, much of which is still a work in progress. Due to the political fallout from Hurricane Katrina, Blanco announced in 2007 that she would not seek reelection (Cillizza, 2007). This choice opened the door for the opposition party, in this case the Republican Party, to put forward a strong candidate who could seize the governor's office and solidify the GOP's control of both the legislative and executive branches in Louisiana.

The GOP opted to support Piyush "Bobby" Jindal as the candidate to run for election. He was a fast-rising star with a strong reputation in Louisiana. In the 2007 Louisiana gubernatorial election Jindal ran against a split field of candidates and won on campaign promises to clean up politics in Louisiana, to maintain the highest ethical practices among his cabinet and state agency employees, and to maintain transparent communication with the state of Louisiana. Despite running on an open ballot against three other candidates, Jindal carried 54% of the vote, winning the governor's race outright. Prior to taking office, he reinforced his position of maintaining ethical standards by creating an ethics team (Nossiter, 2007).

In January 2008, Jindal took office, looking to use his position as a springboard to national office. This motivation was reflected in his actions over the next eight years in office (Bridges, 2015). Further, the administration had a great deal of political capital due to the Republican majority in both legislative chambers, the general shift of Southern states toward the socially conservative planks of the national GOP platform, and the Democratic party's perceived failures in Louisiana under the former governor.

The Situation

To garner national attention in the GOP, Jindal would have to establish a strong reputation as a governor of Louisiana on the national stage. He entered office in 2008 with an approval rating of 77%, and Presidents Carter, Reagan, Clinton, and George H. W. Bush were able to leverage their successes as governors in their home states to win presidential races over the past four decades. Jindal brought in top GOP political operatives to serve on his personal staff. Specifically, two of his press secretaries had successful careers in covering politics and working on previous GOP congressional and presidential campaigns prior to their employment in the governor's office. Jindal was even on Senator John McCain's list of vice presidential candidates during the first year of his administration (Cillizza, 2008).

While the opportunity and goals were clear for Jindal, his administration also faced some strong criticism and early challenges to the identity they were trying to cultivate with voters during the 2007 election. Corruption, in particular, reared its ugly head shortly after Jindal's inauguration in January 2008. During the 2008 legislative session, Jindal signed into law a code of ethics for the state government of Louisiana that included multiple conflicts of interest in maintaining ethical standards for elected officials and state employees, including a shadowy recusal process for members of the state's boards and commissions (Mann, 2014). Furthermore, more than a dozen members of Jindal's cabinet and agency directors resigned in the first 25 months of his administration due to criticism for poor performance and ethics violations (Alford, 2010).

In response to the growing criticism of the Jindal and his administration, and as a way to manage the information shaping public opinion about him, his press secretary strategically centralized communication to control the public information about the Jindal administration. Pragmatically, this move allowed Jindal and his staff to limit information about the administration to one controlled outlet of information, which is valuable in a political context. Functionally, all agencies and the PIOs representing them would share identical talking points in press briefings and in answering reporters' calls. The governor's press office met and coordinated information with each relevant agency PIO and head in advance of every press briefing. Governor Jindal would handle the opening remarks at the briefing to establish a supervisory role before allowing the agency heads to speak on their prepared comments. The comments of the governor and the agency heads would be identical in their central message, with only minor elaboration on the part of the specific agency heads.

While this seems like an effective way to avoid sending out messages that contradicted those of the administration, it created the perception that the agencies were working for the political benefit of the governor rather than in the service of the state's citizens. In the effort to be efficient in centralizing their messages, Jindal's administration was violating the historical role of each agency's PIO to engage in an open dialogue with the public about the individual agency's function and practice.

It was clear to the press corps that the administration and its agencies were working from the same script. This was particularly clear during each legislative session, as specific agencies central to key pieces of legislation championed by the Jindal administration repeated and supported the central themes expressed by the governor's office in talking points during prepared speeches, press briefings, and media releases. Reporters seeking independent comment from agencies were met with the same remarks they had heard at the press briefing, or were redirected to the governor's press office for further comment. The press corps soon grew antagonistic and distrustful of those who were consistently "on message" with or in deference to the governor's office.

From the reporters' perspective, this strategy severely limited their ability to offer comprehensive news coverage that reflected differing viewpoints from the state agencies and the governor's office. The governor's goal was to promote his efforts, to unify the message coming from each agency under his supervision, and to leave individual state agencies to face any blame and criticism for failed policy or practice. The ideal outcome for him would be two successful terms and a public perception of prosperity and executive efficiency in the governor's office. The actual outcome proved to be quite different, though: Both the local and national media began to cover the administration much more critically.

Outcomes

The mixed results of Jindal's two terms in office reflect poor strategy. Jindal's administration did win reelection in 2011 with a strong 66% percent of the overall vote, although this outcome may be attributed to the opposition's timid campaign and a strong fundraising effort on Jindal's part to establish his position. In terms of national prospects, Governor Jindal experienced his high-water mark with his response to President Obama's 2009 State of the Union address (Jindal delivers Republican response, 2009). He made two brief runs for president in 2012 and 2016 and was under consideration for a cabinet post during Governor Mitt Romney's failed 2012 presidential election. During the 2016 GOP presidential primary he suspended his race in November 2015, never contending seriously in a state primary. In addressing why his strategic aims never succeeded, his reception among reporters and the public offers useful evidence.

Journalists interviewed in Louisiana said they had an antagonistic relationship with the governor's office, especially with the press secretaries. A common theme in interviews was that the executive branches under Blanco and Jindal struggled to establish transparency in the aftermath of Hurricane Katrina. A common perception of hostility or contempt for the press damaged the relationship with reporters.

The damage done made it difficult for practitioners in the governor's office to work with reporters to construct a narrative in which the Jindal administration's point of view was present. In reality, the practice primed journalists to view all Jindal communications skeptically. Over time, this led to increasingly negative coverage about the governor, which further damaged his reputation. In short, it is clear that a centralized communication strategy in media relations did not aid Governor Jindal in controlling the media narrative about his administration.

PIOs made it clear that they worked below the governor's office with an eye on managing their agencies and avoiding conflict with what they perceived to be a hostile staff. That said, PIOs in state government often remain within a state government for years, independent of the political forces present in the administrations. One reason for this longevity is that PIOs work to cultivate professional relationships at the individual level with reporters covering state government, which means providing information as honestly and openly as possible, within the practical constraints of the prevailing political forces.

The Jindal administration's pressure to keep all information central to the governor's office led some PIOs to shift from agency to agency, from agency to lobbying organization, or from agency to the private sector. Even with these shifting positions, they usually remained within the same network because of the enduring relationships they maintained with the press.

If the Jindal administration's goal was to take credit for the good news in Louisiana and cast blame on individual agencies, it is clear that the impression did not ultimately have much of an impact on the PIOs interviewed, who are still working in the state government long after Jindal's term expired in January 2016. While the PIOs likely felt compelled to get in line with the administration's message, they often worked to establish a separate identity from the administration with reporters. This is evident among the journalists interviewed, who all differentiated between ethical PIOs committed to open and honest practice and those who were clearly political operatives committed to Governor Jindal.

One name commonly discussed among journalists was Bob Johannessen, who served at the Louisiana Department of Health and Hospitals (DHH). He worked in the Louisiana state government for better than a decade before leaving state government for the private sector with a local healthcare company due to the after-effects of Hurricane Katrina. With the election of John Bel Edwards, Johannessen returned to DHH as its communications director. When asked for an example of a PIO whom they consistently trusted to be honest and ethical in practice, the journalists interviewed offered several different stories about individual experiences in covering DHH and their dealings with Johannessen, and each was a positive testimony to his character and professionalism. Given the new administration's desire to bolster public trust, his hiring was a positive indicator to the state press that there would be an effort to promote greater transparency in public communication.

An examination of public opinion pertaining to the Jindal administration shows the net impact of the administration's media relations in managing perception, regardless of action. Jindal enjoyed a 77% favorability rating among registered Louisiana voters in 2008, but at the end of his tenure in 2015 it had fallen to 20%, including a 55% disapproval rating from registered Republicans (O'Donohue, 2015). Jindal's reputation for being ambitious and in constant pursuit of higher office also ultimately had an impact on public perception, as his economic record in Louisiana proved poor and residents of Louisiana asked, "Where's Bobby?" in light of his frequent absence on campaign visits to Iowa, New Hampshire, and Ohio (Ballard, 2015). In short, Jindal's strategic effort to cultivate a successful record on the national stage failed; in fact, criticism of his record was the impetus for the election of Democratic gubernatorial candidate John Bel Edwards.

While it is clear that adopting a centralized communication strategy for media relations and public communication led to a pragmatic failure for Governor Jindal, it is also important to recognize the ethical implications of his government relations approach in light of the practice of public relations adopted by the PRSA (PRSA Code of Ethics, 2016). First, it is clear that the Jindal administration violated the PRSA code of conduct by trying to inhibit the free flow of information to the media and the public. The Jindal administration also clearly violated the disclosure-of-information provision due to its deceptive practices in controlling the message delivered by PIOs and government representatives to the press and through frequent acts of lying by omission when responding to or ignoring media inquiries. In the conception of the ethical expectations of PIOs offered by both Garnett (1992) and Graber (1992), we see a similar violation of the traditional expectation of the work of PIOs within state government. While it is clear that unethical public relations practices can sometimes yield successful results, we see a clear example here in government relations of an organization using clearly unethical media relations practices that resulted in the steady decline and ruin of an aspiring presidential nominee.

References

Alford, J. (2010, February 12). Bobby Jindal, the good-bye guv. *Gambit*. Retrieved from http://www.bestofneworleans.com/gambit/bobby-jindal-the-goodandmdash bye-guv/Content?oid=1255203.

Ballard, M. (2015, March 13). Special report: Bobby Jindal spent half of 2014 outside of Louisiana; critics: that the best use of time? *The Advocate*. Retrieved from http://www.theadvocate.com/baton_rouge/news/politics/article_85c2b0f3-0134-5ab5-8154-e4aa2584feb0.html.

Bridges, T. (2015, February 5). Bobby Jindal's troubles at home: What he's not talking about on the campaign trail. *Politico Magazine*. Retrieved from http://www.politico.com/magazine/story/2015/02/bobby-jindal-campaigning-114948.

Cillizza, C. (2007, March 21). Louisiana governor announces she won't seek reelection. *Washington Post*. Retrieved from http://www.washingtonpost.com/wp-dyn/content/article/2007/03/20/AR2007032001437.html.

Cillizza, C. (2008, July 29). John McCain to huddle with possible VP pick Gov. Bobby Jindal of Louisiana. *Washington Post*. Retrieved from http://www.huffingtonpost.com/2008/07/21/john-mccain-to-huddle-wit_n_114169.html.

Garnett, J. L. (1992). *Communicating for Results in Government: A Strategic Approach for Public Managers*. San Francisco: Jossey-Bass Publishers.

Graber, D. A. (1992). *Public Sector Communication: How Organizations Manage Information*. Washington, DC: Congressional Quarterly, Inc.

Jindal delivers Republican response [Video file]. *New York Times*. Retrieved from http://www.nytimes.com/video/us/politics/1194838132435/jindal-delivers-republican-response.html.

Mann, B. (2014, August 16). Under Bobby Jindal, Louisiana's culture of corruption hasn't changed: Bob Mann. *Nola.com*. Retrieved from http://www.nola.com/opinions/index.ssf/2014/08/under_jindal_louisianas_cultur.html.

Nossiter, A. (2007, October 21). Indian-American elected Louisiana's governor. *New York Times*. Retrieved from http://www.nytimes.com/2007/10/21/us/nationalspecial/21louisiana.html?_r=0.

O'Donohue, J. (2015, November 12). Even Louisiana Republicans don't approve of Bobby Jindal anymore: UNO poll. *Nola.com*. Retrieved from http://www.nola.com/politics/index.ssf/2015/11/uno_poll_bobby_jindal.html.

Public Relations Society of America. (2016). Member Code of Ethics. Retrieved from https://www.prsa.org/AboutPRSA/Ethics/CodeEnglish/index.html?seMobiPref=true.

Turney, M. (2009). Government public relations. *Online Readings in Public Relations*. Retrieved from http://www.nku.edu/~turney/prclass/readings/government.html/ on April 4, 2011.

Discussion Questions

1. How might a stronger research and evaluation operation have helped the Jindal administration improve perceptions about their effectiveness in office, both in terms of practical and ethical outcomes?

2. Journalists have a reputation for being highly skeptical of institutions, especially in government. Given the outcome we see for the Jindal administration, how might you have approached media relations differently with the state press bureau?

3. We see in this case that the Jindal administration very clearly violated the free-flow-of-information and disclosure-of-information provisions of the PRSA Code of Ethics. Were ethics ever a critical consideration for the Jindal administration in the media relations practice employed? How might you adapt media relations practice to better align government relations with the PRSA Code of Ethics?

MERS OUTBREAK IN SOUTH KOREA: A SNAPSHOT OF GOVERNMENT RESPONSES AND PUBLIC RELATIONS CONSIDERATIONS

Ji Young Kim, Ph.D., *University of Hawai'i at Mānoa*

In May 2015, an outbreak of Middle East respiratory syndrome (MERS) occurred in South Korea and resulted in 186 confirmed cases and 36 deaths—which later became 38 deaths—within just two months (Ki, 2015; Park et al., 2015). Causing a mass quarantine, numerous school closings, and significant economic suffering, the MERS outbreak in South Korea was the first massive outbreak of this infection outside of the Middle East region and was deemed unusual because it involved human-to-human transmission. Before that time, the most widely known transmission route was from dromedary camels to humans through close contact (World Health Organization [WHO], 2015a).

This illness, which kills 3 to 4 of every 10 patients (U.S. Centers for Disease Control and Prevention [CDC], 2015), belongs to the same coronavirus family as severe acute respiratory syndrome (SARS; M. Park, 2015). In 2003, more than 8,000 people became sick with SARS and 774 of them died (National Institutes of Health, n.d.). Like other coronaviruses, MERS is spread via the respiratory secretions of an ill person, such as through coughing (M. Park, 2015). According to the CDC (2015, 1), "MERS-CoV has spread from ill people to others through close contact, such as caring for or living with an infected person. Infected people have spread MERS-CoV to others in healthcare settings, such as hospitals."

After the first case was confirmed on May 20, 2015, it took less than 20 days for the virus to spread significantly throughout South Korea—more than 95 people were infected and 7 had died as of June 9 (BBC News, 2015; Choe, 2015a). The first patient, a 68-year-old Korean man, had taken a business trip to Saudi Arabia, the United Arab Emirates, and Bahrain via Qatar (M. Park, 2015; Park et al., 2015). He had no symptoms during his trip or upon his return until May 11; at that time, he visited several clinics and hospitals until he was reported as a suspected case of MERS on May 19 (Choe, 2015a; Kwaak, 2015b). During this time, he had continuous contact with his family, other patients, and healthcare professionals, so the infection spread rapidly throughout the healthcare facilities. He was treated and discharged on September 25 (Park et al., 2015).

On July 28, South Korea's prime minster, Hwang Kyo-ahn, announced that citizens could return to their normal lives considering that no additional infection had been reported during the past two weeks (Choe, 2015b; Agence France-Presse, 2015).

On December 23, the MERS epidemic officially ended in South Korea according to WHO standards, following a 28-day waiting period (Normile, 2015).

The Situation

During an outbreak of a disease like MERS, rapid, responsible, and accurate communication on the part of the government is critical to help people understand the situation. In this case, the communication efforts by the South Korean government included setting up a MERS portal website (www.mers.go.kr) and offering a call service center. The Ministry of Education launched a Facebook channel so parents could ask questions. Through these multiple channels, the government tried to share guidelines and information about the disease and worked closely with local departmental offices and healthcare facilities.

However, aside from the fact that MERS is an infectious and lethal disease, healthcare practitioners, government officials, the news media, and publics pointed out that a lack (or insufficient evidence) of strategic communication would be one of the foremost factors contributing to the severity of the outbreak (Choe, 2015a; Fantz, Kwon, & Shoichet, 2015). In the beginning, the majority of the patients (19 out of 25 as of June 1) had had direct contact with the index patient due to the lack of proper treatment guidelines, and the fact that there were no vaccines or treatments made the South Korean people scared (Fantz et al., 2015). Several "ghost stories" were spread on social media due to these fears and the information gap between the government and its people (Roh, 2015). Then-president Park Geun-hye and Prime Minster Hwang both acknowledged that the government's initial responses to the case were inadequate (Hanna & Novak, 2015; M. Park, 2015):

> Initial reaction for new infectious diseases like MERS is very important, but there was some insufficiency in the initial response, including the judgment on its contagiousness. (Quoting then-president Park on June 1, 2015; translated in Hanna & Novak, 2015)

Several industrial and academic papers were written about the outbreak between 2015 and 2017, and most of them concluded that the South Korean government should have been better prepared for the MERS crisis (e.g., D. Kim, 2015; E. Kim, 2015 Kim et al., 2017; Lee & Hong, 2016). Many of these analyses drew upon the epidemiology or public administration approach (Cowling et al., 2015; Ki, 2015; Kim et al., 2017; Mizumoto et al., 2015). For example, the study by Ki (2015) examined the transmission of infection and focused on the unusually high infection risk in and between healthcare facilities, suggesting that the unique healthcare system in South Korea—with crowded rooms and frequent visitor rates—was one of the critical factors of the rapid spread of the disease. From a communication perspective, messages on the social networking sites (e.g., Choi et al., 2017; Song et al., 2017; Yoo, Choi, & Park, 2016) or in the news media (e.g., Y. Kim, 2016; Kim & Ham, 2017; Kwon, 2016; Lee & Paik, 2017; Oh et al., 2015) also played an important role in affecting people's perception of the disease. During the MERS outbreak, the South Korean people relied heavily on these sources due to the lack of information from the government (e.g., D. Kim, 2015; E. Kim, 2015; Lee & Hong, 2016). The Ministry of Health and Welfare Department of Korea (2016) also published a book, *The 2015 MERS Outbreak in the Republic of Korea: Learning from MERS*, to review the government's communication efforts during the outbreak and to make suggestions for the future. This case study about the MERS outbreak in South Korea focuses on government communication by reviewing the information it provided and analyzing the news coverage on the epidemic.

Government Communication Responses

The South Korean government raised and maintained its national epidemic and disaster level at "caution" (the levels are "attention," caution, "alert," and "severe") between May 20 and December 1, 2015 (Pyun, 2015). The Ministry of Health and Welfare and the KCDC (2017) published a MERS response manual to provide an overview of the situation. For example, the manual shows what action plans should be followed at the "caution" (yellow) epidemic and disaster level, such as providing a daily monitoring report and strengthening the immigration and quarantine process (KCDC, 2017, 18). A governmental MERS task force was established to respond to the situation; it included several governmental and public offices (C. Lee, 2015). While continuing to perform epidemiologic monitoring together with WHO, the government also provided some guidelines to the public, such as the "MERS Prevention and Reporting Guidance" leaflet, which became one of the most criticized government messages during the crisis. The leaflet cautioned people to avoid making contact with camels because this mode of transmission had been frequently reported as a means of infection in other areas of the world (CDC, 2015). Unfortunately, the Korean government did not consider culture or context when adopting these messages (e.g., Moon, 2015): A camel is a rare sight in Korea!

Key Problems

Using the keyword "MERS," 299 news releases from the government MERS information page (www.mers.go.kr) and 767 news articles from the two selected daily newspapers in South Korea—*Chosunilbo* (371 articles) and *Hankyoreh* (396 articles)—were collected related to the case. A content analysis shows that there were discrepancies between the government's public relations messages and the news media coverage about MERS between May 20 and December 23, 2015. For example, most of the governmental messages were daily monitoring reports and responses to rumors, whereas the media covered more diverse topics, such as MERS rumors/corrections, infection routes, policies and regulations, and patients' status reports. Particularly during the summer (May to July), the news media were mostly interested in how people became infected or how MERS spread. This was the one of the least frequent topics in the government's public relations messages.

Even though the Korean government said it established a MERS management team in 2013 (Park et al., 2015), when the outbreak occurred, it could not manage the crisis. The government gave no clear guidelines to healthcare professionals, and the lack of information about topics such as treatment and infection transmission only intensified the public's fear and concern (i.e., Fantz et al., 2015; Roh, 2015). It took more than two weeks after the outbreak occurred before the Korean government released a list of the names of hospitals where MERS infection transmission had occurred, which caused more unease about the situation (S. Kim, 2015). Prior to that, due to the lack of official information, citizens were collecting information themselves and had developed a "MERS Map" website, which displayed a list of hospitals where infected individuals had been reported based on online users' testimonials (Han, 2015).

When a government fails to share information in a timely manner, it is unable to stop people from sharing false rumors or inaccurate information—also known as secret treatment or false infection news—through social network sites, which only causes more fear in the country (Kwaak, 2015a; Lee, 2015b; Roh, 2015). The government sent its first mobile communication—a disaster alert—a full two weeks after the start of the outbreak, and the KCDC's official Twitter account was inactive in the early stage of the epidemic (Ahn, 2015). In addition, the government first announced that MERS was not very contagious—which was not the case— and kept the names of the affected hospitals confidential in an attempt to avoid provoking confusion or anxiety among residents (D. Lee, 2015).

More Considerations

These information transparency and accuracy concerns draw attention to the need to use ethical considerations in communication practices. When is the right time to release information that may cause public panic? How should epidemiologic data be collected (e.g., patient information) (e.g., O. Kim, 2016; Lee, 2012; Petrini, 2010)? The patients, their families, and quarantined individuals were the important stakeholders because the disease directly affected them. Due to the infection's rapid spread, people were advised to self-quarantine if they had contact with a patient (KCDC, 2017, 140). However, what should the government do if an individual refuses to be quarantined? To what extent can the government force someone to enter quarantine voluntarily? How and to what extent should the government compensate quarantined individuals? What if communities refuse to have quarantine facilities (see also O. Kim, 2016; Lee, 2012)? Public health threats such as MERS raise an important ethical question about balancing "individual rights" against the "security of public health" (Bae, 2016, 15).

Today's global communication environment also requires a broader understanding of ethics and justice encompassing social, community, or population considerations (Bae, 2016; O. Kim, 2016; Plaisance, 2016). Both the government and the media should think about their responsibilities as the main sources of information. For example, the broad spread of false rumors about MERS could have stemmed from the Korean government's insufficient communication plan and from media professionals who sought more sensational news. Also, the information should be provided with consideration of the multiple stakeholders involved in the situation so that they can perform their functions well. In this situation two of the overlooked stakeholders from a strategic communication standpoint were healthcare facilities and foreign audiences. For example, doctors and nurses were the ones fighting MERS on the front lines; however, despite their dedicated patient care and epidemiologic study efforts, people and the media criticized them for their lack of knowledge about the disease and infection route (J. Lee, 2015). Another important set of stakeholders comprised international governments and organizations (such as WHO) and foreign residents or tourists. The South Korean government notified WHO when it confirmed the first case, and it conducted a joint mission with WHO to examine the virus's epidemiologic patterns and to assess public health–related responses (WHO, 2015b). Although WHO said travel restrictions were unnecessary, several Asian countries increased their attention level toward the outbreak in South Korea. For example, Hong Kong raised its crisis response level to "serious" (the levels were "alert," "serious," and "emergency") to advise people to avoid visiting South Korea (Park & Kim, 2015). These international governments' responses could affect the country's economy and reputation. In addition, in the early stage, the Korean government's communication efforts did not reach foreign residents due to the lack of multi-language services. These services became available on June 12 starting with English; soon after, the services were expanded to include 18 other foreign languages, including Chinese and Japanese (J. Park, 2015).

After MERS

The KCDC continued to update the MERS response manual (KCDC, 2017), and the Ministry of Health and Welfare published a review of the government's responses during the 217 days of the MERS crisis and to make suggestions for the future (Ministry of Health and Welfare Department of Korea, 2016). Using multiple assessment methods, including surveys and interviews, the Ministry of Health and Welfare said that the majority of the government's responses were not strong and that system-wide changes were needed to strengthen leadership during the crisis. Those changes would include having experts and an advisory board for science and safety matters; an onsite manual for effective communication; capacity improvement of healthcare facilities; information management; and ethical standards (Ministry of Health and Welfare Department of Korea, 2016).

This case study reviewed the communication strategies of the South Korean government during the MERS outbreak in 2015 to identify some critical challenges and to discuss the key communication and ethical issues associated with the public epidemic. The government's public relations messages and the news media's coverage on MERS were reviewed to summarize the timeline and to identify members of the public who were involved in the case. The need for strategic crisis communication management, the need for an understanding of multiple stakeholders and their interests, and the need to build trust between the government and public were discussed as the key factors of effective government communication. Furthermore, this study drew our attention to ethical considerations in the communication of a public health crisis.

References

Agence France-Presse. (2015, July 28). South Korea: MERS virus outbreak is over. *The Guardian*. Retrieved from https://www.theguardian.com/world/2015/jul/28/south-korea-mers-virus-outbreak-is-over.

Ahn, S. H. (2015, June 8). Government response to MERS, mobile communication is one step behind [in Korean]. *PR News*. Retrieved from http://www.the-pr.co.kr/news/articleView.html?idxno=13099.

Bae, J. M. (2016). Establishing public health ethics related to disclose information for controlling epidemics on 2015 MERS epidemics in Korea. *Korean Public Health Research, 41*(4), 15–20.

BBC News. (2015, June 9). MERS outbreak: Hong Kong warns against S. Korea travel. [Asia]. Retrieved from http://www.bbc.com/news/world-asia-33059049.

Choe, S-H. (2015a, June 8). MERS virus's path: One man, many South Korean hospitals. *New York Times*. Retrieved from https://www.nytimes.com/2015/06/09/world/asia/mers-viruss-path-one-man-many-south-korean-hospitals.html.

Choe, S-H. (2015b, July 27). South Korea: Government declares end to MERS outbreak. *New York Times*. Retrieved from https://www.nytimes.com/2015/07/28/world/asia/south-korea-government-declares-end-to-mers-outbreak.html.

Choi, D. H., Yoo, W. H., Noh, G. Y., & Park, K. (2017). The impact of social media on risk perceptions during the MERS outbreak in South Korea. *Computers in Human Behavior, 72*, 422–431.

Cowling, B. J., Park, M., Fang, V. J., Wu, P., Leung, G. M., & Wu, J. T. (2015). Preliminary epidemiologic assessment of MERS-CoV outbreak in South Korea, May to June 2015. *Euro Surveillance: Bulletin Europeen sur les Maladies Transmissibles: European Communicable Disease Bulletin, 20*(25), 7–13.

Fantz, A., Kwon, K. J., & Shoichet, C. E. (2015, June 2). 2 MERS patients die in South Korea. *CNN*. Retrieved from http://www.cnn.com/2015/06/01/world/south-korea-mers/.

Han, J. H. (2015, June 4). A website publishes MERS hospitals list . . . government reaction is expected [in Korean]. *Yonhapnews*. Retrieved from http://www.yonhapnews.co.kr/bulletin/2015/06/04/0200000000AKR20150604080100017.HTML.

Hanna, J., & Novak, K. (June 5, 2015). South Korea: 1,500 should stay home because of MERS-infected doctor. *CNN*. Retrieved from http://www.cnn.com/2015/06/04/world/south-korea-mers/.

Ki, M. (2015). 2015 MERS outbreak in Korea: Hospital-to-hospital transmission. *Epidemiology and Health, 37*, e2015033.

Kim, D. H. (2015). Structural factors of the Middle East respiratory syndrome coronavirus outbreak as a public health crisis in Korea and future response strategies. *Journal of Preventive Medicine & Public Health, 48*(6), 265–270.

Kim, E. S. (2015). A social analysis of the limitation of government MERS risk communication. *Korean Review of Crisis & Emergency Management, 11*(10), 91–109.

Kim, K. H., Tandi, T. E., Choi, J. W., Moon, J. M., & Kim, M. S. (2017). Middle East respiratory syndrome coronavirus (MERS-CoV) outbreak in South Korea, 2015: Epidemiology, characteristics and public health implications. *Journal of Hospital Infection, 95*(2), 207–213.

Kim, O. J. (2016). Ethical perspectives on the Middle East respiratory syndrome coronavirus epidemic in Korea. *Journal of Preventive Medicine and Public Health, 49*(1), 18–22.

Kim, S. K. (2015, June 7). Choi Kyung Hwan Deputy Prime Minister announces 24 MERS infection hospitals list [in Korean]. *Hankyoreh*. Retrieved from http://www.hani.co.kr/arti/society/health/694604.html.

Kim, Y. (2016). An essay on Korean media's coverage of Middle East respiratory syndrome coronavirus. *Health Communication, Korean Academy on Communication in Healthcare, 11*(1), 39–50.

Kim, Y. W., & Ham, S. K. (2017). The effect of narrative reporting on stigmatization during the MERS incident: Focusing on the moderating and mediating effects of cultural bias, social capital, and message responses. *Crisisonomy, 13*(1), 63–84.

Korea Center for Disease Control & Prevention. (2017). *MERS Manual* (4-2 Edition). Retrieved from http://www.cdc.go.kr/CDC/contents/CdcKrContentLink.jsp?fid=51&cid=73947&ctype=1.

Kwaak, J. S. (2015a, June 5). MERS, rumors spread in South Korea: Five new cases, fourth death reported; Seoul mayor, health minister exchange criticisms. *Wall Street Journal*. Retrieved from https://www.wsj.com/articles/mers-rumors-spread-in-south-korea-1433484078.

Kwaak, J. S. (2015b, June 8). South Korea MERS outbreak began with a cough. *Wall Street Journal*. Retrieved from https://www.wsj.com/articles/south-korea-mers-outbreak-began-with-a-cough-1433755555.

Kwon, H. C. (2016). A study of semantic network analysis of newspaper articles on MERS situation: Comparing conservative and progressive news media. *Health Communication, Korean Academy on Communication in Healthcare, 11*(1), 63–80.

Lee, C. (2015, June 3). Government mobilizes special task force on MERS: Over 1,300 people quarantined for possible infection. *Korea Herald*. Retrieved from http://www.koreaherald.com/view.php?ud=20150603001173.

Lee, D-E. (2015, June 5). As MERS spreads, so do wild rumors. *Korea Joongang Daily*. Retrieved from http://koreajoongangdaily.joins.com/news/article/Article.aspx?aid=3005037.

Lee, J. G. (2015, June 14). Samsung's conceit and government misjudgment boosts MERS case [in Korean]. *Hankyoreh*. Retrieved from http://www.hani.co.kr/arti/society/health/695895.html.

Lee, L. M. (2012). Public health ethics theory: Review and path to convergence. *Journal of Law, Medicine & Ethics, 40*(1), 85–98.

Lee, M., & Hong, J. (2016). Semantic network analysis of government's crisis communication messages during the MERS outbreak. *Journal of the Korea Contents Association, 16*(5), 124–136.

Lee, S. W., & Paik, J. E. (2017). How partisan newspapers represented a pandemic: The case of the Middle East respiratory syndrome in South Korea. *Asian Journal of Communication, 27*(1), 82–96.

Ministry of Health and Welfare Department of Korea. (2016). *The 2015 MERS Outbreak in the Republic of Korea: Learning from MERS*. Retrieved from http://www.cdc.go.kr/CDC/contents/CdcKrContentLink.jsp?fid=20&cid=70039&ctype=1.

Mizumoto, K., Saitoh, M., Chowell, G., Miyamatsu, Y., & Nishiura, H. (2015). Estimating the risk of Middle East respiratory syndrome (MERS) death during the course of the outbreak in the Republic of Korea, 2015. *International Journal of Infectious Diseases, 39*, 7–9.

Moon, Y. P. (2015, June 5). MERS situation diagnosis "barking up the wrong tree" [in Korean]. *PR News*. Retrieved from http://www.the-pr.co.kr/news/articleView.html?idxno=13092.

National Institutes of Health (n.d.). MERS and SARS. Retrieved from https://www.niaid.nih.gov/diseases-conditions/mers-and-sars#top.

Normile, D. (2015, December 23). South Korea finally MERS-free. *Science*. Retrieved from http://www.sciencemag.org/news/2015/12/south-korea-finally-mers-free.

Oh, H., Jo, A., Park, J., & Gil, E. (2015). Contents and quality of online news articles on preventive food for MERS during MERS outbreak in South Korea. *Korean Review of Crisis & Emergency Management, 11*(11), 167–184.

Park, J. M., & Kim, J. (2015, June 8). Hong Kong sets "serious" response to South Korea's MERS outbreak. *Reuters*. Retrieved from http://www.reuters.com/article/us-health-mers-southkorea-idUSKBN0ON14T20150608.

Park, J. Y. (2015, June 17). MERS hotline expands to 19 languages [in Korean]. *Chosunilbo*. Retrieved from http://news.chosun.com/site/data/html_dir/2015/06/17/2015061700280.html.

Park, M. (2015, June 4). South Korea grapples to contain MERS as 1,369 in quarantine. *CNN*. Retrieved from http://www.cnn.com/2015/06/03/world/south-korea-mers/.

Park, Y.-S., Lee, C., Kim, K. M., Kim, S. W., Lee, K.-J., Ahn, J., & Ki, M. (2015). The first case of the 2015 Korean Middle East respiratory syndrome outbreak. *Epidemiology and Health, 37*, e2015049.

Petrini, C. (2010). Theoretical models and operational frameworks in public health ethics. *International Journal of Environmental Research and Public Health, 7*(1), 189–202.

Plaisance, P. L. (2016). Media ethics theorizing, reoriented: A shift in focus for individual-level analyses. *Journal of Communication, 66*, 454–474.

Pyun, H. J. (2015, December 1). MERS national alert level goes down from warning to concern [in Korean]. *Joongang Ilbo*. Retrieved from http://news.joins.com/article/19168597.

Roh, J. (2015, June 3). MERS, the Korean government and its "ghost stories." *Huffington Post*. Retrieved from http://www.huffingtonpost.com/roh-jeongtae/mers-korean-government_b_7503598.html.

Song, J. Y., Song, T. M., Seo, D. C., Jin, D. L., & Kim, J. S. (2017). Social big data analysis of information spread and perceived infection risk during the 2015 Middle East respiratory syndrome outbreak in South Korea. *Cyberpsychology, Behavior, and Social Networking. 20*(1), 22–29.

U.S. Centers for Disease Control and Prevention. (2015). Information about Middle East Respiratory Syndrome (MERS) [Fact sheet]. Retrieved from https://www.cdc.gov/coronavirus/mers/downloads/factsheet-mers_en.pdf.

World Health Organization. (2015a). *Middle East Respiratory Syndrome Coronavirus (MERS-CoV) in the Republic of Korea* [Situation Assessment]. Retrieved from http://www.who.int/mediacentre/news/situation-assessments/2-june-2015-south-korea/en/.

World Health Organization. (2015b). WHO and the Republic of Korea to carry out joint mission for the MERS-CoV outbreak [News Release]. Retrieved from http://www.who.int/mediacentre/news/releases/2015/mers-joint-mission/en/.

Yoo, W. H., Choi, D. H., & Park, K. (2016). The effects of SNS communication: How expressing and receiving information predict MERS-preventive behavioral intentions in South Korea. *Computers in Human Behavior, 62*, 34–43.

Discussion Questions

1. A government may decide not to release some information during a national crisis situation for fear that it would cause public panic. Is this ethical or unethical? What would be the key considerations?

2. In today's modern communication environment, the internet and social media are among the most important and popular communication channels. Even though there can be great benefits, one of the biggest challenges is the accuracy

of information (i.e., fake news). Discuss ethical issues that are likely to arise in the online communication environment (particularly during a crisis situation).

3. Who were the primary stakeholders in this national crisis situation? What conflicts of interest do you see among them? How would you deal with these conflicts?

4. What would you suggest the Korean government do to regain public trust after the epidemic crisis?

5. During a national crisis, journalists and the media are the main information sources. What individual and community-level ethical considerations do they have?

11 INTERNATIONAL

Learning Outcomes

- Recognize the importance of global public relations.
- Analyze ethical principles in relation to global perspectives.
- Apply ethical principles to global case studies.

Definitions

Global: Worldwide reach.

Global public relations: Building and maintaining positive relationships with priority publics in an organization's home country and in other nations where it operates.

Public relations practitioners need to recognize how interconnected the world is. As University of Miami faculty member Donn Tilson says, "The world has really become a global village" (quoted in Sweeney, 2005, 26). While the public relations field is growing around the globe, it is becoming especially important in Asia, Africa, and Eastern Europe (Barnes, 2017). Most public relations theory and knowledge of practice has come from the United States and Western Europe (Domm, 2013). Practitioners need to think about how having this Western perspective shapes their work. A lack of knowledge about the practice of PR across the globe means practitioners can only speculate as to whether these Western ideas will work in other countries, especially when considering how countries differ in terms of their economic development and political systems (Domm, 2013). What might be the influential factor determining the appropriateness of PR practice is local culture.

"Global integration" is a phrase commonly used when describing global public relations practice. This term can mean several things. For example, it could mean sharing best practices among global teams, or using consistent objectives and metrics for communication. However, it does not mean using the same messaging and content across the world market, nor does it mean using the same tactics in every country (Fry, Sosin, & Stein, n.d.) "Good PR gets at insights that are specific to a consumer, or has a flavor that is distinctive to her country, her city, her neighborhood" (Glasgow, 2011, para. 5). In other words, practitioners who are not knowledgeable about the local context should not assume they know all the answers.

Roles of Global PR

Glasgow (2011) suggests there are three distinct roles in global PR: the shepherd, the scientist, and the preschool teacher. The shepherd brings together regional and local team members so they can develop strategies that can be customized to suit local publics while still reflecting global messaging. The scientist evaluates what is working at the local level and determines which elements might be able to work globally if they are applied appropriately and authentically in different locales. Finally, the preschool teacher determines if messaging, strategy, and practitioners work well together and don't overreach and take over another's turf. Cultural understanding is key to fostering communication and cooperation; anyone working in global PR will need to recognize that "local knowledge with global reach" is what is most desired (Hoyt as quoted in Barnes, 2017, para. 34). Practitioners can help bridge the gaps among nations and cultures when they recognize the importance of not only understanding cultural values and attitudes, but also thinking about how varying infrastructure, transportation, and literacy levels affect communication (Domm, 2013; Sweeney, 2005).

References

Barnes, S. (2017, June 9). Global PR networks face political, economic changes. Retrieved from http://www.odwyerpr.com/story/public/8906/2017-06-09/global-pr-networks-face-political-economic-changes.html.

Domm, G. (2013, May). Public relations in emerging nations: What do local practitioners themselves have to say? Retrieved from https://www.ipra.org/news/itle/public-relations-in-emerging-nations-what-do-local-practitioners-themselves-have-to-say/.

Fry, T., Sosin, J., & Stein, S. (n.d.). The new global world of public relations. Retrieved from https://www.webershandwick.com/uploads/news/files/Global_Comms_Trends.pdf.

Glasgow, A. (2011, March). Does global public relations exist? Retrieved from https://www.ipra.org/news/itle/does-global-public-relations-exist/.

Sweeney, K. (2005, January). The year ahead in public relations: A preview of what's in store in 2005. *Public Relations Tactics, 12*(1), 1, 14, 15, 26, 27.

SKOL'S "VIVA REDONDO" ("LIVE ROUND") CRISIS

Deborah de Cillo Ottoni Teixeira, M.A., *Texas A&M University-Corpus Christi*, and Michelle M. Maresh-Fuehrer, Ph.D., *Texas A&M University-Corpus Christi*

In anticipation of the annual *Carnaval do Brasil* festival, Skol—a leading Brazilian beer brand—introduced a new campaign, *Viva Redondo*. What Skol did not foresee was the influence that two upset stakeholders could have on their organization. In February 2015, Skol entered full crisis mode due to the public's perception that their campaign unethically promoted irresponsibility and placed profits ahead of societal values. Outraged stakeholders used social media to express their dissatisfaction with Skol's campaign and garnered widespread community support, leading ultimately to a formal ethical investigation by a regulatory agency.

Background

Ninety-five percent of the Brazilian beer market is shared by the three largest companies—Ambev, Heineken, Petrópolis—while the remaining 5% is represented by 450 small companies (Bigarelli & Frabasile, 2017). According to the Brazilian Federal Revenue Service, in 2014 alone, 14.1 billion liters (equivalent to more than 3.7 billion gallons) of beer were produced in Brazil (Receita Federal, 2015). The Skol brand was established in Brazil in 1967. At the time of the crisis discussed here, Skol was considered the most valuable brand in Brazil and in Latin America, with an estimated brand value of $8.5 billion (Millward Brown, 2016). Owned by Ambev, Skol is the leader in the Brazilian beer market, with a market share estimated at 30% (Young, 2013).

Carnaval is a Christian celebration that occurs 47 days before the Easter holiday, typically in February. Celebration begin on Friday and extend to Wednesday, although parties are commonly held weeks before the actual date and after the end of the holiday. As a result, Carnaval is said to range from one to four weeks, depending on the location. Carnaval is known for its parades, music, dancing, and elaborate costumes. It is one of the largest holidays in Brazil and has an impact on many sectors of the country's economy, such as tourism, hotels, and restaurants. For the 2018 celebration, the Brazilian Department of Tourism estimated its revenue at more than $3 billion in the whole country, with 10.69 million Brazilian tourists and 400 thousand international visitors (Oliveira, 2018). The city of São Paulo estimated its revenue for the 2018 celebration at $213 million (Observatório do Turismo, 2018), while Salvador calculated its revenue at $496 million as over 770,000 tourists visited the city during the holiday (Oliveira, 2018).

Despite the many positive aspects of this holiday, there is also a dark side. An increase in sexual violence, hate crimes, robberies, and automobile accidents plague the celebrations (Froio, 2013; Gomes, 2015; Kaye, 2015; Triginelli, 2014). For instance, there were 429 reported cases of racism, sexism, and homophobia in Salvador, Bahia, during the 2012 Carnaval. Of these incidents, 153 involved violence and abuse toward women (Froio, 2013). Most of the celebrations involve thousands of people concentrated in relatively small spaces and heavy alcohol consumption, which are said to be contributing factors to such outcomes (Gomes, 2015; Triginelli, 2014).

To understand the sequence of events that led to the crisis situation, we must consider the messaging surrounding the Viva Redondo campaign. By the end of 2014, Skol launched a campaign with the slogan "Viva Redondo" (Live Round), inviting consumers to live life fully and say "yes" to life more often. The campaign built upon the traditional slogan "Skol, the beer that swallows round," created in 1995 by the agency F/Nazca Saatchi & Saatchi. (When something is perfect, it is common to hear Brazilians refer to it as "round.")

To unveil this campaign, Skol selected a few consumers and invited them to a bar. During this experience, one of the male consumers was asked to push a button. Without knowing what would happen, he accepted the invitation and was launched into an intensive brand experience: He was trapped in an elevator with a famous actress, participated in an action figure boxing match against Mike Tyson, and parachuted from a helicopter and landed in a party on a cruise ship. Skol recorded each step of his experience and released it to the public in the form of several television and internet commercials. These commercials supported other promotional pieces of the campaign that were aired on the radio and featured in print, involving other consumers in the experience of "living round," or accepting life's invitations.

The Situation

With Carnaval approaching, Skol continued to incorporate new messaging into its Viva Redondo campaign with a focus on the festival to raise brand awareness. The campaign messaging was used in several media channels, including television, radio, magazines, and billboards, and on signage at bus stops, on street clocks, and on social media. Messages encouraging customers to "live round" during Carnaval included "I forgot the 'no' at home," "I accept before hearing the question," and "I'm with you, even not knowing you."

On February 11, 2015—the week before Carnaval—two women, Pri Ferrari and Mila Alves, were on the way to work when they saw one of Skol's "I forgot the 'no' at home" signs at a bus stop. The women were offended by the message, believing that it was promoting a loss of control during a festival that was already vulnerable to such actions. They returned to the bus stop and altered the message with electrical tape to avoid damaging the structure of the billboard, adding "and brought the never" to the end of the message. They took photos posing in front of the billboards using an obscene hand gesture to express their dissatisfaction with the original messaging, and posted the photos on their Facebook pages.

In about an hour the post had generated more than 4,000 likes, dozens of supportive comments, and the hashtag #SkolNunca (Skol Never) on Twitter. Shortly after, the subject gained the attention of news websites, increasing its visibility. In an interview with the website Exame.com, Ferrari explained that she and Alves were outraged because they felt the campaign was encouraging people not to respect their own limits and the limits of others during Carnaval—a period when abuse of drugs and alcohol and sexual violence increase (V. Barbosa, 2015). Ferrari contended that saying "no" is actually necessary during Carnaval: "no to rape, no to drinking and driving, no to sex without condoms" (Martinho, 2015).

The negative attention led Ambev's communication director, Alexandre Loures, to contact Ferrari to explain the intent of the campaign and to listen to her concerns. Shortly after their discussion, Loures called Ferrari and promised

FIGURE 11.1 From left to right, Alves and Ferrari add *"e trouxe o nunca"* ("and brought the never") to Skol's advertisement.

Source: Pri Ferrari's Facebook page

to create a task force to remove the campaign from circulation and substitute new messaging emphasizing "saying yes to the good things" (Martinho, 2015).

Later that day, at 12:42 p.m., Skol released its first official communication in response to the situation, a Twitter post announcing that the company was not supporting or encouraging any act of violence or excessive drinking. In this message, Skol emphasized its commitment to responsible consumption and said it would replace the messages with clearer positive messages about "living round." By 5 p.m., Skol informed the media that it would develop a task force to remove the campaign from circulation, but at 7 p.m., they announced that only the "I forgot the 'no' at home" messaging would be removed and the campaign as a whole would be maintained (Lafloufa, 2015).

FIGURE 11.2 Skol's social media response. Translation: "Folks, we would like to clarify that at no moment did we have the intention to encourage or support any act of violence or excessive consumption. We repudiate all and any type of violence—physical or emotional—and we reiterate our commitment to responsible consumption. Hence, we will substitute the current phrases for clearer and more positive messages that convey the same concept of the campaign 'Live Round'—whose motto is to accept life's invitations to enjoy every moment."

By the end of the day, Ferrari and Alves commemorated the positive outcomes of their initiative on their social media pages. Dozens of websites, including some of the largest news media in Brazil, shared the story. Discussions took place on Facebook, Twitter, and news website forums. The next day, Skol released the new campaign messages: "When one doesn't want it, the other goes to dance," and "Is the game over? Take your team off the field"—both making reference to situations where one should respect another's "no." The new artwork also included a line advising, "In this Carnaval, respect." Several websites announced the changes and users shared them on social media.

Despite the new messaging, the subject was still echoing in the news and on social media, capturing the attention of Conselho Nacional de Autorregulamenta-ção Publicitária (National Council for Self-Regulation in Advertising [CONAR]), a regulatory agency responsible for evaluating cases of inappropriate advertising. CONAR received over 30 complaints about the campaign and opened a formal inquiry (M. Barbosa, 2015).

Outcomes

This case study contains lessons related to three important components of public relations study: ethics, social media, and crisis communication. There are various codes of ethics that guide the actions of public relations practitioners. These codes of ethics do not vary greatly by country, but international codes of ethics tend to place more emphasis on "dignity, respect, and human rights" (Institute for Public Relations, 2016). In Brazil, "the State has the power to interfere in advertisement businesses," but the "industry's activities are mostly self-regulated" (CONAR, 2016). CONAR's code, named *Código de Autorregulação Publicitária*, provides specific guidelines for the promotion of alcoholic beverages: Such promotions "should be structured in a socially responsible way" and should "not encourage consumption in inappropriate situations, illegal, dangerous or socially reprehensible" (CONAR, 2016, n.p.).

Although Skol maintains that the brand did not intend to promote irresponsible actions, the public (starting with Ferrari and Alves) perceived the campaign messaging to encourage irresponsible consumption and socially reprehensible behavior. This perception was strengthened by the campaign's association with Carnaval, as this is a time of increased vulnerability to social ills. As such, Skol's campaign messaging violated not only CONAR's code but also the International Association of Business Communicators' (IABC, 2016) Code of Ethics, which requires communicators to be "sensitive" to cultural values and beliefs." This violation of ethics is what caused the potential for a crisis to emerge.

While the offending campaign message was presented across a variety of channels, social media was the channel Ferrari and Alves used to express their discontent. According to Maresh-Fuehrer and Smith (2015, 621), "social media has been recognized in crisis communication research as facilitating both the spread and mitigation of crises." Furthermore, social media increases the visibility of crisis situations and affects the expectations that the public has for an organization's crisis response efforts (Austin, Liu, & Jin, 2012; Spence et al., 2006). At the time this essay was written, Ferrari's Facebook post had accumulated almost 27,000 likes, 592 comments, and over 8,500 shares.

The visibility and spread of this post led to public outcry and open discussions about how Skol should respond to the situation. Loures reached out personally to Ferrari, an action that demonstrates one of the best practices in risk and crisis communication, which is to listen to the public's concerns to understand the audience (Veil, Buehner, & Palenchar, 2011). This action supports the International Public Relations Association's (2016, n.p.) Code of Conduct regarding dialogue; this code states that practitioners must "seek to establish the moral, cultural and intellectual conditions for dialogue, and recognise the rights of all parties involved to state their case and express their views."

As a result of the crisis, Skol enacted a public relations strategy known as "social listening." Social listening is "the process of monitoring digital conversations to understand what customers are saying about a brand and industry online" (TrackMaven, 2016, n.p.). Consequently, Skol issued its first statement about the Viva Redondo crisis on social media. According to Maresh-Fuehrer (2013, 80), "in most crisis situations, a good rule to follow is to use the channel where the crisis began." Four hours after Ferrari's original Facebook post, Skol responded with a tweet but neglected to post a statement on Facebook. Because the hashtag #SkolNunca was trending on Twitter, it was appropriate for Skol to tweet about the incident; however, it would have been more effective had a response also been posted on Facebook to ensure they were reaching the entire concerned audience.

The statement Skol released on Twitter contained several crisis response strategies that are recommended by Situational Crisis Communication Theory (SCCT). According to Coombs (2007), crises are considered to be part of the accidental cluster when the organization's actions leading to the crisis were unintentional. Appropriate crisis response strategies for crises in the accidental cluster include diminish and rebuild strategies (Coombs, 2007). In its Twitter response, Skol used the diminish strategy of "excuse" when denying the intent to do harm: "At no moment did we have the intention to encourage or support any act of violence or excessive consumption." With this strategy, Skol followed the IABC's code of ethics: "Promptly correct any erroneous communication for which they may be responsible" (IABC, 2016, n.p.).

A secondary bolstering strategy of "reminder" was also incorporated in its response as Skol reminded the public of its stance on violence and responsible consumption: "We repudiate all and any type of violence—physical or emotional—

and we reiterate our commitment to responsible consumption." Finally, Skol used the rebuild strategy of "corrective action" by promising to replace the offensive messaging with more positive messages: "Hence, we will substitute the current phrases for clearer and more positive messages, that convey the same concept of the campaign 'Live Round'—whose motto is to accept life's invitations to enjoy every moment."

Skol's use of ethical strategies during its response to this crisis was perceived favorably by stakeholders. By the third day of the crisis, the company had enacted an action plan to address the problem and the media were no longer generating new stories about the situation. In April 2015, CONAR released the results of their inquiry. Because Skol voluntarily listened to stakeholders, replaced the old messaging, and improved its campaign, the investigation was closed with no further action required and the brand was not significantly harmed by this crisis.

References

Austin, L., Liu, B. F., & Jin, Y. (2012). How audiences seek out crisis information: Exploring the social-mediated crisis communication model. *Journal of Applied Communication Research, 40,* 188–207.

Barbosa, M. (2015, February 13). "Esqueci o Não" da Skol sai de cena, mas cai na mira do Conar. *Folha de S. Paulo.* Retrieved from http://www1.folha.uol.com.br/mercado/2015/02/1589625-apos-denuncias-conar-entra-com-representacao-contra-campanha-do-nao-da-skol.shtml.

Barbosa, V. (2015). Skol billboard causes outrage in SP [in Portuguese]. *Exame.com.* Retrieved from http://exame.abril.com.br/marketing/noticias/outdoor-da-skol-para-carnaval-causa-indignacao-em-sao-paulo.

Bigarelli, B. & Frabasile, D. (2017, February 14). What Heineken gets acquiring Brasil Kirin [in Portuguese]. *Época Negócios.* Retrieved from https://epocanegocios.globo.com/Empresa/noticia/2017/02/o-que-heineken-ganha-ao-comprar-brasil-kirin.html

CONAR. (2016). Código Brasileiro de Autorregulamentação Publicitária. Retrieved from http://www.conar.org.br.

Coombs, W. T. (2007). Protecting organizational reputations during a crisis: The development and application of situational crisis communication theory. *Corporate Reputation Review, 10,* 163–176.

Froio, N. (2013). Hyper sexual Carnival atmosphere has a dark side for Rio's women. *Independent.* Retrieved from http://www.independent.co.uk/voices/comment/hyper-sexual-carnival-atmosphere-has-a-dark-side-for-rios-women-8490306.html.

Gomes, L. F. (2015). Why so much violence in Carnaval? [in Portuguese]. *Instituto Avante Brasil.* Retrieved from http://institutoavantebrasil.com.br/por-que-tanta-violencia-no-carnaval/.

IABC. (2016). IABC code of ethics for professional communicators. Retrieved from https://www.iabc.com/about-us/governance/code-of-ethics/.

Institute for PR. (2016). Ethics and public relations. Retrieved from http://www.instituteforpr.org/ethics-and-public-relations/.

IPRA.(2016).Codeofconduct.Retrievedfromhttps://www.ipra.org/member-services/code-of-conduct/.

Kaye, L. (2015, February 20). Accused of condoning rape, Brazilian beer company drops Carnaval ad campaign. *TriplePundit*. Retrieved from http://www.triplepundit.com/2015/02/accused-condoning-rape-brazilian-beer-company-drops-carnaval-ad-campaign/.

Lafloufa, J. (2015). Women irritated with tone of Skol campaign and change outdoor message [in Portuguese]. *Brainstorm9*. Retrieved from http://www.b9.com.br/55133/advertising/mulheres-se-irritam-com-tom-da-campanha-de-skol-e-alteram-mensagem-de-outdoor/.

Maresh-Fuehrer, M. M. (2013). *Creating Organizational Crisis Plans*. Dubuque, IA: Kendall Hunt Publishing.

Maresh-Fuehrer, M. M., & Smith, R. (2015). Social media mapping innovations for crisis prevention, response, and evaluation. *Computers in Human Behavior, 54,* 620–629.

Martinho, A. (2015, February 11). Accused of vindication of rape, Skol will withdraw campaign from circulation after feminist protest [in Portuguese]. *Folha de São Paulo*. Retrieved from http://f5.folha.uol.com.br/voceviu/2015/02/1588510-acusada-de-apologia-ao-estupro-skol-vai-retirar-campanha-de-circulacao-apos-protesto-feminista.shtml.

Millward Brown. (2016). Top 50 Most Valuable Latin American Brands 2015. *Millward Brown*. Retrieved from http://www.millwardbrown.com/brandz/top-latin-american-brands/2015.

Observatório do Turismo (2018). Carnaval Paulistano 2018 [in Portuguese]. Retrieved from http://www.observatoriodoturismo.com.br/pdf/CARNAVAL_2018_SAMBODROMO_RUA_ALTA.pdf

Oliveira, N. (2018, January 25). Carnaval 2018 will inject R$11 billion into Brazilian economy [in Portuguese]. *Ministério do Turismo* [Brazilian Department of Tourism]. Retrieved from http://www.turismo.gov.br/ultimas-noticias/10648-carnaval-2018-injetar%C3%A1-r$-11-bilh%C3%B5es-na-economia-brasileira.html

Receita Federal. (2015). Control system of beverage production [in Portuguese]. *Receita Federal* [Brazilian Federal Revenue Service]. Retrieved from http://www.receita.fazenda.gov.br/pessoajuridica/bebidas/SistContrProdSicobe.htm.

Spence, P. R., Westerman, D., Skalski, P. D., Seeger, M., Sellnow, T. L., & Ulmer, R. R. (2006). Gender and age effects on information seeking after 9/11. *Communication Research Reports, 23,* 217–233.

TrackMaven (2016). Social listening. Retrieved from http://trackmaven.com/marketing-dictionary/social-listening/.

Triginelli, P. (2014, March 6). Federal highway patrol registering 155 deaths on federal highways during Carnaval in the country [in Portuguese]. *Portal G1*. Retrieved from http://g1.globo.com/minas-gerais/noticia/2014/03/prf-registra-155-mortes-em-estradas-federais-durante-carnaval-no-pais.html.

Veil, S. R., Buehner, T., & Palenchar, M. J. (2011). A work-in-process literature review: Incorporating social media in risk and crisis communication. *Journal of Contingencies and Crisis Management, 19*(2), 110–122.

Young, A. (2013). The top 10 biggest beer brands. *The Drinks Business*. Retrieved from https://www.thedrinksbusiness.com/2013/06/the-worlds-top-10-beer-brands.

Discussion Questions

1. Only two months after the Skol crisis referenced in this reading, Budweiser faced criticism for using a similar tagline in one of its campaigns in the United States: "The perfect beer for removing 'no' from your vocabulary for the night." Consider Budweiser's position in the U.S. beer market and the recent attention placed on "rape culture" on college campuses. What are the ethical implications of disseminating campaign messaging that is socially irresponsible?

2. Select a brand of your choice. What are some current issues affecting your city or state of residence that could lead to an indirect crisis for this brand?

3. Consider the ethical principles for international public relations organizations (such as IPRA and IABC). How do these principles differ from national organizations' codes of ethics?

4. Search for other Skol PR campaigns. Using a codes of ethics system of your choice, discuss whether Skol acted ethically in their overall PR strategy.

TOSHIBA ACCOUNTING SCANDAL: JAPANESE NATIONAL CULTURE, CORPORATE GOVERNANCE, AND PUBLIC RELATIONS ETHICS

Koji Fuse, Ph.D., *University of North Texas*, Jacqueline Sears, *University of North Texas*, and Keyona Adaiah Butler, *University of North Texas*

On April 3, 2015, Toshiba Corporation, a Japanese multinational electric and electronic conglomerate, issued a news release to announce an internal investigation of possible accounting irregularities, stating, "[Toshiba] expresses its most sincere apologies to our shareholders, investors, and all other stakeholders for any concern or inconvenience caused on this occasion" (Toshiba, 2015a, para. 2). Initial findings prompted the company to expand its investigation by establishing a third-party committee (Kim & Cushing, 2015). According to that committee's report, Toshiba had inflated its earnings by more than $1.2 billion (¥151.8 billion) over seven years (Alpeyev, Amano, & Ma, 2015; Toshiba, 2015b; Ueda, Matsui, Ito, & Yamada, 2015). Upon the release of the committee report, then-president Hisao Tanaka announced on July 21, 2015, his and others' resignations during a Japanese ritualistic "apology news conference" where three top executives deeply bowed to apologize before explaining the situation, emphasizing the need to reform the management structure, and answering questions from the media (Alpeyev & Amano, 2015b).

The systemic failure of Toshiba's corporate governance began in FY 2008 when former president Atsutoshi Nishida established the "Challenge" system, in which he and his successors pressured Toshiba's unit presidents, executives, and accountants, as well as their subordinates, to impose unrealistic goals on themselves in a corporate culture that suppressed dissent and disobedience (Alpeyev & Amano, 2015b; Ueda et al., 2015). The "Challenge" system was identified as one of the direct causes for its financial mismanagement. The implication was often that "failure would not be accepted" (Carpenter, 2015, para. 6). Nishida allegedly threatened the president of Toshiba's PC company in a January 2009 meeting by saying, "Do all that you can as if your life depends on it" and "You will become a group subject to reconsideration if you don't do anything. There is no point in keeping this business" (Ueda et al., 2015, 245). Much like other Japanese companies when embroiled in a scandal, Toshiba offered profuse apologies in news releases and news conferences, as well as on its website (e.g., Toshiba, n.d.-d) since its initial public disclosure of the situation. The company also took corrective actions by implementing some recommendations for corporate governance reform made by the committee's report, such as increasing external board directors and enforcing its internal audit structure (Toshiba, 2015c; Toshiba, n.d.-e). Toshiba also created a webpage devoted to news releases regarding the "Actions Taken in Response to Inappropriate Accounting" (Toshiba, n.d.-a). In March 2016 the company discovered seven additional accounting errors, which its spokeswoman described as a lack of "awareness for appropriate disclosure" (Yamazaki, 2016, para. 4), thus indicating internal communication failures caused by ineffective reform measures. Toshiba treated those errors as losses in financial reports but did not publicly announce them because "the amount was below the threshold requiring regulatory disclosure" (Yamazaki, 2016, para. 3).

Japanese corporations have traditionally pursued long-term stability rather than short-term profit and protected themselves against hostile mergers and acquisitions by applying various Japanese-style managerial measures, such as lifetime employment, a board composed almost entirely of inside directors, and the government's administrative guidance (Jackson & Miyajima, 2008, 3–6). However, the burst of Japan's economic bubble, which was built on the enormously inflated valuation of real estate and stocks, in the early 1990s and the subsequent decline of its overheated economy necessitated the acceptance of international standards and greater transparency to attract foreign investments (Jackson & Miyajima, 2008, 6–17). Following a reform of Japanese corporate governance law, in June 2003 Toshiba adopted a new U.S.-style corporate governance system called the "board with committees" (Fuwa, 2009, 255; Shishido, 2008, 321).

However, Toshiba's accounting fraud seemed to reflect a disastrous, superficial move toward a more U.S.-style corporate governance system meant to protect shareholder interests above all else (Zahra, 2014, 79). It also signified disregard for Toshiba's traditional Japanese-style corporate governance, which advances the long-term value of a corporation (Japan Business Federation, 2006) and makes the interests of all stakeholders equal (Miyajima, Saito, Sho, Tanaka, & Ogawa, 2013, 30–31; Yoshimori, 1995, 34–35). While both styles have strengths and weaknesses, adopting a new system of corporate governance without cultural considerations seems to be a perfect formula for a catastrophe. This corporate culture change, coupled with a relatively high superior–subordinate power distance and collectivism (Hofstede, 2001, n.d.-a, n.d.-b; Meyer, 2014a, 2014b), allowed the "Challenge" system to aggressively pursue short-term profit while stifling internal dissent. It took about seven years for "a person related to Toshiba" to tip off Japan's Securities and Exchange Surveillance Commission (Kitanaka & Reynolds, 2015, para. 4). In addition, internal and external communication failures continued to prevent the company from putting the scandal behind itself so it could move forward.

Background

Toshiba's 140-plus-year history started with the founding of two pioneer companies in the development of electrical equipment in Japan: Tanaka Engineering Works (later renamed Shibaura Engineering Works) in 1875 and Hakunetsu-sha Co., Ltd. (later renamed Tokyo Electric Company) in 1890. Their 1939 merger led to the formation of Tokyo Shibaura Electric Co., Ltd., which was changed to "Toshiba" in 1984 (Toshiba, n.d.-f). Toshiba currently employs more than 180,000 people worldwide and provides diverse products and services through four companies: energy systems, infrastructure systems, storage and electronic devices, and industrial information and communication technology (Toshiba, n.d.-b, n.d.-c). While emphasizing on its website its commitment to serving the needs of all people (Toshiba, n.d.-h), Toshiba was also celebrated as one of the most "progressive" Japanese companies when it established a new corporate governance structure similar to the U.S. model in as early as June 2003. At that time, many publicly held Japanese companies were taking easier options, such as strengthening their existing statutory auditor system without making a drastic change by setting up separate independent committees, under the reformed Japanese corporate governance law (Shishido, 2008, 321–322). Toshiba's new corporate structure included three committees: the Nomination Committee, the Audit Committee, and the Compensation Committee. The board consisted of seven executive and seven nonexecutive members, four of whom were outside directors, to perform supervisory roles (Fuwa, 2009, 255–257, 258; Toshiba, n.d.-g). Compounding this cultural shift was the Great Recession, which hit in December 2007 (The Great Recession, n.d.) and had significantly negative effects on many businesses worldwide.

Against this backdrop, Nishida established the "Challenge" system. Although it is not uncommon for Japanese managers to pressure their subordinates to set unrealistic goals (Morita, 2008, 748), the leading cause of unethical behavior in corporate life is often pressure from management to meet unrealistic business objectives and deadlines (Jamrog et al., 2006, 5). Toshiba's business environment was further shaken by the Great East Japan Earthquake and the subsequent tsunamis of 2011, which caused the meltdown of the Fukushima Daiichi nuclear power plant and created negative prospects for Toshiba's nuclear business (Ueda et al., 2015).

Nothing much had changed since Nishida's resignation. Norio Sasaki, who replaced Nishida as president on June 24, 2009, expanded the inappropriate accounting practices. Hisao Tanaka, who succeeded Sasaki on June 25, 2013, also followed the same path as his predecessors, continuing to delay the report of massive financial losses (Ueda et al., 2015). Toshiba had a corporate culture "where employees cannot act contrary to the intent of superiors," as well as a de facto rule "whereby approval from a progressively senior personnel was required before making an accounting treatment" (Ueda et al., 2015, 309). While this accounting malpractice was going on, Toshiba received an order on February 12, 2015, from Japan's Securities and Exchange Surveillance Commission to investigate and report on financial disclosure practices regarding some projects (Ueda et al., 2015, 17).

Proposed in March 2015 and implemented on June 1, 2015, by Japan's Financial Management Agency and the Tokyo Stock Exchange, the "Corporate Governance Code" for its listed companies established the five general principles, which primarily focus on protecting shareholders' interests:

1. Securing the rights and equal treatment of shareholders
2. Appropriate cooperation with stakeholders other than shareholders
3. Ensuring appropriate information disclosure and transparency
4. Responsibilities of the board
5. Dialogue with shareholders (Tokyo Stock Exchange, 2015, 3–4).

In this political-economic climate, the timing of Toshiba's April 2015 announcement about its accounting irregularities could not have been more embarrassing to the Japanese government (Ando, Layne, & Armstrong, 2015).

The Situation

On Friday, April 3, 2015, Toshiba announced in a news release its decision to establish an internal committee to probe whether the accounting method applied to its infrastructure projects in FY 2013 was reasonable, expressing "its most sincere apologies" to all stakeholders for any concern or inconvenience they were experiencing (Toshiba, 2015a, para. 2). The committee's initial findings led to the withdrawal of the company's earnings projections and the cancellation of year-end dividend payments on May 8, 2016 (Alpeyev & Amano, 2015b). Then, Hisao Tanaka, the president at the time, held a news conference on May 15, 2016—the first time Toshiba's top management had discussed the issue in public—to make public apologies, to announce the launching of the independent committee to expand its accounting probe, and to admit that "internal controls may not have functioned, due to the high priority placed on meeting budget targets" (Toshiba admits, 2015, para. 5; see also Ueda et al., 2015, 17).

A report released on July 20, 2016, by the committee revealed that Toshiba's cumulative inflated earnings, which were caused primarily by its obsession with short-term profits, top-down corporate culture, and "Challenge" system, reached more than $1.2 billion (¥151.8 billion) over seven years (Alpeyev & Amano, 2015a; Alpeycv, Amano, & Ma, 2015; Toshiba, 2015b; Ueda et al., 2015). The report also highlights how the three former presidents used "Quarterly Reporting Meetings" and "CEO Monthly Meetings" to demand a significant improvement on earnings and meet "Challenge" targets.

Upon the report's release, Tanaka announced his resignation, along with those of his two predecessors and six other board members, during an "apology news conference" held on July 21, 2015; Masashi Muromachi succeeded him as interim president (Alpeyev & Amano, 2015b; Tomita & Maeda, 2015). Tanaka insisted that "'I have no recognition of directly ordering' inappropriate accounting" (Alpeyev & Amano, 2015b, para. 10). However, the report already determined that he and other top-level executives had been aware of the intentional accounting malpractice but had not given instructions for it to stop (Ueda et al., 2015). In short, Toshiba's switch to the U.S.-style management system to pursue short-term profits above all else, with disregard for stakeholders other than shareholders, led to a vicious cycle of the "Challenge" system and its consequent accounting irregularities.

Many tweets discussed Tanaka's resignation matter-of-factly, but some Japanese tweets criticized him, lamented corporate malfeasance, and even predicted the end of Toshiba. For example, referring to Tanaka, one Japanese tweet said that "I guess people could not get ahead in the Japanese corporate world unless they were this shameless. Honest ones are not that thick-skinned" (Matsuhara, 2015). Another asserted that "Falsified earnings under the name of accounting irregularities. Large corporations would end up being forgiven if they committed a crime" (Toyochi@, 2015).

Toshiba continued to make announcements related to the accounting scandal and offered repeated apologies through its news releases, news conferences, and corporate website, while posts on its Facebook page reflected "business as usual" with no hint of the ongoing scandal (Toshiba, n.d.-i). The company's PR division did not create its Japanese Facebook page ("Toshiba News and Highlights") until September 30, 2016; as of this writing it does not have an official Japanese Twitter account. Not only was the company late in getting into social media, but it also attempted to obfuscate the core issue of its systematic multiyear accounting fraud by not discussing it on any social media platform. Reflecting the Japanese apology culture, which does not necessarily emphasize corrective actions, Toshiba's online communication lacked substance and transparency, a sign of discrepancy between U.S.- and Japanese-style communications despite the company's adoption of the U.S.-style corporate governance structure. Even to its employees, Toshiba simply posted notices about its lenient disciplinary actions against senior officials on its in-house network (Toshiba workers, 2016).

Although Muromachi apologized to Prime Minister Shinzo Abe's office for "inconveniences caused" on August 5, 2015 (Ando et al., 2015), the Tokyo Stock Exchange designated the Toshiba stock as "a Security on Alert" on September 15, 2015, as a punitive measure against its accounting fraud. In the case of Toshiba, the designation indicated that "a listed company has made false statements in a securities report, etc." (Tokyo Stock Exchange, 2016, 85). In recent years, stocks of only a handful companies have been placed on alert annually (Japan Exchange Group, 2017). Unless Toshiba improved its internal governance, it could face delisting (Toshiba stock, 2015) and the trading of its stocks would become nearly impossible.

In response, Toshiba continued to implement restructuring measures to its corporate governance, such as a newly approved board that now included seven outside directors (Yamazaki, 2015a), punishment of 30 more executives identified as being involved in the accounting scandal (Alpeyev, Amano, & Ma, 2015), and additional reduction of the workforce by 6,800, totaling more than 10,000 employees in the year (Yamazaki, 2015c).

However, Toshiba's woes continued. For example, on December 25, 2015, Japan's Financial Services Agency imposed a record $62.1 million (¥7.37 billion) fine on Toshiba; the company's response was again to express apologies to all stakeholders, and shareholders and investors in particular (Schoenberg & Robinson, 2016; Toshiba fined, 2015).

Despite Toshiba's corporate governance reform, in March 2016 seven new accounting errors emerged, which prompted its spokeswoman to admit that "The company 'lacked awareness for appropriate disclosure'" (Yamazaki, 2016, para. 4). Not only did this incident demonstrate the ineffectiveness of Toshiba's internal training and communication, but it also cast "doubts over the company's pledge to improve transparency" (Yamazaki, 2016, para. 1).

On June 22, 2016, Satoshi Tsunakawa, who had led Toshiba's medical unit, became the new president (Alpeyev & Oh, 2016). The next day, Japan's $1.3 trillion Government Pension Investment Fund announced a lawsuit against Toshiba, seeking $8.6 million in damages (Kitanaka & Matsuda, 2016).

Outcomes

As is typical of many Japanese companies, Toshiba's crisis communication practices focused on announcements and apologies. But the company also implemented some measures of corporate governance reform, including the divesture of some of its assets (Toshiba whistleblowers, 2015), the inclusion of more outside directors (Toshiba, n.d.-e), the implementation of new management evaluation and employee survey systems, the reinforcement of the internal audit structure (Toshiba, 2015c), and the strengthening of the whistleblower system that had already existed as a "Risk Hotline" since the year 2000 (Fuwa, 2009, 262; Toshiba whistleblowers, 2015). As a result, Toshiba still received some additional reports in August 2015 from internal whistleblowers, independently from its audits, on improper accounting. During a news conference on August 31, 2015, Muromachi, then the interim president, put a positive spin on the situation, saying, "There is a new-found awareness among employees that whistleblowing helps improve our corporate culture . . . I believe it is important to come to terms with this in order to regain shareholders' trust" (Toshiba whistleblowers, 2015, para. 4).

However, more whistleblowing called into question the credibility of Toshiba's audits, both internal and independent (Toshiba whistleblowers, 2015). Another failure to detect additional new accounting irregularities, which the company belatedly revealed in March 2016 (Yamazaki, 2016), indicated not only the ineffectiveness of Toshiba's audits and internal communication but also its lack of transparency in investor relations.

Furthermore, Toshiba committed some ethically dubious acts, such as (1) promising to "review" the existing, "Challenge"-based budget development process (Toshiba, 2015c) despite the independent committee's recommendation to abolish the "Challenge" policy (Ueda et al., 2015); (2) its lawsuit against only five former executives, including three former presidents, for merely $2.44 million in damages in November 2015 despite a 40% yearly decline in its stock price, which caused significant financial damage to investors (Yamazaki, 2015b; Yan, 2015); and (3) its light punishment of other executives and managers identified as involved in the scandal while laying off a massive number of rank-and-file employees (Toshiba workers, 2016). One employee said, "The disciplinary measures are too lenient. How do they (the officials involved in the scandal) feel about their responsibilities over causing a disturbance in society? There is a gap in respect between managers and employees" (Toshiba workers, 2016, para. 16, parentheses in the original).

Financially, as the accounting scandal led to extensive media coverage and massive financial downward adjustments, both the revenue and the net income in FY 2016 (April 2015–March 2016) took a nosedive to ¥5.67 trillion (−14.83% from ¥6.66 trillion in FY 2015) and ¥831.9 billion in losses (−2,099.34% from ¥37.83 billion in losses for FY 2015) respectively (Annual financials, 2016). Toshiba's stock price plummeted from ¥512.4 on April 3, 2015—when the first announcement about its accounting irregularities was made—to ¥158.0 on February 22, 2016, which was the lowest point in the past five years. However, the stock price had since been recovering slowly (Toshiba Corp., 2016).

It is important to note that Toshiba actually followed U.S. practices of focusing on short-term profit, which was identified in the independent committee's report as one of the direct causes for its accounting scandal (Ueda et al., 2015, 321). In former President Nishida's mind, "building credibility with investors" was a priority to be accomplished no matter what by hitting revenue and profit targets and boosting returns for investors (Layne & Ando, 2015). His misguided idea of investor relations—profits above all else, including honesty, transparency, and long-term reputation—began the saga of Toshiba's accounting scandal. In fact, many of Arthur W. Page's "Page Principles" are applicable in this case: telling the truth with honest and good intention, proving it with action rather than repetitive ritualistic apologies, listening to not only shareholders but also all stakeholders, managing for tomorrow by focusing on a long-term vision rather than short-term profit, and realizing an enterprise's true character is expressed by its employees, the very stakeholders mistreated by the Toshiba management (Arthur W. Page Society, n.d.). In other words, the core issue of the Toshiba case is not just about the structure of corporate governance but also about the nature of leadership and the culture of an organization.

However, anything Toshiba has done and will do to resurrect itself from this crisis may be too little and too late. Since the revelation of its accounting scandal, the company has been selling off some of its business units to restructure its entire business (Alpeyev & Amano, 2016). Additionally, because of massive financial losses related to the March 2017 bankruptcy filing of its troubled U.S. nuclear business unit Westinghouse Electric Co., Toshiba warned on April 11, 2017, that it might not be able to continue as a "going concern" (Swartz, 2017, para. 3). "Toshiba introduced millions of Americans to high-end TVs and portable computers. Now, it could be saying goodbye" (Swartz, 2017, paras. 1–2).

References

Alpeyev, P., & Amano, T. (2015a, July 21). Toshiba executives resign over $1.2 billion accounting scandal. *Bloomberg*. Retrieved from http://www.bloomberg.com/news/articles/2015-07-21/toshiba-executives-resign-over-1-2-billion-accounting-scandal.

Alpeyev, P., & Amano, T. (2015b, July 21). Toshiba scandal grew from numbers "too embarrassing" to show. *Bloomberg*. Retrieved from http://www.bloomberg.com/news/articles/2015-07-21/toshiba-scandal-grew-from-numbers-too-embarrassing-to-release.

Alpeyev, P., & Amano, T. (2016, March 17). Toshiba gets $5.9 billion deal to sell medical unit to Canon. *Bloomberg*. Retrieved from https://www.bloomberg.com/news/articles/2016-03-17/canon-clinches-deal-to-buy-toshiba-medical-unit-for-5-9-billion.

Alpeyev, P., Amano, T., & Ma, J. (2015, November 7). Toshiba sues five former executives over accounting scandal. *Bloomberg*. Retrieved from http://www.bloomberg.com/news/articles/2015-11-07/toshiba-sues-five-former-executives-over-accounting-scandal.

Alpeyev, P., & Oh, T. (2016, June 23). Toshiba's President Tsunakawa warns of long road to recovery. *Bloomberg*. Retrieved from http://www.bloomberg.com/news/articles/2016-06-23/toshiba-s-president-tsunakawa-warns-of-long-road-to-recovery.

Ando, R., Layne, N., & Armstrong, R. (2015, August 5). Toshiba CEO apologizes to Japan PM office for accounting scandal. *Reuters*. Retrieved from http://www.reuters.com/article/us-toshiba-accounting-apology-idUSKCN0QA0II20150805.

Annual financials for Toshiba Corp. ADR. (2016). *MarketWatch*. Retrieved from http://www.marketwatch.com/investing/stock/tosyy/financials.

Arthur W. Page Society. (n.d.). The Page Principles. Retrieved from http://www.awpagesociety.com/site/the-page-principles .

Bakan, J. (2004). *The Corporation: The Pathological Pursuit of Profit and Power*. New York: Free Press.

Carpenter, J. W. (2015, August 13). Toshiba's accounting scandal: How it happened. *Investopedia*. Retrieved from http://www.investopedia.com/articles/investing/081315/toshibas-accounting-scandal-how-it-happened.asp.

Fuwa, H. (2009). Management innovation at Toshiba: The introduction of the company with committees system. In Whittaker, D. H., & Deakin, S. (Eds.), *Corporate Governance and Managerial Reform in Japan* (pp. 254–265). New York: Oxford University Press.

Hofstede, G. (2001). *Culture's Consequences: Comparing Values, Behaviors, Institutions, and Organizations Across Nations* (2nd ed.). Thousand Oaks, CA: Sage Publications.

Hofstede, G. (n.d.-a). *National culture*. Retrieved from https://geert-hofstede.com/national-culture.html.

Hofstede, G. (n.d.-b). *What about Japan?* Retrieved from https://geert-hofstede.com/japan.html.

Jackson, G., & Miyajima, H. (2008). Introduction: The diversity and change of corporate governance in Japan. In Aoki, M., Jackson, G., & Miyajima, H. (Eds.), *Corporate Governance in Japan: Institutional Change and Organizational Diversity* (pp. 1–47). New York: Oxford University Press.

Jamrog, J. J., Forcade, J. W., Groe, G. M., Keller, R., Lindberg, A., Vickers, M. R., & Williams, R. (2006). *The Ethical Enterprise: A Global Study of Business Ethics, 2005–2015*. Retrieved from American Management Association website: http://www.amanet.org/images/HREthicsSurvey06.pdf.

Japan Business Federation. (2006, June 20). Regarding the corporate governance system in Japan [in Japanese]. Retrieved from https://www.keidanren.or.jp/japanese/policy/2006/040.html.

Japan Exchange Group. (2017). Designation of securities on alert: Designation history. Retrieved from http://www.jpx.co.jp/english/listing/market-alerts/alert/archives/index.html.

Kim, M., & Cushing, C. (2015, July 20). Toshiba's accounting probe. *Reuters.* Retrieved from http://www.reuters.com/article/us-toshiba-accounting-timeline-idUSKCN0PU0EF20150720.

Kitanaka, A., & Matsuda, K. (2016, June 23). World's biggest pension fund sues Toshiba for profit scandal. *Bloomberg.* Retrieved from http://www.bloomberg.com/news/articles/2016-06-23/world-s-biggest-pension-fund-sues-toshiba-for-accounting-scandal.

Kitanaka, A., & Reynolds, I. (2015, July 21). Whistle-blower laws fail to curb Toshiba executives' deception. *Bloomberg.* Retrieved from http://www.bloomberg.com/news/articles/2015-07-22/toshiba-scandal-shows-cultural-legal-hurdles-for-whistleblowers.

Layne, N., & Ando, R. (2015, August 24). In Toshiba scandal, the "tough as nails" target setter. *Reuters.* Retrieved from http://www.reuters.com/article/us-toshiba-accounting-nishida-insight-idUSKCN0QT2B520150824.

Matsuhara, K. [keisuke_m]. (2015, July 21). Tweet [in Japanese]. Retrieved from https://twitter.com/keisuke_m/status/623478463282843648.

Meyer, E. (2014a). *Comparing Management Cultures.* Retrieved from https://hbr.org/resources/html/infographics/2014/05/R1405K-Meyer/May_MY_Meyer_v2.html.

Meyer, E. (2014b). *The Culture Map: Breaking Through the Invisible Boundaries of Global Business.* New York: Public Affairs.

Miyajima, H., Saito, T., Sho, H., Tanaka, W., & Ogawa, R. (2013). Where is the Japanese-style corporate governance going? Reading from the survey by "The Questionnaire on Japanese Firms' Corporate Governance" [in Japanese]. (RIETI Policy Discussion Paper Series 13-P-012). Retrieved from Research Institute of Economy, Trade and Industry website: http://www.rieti.go.jp/jp/publications/pdp/13p012.pdf.

Morita, K. (2008). Karoshi. In Clegg, S. R., & Bailey, J. R. (Eds.), *International Encyclopedia of Organization Studies* (Vol. 2, pp. 747–749). Thousand Oaks, CA: Sage Publications.

Schoenberg, T., & Robinson, M. (2016, March 17). Toshiba shares plunge as U.S. unit faces accounting probe. *Bloomberg.* Retrieved from http://www.bloomberg.com/news/articles/2016-03-17/toshiba-said-to-face-u-s-probe-over-westinghouse-accounting.

Shishido, Z. (2008). The turnaround of 1997: Changes in Japanese corporate law and governance. In Aoki, M., Jackson, G., & Miyajima, H. (Eds.), *Corporate Governance in Japan: Institutional Change and Organizational Diversity* (pp. 310–329). New York: Oxford University Press.

Sugimoto, R. (2015, August 19). Why do Japanese corporations constantly apologize? *Tokyo Business Today.* Retrieved from http://toyokeizai.net/articles/-/81045.

Swartz, J. (2017, April 11). Toshiba gave us flash memory and portable PCs—and a lesson in risky nuclear bets. *USA Today.* Retrieved from https://www.usatoday.com/story/tech/news/2017/04/11/toshiba-us-going-concern-americas-tvs/100323986/.

The great recession. (n.d.). *Investopedia*. Retrieved from http://www.investopedia.com/terms/g/great-recession.asp.

Tokyo Stock Exchange. (2015, June 1). *Japan's Corporate Governance Code: Seeking Sustainable Corporate Growth and Increased Corporate Value over the Mid- to Long-Term*. Retrieved from http://www.jpx.co.jp/english/equities/listing/cg/tvdivq0000008jdy-att/20150513.pdf.

Tokyo Stock Exchange. (2016, November 4). *Securities Listing Regulations [Rule 1 through Rule 826]*. Retrieved from http://www.jpx.co.jp/english/rules-participants/rules/regulations/tvdivq0000001vyt-att/securities_listing_regulations_(r1-r826)_20161104.pdf.

Tomita, S., & Maeda, Y. (2015, August 28). Mystery of a resigned Toshiba ex-VP working as an "adviser." *Tokyo Business Today*. Retrieved from http://toyokeizai.net/articles/-/82181.

Toshiba. (2015a, April 3). *Notice regarding establishment of Special Investigation Committee* [Press release]. Retrieved from http://www.toshiba.co.jp/about/ir/en/news/20150403.pdf.

Toshiba. (2015b, July 20). *Notice on receiving report from Independent Investigation Committee, and action to be taken by Toshiba for corrections identified for past financial results* [Press release]. Retrieved from http://www.toshiba.co.jp/about/ir/en/news/20150720_1.pdf.

Toshiba. (2015c, December 21). *Toshiba to execute "Toshiba Revitalization Action Plan"* [Press release]. Retrieved from https://www.toshiba.co.jp/about/press/2015_12/pr2101.htm.

Toshiba. (n.d.-a). *Actions taken in response to inappropriate accounting*. Retrieved from http://www.toshiba.co.jp/about/info-accounting/index.htm.

Toshiba. (n.d.-b). *Companies*. Retrieved from http://www.toshiba.co.jp/worldwide/about/company/index.html.

Toshiba. (n.d.-c). *Corporate data*. Retrieved from http://www.toshiba.co.jp/worldwide/about/corp_data.html.

Toshiba. (n.d.-d). *Corporate information*. Retrieved from http://www.toshiba.co.jp/worldwide/about/index.html.

Toshiba. (n.d.-e). *Directors and executives*. Retrieved from http://www.toshiba.co.jp/worldwide/about/manage/dir.html.

Toshiba. (n.d.-f). *History*. Retrieved from http://www.toshiba.co.jp/worldwide/about/history.html.

Toshiba. (n.d.-g). *Management structure*. Retrieved from http://www.toshiba.co.jp/worldwide/about/manage.html.

Toshiba. (n.d.-h). *The Toshiba commitment*. Retrieved from http://www.toshiba.co.jp/worldwide/about/commitment.html.

Toshiba. (n.d.-i). *Toshiba news and highlights*. Retrieved from https://www.facebook.com/toshiba.newsandhighlights/.

Toshiba admits inflating operating profit over three years. (2015, May 21). *Nikkei Asian Review*. Retrieved from http://asia.nikkei.com/magazine/20150521-GENERAL-MALAISE/Markets/Toshiba-admits-inflating-operating-profit-over-three-years.

Toshiba Corp. (2016). *Bloomberg*. Retrieved from http://www.bloomberg.com/quote/6502:JP.

Toshiba fined record ¥7.3 billion over accounting scandal. (2015, December 25). *Japan Times*. Retrieved from http://www.japantimes.co.jp/news/2015/12/25/business/corporate-business/toshiba-fined-record-%C2%A57-3-billion-over-accounting-scandal/.

Toshiba stock put "on alert" over faulty internal management. (2015, September 15). *Nikkei Asian Review*. Retrieved from http://asia.nikkei.com/Markets/Tokyo-Market/Toshiba-stock-put-on-alert-over-faulty-internal-management.

Toshiba whistleblowers prompt another reporting delay. (2015, September 1). *Nikkei Asian Review*. Retrieved from http://asia.nikkei.com/Business/Companies/Toshiba-whistleblowers-prompt-another-reporting-delay.

Toshiba workers angered by soft stance on management over accounting scandal. (2016, March 18). *The Mainichi*. Retrieved from http://mainichi.jp/english/articles/20160318/p2a/00m/0na/012000c.

Toyochi@. [skytoyopon]. Tweet [in Japanese]. Retrieved from https://twitter.com/skytoyopon/status/623424669333520384.

Ueda, K., Matsui, H., Ito, T., & Yamada, K. (2015, July 20). *Investigation report*. Retrieved from Toshiba website: https://www.toshiba.co.jp/about/ir/en/news/20151208_2.pdf.

Yamazaki, M. (2015a, September 30). Toshiba expands commitment line, shareholders approve new board. *Reuters*. Retrieved from http://www.reuters.com/article/us-toshiba-accounting-banks-idUSKCN0RU02A20150930.

Yamazaki, M. (2015b, November 12). Toshiba lawsuit highlights Japan governance reform still lacking: lawyers. *Reuters*. Retrieved from http://www.reuters.com/article/us-toshiba-lawsuit-idUSKCN0T10AA20151112.

Yamazaki, M. (2015c, December 21). Toshiba to book record loss, cut 5 percent of workforce this year. *Reuters*. Retrieved from http://www.reuters.com/article/us-toshiba-restructuring-announcement-idUSKBN0U40IH20151221.

Yamazaki, M. (2016, March 15). Toshiba finds more accounting errors, promises improvement. *Reuters*. Retrieved from http://www.reuters.com/article/us-toshiba-restructuring-idUSKCN0WH0IG.

Yan, S. (2015, November 9). Toshiba shares tumble after posting loss. *CNN Monday*. Retrieved from http://money.cnn.com/2015/11/09/investing/toshiba-company-accounting-loss/.

Yoshimori, M. (1995). Whose company is it? The concept of the corporation in Japan and the West. *Long Range Planning, 28*(4), 33–44.

Zahra, S. A. (2014). Public and corporate governance and young global entrepreneurial firms. *Corporate Governance: An International Review, 22*(2), 77–83.

Discussion Questions

1. At what point should Toshiba have acted to redress its illegal/unethical actions? Based on Japanese cultural and organizational traits, how could Toshiba transform itself into an ethical organization?

2. It took former President Hisao Tanaka more than a month to apologize in public and more than three months to resign after the company had revealed its accounting irregularities for the first time. How common are CEOs' direct apologies to the public? If they are not common, why not? What is the most ethical and practical course of action for CEOs once they learn that their companies are at fault?

3. Joel Bakan (2004, 69), the author of *The Corporation: The Pathological Pursuit of Profit and Power*, argues that "The corporation, like the psychopathic personality it resembles, is programmed to exploit others for profit. That is its only legitimate mandate." History tells us that corporate scandals, which often originate in corporations' willful disregard for laws and regulations, will never end. Do you agree with Bakan's assessment of corporations? How can public relations professionals alleviate the general public's cynicism about corporations?

4. Japan has an established social ritual called *shazai kaiken*, or "apology news conferences," in which corporate executives and public figures embroiled in a scandal make a brief remorseful statement, deliver a direct, sincere apology, take a deep bow to camera shutters and flashes, discuss details, and answer questions from the media (Sugimoto, 2015). If the accusations are well founded, is this ritual a good practice from the standpoint of public relations? Why or why not? What must follow after an organization makes public apologies?

TAYLOR GUITARS, GUARDIANS OF THE FOREST

Janis Teruggi Page, Ph.D., *The George Washington University*, and William S. Page, *Mediawerks PR*

Guitar players favor instruments made of exotic woods because of their beauty and tonal qualities. No wood is more prized, or under more stress as a species, than ebony, with its high density and dark, rich color. Ebony's journey from a tree in the rain forest of Africa to an instrument in an artist's hands is long, complicated, and fraught with environmental concerns, social issues, and strict regulations. Taylor Guitars, guided by the vision of its owners, took on all of these challenges, and, with an aggressive public relations effort to change the perception of what defined ebony, has, in effect, saved as much as 90% of the world's remaining stock of ebony.

Background

Ebony and other exotic woods used in building musical instruments are among the world's most endangered and protected forest products. U.S. companies that use these materials must follow strict protocols set down in the Lacey Act (U.S. Fish & Wildlife

Service, International Affairs, n.d., para. 1), which makes it "unlawful to export, sell, acquire, or purchase" certain animal products and plants "obtained in violation of U.S. or foreign laws." The act was amended in 2008 to include a ban on "products made from illegally logged woods" (para. 3).

Founded in 1974 by Bob Taylor and Kurt Listug, Taylor Guitars, headquartered in El Cajon, California, builds premium acoustic guitars. They are sold worldwide and are known for their craftsmanship, innovative designs, and technological advances. As a fundamental part of its corporate ethos, Taylor is devoted to "best practices" throughout its building process, starting with sound forest management, ethical sourcing of tonewoods, and rigorous attention to environmental sustainability. Its green practices extend to the final steps in the process, with repurposing of wood scrap and sawdust and the use of recyclable packing materials (Taylor Guitars, n.d.).

In 2011, to maintain a reliable and ethical supply of ebony (used mainly for their guitar fretboards), while observing the strictures of the Lacey Act and other international laws, Taylor Guitars president Bob Taylor and Spanish-based partner Madinter Trade bought Crelicam, the largest ebony mill in the African nation of Cameroon. Once the partners learned more about the social and environmental issues impacting the Cameroonian ebony trade, their goals shifted dramatically and went beyond operating a business that focused only on being a supplier of ebony.

The Situation

Building and sustaining positive relationships with multiple publics was essential to this new direction. Taylor said, "Our focus grew to include the workers in the factory, the citizens of the communities where the ebony grows, the truck drivers who transport the wood, and the forest itself in terms of how we can sustain it and set it up for future stability and harvest" (Kirlin, 2012, 14).

In a series of conversations with the Crelicam workers, the new owners learned most had not received a raise in many years and their working conditions were so primitive there was no ready access to water and toilets. Since the acquisition, workers' wages have doubled; there are now toilets and a water well that serves the factory and the community; and workers' lunches are now provided. Other social and ethical challenges that arose were addressed in a manner that acknowledged local customs without running afoul of any regulation. As the company's supply chain director explained:

> The Cameroonian business culture is much more "family"-centric than businesses in the U.S. or Europe. Because of high unemployment, many family members do not work. Extended family members, such as aunts, uncles, cousins, nieces, nephews, grandparents, and sometimes, village neighbors, all rely on each other and often live in the same household. They are not

their biological brothers, mothers, etc., but they are viewed as such. The employees expect the company to care for them the same as their immediate family, and often that can be up to 20 people in a single family. This is a consideration we must remember when discussing pay and benefits.

For example, employees often have nowhere else to turn if they have a financial hardship, and expect the company to assist. We have had to teach employees personal finance lessons, and will find solutions other than simply giving out loans. One way is to explain the crisis to the rest of the employees, and take a contribution—pass around the hat—so they can help their comrade. Since all employees are viewed as family, no one takes issue with discussing the problem as a family would. (C. Redden, personal communication, June 30, 2016)

Another ethical and legal issue facing U.S. companies doing business in many regions of the world is that some workers or local officials will expect to be given a gratuity (some may call it a bribe) to complete a task or cut through red tape. Although some other countries do not prohibit their companies from engaging in this practice, U.S. companies are bound by the Foreign Corrupt Practices Act (U.S. Department of Justice, n.d.), which not only forbids the paying of bribes but also imposes stiff sanctions on companies and employees that do. How this issue is dealt with by the owners of Crelicam is described by the supply chain director who worked in Cameroon:

When faced with an illegal request, I explain we are a U.S. company and it is against the Foreign Corrupt Practices Act, and we will be fined and probably go to jail. The counter to this is to simply (ask me to) pay from my own pocket. I say to them that even if I pay them from my own pocket, I could lose my job because I disregarded U.S. law.

When I have explained that I could lose my job, they become empathetic to my potential plight, because losing your job in a country like Cameroon is devastating. Usually, only one person in the household of 20 or more has a consistent job. If they lose that job, they could be condemning their entire family to starvation, poverty, and homelessness. As they would never do something that could endanger one's position, including mine, they often finish the job as intended without the bribery. (C. Redden, personal communication, June 30, 2016)

Beyond the various social and political differences, the biggest surprise for the new owners came when the discussion turned to the harvesting process. Cutters for Crelicam described the difficult task of accessing ebony, made even more difficult by the fact that all the easily available trees that grew by the sides of roads and trails had already been harvested, and now they had to go farther into the forest to reach acceptable stock. The cutters also complained about the large discrepancy between what they were paid for the highly desirable black ebony and ebony that is streaked or marbled with lighter tones. The variegated variety was considered to be of inferior quality, so the former owners would pay cutters only a fourth or fifth of the price of the black ebony. The cutters, who had to work just as hard to remove the tree for a quarter or less of the pay, felt it wasn't worth the effort to harvest the variegated ebony. At this point, the cutters were asked how they determined whether a tree was variegated or not.

Their answer changed everything. The color of the wood, the cutters said, could not be determined until the tree was felled. Once on the ground they would look at the stump and examine the grain and color to determine if it were black or variegated. If black, they would haul it out; if variegated, they left it on the forest floor. When asked how many trees they had to cut to obtain the black wood, the reply was, "about ten" (Kirlin, 2012, 14).

This answer was a shock to the new owners, as it meant that fully 90% of the available ebony was being left to decay simply because of its color. On the spot, Bob Taylor announced to the cutters that the company would pay the same for the variegated wood as the black. Despite the cutters' misgivings that "no one will want it," Taylor assured the workers that there was a market for the variegated wood and stood by his decision. "Now that we know this, we can't unknow the realities," he said, adding, "Our ebony reflects the reality of the forest. This is what ebony looks like." Harvesting the variegated ebony along with the black was a wise environmental choice, too, because, as Taylor put it, "Here's the good news . . . there's 10 times as much usable ebony in Cameroon as we thought there was" (Kirlin, 2012, 15).

Outcomes

As environmentally sound as his decision was, Taylor still faced the task of convincing guitar buyers that, after decades of being told that only black ebony was suitable for the fretboards of their instruments, that wasn't necessarily the case. Also needing convincing would be the instrument manufacturers supplied by Crelicam in the past.

To shift the mindset, Taylor Guitars used the industry stature and influence of its CEO to launch a concerted public relations campaign aimed at multiple publics. Bob Taylor began a series of presentations and meetings with other guitar makers who were end users of Crelicam ebony. To these manufacturers, he explained the harsh realities of the ebony trade in Cameroon and the threat to the future of the wood. He then set out the new direction the company was taking to provide ethical, legally sourced, and sustainable ebony. He explained Crelicam's intent to use variegated wood because so many of those trees were being wasted in the harvesting process that favored only black ebony.

He shared what he had learned from his cutters, and the effect was what he wanted. Hearing about the 10 to 1 ratio, and all the waste that meant, was eye-opening, and almost all of the manufacturers Taylor spoke with agreed to use the variegated wood (Kirlin, 2012, 16).

This acceptance of the variegated wood by virtually the entire industry spurred a public relations effort to encourage consumer acceptance, too. Taylor Guitars' public relations campaign aimed at guitar buyers, current owners, and environmentally conscious musicians about the issues involved in the ebony trade was spearheaded by a company-produced 13-minute online video featuring Bob Taylor: "The Truth of the Forest: The State of Ebony in the World" (Taylor, 2012). In the video, Taylor relates the story of the acquisition of Crelicam, explains the threat to the world's supply of ebony, and informs guitar buyers of the inclusion of variegated ebony in new products from Taylor Guitars. Using a guitar with a fretboard made of variegated ebony as an example, Taylor makes the case for the change as being environmentally and ethically sound without compromising the guitar's tone or quality. Released in May 2012, the video has been watched by nearly a quarter-million viewers.

The public relations efforts also included a series of articles on the subject. The acquisition of Crelicam, the obstacles that the owners faced, the ethical and social issues, and the case for using variegated ebony were featured in Taylor Guitars' magazine for owners, *Wood & Steel* (Kirlin, 2012). The magazine, which comes out three times a year, is mailed to 300,000 owners and is also available online.

In addition, the public relations campaign resulted in media coverage about the firm's sustainability efforts in Cameroon that appeared in lifestyle and industry magazines and websites and in major metro U.S. newspapers, according to Chalise Zolezzi, director of brand communications (personal communication, February 12, 2016). For example, an interview with Bob Taylor appeared in the business section of the *Los Angeles Times* (White, 2012), and stories were placed on industry sites, such as the Solutions For Dreamers blog (Beauregard, 2012) and the Woodworking Network website (Bradford, 2012).

The unique feature of this public relations effort was that it had a specific audience to address with a specific message. Although the general public might be interested in a story about a company engaged in an environmentally sound project, it's doubtful many would have an opinion in the variegated versus black ebony issue. The real targets of all of the PR efforts were the guitar-buying public and guitar manufacturers and distributors—all definitely people with an opinion. Bob Taylor's personal presentations, the online video, and the in-depth articles all reached these publics with a consistent message that changed the perception of what is and what is not acceptable ebony. Zolezzi noted the positive reception of Taylor's message: "It is incredibly reaffirming to hear from players who found a new appreciation for their guitar, or someone who requested a Taylor guitar with 'as much color on the fretboard as possible'" (WiMN, 2012).

Bob Taylor's efforts to bring the story of Cameroonian ebony to the fore were recognized by the U.S. government in January 2014. At a ceremony held at the U.S. State Department in Washington, DC, he was presented with an Award for Corporate Excellence (U.S. Department of State, n.d.). The annual award recognizes U.S.-owned businesses that play vital roles around the world as good corporate citizens in support for sustainable development, respect for human and labor rights, environmental protection, open markets, transparency, and other democratic values. At the presentation ceremony, Secretary of State John Kerry said that through Crelicam, "Bob and Taylor Guitars have fundamentally changed the entire ebony trade" (Taylor Guitars, 2014, para. 2).

Accepting the award, Bob Taylor acknowledged the company's commitment to transforming the ebony trade, and the lives of its employees, by applying business solutions to an environmental problem. Taylor emphasized the company's commitment to enrich the lives of employees through training and social events, and to retain the value of ebony wood in Cameroon. "Our vision was to transform the way that ebony is harvested, processed, and sold into a new model of responsible social forestry while enriching the lives of our 75 employees through meaningful work," said Taylor. He continued:

> To accomplish this, we assumed the role of guardian of the forest, and we operate with the philosophy to use what the forest gives us. To us, this means using ebony of all colors and all variegations, including wood that features spotted or streaked coloring, wood which prior to our involvement would have been left to deteriorate on the forest floor. (Taylor Guitars, 2014, para. 3)

Although some guitar enthusiasts will always debate the differences in quality between black ebony and the variegated type, Bob Taylor insists in his video message that the difference is just cosmetic, saying flatly, "There is no difference in tone or density" (Taylor Guitars, 2012). In a stronger explanation of his and Crelicam's ethical stance on the issue, Taylor includes this thought: "The people of Cameroon can't afford the luxury for us to be this picky. Let's embrace what the forest can offer right now."

References

Beauregard, M. (October 30, 2012). Endangered woods: What you need to know before you buy your next acoustic guitar. Retrieved from http://solutionsfordreamers.com/articles/endangered_woods_what_you_need_to_know_before_you_buy_your_next_acoustic_gu/.

Bradford, M. (June 12, 2012). Taylor Guitars' Cameroon ebony mill: The last frontier. Retrieved from http://www.woodworkingnetwork.com/wood-market-trends/woodworking-industry-news/production-woodworking-news/Taylor-Guitars-Cameroon-Ebony-Mill-the-Last-Frontier-158643765.html.

Kirlin, J. (2012, Summer). Ebony's final frontier. *Wood & Steel.* Retrieved from https://www.taylorguitars.com/sites/default/files/W&S_Summer2012_Ebony.pdf.

Taylor Guitars. (n.d.) Taylor Guitars. Retrieved from https://www.taylorguitars.com/.

Taylor Guitars. (2014). Taylor Guitars honored with the Award for Corporate Excellence from U.S. State Department. Retrieved from https://www.taylorguitars.com/news/2014/01/31/taylor-guitars-honored-award-for-corporate-excellence-us-state-department.

Taylor, R. (2012, May 30). *Taylor Guitars: "The State of Ebony"—Bob Taylor* [Video file]. Retrieved from https://www.youtube.com/watch?v=anCGvfsBoFY.

U.S. Department of Justice. (n.d.). Foreign Corrupt Practices Act. Retrieved from https://www.justice.gov/criminal-fraud/foreign-corrupt-practices-act.

U.S. Department of State. (n.d.). Award for Corporate Excellence 2013. Retrieved from http://www.state.gov/e/eb/ace/2013/index.htm.

U.S. Fish & Wildlife Service, International Affairs. (n.d.). Lacey Act. Retrieved from https://www.fws.gov/international/laws-treaties-agreements/us-conservation-laws/lacey-act.html.

WiMN (2012). Front and center: Director of brand communications at Taylor Guitars, Chalise Zolezzi. Women's International Music Network. Retrieved from http://www.thewimn.com/front-and-center-director-of-brand-communications-at-taylor-guitars-chalise-zolezzi/.

White, R. D (June 7, 2012). Taylor Guitars buys ebony mill, pitches sustainable wood. *Los Angeles Times.* Retrieved from http://articles.latimes.com/2012/jun/07/business/la-fi-taylor-ebony-20120607.

Discussion Questions

1. Bob Taylor said Taylor Guitars is "committed to act in the spirit of compassionate capitalism." How would you describe "compassionate capitalism"? How does it compare to corporate social responsibility?

2. Bob Taylor also described his company's role in Cameroon as "guardians of the forest." What other environmental initiatives in other emerging nations can you think of that are being spearheaded by foreign businesses or interests? If so, is it being communicated sufficiently?

3. Is it the ethical responsibility of a foreign company to take action on a major environmental issue affecting another country? If so, how would a PR practitioner encourage this?

4. This case concerns the time period 2012–2014. How has Taylor continued its public relations efforts to promote this cause?

12 NONPROFIT AND EDUCATION

Learning Outcomes

- Recognize the differences between nonprofit and for-profit organizations.
- Analyze ethical principles in relation to nonprofit management.
- Apply ethical principles to nonprofit case studies.

Definitions

Nonprofit: An organization that is tax-exempt and uses all available resources left after normal operating expenses to serve the public interest.

Two-way communication: The process in which a sender and receiver communicate, interact, and use feedback to reach greater understanding.

Nonprofits are tax-exempt and can sometimes be called charities. They come in many types. Some are membership organizations such as the Public Relations Society of America (PRSA). Others focus on social services, such as the United Way, Humane Society, or Boys & Girls Clubs. Still others, like the National Rifle Association or Greenpeace, are concerned with an issue. Most colleges and universities are considered nonprofit organizations, as are religious organizations and churches. Despite their varied agendas and interests, nonprofits do have some common ground: All of them depend on volunteers, staff members, donors, and fundraising.

The Challenges of Working for Nonprofits

In a perfect world, people would understand that nonprofits and their causes are important, but that's not the reality (Selnick, 2005). Instead, PR practitioners who work for nonprofits spend a good amount of time building awareness and informing others about their organization. At the same time, they are often trying to persuade people to support their organization.

Every nonprofit needs staff members who are dedicated to the organization and the cause (Kinzey, 2013). Staff members often serve as a muse to volunteers and donors and inspire them to do more (Kinzey, 2013). Nonprofits should always demonstrate their gratitude to their supporters, donors, volunteers, and staff time and time again (Waters, 2015).

You might be asking, how can ethics affect nonprofits? One of the ways is through transparency. People want to know where their donations go and how those donations are used, so PR practitioners working for a nonprofit need to help their organization to be transparent about these things in order to build trust and better relationships with publics.

The Education Sector

One specialized type of nonprofit is education. The National School Public Relations Association (n.d., para. 1) highlights the complexity of public relations for schools and school districts:

Educational public relations is a planned and systematic management function to help improve the programs and services of an educational organization. It relies on a comprehensive two-way communications process involving both internal and external publics, with a goal of stimulating a better understanding of the role, objectives, accomplishments, and needs of the organization. Educational public relations programs assist in interpreting public attitudes, identify and help shape policies and procedures in the public interest, and carry on involvement and information activities which earn public understanding and support.

Just like any other type of organization, schools and school districts need PR practitioners to help them communicate with their publics such as parents, taxpayers, community organizations, and local government. Communicating with such groups helps schools and districts to build community relations. This communication could include print media, social media, and face-to-face communication. Educational units need a practitioner who can promote the good things students, faculty, administrators, and staff do; they also need practitioners to plan and strategize. By implementing two-way communication, schools can build trust. If publics never hear or see anything positive about a school or school district and if there is no engagement, the opinions of critics are likely to be the ones that will be heard, seen, and remembered (National School Public Relations Association, n.d.).

Higher education also needs the help of PR professionals. Some states have slashed funding for higher education. People are concerned about the high costs of higher education. Parents and students want to know more about how college prepares students for careers and the potential return on their investment. While press releases and media relations are part of what practitioners specializing in higher education do, these practitioners must also plan strategically, counsel, and do research. They need to collaborate with institutional leaders so that their communication efforts advance the institution's visions and goals while balancing the needs of publics such as students, faculty and staff, alumni, prospective students, legislators, and parents (Melichar & Brennan, 2017). To accomplish these goals, practitioners need to do a lot of listening to many constituents and to use the knowledge they gain to create shared narratives and to serve as advocates (Melichar & Brennan, 2017).

References

Kinzey, R. E. (2013, October). Creating nonprofit engagement. *Public Relations Tactics*, *20*(10), 18.

Melichar, C., & Brennan, J. A. (2017, July 11). The future of higher ed PR: Proving the power of strategic public relations. Retrieved from https://www.insidehighered.com/blogs/call-action-marketing-and-communications-higher-education/future-higher-ed-pr.

National School Public Relations Association. (n.d.). Retrieved from https://www.nspra.org/getting_started.

Selnick, D. (2005, August). Public relations and the nonprofit: A necessary alliance. *Public Relations Tactics*, *12*(8), 20 & 23.

Waters, R. D. (2015, October). #GivingTuesday: What's your strategy? *Public Relations Tactics*, *22*(10), 14.

THE WOUNDED WARRIOR PROJECT

Pamela G. Bourland-Davis, Ph.D., *Georgia Southern University*, and William Thompson

Many organizational management experts praise companies that inject fun into the workplace. Silicon Valley startups, in particular, have received attention for their game rooms and company-supplied snacks that built group cohesion while making long hours more tolerable. High salaries and perks like high-end, all-expenses-paid management retreats were viewed as simply a fair trade for the company's 24/7 demands. However, the public holds nonprofit organizations to a different standard and expects its leaders to behave in a certain way. When a nonprofit organization employs unusual practices like those that would be considered acceptable in a Silicon Valley startup, the organization and its leaders may face consequences—as this case study reveals.

Background

Wounded Warrior Project (WWP) was founded by former Marine John Melia in 2003 (Associated Press, 2016), essentially to provide "comfort items" to wounded veterans returning home from post-9/11 military actions (Phillips, 2016). After the group incorporated in 2005, its mission grew to enlist public support and create a group through which injured veterans, or "alumni," could assist each other. Its culture of teamwork (WWP, 2016c), with specific values of fun, innovation, integrity, loyalty, and service, was supported by a variety of social and athletic programs for veterans and employees, often program alumni, as the returning veterans adjusted not only to their injuries but to domestic life.

In 2010, attorney Steven Nardizzi, who was not a veteran, took over from Melia and instituted a far more aggressive fundraising model. Nardizzi focused on investing in fundraising and team building, following a corporate model. His philosophy was echoed by his advocacy of the Charity Defense Council, which promoted business approaches to nonprofits (Mak, 2015b). In a 2015 interview (Center for High Impact Philanthropy, 2:45), Nardizzi said,

> One thing that I realized, . . . the amount of effort and energy that really goes into fundraising—into administration, into having . . . your finances in order, and having a legal department . . . It is nonprofit business, but it is a business . . . The perception, I think, for the public tends to be that charities are all a bunch of volunteers that are working for free and spending very little money on anything other than direct services . . . And the reality is you can't make an extended impact that way.

His approach at WWP appeared to pay off. In his first five years, both WWP's contributions and its beneficiary expenditures jumped 1,200% (Internal Revenue Service [IRS], 2011, 2015).

The Situation

Organizational Success and the Business Model

As 2016 opened, Nardizzi could point to any number of successes since taking the helm: Donations were 12 times higher, and the number of employees had increased nearly 500%. The tracking metrics he had implemented showed his management techniques were on target, with the amount of money generated per employee continuing to climb. That growth represented benefits for the organization's targeted veterans, as expenditures on programming for wounded veterans also jumped over 1,200% (IRS, 2011, 2015).

Public recognition came, too. WWP had been the 2012 charity of the year (Nardizzi, n.d.), and Nardizzi grew WWP into one of the nation's 40 largest nonprofits (Barrett, 2015). In 2015, Nardizzi and his team raised $342 million.

Nardizzi himself prospered as well. His board increased his pay by 300% to nearly $500,000. While that represented an impressive raise, Nardizzi's salary and bonuses significantly declined as a percentage of the organization's total revenue (IRS, 2011, 2015). And his salary, while higher than that of many executives for less successful veterans' charities, was not much larger than the salaries of nonprofit leaders whose organizations raised less.

Nardizzi attributed part of his success to following business assumptions about organizational success. WWP "modeled itself on for-profit corporations, with a focus on data, scalable products, quarterly numbers and branding" (Philips, 2016, para. 17). Phillips (2016, para. 19) quoted Nardizzi as saying, "I look at companies like Starbucks—that's the model. You're looking at companies that are getting it right, treating their employees right, delivering great services and great products, then are growing the brand to support all of that."

Employee Relations

As CEO, Nardizzi acted on his nonprofit business philosophy by treating WWP employees to lots of perks (Kilbride, 2016; Mak, 2016; Phillips, 2016). Free snacks and soft drinks were provided during breaks. Nardizzi created WWP-branded trinkets for employees' desks. Imitating the for-profit corporations he admired, Nardizzi annually flew all employees to resorts for strategy development and team-building. He even staged rousing introductions to the meetings: In successive years, he rode a Segway and a horse and rappelled down a hotel tower to fire up his workers for his opening speech. Corporate travel sometimes included first-class or business-class airline tickets.

Yet Nardizzi's metrics suggested that team-building yielded fundraising success. For instance, while the organization's employee count quintupled during the

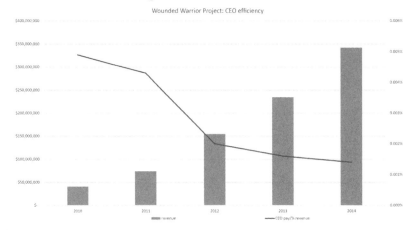

CEO's salary as % of WWP revenue

TABLE 12.1

first five years of Nardizzi's leadership, total travel expenditures only rose 300% (IRS, 2011, 2015). In September 2015, WWP accounts showed that donations had increased $110 million from the previous year (IRS, 2014, 2015).

However, Nardizzi's generosity appeared to come with demands. In an organizational culture wedded to observable metrics, employees were given ambitious performance targets that some employees complained were "numbers based on nothing" (Phillips, 2016, para. 52). Employees, some of them veterans, reported being fired because they didn't seem to fit the company culture or were perceived as working against the team. Others despaired that WWP had wandered off course, becoming a product-licensing behemoth that didn't pay sufficient attention to the veterans it was supposed to serve (Phillips, 2016).

Fundraising

Nardizzi had committed WWP, with board support, to a strategy of rapid financial growth, aggressive branding, and relentless public attention using advertising, social media, and media relations. Public relations was aggressively employed as well. One of WWP's biggest annual expenditures for veterans was the "Soldier Ride," a multiple-day bicycle ride for wounded veterans. WWP purchased custom-fitted bicycles to accommodate veterans' physical limitations, then staged rides. Heavily promoted, the rides generated media coverage across the country (IRS, 2015). To drive the majority of its fundraising, WWP relied on advertising, corporate sponsorships, and direct mail. Combined, these strategies made WWP nearly omnipresent for even the casual television viewer, and social media popup ads made regular appearances on potential donors' computer screens.

Similarly, WWP combined its commitment to hiring veterans with in-person public outreach. WWP employees, to solicit gifts, were deployed to communities nationwide, which stimulated more positive media attention, raised awareness of the organization, and personalized the cause. In line with this philosophy, WWP did not depend on professional fundraisers as part of its fundraising strategy (Hundley, 2013).

Instead, taking his cue from corporate management, Nardizzi capitalized on multiple revenue streams. The huge presence WWP gained from its advertising budgets, public events, and media relations campaigns made the organization's logo a valuable commodity. WWP licensed the right to print the logo on other organizations' products. WWP amassed millions of dollars in interest from its invested earnings (IRS, 2015). Selling donor contact information added to the coffers (Mak, 2015b).

Yet WWP's very success stirred complaints from peers, media, and current and former employees. Other veterans' charities, with longer histories and much smaller budgets, complained about WWP's "bullying" and aggressive advertising and licensing tactics (McCambridge, 2015). They reported being warned of infringement on the WWP brand for using terms such as "wounded warrior" or similar logos (Mak, 2015a). They also criticized the way WWP fulfilled its mission. Because WWP services were restricted to post-9/11 veterans, other veterans' groups felt that WWP attracted funding that should have helped all wounded veterans (Philpott, 2015).

Others speculated whether WWP's services were directed more to helping veterans or generating publicity to build WWP's brand and drive future fundraising (McCambridge & Buchanan, 2016). While the organization offered vocational counseling, educational funding, and rehabilitation services, WWP's fundraising success let it offer nontraditional amenities as well. The organization spent $15 million on the veterans' bicycle rides and offered other recreational activities, such as free sports tickets, fly fishing, hunting parties, and yacht excursions. There were also programs like "Rock 4 Recovery," which offered veterans $10,000 to set up their own rock bands "to express their feelings and thoughts through music" (IRS, 2015, 50). The organization justified these programs as helping veterans reintegrate into civilian society and keeping "feel good" stories about WWP in the media.

WWP also received mixed reviews from charity rating services. In July 2013, the *Tampa Bay Times* (Hundley, 2013) reported that Charity Navigator had given WWP a three-star rating (out of four). While the Better Business Bureau gave WWP its Gold Standard rating for top performance (Kilbride, 2016), Charity Watch (2016) gave the organization a "C" rating. While WWP accountants declared the organization devoted over 80% of its income to charitable programming (Wounded Warrior Project, 2016a), Charity Navigator and Charity Watch evaluators said that only 58% and 48%, respectively, were spent on veterans' programs (Charity Navigator, 2016; Charity Watch, 2016). The rest was spent on "educational materials" that, in the opinion of the two charity watchdogs, predominantly contained fundraising pitches.

Part of the problem was that Nardizzi and the charity evaluation groups used metrics that weren't measuring the same things. The watchdogs expected a larger proportion of current-year revenue to be expended on service programs. While this was an appropriate measure for organizations with stable and predictable fundraising totals, it skewed WWP's evaluation. During a typical two-year planning cycle, WWP's annual income increased $190 million, more than double what it had been two years earlier (IRS, 2013, 2015).

Instead, WWP stashed funds. WWP's net assets grew 3,000% during Nardizzi's tenure, which seemed to ensure the organization's lifetime commitment to severely injured veterans (IRS, 2010, 2015), and each year's program expenditures almost exactly matched the organization's record fundraising totals two years before (IRS, 2011, 2012, 2013, 2104, 2015).

Finally, discontent emerged within the organization itself. Some of the veterans among the WWP speakers complained that their WWP positions made them solicitors with fundraising targets, not honored warriors. Others complained that money should have been spent on veterans' programming instead of first-class flights, a $20,000 WWP yearbook, logo-branded office items, employee apparel, and promotional items distributed to veterans and donors (McCambridge, 2016; Phillips, 2016).

The Crisis

The real blow came on January 26 and 27, 2016, when CBS News aired three reports detailing what former WWP employees labeled "extravagant" spending on executive salaries and employee perks (Reid & Janisch, 2016). The *New York Times* followed with its own report the next day (Phillips, 2016).

As an example of "lavish" spending, both news organization referenced the Colorado Springs' all-employee meeting where Nardizzi rappelled down the hotel tower. Portraying its $3 million cost (WWP's auditing firm later maintained it only cost $970,000) (Wounded Warrior Project, Inc., 2016b) as expenditures taken directly from veterans evoked often emotional accounts like this one from a former employee identified as a Purple Heart honoree, one of the estimated one-third of WWP's staff with military service (Phillips, 2016): "You're using our injuries, our darkest days, our hardships, to make money so you can have these big parties" (Kilbride, 2016, para. 4).

Outcomes

WWP countered on January 27 with a letter to CBS, also distributed widely to the media and through social media (WWP, 2016b). WWP's website (WWP, 2016d) described WWP as an "open book" and complained that CBS News did not contact Richard Jones, the chair of WWP's Audit Committee—who happened to be CBS's executive vice president. Nardizzi and Giordano (2016) announced that WWP had hired an outside accounting consultant and law firm to evaluate the media's allegations.

WWP (2016a) announced the findings in a March 10, 2016, media release. During the previous five years, participation in WWP's many programs had increased from approximately 1,850 to more than 144,000 wounded veterans, it said. Otherwise, the organization simply repeated cost justifications made in its initial complaint letter to CBS (WWP, 2016b). The outside accountant stated that WWP used an alternative, but accepted, accounting procedure. By that standard, WWP dedicated nearly 81% of donations to veterans' programming. And although conference programming costs had grown from $2 million in 2010 to $26 million in 2015, the accounting firm determined that about 94% of WWP's 2015 expenditures were "associated with program services delivered to Wounded Warriors and their families" (WWP, 2016b, para. 5).

Yet, while defending the organization's success and decision-making, the WWP media release announced, almost as an aside, that to "help restore trust in the organization among all of the constituencies WWP serves, the Board determined the organization would benefit from new leadership, and WWP CEO Steve Nardizzi and COO Al Giordano are no longer with the organization" (WWP, 2016b, para. 13). During this time, Nardizzi and Giordano developed a website, TheWoundedTruth.com, to state their case and to highlight news they considered fair and well researched. Nardizzi was replaced by WWP board chairman Anthony

PHOTO 12.1

Odierno and ultimately by Michael Linnington—both veterans. In doing so, the board rejected WWP founder John Melia's offer to return as CEO (Bauerlein, 2016).

Accounting and Accountability

The WWP case reveals how contemporary cultural norms impact the ways citizens perceive obligations toward veterans. In the eyes of many of its constituents and despite its extraordinary financial success, WWP seemed to violate these expectations. For charity monitors, it contradicted budgeting standards dictating that only small proportions of donations should be dedicated to administrative costs.

Of particular interest in this case is Strickland and Vaughan's (2008) application of Maslow's hierarchy of values to nonprofit organizations. The two created an ascending set of ethical values: financial competence, accountability, reciprocity, respect, and integrity. They stressed the centrality of ethics, or values, in the day-to-day work of the nonprofit, which provides useful ethical constructs for analyzing this case.

WWP attained financial competence on many levels, but that depended on the accounting procedures applied. On the basic level, the organization performed exceptionally well, supporting staff and beneficiaries equally. No funding was embezzled or lost, meeting baseline expectations of financial competence.

The second level of accountability involves transparency, which is critical to an organization's public relations and accounting concerns. Having external groups such as the board and independent auditors strengthens this area. Both oversight groups gave WWP their highest ratings for accountability and transparency (Charity Navigator, 2016; Charity Watch, 2016).

Concerning reciprocity, or the "match between donor interests and the nonprofit's mission" (Strickland & Vaughan, 2008, 242), WWP's increased donations signaled success. Still, some donors were upset when WWP sold their contact information (Mak, 2015a), and it bothered charity oversight groups (Charity Watch, 2016).

WWP's recognition as one of 2012's top nonprofits clearly displayed a level of respect. However, respect extends to donors, beneficiaries, other nonprofits, and employees (Strickland & Vaughan, 2008). As such, the organization could have addressed questions regarding its nonprofit business orientation without the defensive overtones of litigation, lobbying, and public relations firms (Phillips, 2016).

The final level is integrity. More of an ideal, it focuses on "preserving incorruptibility and completeness in commitment to the mission" (Strickland & Vaughan, 2008, 237). Central to WWP was the CEO's approach to the nonprofit as a business. While the organization clearly worked to develop a strong culture, not all the constituencies accepted the CEO's vision of how a group like this should operate.

Case Update

The organization and Nardizzi clearly had early warning signs but were unable to rebut them with any lasting impact. WWP's team culture met with internal resistance. Ultimately, its values of fun and innovation came at a high cost by clashing with the values of integrity, loyalty, and service, the latter of which more closely align with public expectations for a nonprofit.

Under new leadership, WWP had to address accountability versus profitability. Founder Melia, in retrospect, commented in an interview, "They [Nardizzi and Giordano] did good work for a long time, but organizations need a conscience. I think in my tenure, while I was there, I was the conscience of the organization" (Gardner & Frazier, 2016, para. 9).

Schaffer (2016) reported in the *Nonprofit Quarterly* that WWP donations were down 25%. At the same time, the organization trimmed its budget, reducing staffing by 15% and closing nine satellite offices. According to Schaffer's assessment (2016, para. 6), "When fundraising by any means is removed as the primary measure of success, transparency, accountability and integrity are restored, along with the wherewithal to very likely raise far more support than ever before thought possible."

References
Associated Press. (2016, March 11). Wounded Warrior Project founder John Melia open to return. *Florida Times Union*. Retrieved from http://jacksonville.com/breaking-news/2016-03-11/story/wounded-warrior-project-founder-john-melia-open-return.
Barrett, W. P. (2015, December 9). The largest U.S. charities for 2015. *Forbes*. Retrieved from http://www.forbes.com/sites/williampbarrett/2015/12/09/the-largest-u-s-charities-for-2015/#7a3f423154e4.

Bauerlein, D. (2016, June 16). Wounded Warrior Project names new CEO. *Florida Times Union*. Retrieved from http://jacksonville.com/news/metro/2016-06-16/story/wounded-warrior-project-names-new-ceo.

Center for High Impact Philanthropy. (2015, October 30). Philanthropy Unfiltered. Retrieved from https://www.youtube.com/watch?v=S2HZV7EDWp4.

Charity Navigator. (2016, June). *Watchlist: Wounded Warrior Project*. Retrieved from http://www.charitynavigator.org/index.cfm?bay=search.summary&orgid=12842.

Charity Watch. (2016, January). *Charity Watch Report: Wounded Warrior Project*. Retrieved from https://www.charitywatch.org/ratings-and-metrics/wounded-warrior-project/559.

Gardner, L., & Frazier, F. (2016, March 17). Founder says wounded Warrior Project grew too fast. Retrieved from http://www.news4jax.cm/news/investigations/wounded-warrior-project-founder-talks.

Hundley, K. (2013, July 21). Wounded Warrior Project spends 58% of donations on veterans programs. *Tampa Bay Times*. Retrieved from http://www.tampabay.com/news/business/wounded-warrior-project-spends-58-of-donations-on-veterans-programs/2132493.

Internal Revenue Service. (2011). *Form 990: Return of Organization Exempt from Income Tax: Wounded Warrior Project Inc.* Retrieved from https://www.woundedwarriorproject.org/media/1065/form-990-2009-2010.pdf.

Internal Revenue Service. (2012). *Form 990: Return of Organization Exempt from Income Tax: Wounded Warrior Project Inc.* Retrieved from https://www.woundedwarriorproject.org/media/1065/form-990-2010-2011.pdf.

Internal Revenue Service. (2013). *Form 990: Return of Organization Exempt from Income Tax: Wounded Warrior Project Inc.* Retrieved from https://www.woundedwarriorproject.org/media/1065/form-990-2011-2012.pdf.

Internal Revenue Service. (2014). *Form 990: Return of Organization Exempt from Income Tax: Wounded Warrior Project Inc.* Retrieved from https://www.woundedwarriorproject.org/media/1067/form-990-2012-2013.pdf.

Internal Revenue Service. (2015). *Form 990: Return of Organization Exempt from Income Tax: Wounded Warrior Project Inc.* Retrieved from https://www.woundedwarriorproject.org/media/1068/form-990-2013-2014.pdf.

Kilbride, L. (2016, January 27). CBS News investigates Jacksonville-based Wounded Warrior Project. *WJCT*. Retrieved from http://news.wjct.org/post/cbs-news-investigates-jacksonville-based-wounded-warrior-project.

Mak, T. (2015a, May 4). "Wounded Warrior" charity unleashes hell—on other veteran groups. *Daily Beast*. Retrieved from http://www.thedailybeast.com/articles/2015/05/04/wounded-warrior-charity-unleashes-hell-on-other-veteran-groups.html.

Mak, T. (2015b, June 8). "Wounded Warrior" charity fights—to get rich. *Daily Beast*. Retrieved from http://www.thedailybeast.com/articles/2015/06/08/vet-charity-s-new-fight-to-waste-your-cash.html.

Mak, T. (2016, March 10). Wounded Warrior Project spent $250,000 on candy and even more on gimmicks. *Daily Beast*. Retrieved from http://www.thedailybeast

.com/articles/2016/03/11/wounded-warrior-project-spent-250-000-on-candy-and-even-more-on-gimmicks.html.

McCambridge, R. (2015, May 5). Is Wounded Warrior Project a "neighborhood bully" among veterans' groups? *Nonprofit Quarterly*. Retrieved from https://non profitquarterly.org/2015/05/05/is-wounded-warrior-project-a-neighborhood-bully-among-veterans-groups/.

McCambridge, R. (2016, February 4). Wounded Warrior hires PR firm to "manage" the crisis they've created—what can we expect? *Nonprofit Quarterly*. Retrieved from https//nonprofitquarterly.org/2016/02/04/wounded-warrior-hires-pr-firm-to-manage-the-crisis-they've-created-what-can-we-expect/.

McCambridge, R., & Buchanan, A. (2016, February 1). Wounded Warrior Project: The fundraising factory issue. *Nonprofit Quarterly*. Retrieved from https://non profitquarterly.org/2016/02/01/wounded-warrior-project-the-fundraising-factory-issue/.

Nardizzi, S. (n.d.). Steven Nardizzi, Social entrepreneur, executive leader. *LinkedIn* [Profile page]. Retrieved from https://www.linkedin.com/in/steven-nardizzi-a066674.

Nardizzi, S., & Giordano, A. (2016, March 30). The wounded truth about the Wounded Warrior Project. *Washington Examiner*. Retrieved from http://www .washingtonexaminer.com/the-wounded-truth-about-the-wounded-warrior-project/ article/2587147.

Phillips, D. (2016, January 27). Wounded Warrior Project spends lavishly on itself, insiders say. *New York Times*. Retrieved from http://nyti.ms/1KbiXKi.

Philpott, T. (2015, March 12). Wounded Warrior Project: Big and getting bigger. *Military Advantage Blog*. Retrieved from_http://militaryadvantage.military. com/2015/03/wounded-warrior-project-big-and-getting-bigger/.

Reid, C., & Janisch J. (2016, January 26). Wounded Warrior Project accused of wasting donation money. *CBS News* [Video file]. Retrieved from http://www.cbsnews. com/news/wounded-warrior-project-accused-of-wasting-donation-money/.

Schaffer, J. (2016, September 6). Wounded Warrior Project loses $100 million and its swagger. *Nonprofit Quarterly*. Retrieved from https://nonprofitquartelry .org/2016/09/06/wounded-warrior-project-loses-100-million-and-its-swagger/.

Strickland, R. A., & Vaughan, S. K. (2008). The hierarchy of ethical values in nonprofit organizations: A framework for an ethical, self-actualized organizational culture. *Public Integrity, 10*(3), 233–251.

WWP. (2016a). *Board of directors of Wounded Warrior Project addresses independent review* [Press release]. Retrieved from https://www.scribd.com/doc/303780121/ WWP-Press-Release?campaign=4417&ad_group=ONLINE_TRACKING_LIN K&keyword=Skimbit%2C+Ltd.&source=impactradius&medium=affiliate&irgw.

WWP. (2016b, January 27). CBS Stories re: Wounded Warrior Project, Inc. [Letter to Al Ortiz]. Retrieved from https://www.facebook.com/wwp/posts/ 10153913530293415.

WWP. (2016c). Mission. Retrieved from www.woundedwarriorproject.org.

WWP. (2016d). Scam information. Retrieved from www.woundedwarriorproject.org.

Discussion Questions

1. At what point should a nonprofit treat CEOs and employees differently from a business CEO? Does being a successful nonprofit CEO or fundraiser mean you have a cap on your salary? Is there a rationale for executives in some nonprofit organizations (e.g., arts, education, health services) to be paid significantly more than in other equally successful nonprofit organizations?

2. If a significant proportion of donations goes toward administration, and that administration benefits veterans who work for WWP, is there a problem? Do you think the fact that this is a veterans' organization affects the case outcomes?

3. As a public relations practitioner for WWP, how would you have addressed accountability and transparency, and to whom? Would those recommendations meld with the organizational culture? How could you make recommendations and still be "part of the team"?

4. What kind of proactive approaches might Nardizzi have used to employ the organization's strong financial performance in defending his business model? And in defending his and Giordano's case after the story broke?

5. Your company has partnered with WWP to use the WWP logo on your product as part of a donation you're making. The products will hit the stores February 1, just after this story breaks. What do you recommend?

WHY ARE THERE SO MANY CRUCIFIXES?

J. J. McIntyre, Ph.D., *University of Central Arkansas,*
and Kristen A. McIntyre, Ph.D., *University of Arkansas at Little Rock*

Businessman Simon Newman, the new president of Mount St. Mary's University in Maryland, looked around and asked, "Why are there so many crucifixes?" (Jaschik, 2016e, para. 24)—and thus began a great experiment in academia. Troubled by financial pressures, the Catholic university had hired a new, non-academic president with a background in fixing troubled financial institutions. However, as you will see in this case study, business and academia have very different cultures. The story of "the Mount" would be described as a failed test case on the corporatization of higher education (Stripling, 2016).

Background

Mount St. Mary's is a private institution in Emmitsburg, Maryland, that was founded over 200 years ago (1808), making it the second oldest Catholic university in the United States. The Mount hosts roughly 1,800 students and enjoys a national reputation in both men's and women's basketball (Mount St. Mary's University, 2016a). Crucial to its mission, "the Mount affirms the values and beliefs central to the Catholic vision of the person and society, and seeks to deepen understanding of faith and its practice in just and compassionate engagement with the world" (Mount St. Mary's University, 2016a, para. 4).

Small, private academic institutions such as the Mount have recently faced financial problems that are predicted to grow in the coming years as enrollment decreases (Woodhouse, 2015). In March 2012, the Mount's creditworthiness rating was downgraded (Moody's downgrades Mount St. Mary's, 2012). Following the lead of other colleges' nontraditional leadership picks (McIntire, 2015), the Mount's board of trustees hired businessman Simon Newman, known for his transformational leadership, to serve as president of the struggling university. Upon his appointment, President Newman described his primary stakeholders as successful students and employers (Weider, 2015, para. 10).

Newman's business background (McIntire, 2016, para. 7) and familiarity with the Mount (Weider, 2015, para. 9) initially garnered positive campus response. However, he quickly made unpopular financial decisions, such as cutting the health benefits of retirees, and the conflict between Newman and the faculty and staff intensified in a debate over his retention strategy (Jaschik, 2016a, 2016b). He proposed administering a survey to identify first-year students who would have difficulty graduating and wanted to encourage them to leave the Mount before being counted in the retention statistics used in rating and ranking institutions of higher learning. While the Mount's retention and graduation rates were well above the national average, they still trailed behind some of their competition (Jaschik, 2016a). Newman said, "My short-term goal is to have 20–25 people leave by the 25th [of September] . . . this one thing will boost our retention 4–5%" (Shisler & Golden, 2016a, para. 12). Students taking the survey were told that "there were no wrong answers" (Shisler & Golden, 2016a, para. 5), and it was not disclosed that their answers would be used to identify whether they were prepared for college.

The strategy was met with resistance by a small group of faculty and administrators (Shisler & Golden, 2016a, para. 6), but most faculty and administrators were unaware of the survey's existence or how the data would be used. The director of the first-year orientation program questioned the use of the survey and was given the controversial explanation that united the faculty against the new president: "Newman said, 'This is hard for you because you think of the students as cuddly bunnies, but you can't. You just have to drown the bunnies . . . put a Glock to their heads'" (Shisler & Golden, 2016a, para. 30). In protest, the Mount faculty waited out two deadlines without forwarding any first-year student names. In response, Newman threatened, "There will be some collateral damage" (Shisler & Golden, 2016a, para. 28).

The debate over the ethically questionable retention strategy received traction when the campus student newspaper, the *Mountain Echo*, broke the story regarding the events of the previous semester on January 16, 2016. Three days later the story was picked up by the media, and the university found itself in the national spotlight.

The Situation

The *Mountain Echo* worked on the story of the president's retention plan for more than six weeks before publishing the story. The article was sent to the president and the board of trustees beforehand for a response, and the board chair responded to the story with a letter to the newspaper's managing editor that was published in a special edition (see Appendix A). The letter called the students' actions irresponsible, denied the article's characterization of the president's retention plan, condemned the use of "private" emails, threatened that the use of emails violated the university's "fair use" policy, and questioned the integrity of the student's actions (see Appendix B). After pushing the article's release back to allow time for diligent research and reflection (see Appendix C), the story was printed just before students returned from holiday break on January 16, 2016, and was followed by a special editorial edition on January 19, 2016.

Phase One: The Dirty Little Secret

The Washington Post, *Inside Higher Ed*, and the *Chronicle of Higher Education*, among others, quickly picked up the controversial and vivid story. President Newman responded first in the *Washington Post*'s article with denial, claiming that he did not recall what was said but acknowledged his use of harsh language at times (Svrluga, 2016a, para. 4). The *Washington Post* article went on to explain the administration's ethical point of view of the retention plan:

> School administrators decided to do much more to try to identify students who weren't happy early on, by tracking things such as whether they were going to events on campus, whether they were attending classes and eating meals, and they created the survey, Newman said. Then he envisioned, for those who seemed to be struggling or withdrawn, "a more serious intervention, a come-to-Jesus meeting, as it were . . ." That talk, he said, that they may be happier at Towson or a community college, could also save students money. (paras. 27–28)

While there may be some merit to this ethical argument, the student handbook explains that students are accepted on the assumption that they will attend the entire academic year (Mount St. Mary's, 2015, 16). As such, the university refunds only a percentage of tuition and boarding fees for the first five weeks. The first of the president's deadlines, September 25, would have resulted in a 40% refund to students who withdrew. The extended deadline of October 2 would have left students only two days (Saturday and Sunday) to withdraw for a 20% refund. After the start of week five *no* refunds are given.

In addition to Newman's response, the chair of the board of trustees provided another voice to the university's administrative response. Heavily steeped in denial, the board chair's statement shifted the blame to "undermining" faculty and restated support of the president's retention program and its goal of helping troubled students (Jaschik, 2016b, para. 4). The board of trustees investigated the allegations made in the student article but found no reason for action and stood in continued support of President Newman. The board also chastised faculty for not "treat[ing] others with dignity and respect and with the highest integrity" when speaking out against the president and threatened that the university "will hold those individuals accountable for these actions" (Jaschik, 2016b, para. 4).

The president and the board of trustees were speaking on behalf of the administration; faculty members also had much to say but only a few sanctioned ways to communicate. Consequently, a group of 12 faculty members formed a campus chapter of the American Association of University Professors (AAUP), giving the Mount faculty a larger and safer voice. The national organization quickly began offering statements to the media on behalf of the Mount's faculty:

> As for the idea that faculty members should check with a public relations office before talking to reporters . . . that was "totally illegitimate." Faculty members should be able to talk to whomever they want, he said, including journalists. (Jaschik, 2016b, para. 24)

As the initial phase of this case came to an end, a battered President Newman escalated the situation even further by making good on the board's threats and catapulted the events at the Mount to a new level of national interest.

Phase 2: The Mount Goes "Nuclear"

Three weeks after the story broke in the *Mountain Echo*, and just over a week after the AAUP comments, President Newman asked for and received the resignation of the university's provost or chief academic officer, David Rehm, who questioned Newman's plan (McGuire, 2016). Days later, two of the Mount's faculty were fired for disloyalty without review or notice (Jaschik, 2016c, para. 1). The first fired faculty member was the advisor of the *Mountain Echo* and the second was a tenured philosophy professor who spoke out against the ethics of the president's policies (Jaschik, 2016c).

The president's actions were not well received at the Mount or nationally. The situation became a focal point in academia for the corporatization of higher education, which increased national attention and the number of vested stakeholders. In addition to the AAUP, other national organizations, such as the Foundation for Individual Rights in Education, offered statements condemning the president's actions, "'Mount St. Mary's went nuclear' . . . 'It's shocking that the university fired faculty members, including a tenured professor, for dissenting from the administration and raising awareness of an issue of great concern to the community'" (Jaschik, 2016f, para. 12). Other universities saw the firings as alarming and as potential warnings to their own institutions (Jaschik, 2016f).

Back at the Mount, faculty voices, while silenced on campus, were being heard in the national media: "'It's terrifying, and nobody is safe'" (Jaschik, 2016c, para. 8).

President Newman's attempt to control the faculty backfired, creating an increasingly tense situation as organizations and faculty across the country rallied behind the Mount faculty and against the president and board of trustees over the seemingly arbitrary dismissals. A week after the two faculty members were fired, nearly 3,000 people had signed a petition demanding that they be reinstated (Jaschik, 2016f).

Phase Three: No "Mercy"

A week after the firings, President Newman reinstated the employees as an act of "mercy." Neither of the faculty members immediately accepted the president's reinstatement offer. Instead, the *Mountain Echo* faculty advisor offered his position at a faculty meeting, stating that Newman's gesture "'was an attempt to placate the faculty to pre-empt a no-confidence vote'" (Thomason, 2016, para. 9). The same day, the university released a statement that was an olive branch, a promise, and a vision of an optimistic future, yet failed to accept any responsibility for the firings (Thomason, 2016). The statement was too little too late. The Mount's faculty were not convinced of Newman's "'solemn commitment to work together to restore our relationship and our school'" (Thomason, 2016, para. 10). Later that day faculty voted 87–3 in favor of "no confidence" in President Newman's leadership and asked that he step down by 9 a.m. the following Monday (Thomason, 2016).

Phase Four: The "Snowdown"

However, that Monday was a snow day, so the university was officially closed. Newman did not step down and was on campus to attend a student rally in his support. Two students made fliers in support of President Newman's bargaining with an athletic apparel maker to bring speakers onto campus and Newman's support for developing courses that would make students "more marketable" (Svrluga, 2016b, para. 4). Three alumni wrote an open letter of support for Newman, praising him for identifying potentially damaging perceptions of a liberal arts education and his ideas for positive rebranding. Supporters also argued that although the bunnies metaphor was "insensitive," the institution's financial troubles were not going away and Newman's "financial acumen and expertise" were still needed at the Mount (Svrluga, 2016b, para. 14). For Newman's supporters, the ends justified the means, and at the rally he told them, "I'm not going to stop" (Mount St. Mary's head rejects demand, 2016, para. 1). Faculty members planned to meet the next week to discuss the president's noncompliance with their demand.

Two weeks after the president refused to step down, the Mount received an inquiry from the Middle States Commission on Higher Education. The university had completed its accreditation process the previous summer, so this inquiry into "core requirements on issues such as integrity, admissions and the way faculty members are treated" at the Mount was unexpected (Jaschik, 2016d, para. 2). The commission's inquiry was the final straw in President Newman's tenure. Three days later he resigned. Two weeks later the chairman of the board of trustees stepped down. Within another month, five more members stepped down (Bauer-Wolf, 2016).

Outcomes

The Mount's crisis lasted only seven weeks—from January 16, when the student article was published, to February 29, when the president resigned—but fallout from the events will continue to be felt both inside and outside of the university. Newman's resignation, which potentially made things worse in the short term, will not fix the financial trouble facing the university. The Mount faces potential costs such as severance pay, hiring an interim president, and conducting a national search, as well as potential reductions in revenue from fundraising and tuition. The fall enrollment (full-time equivalents) following the crisis was down 3.6%, the lowest point in five years (Mount St. Mary's University, 2016b). Full-time equivalent totals for the Mount show that enrollment numbers decreased 6% since 2014, the year before Newman became president.

This situation represents a failed test case on the corporatization of higher education (Stripling, 2016) but has the potential to create opportunities for the Mount. Since Newman's resignation, the Mount has shifted toward putting out a more positive message. The dean of the university's business school took over as interim president but was replaced at the beginning of the 2016 school year by another interim president, Timothy Trainor. Hired to serve as interim president for two years while a national search was conducted to permanently fill the position, Trainor is "a retired brigadier general who was serving as dean of the Academic Board at the U.S. Military Academy in West Point" (Wells, 2016, para. 2). The *Baltimore Sun* reported:

> "Dr. Trainor brings to the Mount extensive experience in leadership and a deep understanding and appreciation of the Catholic liberal arts tradition," Mary Kane, chair of the university's board of trustees, said in a statement. "The hallmarks of his tenure at West Point—a commitment to the liberal arts, to the intellectual life of his students, and to the development of leaders of character—make him an ideal leader for the Mount." (Wells, 2016, para. 10)

With regard to the somewhat daunting task before him, Trainor appears positive and focused on establishing a plan for image restoration:

> "I had some very positive conversations with faculty, staff and students and members of the board," Trainor said. "I heard a lot of good ideas, and I want to engage and learn . . . and figure out the full strategy for the next couple years." (Wells, 2016, para. 4)

It may take the university some time to recover from a crisis such as this, in terms of finances and reputation. Even with a new president, the Mount continues to face challenges. The university's full-time enrollment in spring 2017 showed a drop of 1.2% in student credit hours (Mount St. Mary's University, 2017), the lowest reported spring enrollment in five years. However, this decline shows some recovery from the 3.2% reported in the fall. The resulting drop in tuition revenue may also partially account for the 3.4% tuition increase planned for the following academic year (Mount St. Mary's University, n.d.-a).

The Mount also took a hit to its ranking. In 2015 the university achieved its highest ranking of 19th (Regional Universities North) in *US News & World Report* but fell to 27th in 2017 (Mount St. Mary's University, n.d.-b; *US News & World Report*, 2017).

Newman has remained out of the spotlight following his departure. Nearly a year after the crisis, his LinkedIn profile listed the Mount as his last place of employment.

References

Bauer-Wolf, J. (2016, February 29). Mount St. Mary's President Simon Newman resigns. *The Frederick News-Post*.

Jaschik, S. (2016a, January 10). Are at-risk students bunnies to be drowned? *Inside Higher Ed*. h

Jaschik, S. (2016b, January 25). Drowned bunnies: Part 2. *Inside Higher Ed*.

Jaschik, S. (2016c, February 9). Purge at the Mount. *Inside Higher Ed*.

Jaschik, S. (2016d, February 26). Tough questions for Mount St. Mary's. *Inside Higher Ed*.

Jaschik, S. (2016e, February 15). Turmoil at the Mount. *Inside Higher Ed*.

Jaschik, S. (2016f, February 10). 'We are all bunnies.' *Inside Higher Ed*.

McGuire, P. (2016, February 10). An appalling breach of faith at Mount St. Mary's. *Chronicle of Higher Education*.

McIntire, M. E. (2015, September 10). When nontraditional presidents come to campus, the reception varies. *Chronicle of Higher Education*.

Moody's downgrades Mount St. Mary's University's (MD) rating to Ba2 to Ba1 and removes the rating from watchlist for potential downgrade: Outlook is negative. (2012, March 6). Moody's Investor Services.

Mount St. Mary's University. (n.d.-a). Undergraduate tuition and fees schedule. Retrieved from http://msmary.edu/administration/business-finance/Undergrad_FeeSchedule.html.

Mount St. Mary's University. (n.d.-b). Mount St. Mary's earns high ranking from *US News & World Report*. Retrieved from http://msmary.edu/about-the-Mount/news-and-events/news-archive/2014/9-08-14USNewsBestColleges2014.html.

Mount St. Mary's University. (2015). *2015-16 Undergraduate Catalog*. Emmitsburg, MD: Mount St. Mary's.

Mount St. Mary's University. (2016). *U.S. News & World Report*. Retrieved from http://colleges.usnews.rankingsandreviews.com

Mount St. Mary's University. (2016, September 16). Fall 2016 enrollment, September 16, 2016. Retrieved from http://msmary.edu/administration/administration-pdfs/F16_Enrollment%20of%20Record%209-16-2016.pdf.

Mount St. Mary's University. (2017, March 10). Spring 2017 enrollment, final numbers. Retrieved from http://msmary.edu/administration/administration-pdfs/IR-pdfs/S17Enrollment.pdf.

Prudente, T. (2016, February 15). Mount St. Mary's president says, "I'm not going to stop". *Baltimore Sun*.

Shisler, R., & Golden, R. (2016a, January 19). Editorial statement on the article, "Mount president's attempt to improve retention rate included seeking dismissal of 20-25 first-year students." *Mountain Echo*.

Shisler, R., & Golden, R. (2016b, January 19). Mount president's attempt to improve retention rate included seeking dismissal of 20-25 first-year students. *Mountain Echo*.

Stripling, J. (2016, March 2). The Mount St. Mary's presidency was a corporate test case. It failed miserably. *Chronicle of Higher Education*.

Svrluga, S. (2016a, January 19). University president allegedly says struggling freshmen are bunnies that should be drowned. *Washington Post*.

Svrluga, S. (2016b, February 15). Faculty asked the Mount St. Mary's president to resign. He didn't. *Washington Post*.

Thomason, A. (2016, February 12). As Mount St. Mary's offers to reinstate 2 professors, faculty demand president quit. *Chronicle of Higher Education*.

US News & World Report. (2017). Mount St. Mary's University. Retrieved from https://www.usnews.com/best-colleges/mount-st-marys-university-2086.

Weider, B. (2015, June 8). From managing a private equity fund to leading a Catholic university. *Chronicle of Higher Education*.

Wells, C. (2016, June 20). Mount St. Mary's University names interim president after controversy. *Baltimore Sun*.

Woodhouse, K. (2015, July 17). Closure concerns and financial strategies: A survey of college business officers. *Inside Higher Ed*. Retrieved from: https://www.insidehighered.com/news/survey/closure-concerns-and-financial-strategies-survey-college-business-officers.

Appendix A

MANAGING EDITOR RYAN GOLDEN, ON BEHALF OF
THE EDITORS OF THE MOUNTAIN ECHO

"The time is always right to do what is right."

—MARTIN LUTHER KING, Jr. (1965)

To the Students, Staff, Faculty, Administrators, and Alumni of the Mount:

I will be the first to admit that this week's news article has been the most ambitious, challenging, and detailed assignment that I have ever witnessed a student reporter at this university undertake.

Many will read our special edition issue from Jan. 19 and wonder: why would a student newspaper at a small, close-knit Catholic university dare to publish this report? Why place the spotlight on the words and deeds of the highest officials within the university?

Each member of a university newspaper is called to balance the dual ethical responsibilities of student and journalist. As students at the Mount, we are called to respect the leaders of our community and to uphold the four pillars of community, faith, leadership, and discovery. We are called to seek truth both within our campus community and in the larger world through rigorous inquiry. We are called, in short, to be capable, responsible human beings who work to impact this university in a positive manner within the short span of four years.

In his or her craft, however, the student journalist must seek information about current events on campus and convey them accurately to the public. While most of the time these events are much less serious than those covered in professional journalism (like talent shows, concerts, and sporting events) it is impossible for any respectable journalist to neglect the fact that university leaders make important and often divisive decisions that affect the lives of students, faculty, staff, and other community members for better or worse.

It is not hard to understand the conflict these roles create. Not all truths are easy to swallow, especially for student journalists who may have good relationships with the sources and persons they report on. But in order to facilitate meaningful public discussion about these issues—to give those who are impacted by such decisions the opportunity to read and reflect—we must exercise our role as reporters with the utmost concern for accuracy, fairness, and objectivity.

Having said all of this, I have done my best in the next few paragraphs to give our readers an account of the *Mountain Echo*'s efforts in publishing this week's article.

—

After our staff became aware of the story idea, we followed several leads in order to gather more information about the issue of freshman surveys and retention rates, but only heard back from a few sources.

During the course of the investigation, the *Echo* obtained a copy of the email conversation cited in the article from one of the individuals who was part of the conversation. The transcript's contents were deemed relevant to the investigation because the transcript revealed further detail of the culling plan. It also highlighted opposition from those involved in the president's retention efforts concerning the efforts' execution and overall purpose.

December 1, 2015—By the first day of December, nearly a week before the *Mountain Echo*'s last scheduled publication of the semester, a first draft of the article had been completed. The *Echo*'s editorial board decided that, in the interest of fairness and balance, the article should be sent to the Office of the President and the Board of Trustees for comment that evening.

Less than 25 minutes after the *Echo* sent the article, Chairman of the Board of Trustees John E. Coyne III responded in an email directed to the Board and the *Mountain Echo*'s faculty advisor, Professor Ed Egan. Mr. Coyne wrote that the story was "the product of a disgruntled employee and the creative and destructive imagination of a student being spoon fed his information."

This assertion is highly inaccurate. The reporter in question spent nearly two weeks verifying the claims made by each source, confirming the timing of events and investigating the issue itself thoroughly. The reporter did so while taking into account the advice of the *Echo*'s university-appointed faculty advisor and the advice of outside journalists. In short, the reporter's methods were found by several people to be thorough and exhaustive—highly professional. And by sending this report directly to the Board and President's Office, the *Echo* left a clear channel of communication open for both parties to comment.

The *Echo* practiced fairness by sending this draft before it was published. Mr. Coyne responded, initially, by shooting the messenger.

December 2, 2015—Perhaps not coincidentally, at 9:12 p.m. of the next day, Provost David Rehm sent an email to the entire campus community titled "Fairness and Civility." I will not reiterate the points made in my previous editorial letter written in December. It should be noted, however, that the provost's email addressed the *Echo*'s report on faculty and staff healthcare and retirement benefits. The provost's email was sent over two weeks after that report's publication (Nov. 18).

December 3, 2015—Having received no direct comment from either the president or board concerning the retention rate story, I once again emailed both parties at 5:13 p.m. on Dec. 3 with a notice that the *Echo* had set a deadline on commentary for Friday, Dec. 4 at 12:00 p.m.

As explained in a later email sent by myself to Ms. Pauline Engelstätter, Vice President of University Affairs, the deadline was set so that the author of the story would have time to receive timely additional comment, make revisions, and re-confirm with administrative sources while preparing for final exams over the weekend.

At 10:06 p.m. on Dec. 3, Mr. Egan and I received a lengthy response from Mr. Coyne. Among Mr. Coyne's objections was that the *Echo* had "become privy to confidential email communications among faculty, a violation of Code of Conduct at the Mount and the 'fair use' policy of our electronic email system." The *Echo* has published Mr. Coyne's statement in its entirety on the *Echo*'s official website.

Mr. Coyne is mistaken. The *Mountain Echo* consulted with outside journalists as well as the Student Press Law Center (SPLC), a non-profit organization specializing in student journalism law in Washington, DC. An attorney with the SPLC spoke with the *Echo* over a period of five weeks (after the article's publication had been delayed) and, offering a response similar to that of outside journalists who viewed the report, concluded that the *Echo* was operating on solid legal and journalistic ground.

In a Dec. 3 email, Mr. Paul Palmieri, on behalf of President Newman, requested that the author of the story sit down for an interview with the president on Dec. 4. The *Mountain Echo* denied this request, however, after taking three factors into consideration: a) the feasibility of scheduling such a meeting before the newspaper's deadline; b) the nature of the response from Mr. Coyne; and c) the professional advice of a third-party journalist. Despite this, the *Echo* left open the possibility of comment on the situation via email.

—

The article was originally scheduled to publish on Wednesday, Dec. 9. The *Echo* delayed the article, and the President's Office was notified that the article would not be published on the previously planned date.

Given a period of five weeks after Dec. 9 to offer direct comment, the President's Office has not done so. Instead, on Dec. 22, President Newman took space in an otherwise jovial holiday email to university faculty and staff in order to address the issue of freshman retention rates and other issues in what he termed, "the Mercurial Clairvoyance of the Rumor Mill."

This remark did not explicitly refer to the *Mountain Echo*, but I would like to cast away all such allusions regardless. The culling plan report, as I have stated repeatedly in this piece, is based on fact, documentation, and reliable sources, including those who risked their livelihoods and reputations in order to make this information available to you, the reader.

With staff members at home for winter break in various regions of the country coordinating as closely as possible, we have managed to create what we believe to be the best possible version of this story. We hope our readers will weigh all available evidence and enter the upcoming academic year with a renewed commitment to discourse about the state of our university community and the policies by which it is governed.

We at the *Echo* are proud to produce the Mount's student newspaper. We will continue to serve the truth, and we aim to continue promoting the excellence of the university we call home.

Sincerely,
Ryan Golden
Managing Editor of the *Mountain Echo*
Class of 2016

Appendix B

Ryan,

I am responding on behalf of the Board of Trustees of Mount St. Mary's University. Initially, I am troubled that you have decided to publish an article that categorically provides a grossly inaccurate impression on the subject of the Mount's efforts to improve student retention and to intervene early on to assure that incoming students have every opportunity to succeed at our University. The slant that you have adopted by choosing to publish an article based on selected quotes of confidential email exchanges among senior faculty is quite frankly irresponsible. Equally troubling, however, is the fact that you, as the Managing Editor of the *Echo*, and apparently your faculty advisor, have become privy to confidential email communications among faculty colleagues, a violation of Code of Conduct at the Mount and the "fair use" policy of our electronic email system. Beyond the issue of access is the fact that you propose to use those private, confidential emails to advance your journalistic interests and to do so without any concern for either the individual privacy interests of the faculty involved or the damage you will render to this University and to its brand. In the first instance, we understand that at least one faculty member quoted is quite disturbed that she was quoted verbatim from what she described as a "confidential email" and that she expressed her displeasure to the *Echo*'s faculty advisor, Mr. Egan. Despite her objections, apparently you and he intend to forge ahead. As to the latter point, if this article is published in its present form, it will be both an inaccurate portrayal of the goals and objectives of the Retention Program that President Newman sought to introduce and will render incalculable damage to the reputation of this University and its institutional integrity.

President Newman will be reaching out to you to discuss these matters and, in particular, his Retention Efforts and will do so in the hope that you can meet personally tomorrow.

John E. Coyne, III
Chair, Board of Trustees
("Letter to the Editor: A Message from John Coyne", 2016)

Appendix C

To the Editor,

I write to commend you and your staff for your reporting on President Newman's plan to expel freshmen deemed unlikely to survive until graduation. I offer no opinion on the wisdom of this as a strategy for running a college. Maybe it is a good idea; maybe it isn't.

What has impressed me is the strength and accuracy of the *Echo*'s reporting, and how the paper's editors have handled the difficult task of writing about people you're paying lots of money to for an education and degree. The leaked emails, in which Mr. Newman writes that his "short term goal is to have 20–25 people leave by the 25th [of Sep.]" are crucial to this debate now, rightly, made public. And while it certainly does not indicate any truly violent or weird intentions, the quote comparing struggling freshmen to bunnies to be drowned or shot with Glocks is indicative of Mr. Newman's leadership style and tone. Maybe this is refreshingly clear, blunt language that academia could use more of; maybe it isn't. Both questions seem crucial in local and national debates over where our massively high-priced education system is headed.

The onus is not on the newspaper to explain or defend. The paper does need to be accurate, offer all sides a chance to comment, and relate its facts in clear language, and you have done that. Yes, the result is sometimes messy and people get upset that words they thought private are now public. That is the price to pay for authority and power in a country with a free press—ask Hillary Clinton about emails—which this country guarantees thanks to the First Amendment. Officials in Cuba and North Korea don't have to worry about getting their emails leaked. Is that what we want?

So we seek and when we find we publish, and sometimes we annoy, but if we're accurate and fair, the result is that the governments, institutions, companies and people we cover are made to hold themselves to higher standards of character, clarity and honesty, to the benefit of society. It is a righteous and useful mission.

Already, Mr. Newman has published several letters, including one in the *Washington Post*, clarifying his plans and his argument.

Best regards,
John W. Miller, Staff Reporter, *Wall Street Journal*
MSM Class '99, *Mountain Echo* Editor-in-Chief, 1997–1999
("Letter to the Editor: John W. Miller", 2016)

Appendix D

Message from the Chairman of the Board of Trustees

I want to address the Mount Community on the issues surrounding our retention program, the unfortunate language used by President Newman and our Trustee response when we were made aware of these issues in December.

Reporting by our student newspaper, *The Mountain Echo*, which was subsequently picked up by off-campus media, has characterized the objective of our student retention program as encouraging struggling students to leave the university. Included in that reporting was a metaphor attributed to our president which was controversial in nature.

The Board of Trustees was sent the proposed article in early December by *The Mountain Echo*.

Within days, the board conducted a forensic investigation at Mount St. Mary's with the Trustees' attorneys seeking to understand the following:

- Was this a move to target students for removal, as was alleged by the article, or was this truly a retention program?
- How was the program rolled out?
- What language and metaphors were used by the president, and to describe what?
- Were there any related issues at Mount St. Mary's?

The findings were the following:

1. We found that the retention program, as conceived, is indeed meant to retain students by identifying and helping at-risk students much earlier in their first semester—the first six weeks—than we have ever done before. It takes an innovative approach that includes gathering and analyzing information from a range of sources, including our faculty whom we have

trained on how to have rich, supportive conversations with students. We also noted that the design of a (if necessary) thoughtful, eventual conversation about the student's own discernment process and the refund of tuition was also intended to be in keeping with our Catholic identity.

2. On execution, we found a program with great intent and full consistency with our Catholic values that was beset by several start-up implementation problems. We further found the program itself should be continued and become a key part of future retention efforts. We strongly believe this program will make Mount St. Mary's a better university, and more broadly, because it's the right thing to do for students and families.

3. We found that President Newman did use an inappropriate metaphor in a conversation with Dr. Murry in relation to the retention program, for which he has apologized. We do note that this was a private conversation, later revealed by a professor, which has subsequently been taken out of context and mischaracterized.

4. We found that The Mount has significant work to do in its admissions program, as well as our marketing and branding, in order to create a stronger fit for our incoming freshmen. This has been an area of under-investment and is a tremendous opportunity to advance the university in a bold, new direction.

5. By far, our largest finding was deeply troubling. We found incontrovertible evidence of the existence of an organized, small group of faculty and recent alums working to undermine and ultimately cause the exit of President Newman. This group's issues are born out of a real resistance to positive change at Mount St. Mary's. Apparently they are not done with their personal attacks and are continuing, both directly and through others, to malign and denigrate President Newman and our plans for the university's future by circulating mischaracterized accounts and flat-out falsehoods. This will not stand and cannot be let to stand at our university. One of our hallmarks requires each member of the Mount Community to treat others with dignity and respect and with the highest integrity. As such, the university will hold those individuals accountable for these actions.

Part of our findings included the discovery that the same small group of faculty who launched this initiative also apparently met together and actually "worked on" the very *Mountain Echo* article that resulted in the deliberate mischaracterization of the retention program and whose distribution to the public media by them has caused damage to the reputations of both President Newman and Mount St. Mary's University. The University has a proud history of a student newspaper, and its administration values both the rights and obligations that students working on a student newspaper should enjoy. In this instance, the misuse of our *Mountain Echo* by a small group of faculty violated those rights and obligations and they embarked on this effort solely to advance their own personal agenda.

6. We concluded that President Newman continues to be the right kind of talented leader to be at the vanguard of Catholic higher education growth. We also concluded that President Newman's vision for the future is exactly what will lead to Mount St. Mary's being recognized as a top Catholic University.

On January 10, 2016, more than a month after we learned of the article, and conducted our investigation, the Board of Trustees passed a unanimous resolution of full confidence in President Newman. The board is also continuously being shown that the president enjoys the widespread support of the faculty, student body and broader university community.

We are moving a 200 plus-year-old institution into a new era, with a dynamic and bright future. In higher education, change is hard. We remain committed to the guiding principles that we have been known for, to our Catholic identity, and placing the student at the center of our universe.

President Newman is a transformational leader, and our future direction is incredibly exciting. We invite you to join in the conversation about our vision and plans for our university's future.

Sincerely,
John E. Coyne, Chairman

Discussion Questions

1. Recall the four objectives of the crisis theory of renewal (Ulmer, Sellnow, & Seeger, 2015)—organizational learning, ethical communication, prospective rather than retrospective vision, and effective organizational rhetoric. What examples in this case study support or contradict these objectives?

2. Using each of the four objectives of renewal, what could the president and the board of trustees have done differently to create a renewing response to the president's retention plan?

3. What ethical questions surrounded the *Mountain Echo*'s breaking the story on the president's retention plan for the students and faculty involved (see Appendix A)? Would you have done anything differently? Why or why not?

4. Taking the quotation "Why are there so many crucifixes?" as an example of the president's struggle to understand the culture of a small, private university, what do you think the president's biggest mistake was in this new culture?

5. What are the ethical implications of the president's quote that the Mount's "'core customers' are the university's most engaged and successful students, while its 'ultimate customers' are employers"? What stakeholders does his statement leave out?

CONNECTING ETHICS AND PRACTICE AS PR STUDENTS TRANSITION FROM LEARNERS TO EDUCATORS

Douglas J. Swanson, Ed.D., APR, *California State University, Fullerton*

The 21st-century workplace is one of constant economic, ethical, social, and technological change. "Life-long learning," though something of a cliché, is probably the most important value for today's graduates to manifest. Life-long learning means being able to deal with change and learning how to educate others, particularly to the ethical realities that more seasoned workplace professionals don't always respect.

Millennials—those born in the 1980s and 1990s—are technologically adept. They have no knowledge of a world without Wi-Fi, smartphones, and 200 channels of high-definition TV. But their value system and approach to work differ radically from other demographic groups still active in the workplace. Traditionalists (born before 1946), Baby Boomers (born after World War II but before the Vietnam War), and Generation X (born between 1965 and 1980) think and act differently (Arnold & Williams, 2008). Millennials must constantly adapt—and be adapted to—for an organization to be productive and successful. Such adaptability is especially important in the public relations workplace (Gallicano, Curtin, & Matthews, 2012).

The university student-run communication agency described in this case study creates an exceptional opportunity for public relations students to make the transition from college to the workplace by developing the concept knowledge and hands-on skills the profession demands. The agency experience allows students to demonstrate what they've learned in the classroom while conducting ethically responsible communication campaigns for real clients, with real consequences (Bush & Miller, 2011). There are at least 158 student-run agencies within academe, and the number is growing (Swanson, 2017). As a business that operates within an academic program, the student agency provides unique learning experiences that classroom-centered instruction and hypothetical situations cannot duplicate. The agency facilitates reverse mentoring, a structured workplace relationship between younger or less experienced workers—in this case, university students—and older or more experienced professionals (Hays & Swanson, 2012).

When conducting advertising, public relations, or marketing campaigns for clients aged in their 40s, 50s, or 60s, our students become educators. This role reversal of sorts happens as students work with clients who are not digital natives and may have no social media knowledge beyond tracking "likes" on Facebook. In short, the Millennials who have grown up with digital media but lack perspective on the business workplace educate older people who have a wealth of business knowledge but don't know how to use new media to engage organizational stakeholders.

But what happens when PR students conducting a campaign for a real-world client encounter unprofessional or unethical client conduct? How should students respond when a campaign shows no prospect for reaching its goals? How does the faculty member allow student autonomy while still guiding students to a successful learning outcome? All these questions came up in the context of the situation described here. The questions are relevant not only in regard to a student-run agency but in any public relations education situation involving real-world clients.

Background

This case unfolded in a university student-run agency housed within a mass communication program at a large public university in the western United States. The identities of the agency, students, and client are withheld here to preserve confidentiality. The agency serves as a capstone course option for undergraduate communication students, who typically enroll in the agency as their last subject course before graduation. The agency has four faculty members and has operated successfully for several years. Clients are recruited by word of mouth for a strategically focused campaign lasting one academic term. Clients agree in advance to a set of terms and conditions for the project. For-profit clients typically compensate the agency for services; nonprofit clients are served pro bono.

In this case, a wealthy client came to the agency seeking help in establishing a nonprofit community service organization. The client wanted to provide a unique set of services to impoverished people living on the streets in a nearby urban area. Before the start of the academic term, a supervising faculty member reviewed the client's idea, shared a terms and conditions agreement, and approved the project. At the start of the semester, the client was assigned a team of four students to carry out the campaign.

The Situation

The student team began by conducting research on homelessness in the urban area and existing organizations that offered support services for homeless people. Then, an initial client consultation meeting took place. During that meeting, the team proposed and the client accepted the goals of (1) developing an organizational mission statement; (2) creating a focused organizational brand identity via a new website and existing social media accounts; (3) launching a YouTube page with "short, inspirational videos revolving around [client name] and the people they help"; and (4) drafting a structure to identify and recruit donors and volunteers. Everyone agreed the goals were consistent with professional public relations practice for nonprofits (Bonk et al., 2008) and could be achieved within a 16-week timeframe. The team acquired the client's signature on the terms and conditions agreement.

Immediately following the consultation, the team began working toward a client mission statement. Several drafts were created, but the client rejected each one and followed with recommendations that deviated significantly from the ideas that had been offered in the consultation.

The team began creating the framework for an organizational website. Simultaneously, without informing the team, the client hired a website developer and, according to the team's final report, "launched a live website, against our recommendations, without consulting us on the content." As it turned out, the developer was a homeless man living out of a van. Within a few weeks, and shortly after the students learned of his existence, the developer known as "the man in the van" got in a dispute with the client and quit.

The client had established social media accounts for the nonprofit but was using them for personal communication. The student team acquired the access codes and immediately began what it termed "the purge" to remove dozens of conflicting, irrelevant, off-topic personal posts. The goal was to have the social media all focus consistently on the nonprofit's development and goals. The team communicated to the client the importance of clear, direct organizational brand identity, and the fact that "selfies" were not consistent with that identity. The client ignored the team's advice. As soon as the team would remove inappropriate personal content, the client would repost the messages. "The purge" became an ongoing task for many weeks and consumed dozens of hours of student time.

The student team documented all communication with the client and continued to press the client to return to the agreed-upon goals. The client refused. The client rejected invitations by the student team to meet in the agency's conference room; instead, the client invited the account executive to meet, alone, at Starbucks or for an afternoon at the beach.

At one point, the client pressed the student team to secure an appearance on the *Ellen* television show. Students explained that an organizational identity and track record of newsworthy success needed to be established first. The client became irritated and suggested the team was being uncooperative. Simultaneously, the client excitedly announced that an interview had been pursued and secured with a *Huffington Post* reporter to discuss a topic that had little to do with development of the nonprofit.

The agency's faculty members monitored the situation, met regularly with the team, and offered counsel and suggestions. The only intervention made by faculty came after the client's "meet me at Starbucks or the beach" request. The faculty suspected the client was pursuing an unsolicited personal relationship with the account executive. At this point, the faculty directed a different student to take over as the point of contact with the client. The client offered no further requests for an offsite meeting.

The students were frustrated by the client's actions but not dissuaded. The students had taken ownership of the effort; they supported the client's unique vision for helping the homeless. The members of the student team were following the tenets of the PRSA Code (2015) and were being professionally and ethically responsible. Team members used industry-standard software to manage their productive time and develop a social media outreach strategy. Extensive client communication was conducted by email and telephone and occasionally in person. A cloud storage system stored all records of this communication, along with electronic copies of all team work. The team's strategic plan, tactical steps, and proposed communication tools were in line with accepted public relations practice.

Every time the client drifted from the established goals, the team would politely remind the client of the strategic plan and rhetorically push back in the other direction. The client was alternately sincere and duplicitous; first, there would be agreement to campaign outcomes and then active work to subvert them. When subversion was discovered (such as the hiring of "the man in the van"), students would inquire. The client would in turn use a variety of rhetorical strategies to justify, rationalize, or change the subject. The client did not acknowledge that what the team termed "endless eccentric ideas" and erratic behavior were the source of the campaign's challenges.

What was initially an appearance of great passion by a wealthy individual with altruistic intent turned out to be worthy intent coupled with professional irresponsibility and inability to focus. As the final report stated, "Our team quickly came to the sad realization that the passion was masking the organization's lack of direction and the client's lack of competency."

Outcomes

With about four weeks remaining in the academic term, the team determined that the client's irrational decoupling from the original campaign goals warranted firing the client. The team did so but developed a final report and presentation that made one last effort to educate the client about professional, ethical communication standards and practices.

Prior to terminating the relationship, the client had finally agreed to the team's recommendation for a strong, supportive mission statement for the new nonprofit. This was the only goal realized through the students' work. While the client seemed to understand the need for a strong brand identity, the team was never able to operationalize this identity through a cohesive website and social media. The YouTube testimonials and framework for recruitment were never created because the team was not able to put a basic organizational communication structure in place.

The team delivered a strong, detailed final written report that summarized the actions taken on the client's behalf. It showed how, in a stressful and frustrating situation over many weeks, students transitioned from their role as learners to a new role as educators. The report showed how students were attentive to the interpersonal communication within the team, made the most of peer-to-peer mentoring to come together as a cohesive unit, and utilized reverse mentoring to try to guide a client who demonstrated little or no knowledge or concern about strategic, ethical communication. The report concluded with extensive best practices recommendations and a step-by-step template for the client to follow in future communication with stakeholders. The team's final written report and in-house presentation was judged by the faculty to be among the best ever offered in the agency. It reflected autonomous, self-reliant student learning (Tagg, 2003), which is recognized as a best practice regardless of subject area.

Below are seven points of learning that students and faculty gained from this experience. These are appropriate to seek in any situation where public relations students are working with real-world clients:

- In any team situation, students must come together as a thoughtful, collaborative whole with a shared vision and realistic goals for success (Witmer & Swanson, 2016). A strong, committed team is essential if students are to have any hope of transitioning from learners to educators as they work with clients, particularly clients who are less understanding about the realities of modern communication campaigns.
- The student team must articulate its own set of standards for ethical conduct, individually and collectively. The team's norms must include regularly scheduled meetings, constant communication, message consistency, shared responsibility, and professional conduct always.
- Students and faculty should adhere to the PRSA Code (2015) and other relevant guidelines for professional, ethical public relations practice.
- Students and faculty should be prepared for the eventuality that clients and campaigns can go so far out of control that there is no prospect for recovery.
- If a campaign goes astray without any prospect for recovery, a student public relations team can still provide valuable conceptual guidance for a client. The client's acceptance or rejection of that guidance doesn't diminish its value.
- It is appropriate practice for faculty members to provide ethical guidance and counsel, but they should let students figure out on their own how to frame and solve problems created by clients.
- Sometimes, student teams should stick with an unethical client; other times, they should terminate the relationship. The student team should make the decision, and faculty should provide resources to support that decision.

This particular client was invited to the team's final presentation, but the client chose not to attend. A final communication to the team praised the students for their work and announced the client's decision to change the nonprofit's intended service focus. Instead of providing the services to homeless people, the client decided to help battered women and other victims of domestic violence—a service area already addressed by more than a dozen other nonprofits and charitable organizations in the community. It's not known whether the client will apply any of the students' best practices recommendations.

References

Arnold, K., & Williams, K. (2008, November). Playbook: Dealing With Generational Crosstalk. *Parks & Recreation, 43*(11), 18–19.

Bonk, K., Griggs, H., Sparks, P., & Tynes, E. (2008). *Strategic Communications for Nonprofits*. San Francisco: Jossey-Bass.

Bush, L., & Miller, B. M. (2011). U.S. student-run agencies: Organization, attributes and adviser perceptions of student learning outcomes. *Public Relations Review, 37*(5), 485–491.

Gallicano, T. D., Curtin, P., & Matthews, K. (2012). I love what I do, but . . . a relationship management survey of Millennial generation public relations agency employees. *Journal of Public Relations Research, 24*(3), 222–242.

Hays, B. A., & Swanson, D. J. (2012). Public relations practitioners' use of reverse mentoring in the development of powerful professional relationships. *PRism, The Online Journal of Public Relations.* Retrieved from http://www.prismjournal.org/fileadmin/9_2/Hays_Swanson.pdf.

Public Relations Society of America. (2015). PRSA Member Code of Ethics. Retrieved from https://www.prsa.org/AboutPRSA/Ethics/CodeEnglish/index.html#.Vi_RAmTnulk.

Swanson, D. J. (2017). *Real-World Career Preparation: A Guide to Creating a University Student-Run Communications Agency.* London: Peter Lang.

Tagg, J. (2003). *The Learning Paradigm College.* San Francisco: Jossey-Bass.

Witmer, D. F., & Swanson, D. J. (2016). *Public Relations Management: A Team-Based Approach* (2nd ed.). Dubuque, IA: Kendall Hunt.

Discussion Questions

1. When college students new to the study of public relations are asked what drew them to this field, it's not unusual for students to say, "I want to go into PR because I'm good with people." Of course, it takes much more than that to have a future in public relations. Identify at least five different types of concept knowledge or hands-on skills that are essential for anyone to master to be successful in PR work.

2. Every public relations campaign must begin with sound research to support the campaign planners' ideas for strategies, tactics, and tools. Briefly describe how research support is needed not only to serve as a basis for the campaign but also to demonstrate a student team's credibility to the client.

3. Imagine you're a member of a student public relations team that is planning an event for a nonprofit client. As your team prepares the news release that will be sent to the media to announce the event, the client asks you to falsify background information about the nonprofit to make the organization appear larger and more successful than it really is. If you were to do what the client asks, what elements of the PRSA Code of Ethics might you be violating?

4. Describe the importance of a having a written terms and conditions agreement when a student team is doing public relations work for a client. What kinds of problems would a written agreement help prevent? Is the agreement alone a guarantee that there will never be any misunderstandings? Why or why not?

5. When a client acts so unprofessionally that there is no choice but to sever the relationship, how can a student team take this action without "burning the bridge"? Offer an example of the kind of statement a student team might make to a difficult client to end the relationship in a firm but professional and tactful way.

IV THE FUTURE OF PUBLIC RELATIONS

13 TRENDS IN PUBLIC RELATIONS, COMMUNICATION, AND SOCIETY THAT WILL CHALLENGE ETHICS

Learning Outcomes

- Recognize the future trajectory of public relations.
- Analyze ethical principles in relation to technology, influencers, and fake news.
- Apply ethical principles to future-trend case studies.

Definitions

Artificial intelligence: Computers doing tasks usually done by humans, such as speech recognition, decision-making, and translation.

Augmented reality: Using computer-generated images to enhance someone's view of the real world.

Branding: The messaging and logos used by an organization or product as well as the perceptions people have of that organization or product.

Fake news: News published or written with the intent of misleading others.

Influencers: Individuals who use social media and blogs to reach consumers. They are typically paid by organizations to use their engagement with people to build long-term relationships between brands and consumers.

Measurement: A system for computing and quantifying PR output.

Virtual reality: Technology that creates a simulated environment through computer-generated sights and sounds. This simulated environment is realistic and often the user can determine some of the things that happen within this realm.

It is always difficult to guess where a field may go in the future. After all, who could have imagined the influence of social media a mere 15 years ago? However, based on the opinions of experts and thought leaders in public relations, the following are some areas and changes practitioners may want to watch.

Branding

Although at heart a marketing concept, branding has found a niche in public relations as well. Organizations are using brands in many ways. For example, some organizations share messages about their corporate social responsibility (CSR) efforts and other good acts. These messages can help enhance publics' perceptions and understandings of these organizations to build their reputations (Goldstein, 2017). In addition, when these message points are shared on social media, online newsrooms, and owned channels, they can help to build trust (Goldstein, 2017). Brands want to find ways to build connections and awareness with key publics. Many brands are trying to humanize themselves by bringing personality and experience to their messaging and finding the best ways and outlets for sharing (Hawkins, 2017). However, organizations need to make sure that such messaging is authentic. Otherwise, the messaging and efforts to cast the brand in a positive light might fail, much like the Kendall Jenner Pepsi ad of 2017.

Technology

Technology may be brought into the realm of public relations in many interesting ways. For example, practitioners will likely continue to use social media. Geolocation may also be used to help keep track of members of certain publics or to engage with them through contests or other interactive experiences—remember Pokémon Go? However, the use of technology to build experiences may grow even more through virtual reality and augmented reality.

Virtual reality (VR) and augmented reality (AR) may sound similar, but they are quite different: "As opposed to virtual reality, which constructs a user immersion into a digital experience, augmented reality projects digital images onto objects in the physical world" (Dykes & Morgan, 2017, para. 6). However, it seems practitioners can use VR and/or AR to engage members of priority publics, to allow for interaction between brands and those people, and to tell stories about organizations, brands, and CSR efforts (Alaimo, 2016). Some experts even suggest that artificial intelligence (AI) and robots may soon be used to analyze trends and to manage tasks such as media relations to free humans up for more strategic tasks. Think about how Siri and Alexa have changed the ways you manage some tasks. Soon you may have a voice assistant who can help you generate ideas, conduct basic secondary research, identify appropriate media outlets, and gather trends (Wood, 2017). AI might also be used to determine the content and timing of social media posts, and chatbots can manage some customer relation tasks such as responding to customer questions (Wood, 2017). However, practitioners need to think about the ethical implications of using technology and the influence these tactics can have over people.

Measurement

While not a newcomer to any list of trends, measurement is still an important topic for practitioners. To become members of the dominant coalition, practitioners have found they had to explain what they do, how their efforts affect others, and how public relations fits within and supports their respective organizations, and this situation may continue (Sweeney, 2005). Practitioners may need to remind others that "PR is an extension of everything the organization does" (Elsasser, 2013, 13). Although it may be a challenge, practitioners need to continue their efforts to document their work and to demonstrate its effect on the bottom line.

Influencers

Not only has social media changed the way we distribute and consume news, it has also changed the ways people engage with it (Hawkins, 2017). How many of you rely on crowdsourcing when trying to make a purchasing decision? Or better yet, how many of you look to see what influencers have to say about products and services? Companies have paid influencers a lot to increase awareness and trust and to build engagement with publics (Hawkins, 2017). However, practitioners again have a problem quantifying the worth of influencers (Hawkins, 2017). Influencers may be losing importance since they seem so tied to money; organizations and members of publics are more interested in relationship, trust, and transparency (Hawkins, 2017). Therefore, influencers who connect with people and who are authentic will be key. To harness the power of influencers, practitioners will need to understand no only influencers, but also their level of engagement with followers as well as the psychographics of those followers (Hawkins, 2017). Once practitioners gain an understanding of all those elements, they will better be able to determine the importance of influencers. Practitioners should be mindful to determine how influencers persuade so that manipulation does not occur.

Fake News

An area affecting not only public relations but also journalism is fake news. While not necessarily a new concept, it has become more prominent in the last few years. Media fragmentation, brought about in part by the rise of social media, has caused a loss of trust in national media and traditional subject matter experts and institutions (Hawkins, 2017). In an effort to combat these losses, public relations practitioners need to remind organizational leaders about the importance of third-party validations and what a strong press offers when telling an organization's story.

References

Alaimo, K. (2016, Jan.) A new reality. *Public Relations Tactics*, 23 (1), 13.

Dykes, D., & Morgan, T. (2017, May 3). The future of PR: Technically speaking Retrieved from http://www.odwyerpr.com/story/public/8730/2017-05-03/future-pr-technically-speaking.html.

Elsasser, J. (2013, December). Brian Solis on the future of public relations. *Public Relations Tactics, 20*(12), 13.

Goldstein, S. (2017, October 31). 4 key PR trends to watch in 2018. Retrieved from http://www.prnewsonline.com/prnewsblog/4-key-pr-trends-to-watch-in-2018/.

Hawkins, J. (2017, July 20). Small screens, micro-influences, growing opportunities. Retrieved from http://www.odwyerpr.com/story/public/9090/2017-07-20/small-screens-micro-influencers-growing-opportunities.html.

Sweeney, K. (2005, January). The year ahead in public relations: A preview of what's in store in 2005. *Public Relations Tactics, 12* (1), 1, 14, 15, 26, 27.

Wood, S. (2017, December 8). How AI and voice assistants can help communicators make the important decisions. Retrieved from http://www.prnewsonline.com/how-ai-and-voice-assistants-can-help-communicators-make-the-important-decisions/.

TAKING A SWIPE AT APPLE:
THE FBI V. APPLE, INC.

Heather J. Hether, Ph.D., *University of California, Davis*

In the aftermath of a terrorist attack in San Bernardino, California, that killed 14 and wounded 22, the FBI sought Apple Inc.'s assistance in unlocking the passcode to an iPhone used by one of the terrorists, Syed Farook. Apple refused to create the software the FBI needed; therefore, the FBI pursued and received a court order mandating Apple to provide technical assistance to the bureau. Apple opposed the order and argued that assisting the FBI would weaken digital security for everyone, violate Apple's right to free speech, and set a "dangerous precedent"

(Cook, 2016). Ultimately, the FBI dropped the case because the bureau received assistance from a third party who was able to access the data on the iPhone.

This conflict represented a delicate public relations situation for Apple. American lives had been lost in a violent attack and Apple may have been able to help with the investigation. However, the FBI was asking Apple to undermine the security of its own products by subverting its encryption software. This case attracted significant media attention, fueled by comments made by public figures, including President Obama and the candidate for the Republican presidential nomination, Donald Trump. Despite the intense scrutiny, Apple stood its ground and did not appear to suffer any serious consequences. The company followed through on its values, engaged stakeholders with clear communication, and encouraged dialogue around the issue. This case study illustrates how an organization can manage an emotionally charged issue and stay true to its corporate values even in the midst of public criticism. While this issue could have damaged Apple's reputation and labeled it as unpatriotic, the conflict may have ultimately benefitted Apple's reputation as a steward of privacy and data security.

Background

Homegrown Terrorism

On December 2, 2015, Syed Farook and his wife, Tashfeen Malik, opened fire at a holiday gathering in San Bernardino, killing 14 and injuring 22. Farook and Malik were killed later that day in a shootout with police. Victims of the shooting were primarily employees of the San Bernardino County Department of Public Health, where Farook had worked as an environmental health specialist for five years. Farook had left the party and returned with his wife and attacked the group.

The FBI assumed a lead role in the investigation and concluded that Farook and Malik were self-radicalized terrorists who acted in the name of ISIS (Islamic State of Iraq and Syria), a militant terrorist group. While the investigation indicated that ISIS had no formal involvement in the planning or execution of this attack, this incident, which was described at the time as the "deadliest terror attack on the United States since Sept. 11, 2001" (Serrano, Esquivel, & Knoll, 2015, para. 5) elicited intense media interest and public concern because it was a deadly attack executed on American soil, by an American citizen, inspired by a foreign terrorist organization. The incident was reminiscent of other deadly terrorist attacks carried out in the West, and it provoked anxiety about national security among Americans (Lister et al., 2016; Nakamura, 2016).

The FBI quickly identified the San Bernardino attack as a potential act of terrorism. During its investigation, the bureau collected digital evidence, including social media and email communications, and digital devices used by the assailants. Among these devices were three cellphones. Two of them were crushed and found in a Dumpster near the assailants' home; the third, an Apple iPhone 5c, was found intact in a car registered to Farook's mother. The phone was owned by San Bernardino County and used by Farook. Shortly after the iPhone was collected as evidence, the FBI sought Apple's assistance in accessing data from the passcode-protected device, first with a warrant and then by additional requests (Gibbs & Grossman, 2016).

Apple Inc.

Apple was founded in 1976 by Steve Jobs and Steve Wozniak in a garage in Palo Alto, California. From its beginnings, the company was fueled by Steve Jobs' visionary leadership and innovative ideas about technology. Jobs may be one of the world's most recognizable technological leaders whose reputation as a countercultural, creative "genius" (Isaacson, 2011; Markoff, 2011) was closely aligned with that of the technology company he co-founded. While Jobs passed away in 2011, the company continues to reflect his vision, with its focus on creating innovative products with a strong design sensibility.

Throughout its 40-year history, Apple has become an iconic American brand and the world's most valuable company (Mullaney, 2016; "The World's Most Valuable Brands," 2016). Apple's success, however, wasn't guaranteed. In its early years, Steve Jobs was accused of mismanaging the company and was fired. The company's growth later stalled and, months away from bankruptcy, Apple brought Jobs back to help save the company. As part of its revival, in 1997 Apple launched an advertising campaign, *Think different*, that relied upon images of "transformational figures" such as Martin Luther King, Jr., and Muhammad Ali to communicate "a message to the world that Steve Jobs and his innovative vision had returned to Apple" (Taube, 2014). This groundbreaking campaign solidified Apple's reputation for innovative marketing strategies and helped cultivate a loyal following of passionate users (Glance, 2014; Goodson, 2011), sometimes referred to as the "cult of Apple" (Spence, 2015).

In 2007, Apple introduced the iPhone, an innovative cellphone that eliminated the need for a stylus or trackball by relying on a touch screen (Mangalindan, 2013). The iPhone combined multiple functions into one device, including a camera, telephone, music player, and internet browser. The iPhone quickly became a cultural phenomenon and continues to be a popular device: Apple announced in mid-2016 that it sold the billionth iPhone (Apple, 2016).

Digital Privacy and Security

We increasingly rely on technology to help manage all aspects of our lives. However, there is growing concern over the security of personal data stored on digital platforms, particularly in the aftermath of several high-profile data breaches

(Pew Research Center, 2014; Rainie & Duggan, 2016), such as those at Sony PlayStation in 2011, Target in 2013, and Anthem Blue Cross in 2015. Moreover, pundits have been warning users about privacy intrusions from online services like Google Mail and Facebook, as well as from internet cookies and "big data" (Fox-Brewster, 2016; Lohr, 2013; MacKinnon, 2012; Vega, 2010).

Perhaps no other story in recent years has drawn as much attention to the issue of digital privacy as the revelations from former National Security Agency (NSA) contractor Edward Snowden. Snowden leaked information to the media about surveillance programs conducted by the NSA that revealed the agency overstepped its authority (Gellman, 2013). The Snowden scandal was a watershed moment that illustrated the vulnerability of our digital data, the power and reach of government surveillance programs, and the need to consider more seriously the importance of legislation that preserves digital privacy (Pew Research Center, 2014; Pilkington, 2015).

The Situation

The investigation into the deadly terrorist attack yielded an iPhone used by Syed Farook and owned by his employer, San Bernardino County. Investigators wanted to access the data on this phone, but only Farook knew the passcode. The contents of the phone, however, were backed up to an iCloud server, and while the county did not know that passcode either, they could change it so the backup data could be examined. In the early days of the FBI investigation, the agency had the county change the iCloud passcode so the bureau could access the backup data (Gibbs & Grossman, 2016); however, it was discovered that the phone had not been backed up since October, well before the attack. Later on, the FBI realized that updating the passcode was a serious error: if it had not been updated, Apple could have facilitated a backup of the device that would have captured current data.

During the investigation (see Appendix A), the FBI reached out to Apple for assistance. Initially, the FBI had a warrant for information related to the iPhone and Apple complied with the warrant (Gibbs & Grossman, 2016). Later on, the FBI requested further help from Apple and Apple remained supportive and provided the FBI with information and advice. However, when the FBI was stymied in their attempts to access the data on the iPhone, investigators asked Apple to create software to bypass the security encryption on the device. Apple refused to comply. Therefore, on February 16, 2016, the FBI filed a motion with the Central Court of California to compel Apple's assistance. The FBI filed an application under the *All Writs Act* of 1789, a broad-based law that authorizes federal courts to issue orders that are "necessary or appropriate" for a case to achieve its goals (Davidson, 2016; Limer, 2016).

The court granted the application and ordered Apple to provide technical assistance to the FBI that would enable investigators to electronically submit passcodes, without delay between each attempt, and with no limit to the number of passcodes that could be submitted (current encryption software erased the contents of the phone after 10 failed attempts) (Apple v. FBI, n.d.). The court also stated that should the order be too burdensome, Apple could file an appeal to the court within five days.

Throughout February and March there were multiple interactions between the court and both organizations (see Appendix A). On February 25, Apple filed a motion for the court to vacate, or nullify, the order, arguing that it exceeded the scope of the *All Writs Act* and violated the First Amendment and the Fifth Amendment's Due Process clause (Apple Inc.'s motion to vacate order, 2016). While a date of March 22 was set for the court to hear arguments regarding the order, on March 21 the FBI filed a motion to cancel the hearing, and on March 28, 2016, the case came to an abrupt end when the FBI asked the court to vacate the original order because it had found another way to access the iPhone with the help of a third party.

The conflict between the FBI and Apple played out in public because the FBI chose a public court to hear the case rather than going through a national security court in which the case would have been under seal (Benner & Perlroth, 2016; Fiegerman, 2016; Sullivan, 2016). Moreover, Apple CEO Tim Cook explained that the FBI did not privately inform Apple of its impending claim; instead, he first heard about the claim through the media (Gibbs & Grossman, 2016). Therefore, from its beginning, this issue was public and elicited interest and debate from a variety of stakeholders, including Apple customers, the media, politicians, lawmakers, and Americans concerned about national security.

This was not the first public relations crisis for Apple. The company had confronted previous issues, such as questionable working conditions in its Chinese manufacturing facilities and a malfunctioning iPhone antenna. Therefore, crisis management was not new to the organization. However, the current issue carried significant political implications and brought attention from a variety of high-profile stakeholders. In response, Apple deployed an aggressive public relations campaign to advocate for its position.

Apple's response was swift and relied upon the repetition of key messages, clearly articulated across multiple platforms. Cook explained why the organization refused to acquiesce to the FBI's demands. His key messages were that unlocking the iPhone for the FBI would essentially undermine the security of all iPhone users and ultimately would pose a threat to all Americans.

Apple engaged its key publics, including its shareholders, employees, customers, and the media, through multiple strategies. First, Apple engaged in extensive media relations with a variety of outlets. Media outlets have suggested that, historically, Apple has not been as forthcoming and transparent with the press as they would have liked (Fiegerman, 2016; Greenberg, 2016; Gurman, 2014). In the wake of this conflict, however, Apple launched an aggressive media relations campaign. They held multiple conference calls with reporters, during which the reporters could question the company's attorneys; they emailed backgrounders to support media coverage; and they engaged in several high-profile interviews (Fiegerman, 2016). One of these interviews was a rare television interview in Cook's office with David Muir of ABC News; another interview landed Cook on the cover of *Time*

Magazine with the headline, "Apple CEO Tim Cook on his fight with the FBI and why he won't back down" (Grossman, 2016). Apple's media relations strategy was also notable because the company expanded its outreach beyond its regular cadre of technology and business reporters to include political and policy reporters in Washington, DC (Greenberg, 2016).

Also prominent in Apple's public relations strategy were their direct appeals to customers, employees, and shareholders. On the same day of the initial court order, Apple posted a response on its website in a statement from Cook entitled "A message to our customers" (Cook, 2016). In this letter (see Appendix B), Cook described how complying with the FBI's request would set a precedent for compliance that would ultimately provide the government with "the power to reach into anyone's device to capture their data" (Cook, 2016, para. 19). Cook argued that creating this kind of backdoor software would undermine the security of all iPhone users by compromising the integrity of Apple's encryption software. Cook indicated that the government was asking Apple for something it did not have and was, therefore, demanding that Apple create new software for the government agency.

In addition to this letter, Apple posted on its website a question-and-answer fact sheet about Apple and security. Both of these statements, the letter and the Q&A, issued calls for dialogue among stakeholders. In the letter, Cook wrote that "this moment calls for public discussion, and we want our customers and people around the country to understand what is at stake" (Cook, 2016, para. 2). Similarly, the Q&A fact sheet concluded with Apple indicating its willingness to participate in a dialogue with top experts examining issues related to intelligence, technology, and civil liberties—a suggestion previously made by Congress (Apple, n.d.)

Outreach to employees and shareholders reflected a similar key message. An internal memo from Cook to employees (leaked to the press) reiterated Apple's position on the issue and explained why the organization was standing firm in its convictions (Paczkowski, 2016; Toor, 2016). This letter also referenced the dialogue that was taking place among stakeholders and noted, "Apple is a uniquely American company. It does not feel right to be on the opposite side of the government in a case centering on the freedoms and liberties that government is meant to protect" (Cook, 2016, para. 9, as cited in Paczkowski, 2016). Similarly, at its annual shareholder meeting, Cook explained Apple's position on the issue and why the organization would not comply with the FBI's demands to unlock the phone. Interestingly, after his remarks during the Q&A portion of the meeting, not one shareholder asked Cook about this issue (Weinberger, 2016).

Outcomes

This conflict received significant media attention as both Apple and the FBI courted the favorable opinion of stakeholders. Some opinion leaders made inciting comments, such as Donald Trump's call for a boycott of Apple (Diamond, 2016), while others assumed a more moderate tone, such as President Obama's recommendation that we stop "fetishizing" our phones above all else (Obama, 2016). Former NSA contractor and whistleblower Edward Snowden suggested Apple was now defending privacy rights, where the government should be doing so (Guynn, 2016).

Apple received support in the form of amicus briefs filed with the court from of a variety of organizations and activists working in high-tech in particular. Fewer briefs were filed on the FBI's behalf, primarily from the law enforcement community, as well as the families of the victims from the shooting (see Appendix C). The press largely supported Apple, with newspaper editorials favoring Apple 8:1 (Elmer-DeWitt, 2016). Public opinion was divided, with a slight majority (51%) of individuals supporting the FBI over Apple, although 11% of individuals were undecided (Pew Research Center, 2016).

While both organizations strongly advocated for their positions, the conflict was ultimately unresolved since the FBI found another solution that enabled it to bypass Apple and unlock the phone. The issue, however, has not gone away: Friction between digital privacy and national security will continue as law enforcement agencies grapple with the challenge of increasingly sophisticated encryption software. During this conflict lawmakers held a House Judiciary Committee hearing in Washington in early March 2016 entitled "The Encryption Tightrope: Balancing Americans' Security and Privacy," during which both Apple representatives and the FBI made their arguments on the issue. In late December 2016, the Congressional Encryption Working Group released a report recognizing the complexities of this issue and stating that "any measure that weakens encryption works against the national interest" (Upton et al., 2016, 4). The report called for more cooperation among stakeholders and recognized there is "no one-size-fits-all solution to the encryption challenge" (Upton et al., 2016, 5).

The conflict between Apple and the FBI conflates two important, unresolved issues: digital privacy and national security. Observers suggest the case is a harbinger of more conflict as digital technologies become increasingly secure, thereby making criminal investigations more challenging (Roberts, 2016). While this case aroused intense interest and commentary, it did not provide any solutions, although it did spur the introduction of legislation designed to address the issue (Greenberg, 2016).

Throughout this conflict, Apple strongly advocated for its position and fought for its values and the integrity of its products. Neither the FBI nor Apple made any contingencies for the other. While public opinion slightly favored the Justice Department (Pew Research Center, 2016), Apple sales did not appear to suffer (La Monica, 2016). Ultimately, this conflict may have been beneficial to stakeholders because it provided them with an opportunity to identify their core values and take a stand on an issue. In fact, the position that Apple took may have been a boost to its brand image as it reflected the company's long-established image as contrarian risk-takers. Apple stayed true to its own corporate values and followed its own recommendation to "think different."

References

Apple. (n.d.) Answers to your questions about Apple and security. Retrieved from http://www.apple.com/customer-letter/answers/.

Apple. (2016, July 27). *Apple celebrates one billion iPhones* [Press release]. Retrieved from http://www.apple.com/newsroom/2016/07/apple-celebrates-one-billion-iphones.html.

Apple Inc.'s motion to vacate order compelling Apple Inc. to assist agents in search, and opposition to government's motion to compel assistance. (2016, February 25). Retrieved from https://epic.org/amicus/crypto/apple/#EPIC.

Apple v. FBI. (n.d.) Retrieved from https://epic.org/amicus/crypto/apple/.

Benner, K., & Perlroth, N. (2016, February 19). How Tim Cook, in iPhone battle, became a bulwark for digital privacy. *New York Times*. Retrieved from http://www.nytimes.com/2016/02/19/technology/how-tim-cook-became-a-bulwark-for-digital-privacy.html.

Cook, T. (2016, February 16). A message to our customers. Retrieved from http://www.apple.com/customer-letter/.

Davidson, A. (2016, February 19). The dangerous All Writs Act precedent in the Apple encryption case. *New Yorker*. Retrieved from http://www.newyorker.com/news/amy-davidson/a-dangerous-all-writ-precedent-in-the-apple-case.

Diamond, J. (2016, February 19). Donald Trump calls for Apple boycott. *CNN Politics*. Retrieved from http://www.cnn.com/2016/02/19/politics/donald-trump-apple-boycott/.

Elmer-DeWitt, P. (2016, February 19). Newspaper editorials back Apple over FBI 8 to 1. *Fortune*. Retrieved from http://fortune.com/2016/02/19/apple-fbi-newspaper-editorials/.

Fiegerman, S. (2016, February 26). Apple faces the most important PR battle in its history with the FBI. *Mashable*. Retrieved from http://mashable.com/2016/02/26/apple-pr-battle-fbi/#WzV7WMAeMPqw.

Fox-Brewster, T. (2016, June 29). Facebook is playing games with your privacy and there's nothing you can do about it. *Forbes*. Retrieved from http://www.forbes.com/sites/thomasbrewster/2016/06/29/facebook-location-tracking-friend-games/#310b5ebb3348.

Gellman, B. (2013, December 23). Edward Snowden, after months of NSA revelations, says his mission's accomplished. *Washington Post*. Retrieved from https://www.washingtonpost.com/world/national-security/edward-snowden-after-months-of-nsa-revelations-says-his-missions-accomplished/2013/12/23/49fc36de-6c1c-11e3-a523-fe73f0ff6b8d_story.html.

Gibbs, N., & Grossman, L. (2016, March 17). Here's the full transcript of TIME's interview with Apple CEO Tim Cook. *TIME*. Retrieved from http://time.com/4261796/tim-cook-transcript/

Glance, D. (2014, September 15). The psychology behind Apple's obsessive 'iSheep' fans. *Washington Post*. Retrieved from https://www.washingtonpost.com/posteverything/wp/2014/09/15/the-psychology-behind-apples-obsessive-isheep-fans/.

Goodson, S. (2011, November 27). Is brand loyalty the core to Apple's success? *Forbes*. Retrieved from http://www.forbes.com/sites/marketshare/2011/11/27/is-brand-loyalty-the-core-to-apples-success-2/#4daa08b4677f.

Greenberg, A. (2016, April 8). The Senate's draft encryption bill is "ludicrous, dangerous, technically illiterate." *Wired*. Retrieved from https://www.wired.com/2016/04/senates-draft-encryption-bill-privacy-nightmare/.

Grossman, L. (2016, March 17). Inside Apple CEO's Tim Cook's fight with the FBI. *Time*. Retrieved from http://time.com/4262480/tim-cook-apple-fbi-2/.

Gurman, M. (2014, August 29). Seeing through the illusion: Understanding Apple's mastery of the media. Retrieved from https://9to5mac.com/2014/08/29/seeing-through-the-illusion-understanding-apples-mastery-of-the-media/.

Guynn, J. (2016, February 16). Edward Snowden, Sundar Pichai back Apple in fight over iPhone. *USA Today*. Retrieved from http://www.usatoday.com/story/tech/news/2016/02/17/edward-snowden-apple-san-bernardino-google/80508036/.

Isaacson, W. (2011, October 29). The genius of Jobs. *New York Times*. Retrieved from http://www.nytimes.com/2011/10/30/opinion/sunday/steve-jobss-genius.html?_r=0.

La Monica, P. R. (2016, February 24). Apple's stock has worms but FBI isn't one of them. *CNN Money*. Retrieved from http://www.scrible.com/contentview/page/MKGQ0400224QO36O348143J28I0446AM:228660696/index.html.

Limer, E. (2016, February 24). Most useful podcast ever: Why is the FBI using a 227-year-old law against Apple? *Popular Mechanics*. Retrieved from http://www.popularmechanics.com/technology/a19483/what-is-the-all-writs-act-of-1789-the-225-year-old-law-the-fbi-is-using-on-apple/.

Lister, T., Sanchez, R., Bixler, M., O'Key, S., Hogenmiller, M., & Tawfeeq. M. (2016, July 26). ISIS goes global: 143 attacks in 29 countries have killed 2,043. *CNN*. Retrieved from http://www.cnn.com/2015/12/17/world/mapping-isis-attacks-around-the-world/.

Lohr, S. (2013, March 23). Big Data is opening doors, but maybe too many. *New York Times*. Retrieved from http://www.nytimes.com/2013/03/24/technology/big-data-and-a-renewed-debate-over-privacy.html.

MacKinnon, B. R. (2012, January 29). We're losing control of our digital privacy. *CNN*. Retrieved from http://www.cnn.com/2012/01/26/opinion/mackinnon-sopa-government-surveillance/.

Mangalindan, J.P. (2013, September 26). A history of the iPhone. *Fortune*. Retrieved from http://fortune.com/2013/09/26/a-history-of-the-iphone/.

Markoff, J. (2011, October 5). Apple's visionary redefined digital age. *New York Times*. Retrieved from http://www.nytimes.com/2011/10/06/business/steve-jobs-of-apple-dies-at-56.html?_r=0.

Mullaney, T. (2016, April 29). Apple product innovations that changed the world. *CNBC*. Retrieved from http://www.cnbc.com/2016/04/29/apple-product-innovations-that-changed-the-world.html.

Nakamura, D. (2016, December 6). Obama tries to ease anxiety over terrorism with Oval Office address. *CNN*. Retrieved from https://www.washingtonpost

.com/politics/obama-tries-to-ease-anxiety-over-terror-attacks-with-oval-office-address/2015/12/06/95d9a34c-9c72-11e5-bce4-708fe33e3288_story.html.

Obama, B. (2016, March 12). Transcript of Obama's remarks at SXSW. *Boston Globe.* Retrieved from https://www.bostonglobe.com/news/nation/2016/03/11/transcript-obama-remarks-sxsw/6m8IFsnpJh2k3XWxifHQnJ/story.html.

Paczkowski, J. (2016, February 22). Tim Cook asks FBI to withdraw order to hack terrorist's iPhone. *BuzzFeed News.* Retrieved from https://www.buzzfeed.com/johnpaczkowski/apple-ceo-calls-on-feds-to-drop-iphone-unlock-order?utm_term=.rgkX1B3Om#.ygK6mbKyn.

Pew Research Center. (2014, November). Public perceptions of privacy and security in a post-Snowden era. Retrieved from http://www.pewinternet.org/2014/11/12/public-privacy-perceptions/.

Pew Research Center. (2016, February). More support for Justice Department than for Apple in dispute over unlocking iPhone. Retrieved from http://www.people-press.org/2016/02/22/more-support-for-justice-department-than-for-apple-in-dispute-over-unlocking-iphone/.

Pilkington, E. (2015, September 24). Edward Snowden calls for global push to expand digital privacy laws. *The Guardian.* Retrieved from https://www.theguardian.com/us-news/2015/sep/24/edward-snowden-international-laws-digital-privacy-video.

Rainie, L., & Duggan, M. (2016). Privacy and Information Sharing. Pew Research Center. Retrieved from http://www.pewinternet.org/2016/01/14/2016/Privacy-and-Information-Sharing.

Roberts, J. J. (2016, March 23). Why Apple won round 1 vs. the FBI, and what comes next. *Fortune.* Retrieved from http://fortune.com/2016/03/23/apple-fbi-qa/.

Serrano, R. A., Esquivel, P., & Knoll, C. (2015, December 17). Marquez and Farook plotted campus and freeway attacks, prosecutors allege. *LA Times.* http://www.latimes.com/local/lanow/la-me-ln-san-bernardino-marquez-20151217-story.html.

Spence, E. (2015, October 13). The cult of Apple and the church of Cook. *Forbes.* Retrieved from http://www.forbes.com/sites/ewanspence/2015/10/13/apple-store-design-church-cult-apple/#35bc80de4791.

Sullivan, M. (2016, February 22). Why the FBI chose to try the Apple encryption case in the media. *Fast Company.* Retrieved from http://www.fastcompany.com/3057033/why-the-fbi-chose-to-try-the-apple-encryption-case-in-the-media.

Taube, A. (2014, May 23). Steve Jobs thought the "Think Different" ad that went viral after his death was "horrible." *Business Insider.* Retrieved from http://www.businessinsider.com/steve-jobs-hated-apple-think-different-ad-2014-5.

The World's Most Valuable Brands. (2016). *Forbes.* Retrieved from http://www.forbes.com/powerful-brands/list/.

Toor, A. (2016, February 22). Read Tim Cook's email to Apple employees about its fight against the FBI. *The Verge.* Retrieved from http://www.theverge.com/2016/2/22/11092028/apple-tim-cook-fbi-encryption-internal-memo.

Upton, F., Pallone, F. Johnson, B., Clarke, Y. D., Goodlatte, B., Conyers, Jr., J., et al. (2016). *House Judiciary Committee & House Energy and Commerce*

Committee—Encryption Working Group. Retrieved from http://energycommerce. house.gov/sites/republicans.energycommerce.house.gov/files/documents/114/ analysis/20161219EWGFINALReport_0.pdf.

Vega, T. (2010, September 20). Code known as flash cookies raises privacy concerns. *New York Times.* Retrieved from http://www.nytimes.com/2010/09/21/ technology/21cookie.html.

Weinberger, M. (2016, February 26). Not a single Apple shareholder asked Tim Cook about its fight with the FBI. *Business Insider.* Retrieved from http://www.business insider.com/apple-ceo-tim-cook-addresses-shareholders-on-fbi-case-2016-2.

Weise, E. (2016, March 16). Apple v FBI timeline: 43 days that rocked tech. *USA Today.* Retrieved from https://www.usatoday.com/story/tech/news/2016/03/15/apple-v-fbi-timeline/81827400/

Zetter, K. (2016, March 28). The FBI drops its case against Apple after finding a way into that iPhone. *Wired.* Retrieved from https://www.wired.com/2016/03/ fbi-drops-case-apple-finding-way-iphone/

Appendix A

Timeline of Key Events

December 2, 2015	Syed Rizwan Farook and Tashfeen Malik open fire at a holiday party at the Inland Regional Center in San Bernardino, California, killing 14 and wounding 22. Farook and Malik are killed later that same day in a shootout with police.
December 2015	An iPhone 5c, owned by Farook's employer, the San Bernardino County Department of Public Health, was lawfully seized by the FBI during the execution of a search warrant of Farook's mother's Lexus.
February 16, 2016	FBI filed an application with the Central Court of California for an order of assistance under the All Writs Act, 28 U.S.C. § 1651. The court granted the application the same day and issued a three-page order requiring Apple to assist the FBI.
February 16, 2016	In response to the court order, Apple CEO Tim Cook posted an open letter on Apple's website indicating Apple's intentions not to comply with the order.
February 18, 2016	The court held a status conference and heard the positions of the government and Apple with respect to a briefing schedule for Apple's application for relief.
February 19, 2016	The government filed a *Motion to Compel Apple Inc. to Comply with the Court's February 16, 2016 Order Compelling Assistance in Search.*

February 19, 2016	The court issued a scheduling order and established deadlines for briefs and reports. Court hearing regarding Apple's appeal for relief from the court order was scheduled for March 22.
February 25, 2016	Apple files a motion to vacate the court's order.
March 2016	Court documents are filed by both the FBI and Apple supporting their positions for and against mandating Apple's assistance with unlocking the iPhone.
March 21, 2016	FBI files a motion to delay the March 22 hearing.
March 28, 2016	FBI asks court to vacate the original February 16 court order because they had found another way to access the data on Farook's iPhone.
March 29, 2016	Original court order was vacated.

(Apple v. FBI, n.d.; Weise, 2016; Zetter, 2016)

Appendix B

COMPLETE TEXT OF COOK'S LETTER POSTED ON APPLE'S WEBSITE.
February 16, 2016
A Message to Our Customers

The United States government has demanded that Apple take an unprecedented step which threatens the security of our customers. We oppose this order, which has implications far beyond the legal case at hand.

This moment calls for public discussion, and we want our customers and people around the country to understand what is at stake.

Answers to your questions about privacy and security

The Need for Encryption

Smartphones, led by iPhone, have become an essential part of our lives. People use them to store an incredible amount of personal information, from our private conversations to our photos, our music, our notes, our calendars and contacts, our financial information and health data, even where we have been and where we are going.

All that information needs to be protected from hackers and criminals who want to access it, steal it, and use it without our knowledge or permission. Customers expect Apple and other technology companies to do everything in our power to protect their personal information, and at Apple we are deeply committed to safeguarding their data.

Compromising the security of our personal information can ultimately put our personal safety at risk. That is why encryption has become so important to all of us.

For many years, we have used encryption to protect our customers' personal data because we believe it's the only way to keep their information safe. We have even put that data out of our own reach, because we believe the contents of your iPhone are none of our business.

THE SAN BERNARDINO CASE

We were shocked and outraged by the deadly act of terrorism in San Bernardino last December. We mourn the loss of life and want justice for all those whose lives were affected. The FBI asked us for help in the days following the attack, and we have worked hard to support the government's efforts to solve this horrible crime. We have no sympathy for terrorists.

When the FBI has requested data that's in our possession, we have provided it. Apple complies with valid subpoenas and search warrants, as we have in the San Bernardino case. We have also made Apple engineers available to advise the FBI, and we've offered our best ideas on a number of investigative options at their disposal.

We have great respect for the professionals at the FBI, and we believe their intentions are good. Up to this point, we have done everything that is both within our power and within the law to help them. But now the U.S. government has asked us for something we simply do not have, and something we consider too dangerous to create. They have asked us to build a backdoor to the iPhone.

Specifically, the FBI wants us to make a new version of the iPhone operating system, circumventing several important security features, and install it on an iPhone recovered during the investigation. In the wrong hands, this software—which does not exist today—would have the potential to unlock any iPhone in someone's physical possession.

The FBI may use different words to describe this tool, but make no mistake: Building a version of iOS that bypasses security in this way would undeniably create a backdoor. And while the government may argue that its use would be limited to this case, there is no way to guarantee such control.

THE THREAT TO DATA SECURITY

Some would argue that building a backdoor for just one iPhone is a simple, clean-cut solution. But it ignores both the basics of digital security and the significance of what the government is demanding in this case.

In today's digital world, the "key" to an encrypted system is a piece of information that unlocks the data, and it is only as secure as the protections around it. Once the information is known, or a way to bypass the code is revealed, the encryption can be defeated by anyone with that knowledge.

The government suggests this tool could only be used once, on one phone. But that's simply not true. Once created, the technique could be used over and over again, on any number of devices. In the physical world, it would be the equivalent of a master key, capable of opening hundreds of millions of locks—from restaurants and banks to stores and homes. No reasonable person would find that acceptable.

The government is asking Apple to hack our own users and undermine decades of security advancements that protect our customers—including tens of millions of American citizens—from sophisticated hackers and cybercriminals. The same engineers who built strong encryption into the iPhone to protect our users would, ironically, be ordered to weaken those protections and make our users less safe.

We can find no precedent for an American company being forced to expose its customers to a greater risk of attack. For years, cryptologists and national security experts have been warning against weakening encryption. Doing so would hurt only the well-meaning and law-abiding citizens who rely on companies like Apple to protect their data. Criminals and bad actors will still encrypt, using tools that are readily available to them.

A DANGEROUS PRECEDENT
Rather than asking for legislative action through Congress, the FBI is proposing an unprecedented use of the All Writs Act of 1789 to justify an expansion of its authority.

The government would have us remove security features and add new capabilities to the operating system, allowing a passcode to be input electronically. This would make it easier to unlock an iPhone by "brute force," trying thousands or millions of combinations with the speed of a modern computer.

The implications of the government's demands are chilling. If the government can use the All Writs Act to make it easier to unlock your iPhone, it would have the power to reach into anyone's device to capture their data. The government could extend this breach of privacy and demand that Apple build surveillance software to intercept your messages, access your health records or financial data, track your location, or even access your phone's microphone or camera without your knowledge.

Opposing this order is not something we take lightly. We feel we must speak up in the face of what we see as an overreach by the U.S. government.

We are challenging the FBI's demands with the deepest respect for American democracy and a love of our country. We believe it would be in the best interest of everyone to step back and consider the implications.

While we believe the FBI's intentions are good, it would be wrong for the government to force us to build a backdoor into our products. And ultimately, we fear that this demand would undermine the very freedoms and liberty our government is meant to protect.

Source: Cook, 2016

Appendix C
Amicus briefs (court documents) filed during the case.

Briefs filed in support of Apple:

> 32 law professors
> Access Now and Wickr Foundation

ACT/The App Association

Airbnb, Atlassian, Automattic, CloudFlare, eBay, GitHub, Kickstarter, LinkedIn, Mapbox, Medium, Meetup, Reddit, Square, Squarespace, Twilio, Twitter and Wickr

Amazon, Box, Cisco, Dropbox, Evernote, Facebook, Google, Microsoft, Mozilla, Nest, Pinterest, Slack, Snapchat, WhatsApp, and Yahoo

American Civil Liberties Union, ACLU of Northern California, ACLU of Southern California, and ACLU of San Diego and Imperial Counties

AT&T

AVG Technologies, Data Foundry, Golden Frog, the Computer & Communications Industry Association (CCIA), the Internet Association, and the Internet Infrastructure Coalition

BSA | The Software Alliance, the Consumer Technology Association, the Information Technology Industry Council, and TechNet

Center for Democracy & Technology

Electronic Frontier Foundation and 46 technologists, researchers, and cryptographers

Electronic Privacy Information Center (EPIC) and eight consumer privacy organizations

Intel

iPhone security and applied cryptography experts including Dino Dai Zovi, Dan Boneh (Stanford), Charlie Miller, Dr. Hovav Shacham (UC San Diego), Bruce Schneier (Harvard), Dan Wallach (Rice), and Jonathan Zdziarski

Lavabit

The Media Institute

Privacy International and Human Rights Watch

Richard F. Taub

Briefs filed in support of the FBI

- Federal Law Enforcement Officers Association, Association of Prosecuting Attorneys, and National Sheriffs' Association
- California State Sheriffs Association, California Police Chiefs' Association, and the California Peace Officers' Association
- Families of victims in the San Bernardino shooting
- San Bernardino County District Attorney on behalf of the People of California

(Apple v. FBI, 2016)

Discussion Questions

1. Do you think Apple was solely motivated by their values of data security and privacy in how they addressed this conflict? What might be some other motives?
2. If this case had gone to court, do you think Apple's reputation and product sales would have suffered?
3. Reports indicate the FBI did not share with Apple how they bypassed the iPhone's security encryption (with the help of a third party). What are the ethical implications of the FBI's decision not to share this information?

CHIQUITA BRANDS, ITS ILLEGAL PAYMENTS TO PARAMILITARY GROUPS IN COLOMBIA, AND THE TRANSNATIONAL PUBLIC RELATIONS CRISIS THAT FOLLOWED

Vanessa Bravo, Ph.D., *Elon University*, Juan Carlos Molleda, Ph.D., *University of Oregon*, Andrés Felipe Giraldo-Dávila, M.A., *Universidad de Medellín*, and Luis Horacio Botero-Montoya, Ph.D., *Universidad Pontificia Bolivariana*

Chiquita Brands International is "a leading global company with 20,000 employees across 70 countries" (Chiquita, n.d.-a, para. 1) that mainly produces bananas, other fruits, green salads, and snack products. Chiquita found itself in the middle of a transnational public relations crisis when the company disclosed, in the United States, that it had paid $1.7 million to paramilitary groups and left-wing organizations in Colombia from 1997 to 2004 (Anderson, 2009). Chiquita sold its Colombia-based banana production and port operations after the crisis erupted (Chiquita, n.d.-b). The crisis moved to the United States in what is known, in global public relations, as a cross-national conflict shift (Bravo et al., 2013; Molleda 2010, 2011). The crisis triggered reactions from the governments of both countries. As a result of its illegal payments, in 2007 Chiquita had to pay a fine of $25 million to the U.S. government (Anderson, 2009; Lawsuits follow, 2008), and it faced several lawsuits in Florida, which were finally dismissed in 2014 (Lawsuits follow, 2008; Walker, 2014a, 2014b).

This reading describes the Chiquita Brands crisis, the way it shifted from the corporation's host country (Colombia) to Chiquita's home country (the United States), and the strategies and tactics Chiquita used to handle the situation. The authors of this case study analyzed 162 news stories, published in seven U.S. newspapers and five Colombian newspapers, and written also by the Associated Press, between the years of 2007 and 2014.

Background

Chiquita Brands International is a powerful multinational corporation founded in 1870. Through its history, it has had several brand names: Boston Fruit Company (1885), United Fruit Company (1899), Chiquita (1944), United Brands Company (1970), and Chiquita Brands International (1990) (Chiquita, n.d.-b). The company's stock is traded on the New York Stock Exchange. Chiquita sells billions of bananas and other products every year (Chiquita, n.d.-b).

In its almost 150 years of existence, the company has faced several controversies regarding its political influence in Central American nations (deemed "banana republics," given the power that the United Fruit Company had on the actions of Central American governments in the past), the harsh working conditions on the banana plantation, and the lack of workers' rights (Chapman, 2009; Koeppel, 2008). The company also filed for bankruptcy in 2001, but it was able to overcome the situation by 2002 (Chiquita, n.d.-b).

The Situation

This crisis started when Chiquita alerted the U.S. Department of Justice that it had been paying paramilitary groups in Colombia for the last seven years through its Colombia subsidiary, Banadex, allegedly to protect the safety of its employees. Colombia has faced decades of problems with paramilitary and guerilla groups' violence, as well as with drug production and trafficking (CIA World Factbook, 2016). Chiquita sold Banadex in 2004.

It seems that the company understood, early on, the implications of the payments. In a handwritten 1997 note, one Chiquita executive wrote that the payments were "the cost of doing business in Colombia." The note added, "Need to keep this very confidential—People can get killed" (Anderson, 2011, para. 11 and 12).

In March 2007, U.S. federal prosecutors charged Chiquita with "doing business with a terrorist organization" (Lawsuits follow, 2008), saying that Chiquita agreed to pay about $1.7 million between 1997 and 2004 to an organization that, in 2001, was identified by the U.S. government as a terrorist group. As the U.S. Justice Department said in court filings in 2007, "Chiquita's money helped buy weapons and ammunition used to kill innocent victims of terrorism. Simply put, defendant Chiquita funded terrorism" (Lynch, 2007).

Chiquita pleaded guilty in the U.S. District Court in Washington, DC, to one count of doing business with a terrorist organization. The company said that it was "forced to make payments to ensure workers' safety" (Lawsuits follow, 2008) but agreed to pay a $25 million fine.

Between June and November 2007, human rights groups and relatives of victims allegedly killed or injured by paramilitary groups in Colombia that received payments from Chiquita's former subsidiary sued the company. Four civil lawsuits were filed in U.S. federal courts in the District of Columbia, Florida, New Jersey, and New York. The lawsuits claimed that Chiquita should have been held legally responsible for the deaths of hundreds, maybe thousands, of people in Colombia because of the company's support to the paramilitary groups. Three suits sought "unspecified damages"; the fourth sought $7.86 billion in damages (Lawsuits follow, 2008). One of the three "unspecified damages" suits was asking for more than $13 billion for 600 plaintiffs (Anderson, 2009).

In February 2008, all four lawsuits were transferred to the U.S. District Court in Miami. Chiquita asked the judges to dismiss the lawsuits, insisting that the money the company paid to the right-wing United Self-Defense Forces of Colombia (AUC, Spanish acronym) had no direct connection to the criminal acts AUC committed in the region (Anderson, 2009). To add to the complexity of the situation, Chiquita also acknowledged that it paid money to the left-wing Revolutionary Armed Forces of Colombia (FARC). The United States lists both FARC and AUC as terrorist groups that engage in murder, torture, kidnappings, and violence (Anderson, 2009). The lawsuits also claimed that Chiquita provided AUC with cash, weapons such as AK-47s, military supplies, and access to the banana ports for trafficking cocaine (Anderson, 2009). With this material support, according to the lawyers for the hundreds of Colombian plaintiffs, the AUC injured or killed Colombian labor leaders, attacked FARC guerrillas, and became "rulers" of a region formed by about 200 Chiquita farms. The lawsuits were brought under the Alien Tort Statute, which allowed non-U.S. citizens to make claims in U.S. courts for acts that violate international law (Anderson, 2009).

In 2014, the lawsuits were dismissed when the 11th Circuit Court of Appeals in Florida said that "the plaintiffs could not sue Chiquita for damages under the alien tort statute, because the relevant conduct had taken place outside the US" (Walker, 2014b). Not all the judges agreed: in her dissent Judge Beverly Martin wrote that Chiquita executives "participated in a campaign of torture and murder . . . from their corporate offices in the territory of the US" and that "by failing to enforce the ATS under these circumstances, I fear we disarm innocents against American corporations that engage in human rights violations abroad" (Walker, 2014b).

Outcomes

Part of understanding a cross-national public relations crisis should involve analyzing the types of responses that a corporation provides in light of the situation. For this study of the Chiquita Brands' cross-national conflict shift, we used the typology of corporate apologies advanced by Benoit and Brinson (1994) as part of image restoration theory to categorize Chiquita's responses, both in Colombia and the United States. Benoit and Brinson wrote that apologies can be placed into one or several of the following categories: denial of the situation, blame shifting, evading responsibility by arguing that there was provocation, evading responsibility by arguing that there were good intentions involved, reducing the offensiveness of the event by minimizing the importance of the situation, offering corrective action, showing mortification (admitting the wrongful act and asking for forgiveness), or some other response.

In its apology, Chiquita mainly used the strategy of "evading responsibility by arguing that there were good intentions involved." Even after pleading guilty, the company argued that it had paid the paramilitary groups with good intentions (to protect the safety of its employees). The second strategy used was "evading responsibility by arguing that there was provocation." Chiquita argued that it paid the money because it was forced to do so by the paramilitary groups. This position is weakened, however, if we remember that the Chiquita executive referred to the payments as "the cost of doing business in Colombia," acknowledging that "people can get killed" (Anderson, 2011, para. 11 and 12).

The corporate response was issued through statements offered by Chiquita's CEO in two news releases in 2007. They were distributed only in the United States, although they were readily available on the company's website (Chiquita, 2007a). In the March 14, 2007, news release, CEO Fernando Aguirre announced that the company would pay the $25 million fine, stating, "The information filed today is part of a plea agreement, which we view as a reasoned solution to the dilemma the company faced several years ago" (Apuzzo, 2007, para. 9). Aguirre said in the news release that "The payments made by the company were always motivated by our good faith concern for the safety of our employees" (Apuzzo, 2007, para. 9).

In the second news release, distributed on September 11, 2007 (Chiquita, 2007b, para. 3), Aguirre said he was pleased that the Department of Justice did not charge any corporate executives of Chiquita: "We believe this is the right decision and one that reflects the good faith efforts of the company—and its officers, directors, and employees—to address a very difficult situation involving the life and safety of our employees."

A few short statements were also offered to the U.S. news media by a company spokesperson, but press releases were scarce. The corporate response was centralized, was offered almost exclusively by Aguirre, and was given only in the United States. Colombian media had only indirect access to the corporate response because the response to the crisis was managed in the United States, not Colombia.

Hundreds of news stories have been published about this controversy, in the United States, in Colombia, and around the world. Chiquita's argument that it was protecting its employees was present in roughly 70% of the stories published in the United States, but only about 48% of the Colombian news stories. More stories were published in Colombia about this crisis than in the United States, but the U.S. news stories were longer and tended to include more sources of information. And while the tone of the news stories was mainly negative in both countries, this was especially true in the case of the U.S. stories.

In the court of public opinion, having just two news releases with comments by the CEO and a few more statements by a company spokesperson did not seem to be enough to repair the company's reputation, given that many of the news stories published both in Colombia and the United States had a negative tone to them. But in the court of law, Chiquita obtained a legal victory in 2014: The lawsuits initiated by 4,000 Colombian victims of paramilitary groups were dismissed (Stempel, 2014; Walker 2014a, 2014b).

References

Anderson, C. (2009, February 27). Chiquita seeks dismissal of Colombia death lawsuit. *Associated Press*.

Anderson, C. (2011, May 31). Bananas, Colombian death squads, and a billion-dollar lawsuit. *Associated Press*. Retrieved November 29, 2016, from http://www.nbcnews.com/id/43221200/ns/world_news-americas/t/bananas-colombian-death-squads-billion-dollar-lawsuit/#.WD8URJIpa9c.

Apuzzo, M. (2007, March 15). Chiquita to pay $25 million fine in terror case. *Associated Press*. Retrieved November 28, 2016, from http://www.washingtonpost.com/wp-dyn/content/article/2007/03/15/AR2007031500354.html.

Benoit, W. L., & Brinson, S. L. (1994). AT&T: Apologies are not enough. *Communication Quarterly, 42*(1), 75–88.

Bravo, V., Molleda, J. C., Dávila, A. F. G., & Botero, L. H. (2013). Testing cross-national conflict shifting theory: An analysis of Chiquita Brands' transnational crisis in Colombia. *Public Relations Review, 39*(1), 57–59.

Chapman, P. (2009). *Bananas: How the United Fruit Company Shaped the World*. New York: Canongate US.

Chiquita. (n.d.-a). Meet Chiquita. Live Better, Live Chiquita website. Retrieved July 18, 2016, from http://www.chiquita.com/Our-Company/Meet-Chiquita.aspx.

Chiquita. (n.d.-b). The Chiquita Story. Live Better, Live Chiquita website. Retrieved November 29, 2016, from http://www.chiquita.com/Our-Company/The-Chiquita-Story.aspx.

Chiquita. (2007a, March 16). Financial Release: Chiquita statement on agreement with U.S. Department of Justice. Live Better, Live Chiquita website. Retrieved November 29, 2016, from http://investors.chiquita.com/phoenix.zhtml?c=119836&p=irol-newsArticle&ID=974081.

Chiquita. (2007b, September 11). Financial Release: Chiquita Brands International statement on U.S. Department of Justice Sentencing Memorandum. Live Better, Live Chiquita website. Retrieved November 29, 2016, from http://investors.chiquita.com/phoenix.zhtml?c=119836&p=irol-newsArticle&ID=1050372.

CIA World Factbook (2016, July 11). Colombia. Retrieved July 19, 2016, from https://www.cia.gov/library/publications/the-world-factbook/geos/co.html.

Koeppel, D. (2008). *Banana: The Fate of the Fruit That Changed the World*. New York: Penguin.

Lawsuits follow Chiquita guilty plea (2008, March 5). *Associated Press*.

Lynch, D. J. (2007, October 30). Murder and payoffs taint business in Colombia. *USA Today*, 1B.

Molleda, J. C. (2010). Cross-national conflict shifting: A transnational crisis perspective in global public relations. In Heath, R. (Ed.), *Handbook of Public Relations* (2nd ed., pp. 679–690). Thousand Oaks, CA: Sage Publications.

Molleda, J. C. (2011). Advancing the theory of cross-national conflict shifting: A case discussion and quantitative content analysis of a transnational crisis' newswire coverage. *International Journal of Strategic Communication, 5*(1), 49–70.

Stempel, J. (2014, July 24). Chiquita wins dismissal of U.S. lawsuits over Colombian abuses. *Reuters*. Retrieved November 29, 2016, from http://www.reuters.com/article/chiquita-colombia-decision-idUSL2N0PZ28P20140724

Walker, T. (2014a, July 26). Chiquita do not need to pay banana terror victims, US court rules. *The Independent* (London), 28.

Walker, T. (2014b, July 25). Colombians lose torture claim suit against Chiquita Bananas in US court. *The Independent* (London), 1.

Discussion Questions

1. What were the main events involved in this crisis? Summarize them in a brief timeline.
2. Did Chiquita Brands cross any ethical lines in this case? If so, what were those ethical lines? If your answer is no, explain why you think Chiquita Brands acted in an ethical manner.
3. If you were a public relations counselor for Chiquita Brands, how would have you managed the situation? What would you have done the same? What would you have done differently?

MAKING PLASTIC GREEN: CAPITAL ONE'S COMMITMENT TO SUSTAINABILITY

Stephanie A. Smith, Ph.D., APR, *Virginia Tech*

Americans typically don't associate credit cards with environmental sustainability. For Americans, credit card companies are simply a means to an end; we generally don't even think of them as business organizations. But Capital One is one of the largest financial companies in the world and is responsible for far more than the plastic we carry. In fact, Capital One is doing its part as a Fortune 500 organization to ensure that our environment can sustain our lifestyles for decades of future credit card spending.

Background

Capital One Financial Corporation is a global financial services company with banking and non-banking components. It is headquartered in McLean, Virginia, and as of 2014, it employed over 40,000 associates worldwide (Capital One, 2015). Although it is most commonly associated with credit cards, Capital One has many brands and businesses, including credit cards, home and auto loans, and commercial and consumer banking products (Capital One, 2015). As a Fortune 500 company, Capital One is a widely recognized brand in America—but with widespread recognition also comes responsibility.

From an operational standpoint, Capital One has a focus on quality and history of innovation. Created as a spinoff from another company, as a credit card branch, Capital One became its own entity in 1995. For the next several years, Capital One focused exclusively on providing credit cards to consumers before expanding into loans, insurance, and banking. Currently, the company is integrating its business with new technologies and digital platforms. However, Capital One credits its success to three things: employees, culture, and customers (Capital One, 2015). Named as one of Civic 50's most community-minded companies for three years running, and with over 360,000 hours of community service in 2014, its values of "excellence" and "do the right thing" are embodied throughout the organization's commitment to corporate social responsibility (CSR; Capital One, 2015).

The Situation

CSR efforts are not new to large organizations such as Capital One. However, the communication surrounding how CSR efforts are demonstrated has evolved over the last decade and has become increasingly important for engaging and retaining both internal and external audiences. Capital One's CSR initiatives are focused on three core elements: people, community, and environment, with the environment being the focus of this case study.

Capital One's environmental efforts are rooted within its sense of accountability to stakeholders and society (Capital One, 2015). The company's environmental initiatives engage people and the community, making it a trifecta of its CSR goals. Capital One is committed to building strong, thriving communities where people can succeed, and sustainability is a critical component of this goal. While general CSR efforts include basic business operations, customer advocacy, and community development, the company's environmental efforts have had the most impact on its CSR goals and objectives over the last five years. Thousands of Capital One associates actively support its sustainability efforts by opting in to receive environmental updates and engage in discussion via email listservs and an internal intranet. This is the primary form of communication Capital One uses to showcase, promote, and enhance the firm's environmental and sustainability CSR efforts. Through the online channels, many associates have banded together to form more than two dozen "Green Teams," which support local sustainability projects.

The company's environmental goals can be divided into three main categories: operations, products and services, and associates and communities. Operations works to make Capital One facilities "green" by reducing energy use, water use, and waste. For products and services, Capital One considers the environment by making better choices in product materials, including paper, and by relying on digital technology to communicate with customers. Finally, the company engages its employees while helping to "green" local communities through events like Earth Day celebrations and volunteer opportunities (Capital One, 2015).

These goals are communicated to internal and external publics in various ways. Employees receive their information from the intranet and by word-of-mouth throughout the office. For example, communicating recycling services to employees helped reduce waste because it educated employees about onsite recycling options. The locations of garbage cans were moved and personal garbage cans were replaced with a dual recycling/wastebasket to encourage recycling. This emphasized the messaging that recycling is easy and convenient. The intranet allows employees to take action through volunteer opportunities and carpool initiatives to help reduce their carbon footprints and give back to the Earth and others. The intranet and opt-in listservs are also used to communicate progress regarding CSR initiatives, such as how the company has reduced greenhouse gas emissions over the last several years. Capital One has also committed to building more "green buildings" and communicates these efforts to internal and external audiences through its website and company reports. External audiences are informed about Capital One's CSR initiatives through publications such as the annual CSR report, award recognition, online content, and community engagement. The annual CSR report highlights the key performance areas and shows the positive impact Capital One is having on the environment. The report is published online for internal and external audiences and shared with internal audiences via email.

Outcomes

This section will discuss the short- and long-term outcomes of the company's three categories—operations, products and services, and associates and communities—and outlines the tactics used to reach each public.

Operations

Capital One set a goal to reduce its greenhouse gas emissions by 10% within five years, and the company reached the goal one year early: By 2012, emissions were reduced by 18% (Capital One, 2015). This reduction is one of the largest contributions of Capital One since it has over 1,000 offices across the country. In 2015, Capital One received a climate leadership award for excellence in greenhouse gas management on behalf of the U.S. Environmental Protection Agency.

Capital One has taken other steps to minimize its environmental impact across operations. For example, the company has sought out green power sources, applied green building principles in new construction and renovations, offers recycling services, and provides sustainable travel options for employees (Capital One, 2015). The company has also implemented water-saving measures within its operations.

Low-flow fixtures are installed in office buildings and native landscaping is used to decrease the need for irrigation. Small changes like these led to a decrease in water use between 2013 and 2014.

Capital One has consistently committed to the 3 "R"s (reduce, reuse, recycle) to minimize the use of materials and waste. As part of this commitment, the company has participated in food donation and composting efforts: In 2014, more than 20,000 meals were donated and almost 60,000 pounds of scraps were collected and composted (Capital One, 2015). These efforts have provided Capital One with cost savings in addition to having a positive impact on the environment.

Capital One shares its progress related to operations primarily through the annual CSR report. Within the report, data are simplified for the broad audience the report reaches. Graphs, percentages, photos, and brief explanations are used to demonstrate changes over time and positive contributions. Goals for the future are discussed. The report highlights the cumulative effects that Capitol One employees have had throughout the year, which were promoted through the intranet and local offices and spearheaded by passionate employees.

Products and Services

The three biggest areas where Capital One has increased sustainability with regard to products and services are paper, online and mobile tools implementation, and financing activities (Capital One, 2015). Paper is essential to business operations, products, and services. Capital One recognizes this necessity but has created programs to reduce the environmental impact of paper use. In 2009, the company created its "Paper Procurement Policy," which helps procure paper from environmentally preferred sources (Capital One, 2015). By 2014, 70% of its paper came from environmentally preferred sources (Capital One, 2015). Further, ATMs no longer require an envelope for deposits (Capital One, 2015).

These efforts were shared with both internal and external audiences through email, notices at ATMs, and brief blurbs on credit card statements. The outcomes are continuously highlighted in the annual CSR report as well. Capital One has been careful not to use paper channels to share its paper-reduction strategies so as not to be hypocritical.

Capital One also incorporates sustainability into its products and services and financing activities. For example, ATM fees and policies encourage people to reduce their travel for ATM transactions and, instead, to use mobile deposit and mobile banking options. The company supports customers by helping them fund sustainable choices such as onsite renewable energy and green buildings, which typically deter consumers based on the upfront financial investment required. Capital One has an ongoing partnership with SolarCity, which helps American homeowners install solar panels at no cost, resulting in utilities savings and reduced environmental impact (Capital One, 2015).

This information is shared with consumers through Capital One's mobile application, website, emails, employees, and mailed statements to ensure consumers are informed and see the information via multiple channels for better recall and understanding.

Associates and Communities

Capital One is highly reliant on its intranet to communicate with associates. Through the intranet, employees are made aware of opportunities to get involved within their community. In 2014, almost 8,000 employees completed more than 38,000 volunteer hours to help "green" their communities (Capital One, 2015). Some of the activities included restoring native vegetation in Upper Fanno Wetland in Oregon, packaging and distributing donated food to hunger-relief organizations, partnering with nonprofits such as Habitat for Humanity, and planting community vegetable gardens (Capital One, 2015).

More micro-level sustainability changes have impacted employees and business operations alike. For example, company shuttles provided over 70,000 rides in 2014, and hundreds of employees are registered carpooling users (Capital One, 2015). The intranet is the main portal for advertising transportation opportunities and helping employees organize their group travel. Capital One also has a "Work@Home" program and flexible work solutions to help employees avoid peak travel times and therefore reduce their emissions (Capital One, 2015). Although this is also promoted on the intranet, word-of-mouth from managers and human resources associates is the primary way of promoting the "Work@Home" program. Finally, many locations include electric vehicle charging stations (Capital One, 2015). Signs in parking areas denote charging stations, and the annual online report demonstrates the usage and value of having the charging stations.

Although Capital One relied on its annual CSR report to communicate with internal and external audiences, one has not been published since 2015. It served as a way to advertise programs to employees who may not have previously been aware of them, and to recognize the hard work of employees. It is now unclear how Capital One is communicating its efforts with internal and external audiences. To date, the company has received some national recognition for its CSR efforts, but not since 2015. This lack of recognition could be attributed to the lack of a published report. It is likely that internal communication strategies such as communicating through online portals and email are still being used, but without the publication of any data, audiences have no knowledge of Capital One's efforts. A key public relations principle is to tell people what a company is doing. Although Capital One has been good at this in the past, currently the firm is missing an opportunity to share its environmental initiatives with others. The decrease in sharing information could have implications for retaining and recruiting employees and could affect the company's overall reputation in the marketplace.

In conclusion, CSR programs, especially those related to the environment and sustainability, have many benefits internally and externally, and on the micro and macro levels. However, without proper communication of CSR efforts, no one knows they exist. Effectively communicating CSR efforts to internal and external audiences, using measurable results and explaining the tactics used to achieve the results, is just as important as participating in CSR, making it highly relevant to public relations practitioners. CSR activities also provide organizations with a platform for sharing their ethics and values and showing how organizations embody those values in their operations.

References

Bhattacharya, C., Sen, S., & Korschun, D. (2007). Corporate social responsibility as an internal marketing strategy. *MIT Sloan Management Review*. Retrieved from http://www.people.fas.harvard.edu/~hiscox/Bhattacharya.pdf.

Capital One. (2015). *In Pursuit of the Greater Good: Corporate Social Responsibility Report 2014*. Retrieved from https://www.capitalone.com/about/social-responsibility/.

Glavas, A., & Godwin, L. (2013). Is the perception of "goodness" good enough? Exploring the relationship between perceived corporate social responsibility and employee organizational identification. *Journal of Business Ethics, 114*, 15–27.

Lee, E., Park, S., & Lee, H. (2013). Employee perception of CSR activities: Its antecedents and consequences. *Journal of Business Research, 66*, 1716–1724.

Mamantov, C. (2009). The engine behind employee communication. *Communication World, 26*, 33–35.

McGlone, T., Spain, J., & McGlone, V. (2011). Corporate social responsibility and the Millennials. *Journal of Education for Business, 86*, 195–200.

Rodriguez, L., & LeMaster, J. (2007). Voluntary corporate social responsibility disclosure SEC "CSR Seal of Approval." *Business & Society, 46*, 370–384.

Smith, N. (2003). Corporate social responsibility: Whether or how? *California Management Review, 45*, 52–76.

Swann, P. (2014). *Cases in Public Relations Management: The Rise of Social Media and Activism* (2nd ed.). New York: Routledge.

Discussion Questions

1. Which values of the PRSA Code of Ethics does this case address?
2. How can Capital One further promote its CSR efforts with internal and external audiences outside of its annual report?
3. What are some criticisms companies like Capital One often face based on their CSR efforts?
4. What PR theory or theories best describe how Capital One communicates its CSR efforts to its audiences?
5. Which PR model best describes how Capital One communicates its CSR efforts to its audiences?

INDEX

advertising, 65, 71, 133, 157, 186, 295
  campaign, 97, 125, 317
  equivalency value, 108
  inappropriate, 267
  native, 61
  services, 73
  television, 133
advertorials, 61, 133
Airbnb, 49–54, 56–57, 342
apology, 25, 175
  carefully worded, 27
  corporate, 35, 81, 346
  cultural, 276
  formal, 29
  news conference, 272, 275
  public, 31–32
Apple, 121, 328–334
Applebee's, 77–82
artificial intelligence (AI), 325–326
astroturfing, 232–233
athletics, 180, 183–184, 186, 188, 202–203
augmented reality (AR), 325–326

Belk, 103–110
Belk Mobile Mammography Center
  (BMMC), 107–108
Blackfish, 129–134
blame, 62, 125, 169, 174, 194, 202, 239
  cast, 248
  face, 247

ownership of, 171, 175–176
  shift, 99–100, 175, 304, 345
Boston University Medical Center
  (BMC), 211–213, 215–216
branding, 142, 294–295, 315,
  325–326
breast cancer, 107, 109, 115

Cameroon, 284–288
Capital One, 348–352
Carnaval, 263–265, 267
Carolina Commitment, 201–204
case method, 4, 6
categorical imperative, 11, 212
chemical spill, 160
Chiquita, 343–346
Chronic Traumatic Encephalopathy
  (CTE), 191–196
Coca-Cola, 86, 95–101
collectivism, 273
Colombia, 343–346
communication ethics, 36
community, 10, 82, 139, 148, 160, 228,
  235–238, 242, 255, 260, 284, 305,
  318, 321, 334, 352
  active, 115
  activists, 212
  Airbnb, 52–53
  brand-controlled, 79
  building, 219–220, 233

campus, 310–312
colleagues, 5
decisions, 208–209
definition of, 154
development, 86–87
engagement, 109, 349–350
forum, 168
global, 63
management, 78
members, 85, 108, 174, 179,
    220, 239
Mount, 314–316
needs, 106
online, 78
organizations, 291
outreach, 241
panic, 171
relations, 108, 154–155, 291
religious, 31–32
sections of website, 112
social, 222
strengthening, 107–108
support, 176, 263
trusted, 50
UNC, 203
youth, 63
concussions, 191–196
constituents, 37, 40, 114, 154–155, 232,
    292, 298
    informing, 233
consumer relations, 119, 131, 133, 209
contamination, 171, 173
Cook, Tim, 38, 332–333
core values, 15, 229, 334
corporate behaviors, 126–127
corporate communications, 18, 31, 157
corporate governance, 272–273, 276–278
corporate image, 64, 111
corporate social responsibility (CSR),
    63, 88, 95, 102–103, 105–106,
    109–110, 114, 126
    activities, 114, 353
    communication, 100, 115, 116

definition of, 85
efforts, 86, 87, 96–99, 326, 349–353
expert, 91
goals, 101
initiatives, 99, 101, 111–112, 123
policies, 116
programs, 99
report, 350–352
corporate transparency, 63, 68
corporate values, 116, 329, 334
cowbells, 182
crisis communication, 81, 239, 241–242,
    267–268
    definition of, 23
    management, 23–25, 46, 140, 175, 332
    practices, 277
    typology of, 25
deontology, 10–12, 212–213
disclosure, 60–61, 95, 148, 150, 203, 276
    corporate, 149
    demands for, 146, 151
    financial, 274
    implications of, 145
    information, 16–17, 219, 249
    public, 272
distributive justice, 46

ebony, 283–288
Elk River, West Virginia, 157–162
employee relations, 154, 294
environmental racism, 174
environmental sustainability,
    284, 348
ethical practices, 14, 63, 174, 176, 233, 245
ethics of care, 12

Facebook, 50, 53, 60–61, 78–82,
    132–133, 138–141, 146, 202, 240,
    252, 265, 317, 331, 342
    account, 133
    channel, 252
    comment, 81
    group, 240

Facebook (*continued*)
    page, 29–30, 32, 52, 64, 68, 140, 144,
      174, 221–223, 276
    post, 29-30, 139, 223, 268
    shares, 66
Fair Labor Association, 89–90
fake news, 325, 327
fan relations, 180
FBI, 328–334, 338–342
Federal Trade Commission (FTC),
    59, 61, 74, 127
Flint, Michigan, 171–176
Food Babe, 145–152
Freedom Industries, 156–162
Freedom of Information Act, 244

ghost social media, 59
global, 64, 95, 106, 111–112, 129, 348
    activities, 114
    campaign, 97, 343
    communication, 255, 262
    community, 63, 96, 97
    conglomerate, 157
    definition of, 261
    inclusion, 113
    integration, 261
    issue, 92
    leader, 134
    public relations, 88, 97,
      261–262, 343
    society, 124
    stakeholder, 98
good intention, 17, 203–204, 278, 345–346
goodwill, 17, 115, 204
government communication, 241–242,
    253, 256
government relations, 86, 232–233,
    244, 249
Ground Zero, 35–40

Harris Corporation, 111–115
health, 12, 112, 127, 158, 208–212,
    218–222
    benefits, 303

campaigns, 192
communication
    concerns, 97
    conditions, 175
    data, 339
    decisions, 192
    economic, 185
    experts, 99, 329
    information, 220–231
    issues, 98, 192–193, 195, 215–216
    organizations, 112
    promotion, 123
    public, 98, 192, 254
    records, 341
    risks, 159, 161, 171
health advocacy organization, 208–209
healthcare 111, 311
    company, 248
    facilities, 252, 254, 256
    industry, 218–220
    information, 220
    organizations, 212, 215, 218, 225, 229
    practices, 213, 216
    professionals, 210–211, 214,
      251–252, 254
health communication, 192, 208–209
Health Insurance Portability and
    Accountability Act, 208–209
health promotion, 123, 208–209
Hurricane Sandy, 234–235, 237–238,
    241–242

illegal payments, 343
image repair, 134, 175
influencers, 61, 64, 121, 325, 327
    definition of, 106
internal communication, 31, 108, 244,
    272, 277, 352
    management of
    strategy

Jindal, Bobby, 244–249

Kant, Immanuel, 11. 203–204

Lands' End, 26–32
laws, 10, 17, 50, 155, 209, 212, 215, 284
leadership, 96, 99, 137, 278, 310
    changes, 35, 140
    corporate, 104, 106–107, 109
    institutional, 203, 306–307
    new, 176, 297, 299
    senior, 67, 88, 92
    skills, 5
    strengthening, 256
    styles, 142, 313
    temporary, 172
    transparency in, 202
    visionary, 330
lobbying, 232–233, 244, 248, 299
Louisiana, 244–249

maleficence, 213
Market Basket Supermarkets, 136–137
McDonald's, 63–69, 145
Mercedes-Benz, 183–184
Michigan Department of Environmental
    Quality (MDEQ), 171–177
Middle East Respiratory Syndrome
    (MERS), 251–256
Migrant Worker Standard, 91
Minneapolis, Minnesota, 41, 42, 45
Mississippi State University, 181–185, 187
Mixed Motives Model of Conflict
    Resolution, 35, 36
morals, 10, 14
Mount St. Mary's University, 302, 305,
    312, 315

National September 11th Memorial and
    Museum, 37–39
native advertising, 61
natural disaster, 24, 175, 242
news conference, 168, 204, 272, 275–277
NFL, 191–196
NFL Commissioner, 193
nonprofit, 293, 299, 311, 321, 352
    business, 292, 294
    clients, 318–320

    definition of, 290
    goals, 319
    healthcare system, 222, 229
    organizations, 28, 89, 91, 104,
        292, 298
    needs, 291

online review, 71
organizational culture, 13, 295
organizational justice, 46
organizational relations, 180
organizational reputation, 225

Page Principles, 14, 17, 278
paramilitary groups, 343–346
Patagonia, 85, 88–92
patient safety, 208–209, 213–214,
    216, 226, 228
pay-for-play, 59, 61
physicians, 192, 194, 211
Port Authority of New York and
    New Jersey, 35–38
post-crisis, 42, 46, 239
power distance, 273
privacy, 209, 313, 329, 339, 342–343
    breaching, 220, 331, 341
    customer, 78–79, 342
    digital, 331, 334
    issues, 208
    laws, 212, 215
    medical, 213
    patient, 218–219, 221, 223
    right to, 79-80, 334
professional codes, 9, 13
profits, 138, 152
    business, 99
    to increase, 115
    prioritizing, 229, 263, 278
    short-term, 275
PRSA Code of Ethics, 14, 82, 168,
    203–204, 245
public affairs, 232–233
public health beneficence, 215
public health crisis, 256

Public information officers (PIOs),
    244–246, 248–249
public opinion, 100, 249, 334, 346
    court of, 247
    to influence, 79, 176, 244, 246
public relations crisis, 126, 332, 343, 345
Public Relations Society of America
    (PRSA), 13–16, 60–61, 169,
    223, 290

Reddit, 78, 82, 342
regulations, 49–51, 54, 97–98, 130, 161
    EPA, 173
    German, 124
    healthcare, 218, 220, 226, 254
    SEC, 114
    utility, 166
    US, 126
rhetoric, 109, 113, 147, 200–202
risk communication, 23–24

scandal, 228, 273, 276–278
    academic, 200–202
    accounting, 271–272
    athletic, 200–202
    emissions, 123–127
    Snowden, 331
school uniforms, 27–28
scoreboard, 183–186
scrubbing, 71–76
SeaWorld, 129–134
Securities Exchange Commission (SEC)
    114, 116
Situational Crisis Communication
    Theory (SCCT), 25, 238, 268
Skol, 263–269
social media, 87, 98, 108, 145–146,
    235, 241, 266–268, 291, 295, 297,
    325–327, 329
    accounts, 78, 318, 319
    channels, 142, 264
    definition of, 89
    engagement, 187
    feeds, 120

networks, 174
    pages, 142, 204, 217, 219–220,
        252, 264, 276
    policy, 218, 222
    presence, 81, 132
    response, 223, 241
    services, 60
    strategy, 218–219, 224
    use of, 27, 29–32, 52–54, 65–68, 82,
        222, 263
social responsibility, 13, 90, 105,
    112, 114–115
Southeastern Conference (SEC),
    181–183, 185, 187
sponsored content, 61
sports, 123, 188, 192, 195, 220, 296
    collegiate, 200–202
    communication, 179
    fans, 180
    industry, 179–182
    leagues, 182, 187
    medicine, 222
St. Joseph's Hospital, 225–229
St. Rita's Medical Center, 220–223
stakeholder relations, 42, 46, 127
stakeholders, 17–18, 46, 49, 54, 65, 68,
    87, 95–96, 161–162, 192, 194,
    203–204, 227, 229, 272–276, 278,
    305, 317, 320, 329, 349
    conflicts, 35–37
    concerns, 39
    diverse, 18, 40, 98, 116, 332
    engagement with, 17, 79,
        95–96, 113
    expectations of, 23–24
    key, 141, 158, 180, 218–219,
        254–255, 303
    listening to, 269
    outraged, 263
    response, 99
    socially minded, 95, 101
    values, 114
    VW, 123, 124, 126
stances, 236

strategic communication, 109, 114,
    208, 252, 255
strategic philanthropy, 106, 108
student-run agency, 317–318
subsequent crisis, 235
sustainability, 87, 96, 126, 287, 351–353
    environmental, 349
    food, 67–69

Taylor Guitars, 283–284, 286–288
The Footprint Chronicles, 89
third-party review site, 71
Toshiba, 271–278
transparency, 25, 66–69, 92, 125, 138,
    201–203, 239, 241–242, 254,
    276–278, 288, 291, 298–299, 327
    campaign, 65
    complete, 123
    consumer, 157
    culture, 88
    definition of, 59, 61
    enhance, 65, 225, 274
    establish, 247
    inadequate, 175
    increasing, 146, 147, 150, 237, 248, 273
    lack of, 276–277
    maintaining, 169
    strategy of, 63, 236
    supply chain, 90
trust, 17, 63, 71–72, 74, 79, 122–123,
    147, 151, 159, 235, 291
    broken, 125–127, 161
    building, 60, 75, 120, 155, 256
    client, 16
    consumer, 125, 131
    increasing, 327
    maintaining, 61, 216
    public, 14, 214, 248
    restoring, 125, 134, 196, 297
    shareholder, 277
tuberculosis (TB), 210–212, 214–216
tweets, 66, 99, 184
    examples of, 53, 57
    fan, 184

Japanese, 275
    replies to, 68, 183
    responding to, 67
    steamrolling of, 146
Twitter, 53, 61, 65, 68, 134,
    183, 342
    account, 68, 98, 254, 276
    campaign, 132
    feeds, 187
    followers, 64, 78
    platform, 53
    posts, 61, 99, 266
    response, 268
two-way communication,
    67, 222
    channels of, 113
    definition of, 290
    meaningful, 218–219
    opportunities for, 203–204
    process of, 291
    strategy, 35

University of North Carolina at
    Chapel Hill (UNC), 199–204
utilitarian, 12, 75, 213
utilitarianism, 10, 12

victim compensation fund (VCF),
    42–43, 45–46
viral activism, 145–146, 148
virtual reality (VR), 325–326
virtue, 10–12
Volkswagen (VW), 123–127

water, 100, 123, 165, 284, 350–351
    crisis, 3, 171, 174, 176
    pollution, 160
    stewardship of, 95
    supply, 171
    testing kits, 175
    use, 349
Wounded Warrior Project (WWP),
    293–299

Yelp, 71–75